Psychoanalysis, Creativity, and Literature
A French–American Inquiry

Psychoanalysis, Creativity, and Literature

A French–American Inquiry

ALAN ROLAND,
Editor

New York   COLUMBIA UNIVERSITY PRESS   1978

Library of Congress Cataloging in Publication Data
Main entry under title:

Psychoanalysis, creativity, and literature.
Includes bibliographical references and index.
1. Psychoanalysis—France.   2. Psychoanalysis—
United States.   3. Psychoanalysis and literature.
4. Creation (Literary, artistic, etc.)   I. Roland,
Alan, 1930–
RC506.P77   150'.19'50944   77-26613
ISBN 0-231-04324-4

COLUMBIA UNIVERSITY PRESS
NEW YORK   GUILDFORD, SURREY

COPYRIGHT © 1978 COLUMBIA UNIVERSITY PRESS
ALL RIGHTS RESERVED
PRINTED IN THE UNITED STATES OF AMERICA

To
Jackie, Tika, and Ariel

CONTENTS

Psychoanalysis, Creativity, and Literature
A French–American Inquiry

Introduction

ALAN ROLAND

IN AN ERA when psychoanalytic publications of all kinds flourish, it must be considered more than a little odd that French psychoanalysis, which has received an interested reception in American literary circles, is almost unknown in psychoanalytic ones. This is clearly reflected in recent translations and essays on French psychoanalysis. *French Freud*, published in 1972 by *Yale Review* as a varied compilation of translations of French psychoanalysis, was essentially a *literary* endeavor, not a psychoanalytic one. The same may be said of Delta's publication of Jacques Lacan's *The Language of the Self* in 1975. A lengthy and lucid exposition of Lacan's theories was written by a professor of literature, Anthony Wilden, not a psychoanalyst. Only very rarely has a French psychoanalytic book been published in English, or a paper translated into English in a psychoanalytic journal.

Is this lack of translations responsible for American analysts' unawareness of French psychoanalytic thought? Or is it rather, that until very recently, a vague policy of benign neglect has prevailed on the part of the American psychoanalytic movement toward their French relations? And if the latter be the case, as I believe it essentially is, why should the analysts be so uninterested in the French movement in contrast to their literary counterparts?

I shall try to examine this question from several vantage points. To consider French and American psychoanalysis seriously is not simply to discuss, compare, and argue comparative theories—as has been done for years with the work of Melanie Klein. Rather, we must consider the total gestalt of each movement in its respective country: the place of psycho-analysis in its sociocultural context; the institutionalization of psychoana-lysis, including who is allowed to be trained; the relation of psychoanalysis to other intellectual disciplines; and the theoretical thrusts and concerns. One could well argue the point that the strengths and weaknesses of the French and American movements are diametrically opposite. For ex-ample, through the work of Jacques Lacan, French psychoanalysis was able to break through its narrow medical orthodoxy and become closely associated with philosophy, linguistics, literature, and structural anthro-pology—a transdisciplinary approach totally alien to medical psychoanal-ysis in the United States. On the other hand, American analysts, being less exclusively committed to Freud than Lacan and the French, have made significant new clinical observations with resultant major additions to the theories of Freud, such as Kohut's observation of idealizing and mirroring transferences, Mahler's work on separation-individuation, and Erikson's theory of identity conflicts and syntheses—in its transdis-ciplinary orientation, a notable exception to the main thrust of American psychoanalysis.

The first two papers in this book describe the basic sociocultural milieu of each movement. They are in effect a sociology of psychoanalysis. Similar to the sociology of knowledge, these essays delineate how socio-cultural contexts significantly influence theoretical concerns and exposi-tions. The papers are written by "outsiders," affording perspectives that only a visitor could have. In the paper comparing French and American psychoanalysis, Julien Bigras, who moved from North American training in psychiatry in Montreal to psychoanalytic training in Paris, outlines the cultural climate within the French institutes, with some of its advantages and disadvantages; while François Peraldi, who journeyed the other way, offers a detailed critique of the institutional framework of American psy-choanalysis. The second paper is a result of a year's intense research work by Sherry Turkle, an American sociologist in Paris, who, being the out-sider, had unusual access to the various factions of French psychoanalysis. She has thus been able to compose a broad sociological overview of French psychoanalysis and its relation to French society and culture.

Another perspective on the enigmatic relations of the American psy-choanalytic and literary communities to French psychoanalysis involves

the stereotyped image many American psychoanalysts have of psychoanalysis in France. Except for the puzzling and disquieting figure of Jacques
Lacan, French psychoanalysis has been considered a backwater bypassed
by the pre-World War II surge of refugee psychoanalysts from the original
centers of the psychoanalytic movement in Vienna and Germany to England and the United States, and secondarily to Latin America. In retro-
spect, the French movement was not so much a backwater as an underground stream, slowly gaining strength and force over the years. As
Sherry Turkle's paper clearly delineates, for many years it was a small
movement, largely ostracized by the mental health community in France
and shunned by most elements of French society. It was only accorded a
warm reception by certain elements of the artistic, literary, philosophical,
and anthropological communities. Unlike its post-World War II American
counterpart, which has basked in the public eye, French psychoanalysis
struggled for years as a minor, rejected segment of French culture. Perhaps because of this status, it was easier for a charismatic figure such as
Jacques Lacan to break through medical orthodoxy and thus transform, re-
vitalize, and stamp his own imprint on psychoanalysis in France. When
the student uprisings in 1968 brought about profound changes in France
that finally enabled psychoanalysis to surface and become a highly significant force in French cultural and social life, the psychoanalysis that
emerged was far more transdisciplinary in its nature and direction than
the major psychoanalytic movements in England and the United States.

The genesis of this book also reveals the different attitudes toward
French psychoanalysis prevailing in American literary and psychoanalytic
circles. To help remedy the communication chasm, Professor Serge Doubrovsky—of the graduate department of French and Italian at New York
University and the NYU Center in Paris—met with Dr. Alan Roland—
then director of the institute and chairman of scientific programs of the
National Psychological Association for Psychoanalysis (NPAP)—in the
summer of 1974 to plan a comprehensive conference dealing with the
main psychoanalytic and literary concerns of French and American psychoanalysis. The papers would be the basis for a book. It was particularly
fitting for a university and a psychoanalytic institute to cosponsor this
event as the French movement, through the impetus of Lacan, has maintained such integral ties with other intellectual and artistic disciplines.
Through his position at the NYU Center in Paris, Professor Doubrovsky

had established contact with a number of important French psychoanalysts, and was thus able to invite representatives of a broad spectrum to the conference.

It was also most appropriate for the sponsoring psychoanalytic institute to be the NPAP—*not a member of the American Psychoanalytic Association.* The NPAP, founded by Theodor Reik in 1948, became the first and remained almost the only American psychoanalytic institute to admit candidates freely for training from a variety of disciplines and fields outside of the traditional mental health professions. This of course is far more consonant with French psychoanalysis than the American Psychoanalytic Association. Equally fitting, the NPAP publishes *The Psychoanalytic Review*, considered by many to be the foremost journal of psychoanalysis and culture in the United States. In fact, the NPAP has been the spearhead of what has now become a strong nonmedical psychoanalytic movement that has survived the American Psychoanalytic Association's pruning of candidates from all other disciplines than medicine and psychiatry—with the occasional rare exception.

The assertion of medical orthodoxy in psychoanalysis is primarily responsible for severing psychoanalysis from other intellectual disciplines in the United States; it has been only partially offset in such large urban centers as New York City by the large influx of refugee analysts in the 1930s from Vienna and Germany—many of them, like Theodor Reik and Erich Fromm, nonmedical. To complete this severance from other intellectual disciplines and to establish new monopolies in psychoanalysis, psychology associations in New York and other states has taken up the clarion call of the medical model to restrict nonmedical psychoanalysis almost exclusively to psychologists and social workers. The NPAP thus remains one of the only nonmedical psychoanalytic institutes still committed to Freud's view of admitting candidates from a variety of disciplines—thus maintaining significant ties to other fields.

The picture of why American literary rather than psychoanalytic circles have been interested in French psychoanalysis now comes more clearly into focus. First, through medicine and now through psychology, American psychoanalysis has been largely truncated from any meaningful discourse with other intellectual disciplines. Oddly enough, reverse discrimination has not taken place: persons in the humanities and social sciences have maintained interest in and knowledge of psychoanalysis. But the interested professional or student of the humanities and social sciences often has a limited understanding of the complexities and controversies of psychoanalysis because he or she is not allowed to have full psychoanalytic training at any institute of the American Psychoanalytic Association—with the very occasional exception. An earnest attempt by the Chicago Psychoanalytic Institute to admit an entire class of persons with doctorates from other disciplines has been recently rejected by the American Psychoanalytic Association. *Psychoanalysis, overly restricted to a medical or psychological model of restricted training of candidates, severed from other intellectual disciplines, and thus turned in on itself, finds itself largely unable to relate to the French psychoanalytic movement, transdisciplinary in nature.*

To return to the conception of this book, a three-day series of four symposia was held at New York University in May 1976, titled: "A Franco-American Dialogue: Self and Culture Today." The meetings were attended by large numbers from psychoanalysis and the Humanities, and applauded by both. Rarer still, the dialogue did not die on the vine. Through the subsequent good offices of François Peraldi and Alan Roland, small meetings are still being regularly held between French psychoanalysts from Paris and Montreal, and American psychoanalysts and literary figures. For one of the first times, interested American medical and nonmedical analysts are sitting regularly side by side, and beside those from other disciplines.

This exchange, of which this book is now but one part of an effort that also includes translations of Lacan and other major French psychoanalysts, should make French psychoanalysis more accessible, and should contribute to broadening the perspectives of American psychoanalysis. Needless to say, a comprehensive picture of the theoretical directions and contributions of French psychoanalysis can only come from a variety of translated works. In the second section of the book, a very readable and lucid sampling is given in the papers by Serge Leclaire, François Peraldi, and J. B. Pontalis. The papers by the first two, both "Lacanians," are good examples of such central Lacanian concerns as the unconscious being related to linguistic structures, "listening without knowing" (or the need to approach the patient's associations without preconceived categories), the issue of authenticity, and the need to be in touch with the patient's unconscious desire. Peraldi's paper also deals with social and political concerns, another central interest of French psychoanalysis. Pontalis's paper, on the other hand, illustrates a brilliant reworking of Freud's concept of the death drive—a concept largely moribund in American psychoanalysis—through close textual analysis of Freud's writings, letters to Fleiss, and biographical material on Freud. With each of these writers, literary style is obviously of central importance. The last paper in this section, by Ernest Wolf, a close associate of Heinz Kohut, counterpoints and highlights the French approach by lucidly delineating Kohut's seminal work on narcissism and the self. As the paper illustrates Kohut's theories by literary examples, it affords a further interesting comparison with the literary papers of Doubrovsky and Girard in the fourth section.

The third section, on creativity, is all-American, dividing equally into cognitive-linguistic dimensions and motivational ones involving self and identity—reflecting some of the same divisions of the psychoanalytic papers. The first paper, by Kenneth Burke, one of America's foremost philosophers of language and literary critics, testifies to the fundamental dualism of experience and physicality on the one hand and man's constant predilection to symbolize on the other. Burke's emphasis on the essential role of language and symbolicity ties him to the French viewpoint. His formulation of this fundamental duality has an obvious relationship to the Lacanian concern (in Leclaire's paper) with the gap between the essential experience and what is symbolized in memory.

Albert Rothenberg's work differentiates in an unusually clear way the cognitive and linguistic processes and structures involved in creative work in literature and science from those involved in the unconscious—or the primary process. This paper describes the results of more than ten years of research into the actual processes of creativity with major American writers, later supplemented by interviews with highly creative scientists.

As Rothenberg's paper relates to Burke's in the stress on cognitive integrations of antitheses, Menaker's and Brenman-Gibson's papers are also remarkably related in emphasizing the artist's self-appointed task first to forge within himself or herself a self or identity based on new integrations of basic dualities in life, and then to present this new resolution meaningfully to the collectivity. Menaker, in a new interpretation of Rank's neglected psychology, shows how Rank took the artist as the paradigm of creativity, motivated by the fundamental duality of mortality versus strivings for immortality. Brenman-Gibson, by using the specific example of Clifford Odets, illustrates her broader thesis that the playwright is preoccupied with issues of creativity and the communication of new identity resolutions.

The fourth section of the book explicitly treats psychoanalytic literary criticism, although all the papers on creativity have strong implications for literary criticism, as do some of the papers on psychoanalysis. Thus, the crossings between psychoanalysis and other disciplines are rich and varied. The first two papers in this section offer an American overview on the relationship of psychoanalysis to literary criticism. In the first paper, Norman Holland delineates the progress in American psychoanalysis from an id to an ego psychology, and now to a psychology of self and identity—relating different approaches in psychoanalytic criticism to each of these phases. The second paper by Alan Roland addresses itself to the pervasive reductionism in much of psychoanalytic criticism by challenging the usual assumptions on the relationship of structures in dreams to those in art. In its investigation of structures this paper is closely related to French psychoanalytic concerns as well as to Rothenberg's work on creativity; in its emphasis on the relevance for criticism of contemporary psychoanalytic theories of the self, it repeats similar themes in Holland's and Wolf's papers.

A counterpoint to the American orientation to psychoanalytic criticism is provided by André Green's paper—at once a manifesto of psychoanalytic criticism within the French context as well as an approach to literary creativity. His exposition of Henry James's "Private Life" is an interesting variation on Brenman-Gibson's theme of the writer directly concerned with issues of creativity in his work. Green's and Doubrovsky's papers are excellent examples of the close textual analysis and emphasis on linguistic structures characteristic of French psychoanalytic criticism. Doubrovsky's analysis of an interesting episode in Sartre's *Nausea* offers an informative contrast to Wolf's approach: the psychosexual versus the self. René Girard's incisive critique of Freud's theory of narcissism, made through analyzing the writings of Proust, presents a totally different perspective on narcissism—one actually far more congruent with Wolf's and Kohut's orientation. Roland's and Rizzo's paper on Pirandello continues the dialogue on structural analysis and the self, showing both to be intrinsically valuable for psychoanalytic criticism of Pirandello's *Six Characters in Search of an Author* and *Henry IV*.

What therefore emerges from the various papers in this book is a preoccupation with linguistic, literary, and psychological structures on one hand, and issues involving self, identity, and narcissism on the other. The division is by no means strictly French and American. Certainly, Burke,

Rothenberg, and Roland and Rizzo are strongly oriented toward analyzing a variety of structures, while Girard concerns himself with important issues in narcissism. What further emerges is an interrelationship of psychoanalysis to literary and philosophical concerns from both sides of the Atlantic. It is hoped that this book not only makes French psychoanalysis more readily accessible; but in a broader context helps build another bridge between psychoanalysis and the humanities—part of Freud's original vision of psychoanalysis.

SECTION I
A Sociology
of
Psychoanalysis

❦ 1 ❧

French and American Psychoanalysis

JULIEN BIGRAS
AND FRANÇOIS PÉRALDI

FRENCH PSYCHOANALYSIS
by Julien Bigras

ONE WAY OF discussing the differences between the French and American schools of psychoanalysis is to examine the major prejudices that seem to be inherent in their respective ways of judging each other. French psychoanalytical thought, according to the Americans, is too steeped in philosophy; the French, on the other hand, criticize American analysts for the seemingly total infiltration of their profession by medical influences.

Naturally both prejudices are not always so clear-cut: in certain circles, American as well as French, completely opposite points of view are held, while in other circles utter and reciprocal ignorance prevails.[1] This fact recently prompted a colleague of mine in New York to write to me, "American analysts, as you know, are as a rule blithely ignorant of French contributions; and my impression of analysts from France is that they are not completely open-minded to American psychoanalysis."

Be that as it may, I think it useful, without going into too much detail, to indicate the major obstacles that I personally had to overcome before I was able to familiarize myself with French psychoanalytic thought in France. My initiation into psychoanalysis occurred about fifteen years ago in Paris. I had come from North America and planned to return there as a practicing analyst; for these reasons my stay in France was most illuminating as regards the issues discussed here.

After being admitted as psychoanalyst-in-training in Paris, I became acutely aware of certain tacit but strong requirements imposed on aspiring psychoanalysts—in particular the emphasis on theory. I was amazed at the seeming facility with which my French colleagues assimilated the concepts of Freudian thought—no matter how complex—and their ease in discussing these concepts. This requirement did not stop there: from the outset of their training, it was mandatory for students, or at least the ones considered brilliant, to become familiar with the main ideological trends of the day and to be able to discuss them and their pertinence to psychoanalytical theory. I feel certain that today as well young French analysts who intend to be truly successful must be familiar with the works of Barthes, Derrida, Foucault, Deleuze, in addition to Marx, Hegel, and many others.

As far as I was concerned, there were serious dangers inherent in this requirement even though, judging from the results, it constituted a highly useful, efficacious tool in the training of some analysts. The danger of intellectualism is the first observation I would like to point out here. Coupled with the awesome emphasis placed on theory, intellectualism was particularly manifest whenever the student-analyst had to discuss a patient's case. In fact he was often incapable of doing so: the patient was often little more than a pretext for performing what might be called theoretical gymnastics. North American training had taught me to discuss a patient's case only in terms of the facts and to be extremely circumspect with regard to the theoretical implications of a given case history. However, at that time, when I was at the beginning of my career, I did not yet realize that this approach was also illusory. I was laboring under the delusion that psychoanalysis was an exact science based exclusively on factual observation; in reality it is an interpretation of facts (rather than an observation of facts), and the interpretive aspect is the core of psychoanalysis, indeed, its very object. I was thus torn between two extreme positions, somewhat suggestive of a Pascalian dilemma; the splendor of Theory on one hand and the affliction of the Clinically Objective Approach on the other.

But let us proceed in our analysis. I mentioned that some students could talk nonstop for hours without really including the patient in their discussions, even though it was the patient's case they were supposedly presenting. I have listened to their brilliant discourse many times, noticing that their eloquence was hollow. I even detected this hollowness in the discourse of our "master thinkers" who watched over our training; this censorship was discreet but efficacious.

It is true of course that France has always produced exceptionally good clinicians. In my opinion psychoanalysis has benefited from this tradition. Excellent clinicians, trained in medicine and neurology among other specializations, initiated us into the tact and subtlety of close clinical observation. It should be noted therefore that medicine has had much influence on French psychoanalysis, although compared with its influence on American psychoanalytical schools, it has taken different directions and has had less impact. For us students, the problem was centered around reconciling theory and clinical methods. It may appear curious to state that we looked upon theory and the clinical approach as two distinct and separate fields. Theory was naturally considered to be superior: we were firmly convinced it was the door to the most brilliant careers.

Students were accepted or rejected by their professors according to one criterion only: their discourses in terms of theory had to conform strictly to Freudian thought. This is the touchiest part of the present analysis; much time elapsed before I realized that there were two kinds of orthodoxy: the first kind, which had a great deal of influence on me for years, was the orthodoxy defended by those we might call "the custodians of doctrine." Another name might also be "the custodians of technique," since these two functions went together. Some of our professors had all of Freud's thought at their fingertips, which was the source of their enormous influence. Many a time I have seen a student stand helpless and embarrassed as some interminable quotation, lifted directly from a Freudian text, came tumbling down about his ears! Some students, either because of this or in spite of it, coped with the situation, making haste as one can imagine to learn all of Freud by heart.

This kind of fidelity to Freud constituted what may be termed "external" rather than true orthodoxy; the constraints thus imposed upon the students were all the more binding as they were dispensed in the highest spheres of the institution. The last word, the word that closed the discussion in scientific conferences, was nearly always uttered by that professor who referred the most to Freud's text itself. One may say therefore, given that this fidelity had force of law within the institution, that it was directed as much—if not more so—toward those who held the reins of power as toward Freud's thought.

I do not mean to suggest that our professors were speaking untruths; on the contrary, I have someone in mind who influenced me greatly at a very early stage, and it seemed to me then that his words were rooted in fact: what I do contest was the authoritative and dogmatic manner in which those words were delivered. I was very fond of the professor I mentioned, and I believe the feeling was mutual. There was nothing unfamiliar to me in his authoritarian attitude; my religion-permeated upbringing as a child had made me thoroughly familiar with it. As a matter of fact, at that time it was a nearly inescapable necessity. I imagine that it is obvious that there is a lot of analytical work to be done by the student when he is faced with this type of transferance: in a word, when he is inevitably a discreet participant in established authority and power.

I am reminded of something worth mentioning here. Sexuality is one question that absolutely cannot be discussed peremptorily. How can the lover speak of "authority" when it is a fact, as Freud points out, that the lover is humble before the desired object? Can the lover of psychoanalysis (and we all were to varying degrees) be different from other lovers? Why should he be inflexible or dogmatic before psychoanalysis, the object of his love?

But orthodoxy (especially when rigidly authoritative) implies marginality as well: orthodoxy on one side and marginality on the other. For France is one of the very few countries in which personal and original works on psychoanalysis are produced in quantity, especially within the past fifteen or twenty years. How to explain this fact?

In certain milieux in present-day France, a minor author is defined as someone who has not yet produced an original piece of work. Orthodoxy, over the past years, has shifted direction: the major writers (those who have produced a work of their own) are considered as marginal, on a temporary basis for some, on a definitive basis for others. But the point is that these writers are marginal by virtue of the same principle as the one held by the custodians of doctrine: fidelity to Freud.

I have an example to illustrate what I have been saying: it concerns the discussions centred around the death drive. I have lost track of the number of times, in France and elsewhere, I have had to sit through exposés on the thorny question Freud left us: does the death drive exist?

This question, set forth in the terms of "scholastic" orthodoxy, that is, in the sole terms of the manifest Freudian text (which was precisely how the question was posed in Freud's time), finally exhausted my patience with the result that I refused to discuss it for at least ten years. For me, the question had become inert and lifeless; in a word, so far as I was concerned it no longer had any dynamic role to play in the actual cure process. This is where I stood thanks to my reading of *Beyond the Pleasure Principle*, done exclusively in terms of the explicit Freudian text.

But now, one text included here in this series, entitled "On Death-Work," is sufficient in itself to incite me to examine this question left unresolved by Freud and to which he attached so much importance. How does death work within the cure process?

In New York, listening to the text "On Death-Work," what really occurred some time ago between myself and a young patient of mine, a girl, became clear to me. She had been sent to me on the advice of her school-teacher because she had shown absolutely no reaction after her mother had been killed in a car accident. The girl had also been involved in the crash but had suffered only a very slight brain concussion.

Her teacher could not understand why the girl's conduct at school had not changed in any way whatsoever; she behaved as though absolutely nothing unusual had occurred. I too was at a loss to understand the phenomenon. I therefore accepted her as a patient. I had already dealt with several cases of traumatic neuroses and thus knew that spontaneous sketches, dreams, and fantasies of the patient should reveal violent scenes linked to the accident in which her mother had been killed. This was not the case; the girl would say, "I don't have dreams. No, I'm not afraid. Everything is fine, I assure you."

There was nothing left but to hope that, as a last resort, the spontaneous sketches done by the girl would clear up the mystery. But here also I drew a blank: a cozy little house, a road, a tree; in short, the ingredients of the typical child's drawing. True, a little star or two were in the first drawing, but who would have paid any attention to them? And since it was around Christmas, who would see anything unusual in stars at the tips of the branches of a Christmas tree? Yet in subsequent drawings the stars reappeared again and again scattered among blue flowers or atop a mountain and even at times next to a dazzling yellow sun. Six months went by and still I saw nothing significant in this fact.

Then one day I had a kind of illumination.

"Tell me,"[2] I said, "when the accident happened I'll bet you saw stars."

She had indeed seen stars at the moment of impact. She immediately burst into tears and told me that she saw stars every night. She was afraid to fall asleep and see them appear again. In addition, from that day forward, she became sad both in my presence and at school. Only at that point was she able to comprehend that before then it was neither possible nor permissible for her to mourn her mother's death.

As I listened to "On Death-Work" it was my turn to become aware of something: the subtle and cunning ways in which the death drive works. Suddenly this notion became tangible and vital. It was the "work of death" which, without my young patient or myself being aware of it, had held constant and silent sway over the life of a child and continued to exert its influence upon the cure process she was going through with me. Surely it is striking to see how awesomely the death drive worked its way into the very cure, even concealing itself beneath the things children are so fond of, like wonderful scenes depicting nature or Christmas. It was the author of "Death-Work," therefore, who made the notion of the death drive vital and dynamic to me; in Freud's text, on the contrary, the strength of this drive is directed toward rendering lifeless and inert all that moves within us.

We should go slowly here because we are dealing with a specific point of doctrine in Freud's work that even his own disciples found difficult to accept. Let us therefore compare Freud's explicit text, "Beyond the Pleasure Principle," with "On Death-Work." Freud feels bound, in his text, to establish the existence of the death drive. So as not to prolong the discussion too much, let us stick to the most moving illustration of the death drive that Freud has bequeathed to us: the *fort-da* game invented by his grandson when he was eighteen months old.[3] Freud was undoubtedly aware of the immense solitude this child felt whenever Sophie, his mother (and Freud's favorite daughter; "my Sunday child" as he called her), was away from the house. The child made up a complex yet very simple game: he learned to make a spool attached to a thread he held in his hand disappear whenever he shouted "O-O-O," and make it reappear every time he shrieked a joyous "A-A-A-." O–A. *Fort-da.*

The child played and played at the game. The compulsion on the child's part to repeat the game over and over again indicates that he had a control instinct and that he automatically used it in order to protect himself from his solitude. Mother away, mother dead. Freud also speaks of a revenge instinct in the child since he can make his mother disappear whenever he chooses by playing his game of make believe with the spool.

In short, the passive situation imposed upon the child when the mother was absent was transformed into an active reaction from the child. Henceforth he could control the trauma; he could even have his revenge. This was compulsively repeated, which induced Freud to postulate the notion of the death drive, since the aim of this ritualistic repetition is not to obtain pleasure but to ward off death.

Thus the *fort-da* game as presented by Freud is like an incantation, or again like the tip of an iceberg. What about the hidden part of the painful incident the child was experiencing? What about the drive itself? Freud describes the defense aspect only. The processes of the child's psyche, subjected to the absence of his mother, to her "death," certainly went deeper, were more complex and more difficult to grasp than Freud tells us.

It has already been suggested that the conjuring ritual effected by the child (making the spool disappear then reappear) is nothing more than a mere illusion of control if one compares it to the painful solitude and profound distress the child had to endure.

It is absolutely astounding that Freud attached no importance to the fact that the same child, his grandson, showed no grief at his mother's death, which occurred when he was five years and nine months old. The child's denial of death was interpreted by Freud to be the result of the fierce jealousy his grandson felt toward a second child that had come into the family.

It is here that the notion of "death-work" is helpful to me. My little patient, once her defenses weakened, manifested a state of such utter desolation, of such total devastation, that all that was left for her was to play dead, "as though absolutely nothing had happened." Thus it was not only a question of the mother's death but also and in particular of the child's death. The real work in progress here was a "fundamental process of unbinding, of fragmentation, of breaking up, of separation, of bursting but also enclosing, process which has no aim but its own accomplishment and whose repetitive nature brands it as instinctual, it is here that the death instinct operates."

The girl no longer wanted to live, which does not mean that she wanted to die. It is more a question of the death within her of the desire (to live) rather than the desire to die.

There is too strong a tendency to emphasize the desire to conquer (as

Freud did in terms of himself), or if one prefers, to emphasize the desire to challenge death. There were countless times that Freud, juggling Fliessian numbers, predicted that he would die a premature death. But was this not a way of wanting to die by his own will and not "because of internal reasons"? Is this not a way of wanting to be immortal? The Oedipus who survives his childhood murder exists; the Oedipus who becomes a conqueror later on exists. But there is also the Oedipus slain as a child (and who still remains active); there are also Jocasta and Oedipus who commit suicide after their transgression, as the author of "On Death-Work" points out: "Two remarks here—his words "I hold firmly," etc., reveal Freud's wish: if only the whole affair could be taken care of by Oedipus, and by a *conquering* Oedipus—this while ignoring the attempt to murder Oedipus the child and also forgetting that besides the parricide, Oedipus's and Jocasta's suicides are the price exacted by the transgression."[4]

In other words, we have to take into consideration the weak, the submissive, and those conquered by death. And in a way, does this not apply to all of us?

There is another step to be taken if one is to establish a real link with what Freud truly intuited here. I would have to show that the accident involving the mother's sudden disappearance was merely a trigger mechanism in the workings of the patient's psyche; and that these workings of her psyche continued relentlessly no matter what else might happen to her. It would be necessary therefore to show that the external signs of these workings, i.e., the child's distress, were anaclitically related to the death drive.[5] The latter, though, is an utterly blind force, untranslatable into words, indefinable, having no known assignable place in the psyche except that we do know it is at the very foundations of the unconscious. Personally, I have not yet reached this point, but I feel what I have said to be valid; in any case it would shed light on the mysterious cleavages and awesome fissures we find in borderline cases and psychotics. Don't we always find within such patients something broken, foreclosed, ungraspable? How can these patients be touched by the psychoanalysts when, supposedly, the death drives which are unlinked from the libidinal drives, have overcome the subject, making any kind of true dialogue impossible?

I would like to emphasize that a contemporary author, by taking a Freudian notion and reworking it from the inside, has been able to give it new life, at least for me. No matter what the custodians of doctrine and technique may say, we must never look upon Freud's theories or techniques as rigid, closed, or static for all time. I feel that fidelity to Freud consists in such reworking and not in any blind allegiance to his technical and theoretical precepts—even less so in the pure and simple repetition of what his texts enunciate.

In France at present, many authors have succeeded in constructing a work of their own based on Freud's works. Like Freud, they also have had to learn or relearn to explore the secrets of unconscious desire, to let it speak and at the same time to invent a language that would describe it with scientific rigor. They are not trying to prove at any cost that Freud was right, nor that Freud is unsurpassable or unsurpassed. What strikes me, on the contrary, as I read these authors, is a kind of harmony or internal coherence spontaneously established between their writings and Freud's, even though their style may be very different. In France, therefore, Freud's works remain the sole cornerstone of psychoanalytic thought, both for the orthodox thinkers (the custodians of doctrine) and for the true creative theorists. In the United States, on the other hand, this does not appear to be true, as the notions of orthodoxy or fidelity to Freud are subject to other and different criteria.

One work in particular has probably been recognized among those I have mentioned. In fact, among those who, in France, are the greatest sources of inspiration to me, those who have written or are still writing personal and original texts on psychoanalysis—those who, in other words, have written a work—all (or nearly all) have been influenced in one way or another by the presence and teachings of Jacques Lacan. This is true even if they are no longer with him or if they belong to one of the four existing groups.

Lacan is a unique and typically French phenomenon. One day someone should analyze his extraordinary secret of arousing people and passions. An undertaking of this kind is out of the question in these few pages about French psychoanalysis. Nevertheless we should like to point out that Lacan, in terms of fidelity to Freud, is definitely in our second group and is in fact its prototype. He examines the principal philosophical currents of thought and becomes intimately involved with them; yet he is the most ardent partisan of a return to the sources of psychoanalytical thought, and therefore to Freud himself. It is superfluous, of course, to mention Lacan's personal, unique style, which has made him famous. It is disquieting, however, to note that within his own school, "the Freudian

School," there is a tendency to perpetuate the same difficulty regarding fidelity to Freud that we have noted in French psychoanalytic circles in
general. Among Lacan's pupils, some are totally inflexible custodians of
doctrine—Freudian doctrine as well as Lacanian doctrine, which now exists. These pupils copy Lacan's style and thus claim to speak in his name.
Fortunately other disciples, through reflection, research, and analysis,
have succeeded in developing their own way of thinking based on Freud
and Lacan, which of necessity leads to a style of their own and new and
original works.[6] I repeat: the thinkers I have just mentioned are playing
the most vital and dynamic roles in psychoanalytic thought today. A genius like Lacan, even though incapable of solving the age-old problem of
power, since his own custodians of doctrine lay down the law within his
group, has nevertheless produced a work so powerful and vital that other
works have already sprung from it; it has undoubtedly influenced the
whole spectrum of contemporary French thought.

We can now further narrow down our analysis of fidelity to Freud in
present-day French psychoanalysis by stating that the truly creative analysts, the majority of whom, I repeat, have been influenced by Lacan's
teachings, do not repudiate in any way Freud's own teachings. On the
contrary. They are thoroughly familiar with metapsychology. They hold
that the unconscious as defined by Freud has a definite structure (structured the way a language is structured). Thus the unconscious has an
order. In spite of this adhesion to the Freudian notion of the unconscious,
psychoanalytical interpretation can never apply a leveling or reducing
principle: the patient is individual and unique in the same way his unconscious desire is individual and unique. Thus the psychoanalyst must not
only develop his own style—establish a distinction between himself and
his mentor—but must also train his ear to listen to the uniqueness of his
patient. As one of Lacan's most important disciples, Leclaire, has said:
"the rigour of unconscious desire, the logic of desire do not reveal themselves to those who do not respect at one and the same time the following
apparently contradictory exigencies: order and uniqueness."

We can thus draw the conclusion that, far from being intellectual,
philosophical, or abstract, this type of psychoanalysis leads directly into
practice—in a word, it is basically clinical. Its adherents of necessity must
love their patients—and children. It also is conducive to the creation of
new works, as I have said. Ultimately, doesn't writing a work mean to
rewrite Freud? Isn't it the rediscovery and redefinition of order, or in

other words a reworking of what has already been written? Pushed to extreme limits, does not the writing of a work always mean to lay siege to the Tables of the Law, to the death drive?

This is, broadly speaking, what I have learned and am still learning from French psychoanalysis.

POSTSCRIPT

I have to reveal that I made a serious omission in what I have said. I found it important not to mention any names except Lacan's among the French psychoanalytic authors. But now that my article is written I suddenly realize that this has already been done before me, by Conrad Stein in his book *The Imaginary Child.*[7] I have, therefore, to reveal that Conrad Stein has had the greatest influence on my evolution as a psychoanalyst and on my writings, including this text. So my slip of the pen reflects my unconscious will to pay tribute to him. In the final analysis, it is not any school that Stein may belong to or any institutional power he may have that interests me; what truly attracts me is the intrinsic quality of the psychoanalytic investment of the friends gathered around Stein and their personal participation in the quest Freud originated.

NOTES

1. It seems, however, that on both sides, French psychoanalysts and American psychoanalysts have shown a strong and powerful desire to get closer: psychoanalytic works by French authors are being translated into English, and colloquiums are being organized. (A.N.)

2. The French says *ma petite chérie*, which in English would be rendered ordinarily by the use of the patient's name (not given by the author for obvious reasons). The tone of voice, of course, would be very important as well. (T.N.)

3. See *Essais de Psychanalyse; Au-delà du principe de plaisir* (Paris: Payot, 1927), ch. 2, p. 16; *Jenseits des Lustprinzips* (1920), ch. 13, pp. 11–14; *Beyond the Pleasure Principle* (Paris: Revue par Hesnard, 1970), ch. 18, pp. 14–16.

4. In a text entitled "La Souffrance," to be published in *Etudes Freudiennes,* no. 13–14 (Paris: Denoël), I have tried to understand the relationship between a suffering, old, and ill Oedipus (at Colonnus) who wishes to die, and Oedipus the conqueror, whose destiny is to become a god. (A.N.)

5. There is no English verb to translate *étayer* used in this technical sense; the noun "anaclisis" *(anlehnung)* has an adverb, "anaclitically," which has been used here. (T.N.)

6. As an example, see Serge Leclaire's essay in this book.

7. Conrad Stein, *L'enfant Imaginaire* (Paris: Denoël, 1971).

AMERICAN PSYCHOANALYSIS
by François Péraldi

AS HE WAS about to land in New York City, Sigmund Freud said to Carl Gustav Jung: "They don't know yet that we are bringing them the plague." As usual he was right, but still ignorant that there were many good medical doctors in the States, many good physicians who, by taking him absolutely at his word, had nothing better to do than to treat psychoanalysis as they treat the plague, i.e., by considering psychoanalysis as a medical question.

Freud never liked the States as, in spite of all his discretion, Ernest Jones could not help indicating: "Despite his gratitude for his friendly reception there, with the recognition of his work and the honour bestowed on him, Freud did not go away with a very favorable impression of America."[1] There were perhaps many good reasons for this unfavorable impression: "a lasting intestinal trouble, an old appendicular pain, a prostatic discomfort . . . and even his difficulties with the English language and to adapt himself to the free and easy manners of the New World."[2]

But we cannot presume that these reasons drove him to say to Jones: "America is a mistake, a gigantic mistake it is true, but none the less a mistake." In spite of his frequent contacts with American psychoanalysts, Freud always remained very reticent—unless his reticence was caused by these contacts.

Seventeen years after his visit to New York, Freud had to take up a position against medical doctors, intent to take over psychoanalysis. It was no doubt in response to this that Freud wrote "The Question of Lay-Analysis" to protect Theodore Reik who, like many others at that time, was a lay analyst. But this short text has a much broader scope than the protection of nonmedical psychoanalysts.

In fact, Freud's text more or less explicitly indicates the awesome epistemological severance between psychoanalysis and all the medical or psychological sciences of his time. By epistemological severance we mean the "point of nonreturn" at which psychoanalysis begins in the historical process of formation of psychoanalytic science.

Among the epistemological effects of such a severance, Freud emphasizes the relative autonomy of the new science in comparison with all the other existing sciences among which it appeared and especially with both the medical and psychological sciences.

Another consequence is the necessary rupture with all the ideological or philosophical discourse preexistent to the severance.[3] A well-known severance of this type separates pre-Copernican astronomy and its object, the cosmos, from Copernican astronomy and its object, the infinite universe.[4] An epistemological severance has to be understood, historically speaking, as a revolution.

One year after Freud answered the question of lay analysis, American psychoanalysts tried to prevent nonmedical students from being trained as psychoanalysts, and lay analysts from practicing psychoanalysis. It is possible, as Jones suggested, that American psychoanalysts were trying to protect psychoanalysis from the charlatans that were all the freer to practice wild analysis since, as Freud pointed out, "the discussion about lay-analysis in the States can only be theoretical since in this country, anyone can choose whoever he wants to be treated by."

But it is precisely at the theoretical level that the question is of paramount importance because it implies the acknowledgment of this epistemological severance outlined in Freud's text. The assimilation of psychoanalysis by medicine is nothing else but a reduction which can only be made through a distortion of psychoanalytic theory and the suppression of some of its most revolutionary concepts.

No decision has yet been made at the governmental level, as was obvious quite recently when both the representatives of the American Psychoanalytic Association and the National Accreditation Association for Psychoanalysis, who defended opposite positions on the issue of lay analysis, were sent on their separate ways by governmental agents of mental health. But the absence of any decision at such a level does not mean anything: the destiny of psychoanalysis is to be resolved at another level, that of the institution where the decisions are made concerning the selection and the training of psychoanalysts.

It is worthwhile relating an anecdote concerning Ernst Kris as an example of what I am trying to say. Shortly after his arrival in the States, Kris agreed to take a nonmedical student in a supervised control analysis. During one of the sessions an officer of the society that had accepted Kris called him on the phone and told him that he knew who was with Kris then, that no nonmedical students were to be trained in the society, and that he had to get rid of him at once or suffer the consequences for breaking the rules as decided by the "Professional Standards." Kris obeyed but was reported to have felt conflicted long afterward.

Unlike Theodore Reik, Kris had chosen to be accepted and integrated into the "official psychoanalytic movement" represented in the States by the American Psychoanalytic Association. Reik opted for marginality, and, together with a few friends, created the National Psychological Association for Psychoanalysis, where nonmedical students are trained. So, whoever comes to the States to practice psychoanalysis or wants to be trained as a psychoanalyst has the choice between conformism or marginality.

At the individual as well as at the governmental level, the question of conformism versus marginality is of no importance. But as I said, it becomes a critical question at the institutional level for the following reasons. We are in America, the land of liberal politics. In such systems of liberal politics, power is segmented into all sorts of "machineries of power" that function in seemingly autonomous institutions. The psychoanalytic machinery of power can only be analyzed at the institutional level.

In fact, the analysis of the position of psychoanalysis in its socioeconomic and historical context is impossible at the individual level, because the differences between individuals are too numerous to be significant. Nor can it be carried out at the state level, because no law regulates the future of psychoanalysis.

Only institutions (associations, societies, institutes, academies, etc.) have a definite social function in regulating the training and practice of psychoanalysis. These regulations can be unmasked according to their ultimate goals and described in terms of a psychoanalytic machinery of power.

The training in such institutions consists mainly of building the filiation between the analysand who wants to become a psychoanalyst, and the very first psychoanalyst: Freud himself. It is only when this filiation has been fabricated in a very specific way that the newborn psychoanalyst can be affiliated with the society where he has been trained, or, should I say, *tamed.*

The relation to Freud remains the axis of the psychoanalytic machinery of power, whether it be conceived as a protection of Freud's system (Pashe, Benassy) or as return to Freud's text (Lacan) as in France; or as an adaptation of the theory (ego psychology) to the dominant ideology rendered necessary by its transplantation within another cultural context as in the United States.

THE QUESTION OF THE DIFFERENCE

When a French psychoanalyst comes to North America in order to practice psychoanalysis, he is already biased. On the one hand, he knows the main historical events we have mentioned in our introduction; on the other hand, he is more acutely aware of the difference between European and American psychoanalysis because of a very specifically French phenomenon: Jacques Lacan.

The question of the difference has been constantly and powerfully raised in France by Jacques Lacan ever since 1936, but with an increasing insistence after the Second World War, after the departure from Europe of most of the leading figures in psychoanalysis, expelled by the threat of Nazism, and their arrival in the States. Let us mention Ernst Kris, Heinz Hartmann, and Rudolph Loewenstein or even Otto Fenichel, Theodore Reik, Karen Horney, Frieda Fromm-Reichmann, Sandor Rado, the late René Spitz, and many others who fled Berlin or Vienna.

Jacques Lacan, in spite of all the repressive measures taken against him by the psychoanalytic machinery of power, denounced, in the name of a return to Freud's text, the adaptation of psychoanalysis to American ideology, and the development of ego psychology as a recuperation, a reduction, a negation of the epistemological severance introduced by Freud.

Such an adaptation is denounced by Lacan as a malversation of Freud's theory, as an antirevolutionary maneuver in which one can clearly recognize the historical characteristic of American culture, as well as the most violent negation of the importance of history and of its determinism in the course of human affairs.

At the Institutional Level

If the analysis of the American psychoanalytic machinery of power has to be made at the institutional level, where must we start?

There are a lot of so-called psychoanalytic associations, societies, and institutes in North America. They all differ in orientation and importance, but they all recognize each other as psychoanalytic even if they are in a perpetual state of conflict or competition.

Freud created the International Psychoanalytic Association (IPA) to protect the newborn psychoanalytic science against the attacks of all sorts of machineries of power—medical, psychological, and governmental. Its tasks were to protect psychoanalysis and its development and to ensure its diffusion and transmission. In other words, the IPA was the organism charged with overseeing the general laws of filiation.

We may therefore start with the question of the affiliation of psychoanalytic institutions to the IPA. There are three categories: (1) affiliated societies, (2) dissident societies, and (3) Jacques Lacan (and his Ecole Freudienne de Paris). Lacan's expulsion from his former society was the price this society (Société Française de Psychanalyse) had to pay in order to be affiliated to the IPA. This represents a unique case in the history of the psychoanalytic movement.

In America every psychoanalytic institution that wants to be affiliated with the IPA has first to be affiliated with, i.e., recognized by, the American Psychoanalytic Association (APA). This is not the case for individuals.

A second distinction is then possible in the States between institutions affiliated with the APA and those not.

IPA Versus APA

As I was trying to find my way through the psychoanalytic institutional maze, I met one of the leading figures of the APA, the vice president of the IPA, Dr. Kenneth Calder, who is my source for what follows.

I wanted to know the real nature of the relationship between the IPA and the APA. At first glance the APA can be considered as autonomous, the IPA's functions and power being considered by the APA as "moral" ones. The IPA has to oversee the standards for the transmission and practice of psychoanalysis. But in fact it appeared when I dug a little deeper that the majority of the members of the IPA were members of the APA, which in other terms means that if the APA is autonomous with regard to the IPA, it is simply because it controls it entirely.

One understands now why Jacques Lacan concentrated his attacks against American psychoanalysts, although he was expelled from the official psychoanalytic movement by the IPA. Allow me to emphasize, *en passant*, a very familiar pattern: the indirect control by the States of most of the Western world's affairs behind the facade of international institutions. It is in this respect that Freud himself was very naive when he thought that he was bringing the plague to America, because America, by taking him literally, sent back the plague to his association.

But what kind of plague did America send back to the psychoanalytic world? They sent a vaccine, because it is well known that the best way to cure an infectious disease is to prevent it and the best way to prevent it is vaccination; vaccination, as everyone knows, consists in innoculating people with the disease itself in an attenuated form: a vaccine. Innoculation tends to reinforce the body's defense mechanisms. American medical doctors produced and sent back to Europe a psychoanalytic vaccine.

The Psychoanalytic Vaccine

As we said in our introduction, American medical doctors, taking Freud absolutely at his word, at first considered psychoanalysis as a medical question.

In a booklet published in 1971 by the APA and entitled *Standards for Training in Psychoanalysis*, eligibility for psychoanalytic training is defined thus: "The applicant must present evidence of integrity of character, maturity of personality and reasonable evidence of analyzability." In other words, he must be obsessional. The authors continue: "Students are to be informed by their institutes and to understand that they are not accredited to conduct psychoanalysis, or to represent themselves as psychoanalysts until so authorized by their institutes." But a footnote indicates that "sections A, B and C of the earlier 'Standards' have been referred to committee for possible revision." The committee is one of the most important collective agents of the psychoanalytic machinery of power. The above-mentioned sections state that:

1. the applicant must have received a class-A medical training in a medical school;
2. the applicant must have spent one year of internship in a hospital recognized by the American Medical Association;
3. the applicant must have followed a one-year psychiatric training in a hospital recognized by the American Psychiatric Association.

These criteria clearly indicate that the whole psychoanalytic machinery of power is in fact controlled by powerful medical and psychiatric
machineries of power which function in the American Medical Association
and the American Psychiatric Association. Such a subjection of psychoanalysis to medical power is also clearly indicated in the by-laws of the American Psychoanalytic Association: "it shall be the purpose of the American
Psychoanalytic Association . . . to foster the integration of psychoanalysis
with other branches of medicine." This is a law running counter to the
ways explicitly designated by Freud's "Question of Lay-Analysis."

Have sections A, B, and C been referred to committee to be attenuated or suppressed? Certainly not! Nothing is to be changed yet. According to our source, barely 4 percent, and perhaps even only 1 percent,
of the members of the APA are lay analysts, and they have been chosen individually by the Board of Professional Standards.

This "individually" is very important because it means that virtually
any kind of individual derogation is possible. But when the powerful Institute of Psychoanalysis of Chicago asked to be allowed to open a new section for the training of nonmedical students, the APA refused, arguing
that such an innovation would lead to an official recognition of the eligibility for psychoanalytic training of nonmedical students, and that such a recognition would be very dangerous for the supremacy of medical power.

Individual derogations allow for strict control of the selection and the
percentage of the nonmedical individuals admitted to receive psychoanalytic training, and at the same time they keep up the illusion of liberalism.

It is also interesting to indicate that in the APA the percentage of
women is barely higher than the percentage of nonmedical members.
This is certainly due partly to the fact that until recently very few women
had access to the medical profession; but also responsible is the deep
"homosexual structure" on which most of the international movements are
grounded, and is exemplified in the case of the psychoanalytic movement
by "the fellowship of the rings."

To my question why, in spite of Freud's explicit statements on lay
analysis, the APA maintained such a policy, my interlocutor answered
very frankly, "for economic reasons!" Too many lay analysts would constitute an economic threat to medical psychoanalysts. He then mentioned a
few other reasons, among them:

1. the credibility of the medical profession, which seems to me minimal when I think of all the lawsuits brought against medical doctors in the

States, or when I watch the increasing number of TV programs like "Marcus Welby M.D.," the purpose of which is to enhance the credibility of the medical profession

2. confidentiality, a myth we will not even discuss because it is not legally recognized.[5]

3. the medical psychoanalyst's ability to make a distinction between organic or psychological illness. But then, what is the meaning of the preliminary interviews, and how can they be technically conducted to allow such a diagnosis to be made and remain psychoanalytic at the same time? On the other hand, if a medical psychoanalyst has any physical contact with his analysand, how can he handle the transferential reactions he has induced in the Real, especially with hysterical analysands? Freud insisted very strongly on the fact that a medical act can only be made by another physician and certainly not by the psychoanalyst himself. But who reads Freud in the States?

American Psychoanalytic Ethics

Principles of Ethics for Psychoanalysts published by the APA, states: "The honored ideals of the profession of psychoanalysts imply that the responsibilities of the psychoanalyst extend primarily to the individual, but also to society." Psychoanalytic ethics is thus defined as characterized by a complete submission to the necessities included in the fact of offering medical support to individuals who need it. As Greenson points out, the analysand must understand first that he is a patient. Whereas the responsibilities in terms of society are not as important, apparently, as the "but also" indicates in an ambiguous way.

In fact, it appears quite clearly that by overestimating their responsibilities to the individual (one of the main characteristics of medical ideology), psychoanalysts simply disregard their social responsibilities, i.e., their political position.

When I asked my interlocutor if the APA had ever taken positions on political issues, he answered abruptly; "Certainly not, the APA is apolitical." Then he tried to attenuate the brutality of his statement by developing the usual considerations on transference, neutrality, etc., but he clearly indicated that if an individual is allowed to take political positions (we are in a liberal country) it had to be in such a way as to have nothing to do with his belonging to a psychoanalytic society; otherwise it would be a cause for exclusion.

But what is apolitism if not a political position of a certain type, a complete submission to the recognized political power? The silence of

Pius XII is a good example of such a political position, although it never completely concealed his interest in the Nazi party, which he expected would save the Catholic church from Communism.

But even if psychoanalysts are allowed to take political positions privately, they must not be too extreme. It is interesting to see the delicate position of a young immigrant student at the New York Psychoanalytic Society who must hide his involvement in communism at both levels, professional and political: his own analysis and psychoanalytic training and his residence in the States would be threatened since he could be expelled from his institute and deported from the States. One wonders what the meaning of psychoanalysis is when the analysand must conceal his political investments.

Who cares about the blustering statements of those for whom mental illness is only a myth, if such statements have absolutely no impact on the psychoanalytic machinery of power concealed within the institutions where they work? Such statements have only one function: to maintain the myth of liberalism, that every individual can do and think what he pleases. Why not, if no power exists at the individual level?

To introduce what follows, let us say that the machineries of power are completely heterogeneous to what is designated by the term "ego," whether this ego be weak or strong, lay or analyzed.

INSTITUTIONALIZED PSYCHOANALYSIS

The Ego and the Defense Mechanisms

The *Standards for Training in Psychoanalysis* indicate that "it is expected that all candidates will have read and studied during the course of training, Freud's writings, and the other relevant literature." There is no indication as to whether "The Question of Lay-Analysis" is included or not. The relevant literature is made up of the development by Kris, Hartmann, and Loewenstein of some of Freud's ideas, but mainly of Anna Freud's developments of some of her father's ideas. These developments are called ego psychology.

We must of course keep in mind the distinction between the individual and the institutional level, because it appears clear that such authors as René Spitz, Margaret Mahler, or Otto Kernberg would not consider these assigned readings as their main theoretical references. We can give reasons for this: An individual deviance that does not imply any change in the society to which such a deviant individual belongs is considered as harmless and useful, insofar as it maintains the liberal facade of the institution. A Lacanian can become a guest in an American society if he can be used as an extra-value by this society.

But at this point, the question raised by Lacan is of crucial importance. His fight against the APA cannot be considered a tempest in a teapot, or the result of misbehavior on his part, sexual misbehavior with patients, an excessive suicide rate among his patients, the shortening of the length of the session, etc.

The question is whether ego psychology constitutes a real development of Freud's discovery, or, more likely, an attempt to reduce or annihilate the epistemological severance introduced by Freud by interpreting psychoanalysis into the ideology prevalent in the States. This way of putting the question raised by Lacan is quite different because it emphasizes the real situation, i.e., the future of a scientific revolution.

We cannot analyze a question of this scope here, but we want to emphasize what Lacan has vigorously stated for many years; that psychoanalysis is not the science of the reunification of the human subject, that in this respect psychoanalysis has nothing to do with Cartesian philosophy which permeates the medical and psychological ideologies and sciences and that, last but not least, the specific object of psychoanalytic science is not the ego or even the self, but the *unconscious*. Only the unconscious can be considered the specific object of psychoanalysis because it defines psychoanalysis as a science.

The epistemological severance introduced by Freud is as follows: the human subject is not a unified (or unifiable) subject in the light of consciousness. The human subject is radically and fundamentally divided: "I am an Other" as Rimbaud said. It is in such a way that the very formula of Freud's discovery, "Wo es war soll ich werden" has to be understood.

A formula as intense as the pre-Socratic "$\epsilon \nu \pi \alpha \nu \tau \alpha$" cannot be translated into the French by "le Moi doit déloger le ça" (The ego must dislodge the id); it should not be translated into English as the syntax determines the translation by "where the id was the ego shall be." It should not in fact be translated at all without a structural commentary, along the lines of the Lacanian analysis: "Wo es war, soll ich werden," a formula where the structuring of the signifier prevails.

Let us look at it closely. Freud did not say *das Es* nor *das Ich*, as he usually does when designating those instances he uses to structure the new topic, and, given the rigor of his style, this presupposes a special emphasis in their use in the sentence. In any case, without even referring to any internal critique of Freud's text to prove that he states *das Ich* and *das Es* to establish the basic distinction between the true subject of the unconscious and the ego as made up in its core by a series of alienating identifications,[6] it appears that it is at the place: *Wo*, where; *Es*, subject devoid of any *das* or other objectifying article; *war*, was, a place of being in other words, and at this place; *soll*, a duty in the moral sense here, as the only sentence after this one, and which ends the chapter, indicates ("es ist Kulturarbeit, etwas wie die Trockenbegung der Zuydersee"); *Ich*, I, there must I (like announcing: "I am the one who" before saying "it is I [my ego] who"); *werden*, becoming, i.e., not *sur-coming* nor even *after-coming* but *be-coming* because the place is the place of being, where it is my duty to *be-come"*[7] There is undoubtedly a profound difference between such an approach and Hartmann's, a difference due on the one hand to different conceptions of the *activity of reading,* and on the other, to the fact that Lacan primarily read Freud's text whereas Hartmann mainly refers to Anna Freud's writings.

When Hartmann introduces the notion of Ego, he uses a very significant detour. He does not try to understand the difference between psychoanalysis and the other sciences of the human psyche, which would have constituted an epistemological approach. He tries first to develop the notion of adaptation which constitutes an ideological approach. When he introduces the distinction between the state and the process which leads to adaptation, he does not analyze carefully what the human subject has to adapt himself to. The environment, which necessitates an adaptation, is understood by him as a reality, a state of things that appears as equivalent to the Real, a reality that does not seem in Hartmann's mind to have already been analyzed by Marx or even Hegel: a reality that is historical. It is very surprising to see how, when he reached the other side of the Atlantic, Hartmann immediately forgot, along with his bad impressions, the meaning of a historical reality from which he had to escape.

In fact, Hartmann presents adaptation as the adaptation to the Real, and this is why he chooses his examples in the field of natural history, mostly in the style of behaviorists for whom human adaptation can be understood from the adaptation of a monkey to his *Umwelt.*

The confusion between reality and the Real allows Hartmann to dismiss the necessary political and historical analysis that would be implicated if he had considered reality as it is: an historical reality, a socioeconomic context that has no meaning unless situated in its historical development. On the contrary, reality appears to Hartmann as the divine, the eternal order of things, an order that therefore cannot be questioned, but rather implies the necessary adaptation of the human subject to its everlasting laws.

Failing to understand that reality is the historical field of contradiction and the battlefield of the social classes, Hartmann also fails to understand the fundamental *Spaltung* of the *Ich*.

In fact, Hartmann's conception of the subject is nothing other than an enlarged Cartesian conception of the subject, a subject, American of course, who can claim to be master of himself as he is of the universe.

For Hartmann the unconscious is not the part, which only appears in the discourse of the *Other*, of an irretrievably divided subject; it has become a forgotten land which has to be rediscovered so that the subject can finally be reunified in a reality that he confuses with the Real, the natural order of the world.

I hope that it is now clear what I mean by this severance between two groups of psychoanalysts. On one side there are those who believe in the subject as a whole and in history as a constant and inevitable evolution of a natural state of things. Psychoanalysis is thus reduced to a technique consisting in adapting a subject to the complexity of his self and to the social order (taken for granted). On the other side there are those who think that the subject is an irrevocably divided being. The ego is the part of the subject manufactured through a series of alienating identifications; on this side people think that reality is the field of a lasting conflict between social classes, the field of contradiction itself, on the mute and amorphous body of the Real. In this case psychoanalysis has nothing to do with the adaptation of the ego. Psychoanalysis is a process through which a subject can apprehend his own decentering in the three following fields: *the Imaginary* (the field of alienating identifications), *the Symbolic* (the field of reality and language as structured on the same system of laws), and *the Real* (this unutterable field where among other things, something absolutely essential in Freud's discovery functions: the *TodesTriebe*, Death Drive).

The Death Drive

It is amazing to observe how puzzled most psychoanalysts are when they are confronted with the concept of the death drive, which is both the core and the most scandalous and revolutionary concept in Freud's theory. This feeling of puzzlement has been so unbearable for Hartmann and most of the American psychoanalysts that they have simply thrown it out of psychoanalytic theory. It is a rejection based on what appears as a misleading translation of *TodesTriebe* into English. It was voluntarily introduced by Kris, Hartmann, and Loewenstein in one of their common writings, "The Theory of Aggression." When they speak of *TodesTriebe*, the three men speak of death instincts, which allows them to relegate these specific instincts to the field of biology along with all the other instincts—that is to say, to remove them from the field of psychoanalysis. One could forgive this unfortunate error in translating if a few pages further on, the three men had not insisted on a very important distinction between the German words *Trieb* and *Instinkt*, which they correctly translate this time as "drive" for *Trieb* and "instinct" for *Instinkt*. They stress that drives are the very specific objects of psychoanalysis. But Freud never spoke of *Todes Instinkt;* from the very beginning of the second topic, starting with "Beyond the Pleasure Principle" to the end of his life, he always explicitly spoke of *TodesTriebe*, which should have been translated as death drives, and kept in psychoanalytic theory as something entirely different from what has been substituted for them: the aggressive drives.

By uprooting the death drives from psychoanalytic theory, American psychoanalysts have devitalized it. They have cut off one of the most revolutionary and dynamic concepts ever formulated and have therefore reduced psychoanalysis to a pure and formal technique of manipulation. It is very revealing to realize that the recognition of psychoanalysts is based on technical criteria and that psychoanalysis has therefore been reduced to a kind of therapy, or orthotherapy, adapted to the requirements of a technocratic society.

The acceptance of ego psychology as the main development of Freudian psychoanalysis today in the States has two consequences: the hyperdevelopment of a more or less technocratic orientation at the expense of a solid theoretical reflection backed up by a rigorous epistemological critique; and the complete inefficiency of orthodox psychoanalysis in terms of psychosis, resulting in the appearance of the main deviant trends in the American psychoanalytic world: Harry Stack Sullivan, Frieda Fromm-Reichmann, Wilhelm Reich, and others.

THE HYPERDEVELOPMENT OF THE TECHNIQUE

We can grasp the importance of the development of the technique from the enormous number of writings published, from Otto Fenichel's texts right up to Greenson's. The technique includes all the technical developments of audio-visual aids. They are too numerous for us to analyze here. Nevertheless, we would like to indicate that the technical criteria and the ethical standards mentioned by our interlocutor, which prevail in the training and the recognition of psychoanalysts by the psychoanalytic institutions where they are trained, are the same, and are directly imported from medical ideology. Let us review them quickly:

1. sexual conduct in relation to patients, reduced to the period of the so-called therapeutic relationship in analysis. When the cure is supposedly over, who cares? It may be amusing here to indicate that the specialist on narcissism in France is precisely a psychoanalyst who married an ex-analysand much younger than he is.

2. the suicide rate, which constitutes one of the most powerful mechanisms of the medical machinery of power. Suicide can always be considered as a professional mistake for any kind of worker in the field of health, but only medical doctors are considered competent enough to produce a definite judgment on each particular case. Death in the medical world is always interpreted as a failure of medical techniques. The only question is to judge whether it is acceptable in terms of technical standards. It is very easy to understand the immense difference between this medical conception of death and the one put forward by Freud and analyzed in this volume by J. B. Pontalis and Julien Bigras.

3. the frequency and length of the sessions. Everybody knows about the scandalous brevity of Lacan's psychoanalytic sessions, but they always forget the importance of how they are terminated, because the termination constitutes an interpretation.

4. other technical criteria and ethical standards: money, neutrality, confidentiality, etc.

What is the significance of all this emphasis on technique? It is a submission to the requirements of medical ideology. The emphasis put on the clinical aspect is also a means of avoiding the importance of the theoretical aspect which is reduced to a privilege for the happy few. It is also a way to practice dogmatic orthodoxy where, on the contrary, a constant criticism and analysis should always prevail.

When one has to work with an instrument as precise and detailed as that described by Greenson, one wonders what happens to elements such as suspended attention, listening with the third ear (Theodore Reik) or the not-knowing ear, or surprise. On the other hand, one wonders where the place is for disciplines such as anthropology, history of myths, literary criticism, etc. in the training of psychoanalysts. There is no place for such studies in most of the psychoanalytic institutes in spite of the strong recommendation made by Freud. This is a shame because only an effective transdisciplinarity might have allowed for the development of psychoanalysis as it was invented by Freud: a revolutionary anthropology.

Psychosis and Deviant Trends in Psychoanalysis

The total failure of ego psychology in treating psychosis is both an interesting and a revealing phenomenon. We cannot discuss it here, but it would be advisable to use this failure as a springboard to undertake a radical criticism of psychoanalysis reduced to an ego psychology, which cannot explain psychosis in any other terms than organic ones.

Personally, I think that we should start from the question that psychosis poses for us, a question left open by Freud and foreclosed by ego psychologists. However, we would like to make another point here, namely, that most of the great deviant psychoanalysts left the orthodox psychoanalytic movement as soon as they tried to answer the question of psychoses.

It is not a coincidence that Jacques Lacan entered the psychoanalytic movement after he had finished his thesis on a case of paranoïa, circa 1932–36, and left it in 1954 as he was directing his seminar on psychosis and the Schreber case.

The careers of Harry Stack Sullivan and Frieda Fromm-Reichmann are very good examples of the point I am trying to make. Sullivan received a very orthodox training in psychiatry and psychoanalysis but—and perhaps because, as he used to say about himself, he was schizophrenic—instead of working on the usual cases considered suitable for psychoanalytic treatment, he dedicated his whole career to the treatment of schizophrenia. As he was working in psychiatric institutions, he was unable to focus his attention on the individual. Very quickly he became aware of the importance of the social and historical context in which schizophrenia appears, and, sometimes, disappears. Thus he could not help but leave a psychoanalysis permeated with an individualistic ideology to try to develop his own conception of what he called interpersonal theory, by a fusion of psychoanalysis, psychiatry, and social sciences.

Our interlocutor agreed with us when we put forward the hypothesis that the main deviant trends in psychoanalysis elaborated this separation on such topics as: the importance of socioeconomic context in the etiology of madness and the deep modification of psychoanalytic technique required in the treatment of psychosis by the social interpretation of the psychotic process. I would personally add that the question of psychosis forces us to deal with the death drives, on both a theoretical and practical plane. As P. C. Racamier said in his book on the analytic treatment of psychosis, "When we deal with psychosis, we deal with death."[8] But he does not say whose death, the psychoanalyst's or the analysand's. Harold Searles attempts to answer these vital questions.

These three criteria constitute perhaps the common link between the psychoanalytic associations that left the American Psychoanalytic Association and the main differences between affiliated and nonaffiliated societies.

On the one hand (the APA), one finds medicalized psychoanalysis, working under the total control of the medical machinery of power, and dealing only with the type of treatment of neurosis and psychoneurosis according to a very rigid technique, a sort of ritual, which also furnishes the criteria of recognition *by*, and affiliation *to* the APA a technique centered around the individual. On the other hand, in more or less autonomous associations with respect to the medical machinery of power, one finds a more socialized (or even politicized) psychoanalysis. This type of psychoanalysis has been modified and enlarged so that it may be used to answer the question of psychosis, and its theory is reconsidered in such a way that the delicate and difficult question of the death drives has to be raised again. It does not avoid the social aspect of madness and the political implications of its position.

NONCONCLUSION

Of course we cannot draw any conclusion because our work is only a sketch of what could be the major orientations of a serious study of the question of the difference between French and American psychoanalysis. It has to be done if French and American psychoanalysts are to pursue the dialogue that started at NYU in May 1976. And it is to be done by paying more attention than we did to individual deviances within orthodox societies, and to other deviant trends which have not even been mentioned, those of Erich Fromm, Karen Horney, and, of course, Wilhelm Reich.

When I wrote this text I had not yet read the remarkable study that K. R. Eissler has written on the question of lay analysis. It would have provided me with much more information but would not have changed my opinions on the question.

François Péraldi

NOTES

1. Ernest Jones, *The Life and Work of Sigmund Freud* (London: Penguin, 1964), p. 347.

2. *Ibid.*

3. Michel Fichant and Michel Pêcheux, *Sur l'Histoire des Sciences* (Paris: Maspero, 1974).

4. Alexandre Koyré, *From the Closed World to the Infinite Universe* (Baltimore: Johns Hopkins University Press, 1957).

5. The question of confidentiality is thus raised in *The Principles of Ethics for Psychoanalysts,* published by the American Psychoanalytic Association: "Except as required by law, a psychoanalyst may not reveal the confidences entrusted him in the course of his professional work, or the particuliarities that he may observe in the characters of patients. Should he be required by a court of law to give testimony relating to the confidences of his patient, he should conduct himself responsibly toward his patient and should disclose only such information as may be required by law." But the law can require any kind of information, especially because it does not give anyone the right to remain silent under the cover of professional secrecy.

6. In a now classic paper which he presented on July 17, 1949 at the International Congress of Psychoanalysis, in Zürich, Jacques Lacan developed his conception of the ego, the structuration of which begins as soon as the infant is able to apprehend his own image in the mirror, as the title of the paper indicates clearly: "The Mirror Stage in the Formation of the Ego." This ability of the child should be considered, according to Lacan, as the very first form of identification which is also a form of alienation from one's own image. Cf. J. Lacan, *Ecrits* (Paris: Seuil, 1966).

7. J. Lacan, *Ecrits.* This passage has been translated by Daniel Slote.

8. Paul-Claude Racamier, *Le psychanalyste sans divan* (Paris: Payot 1970).

❧ 2 ❧

French Psychoanalysis: A Sociological Perspective

SHERRY TURKLE

THE RESISTANCE to psychoanalytic ideas and practice in France, particularly in contrast to the enthusiastic American response, has until recently been a cliché in the intellectual history of the twentieth century. But within the last decade, and particularly since the French student revolt of May–June 1968, the French attitude toward psychoanalysis has gone from resistance to a kind of infatuation, in what is perhaps one of the most dramatic social reversals of an intellectual position in modern history.

However, the psychoanalysis that the French are now so involved with is very far in both style and substance from the kind of approach that has become somewhat "standard brand" on the American scene. "French Freud" and "American Freud" are very different, not just on an intellectual level, but in terms of their social and political involvements. In America, psychoanalysis was fairly easily accepted in psychiatric cycles. It appears that American psychoanalysis paid a price for popularity: the dilution of those aspects of Freud's vision that can form the basis for a radical critique of society as well as of commonsense ways of thinking about the self. Although some American analysts do stand as exceptions to the general trend, in America, psychoanalysis did not develop a strong cutting-edge as a language for social criticism. In France, things were quite different. Until recent years, French psychoanalysts made up of a small and stigmatized community, and psychoanalysis was marginal to established psychiatry and medicine. From this position as an outsider, French psychoanalysis, unlike its American counterpart, developed in close association with radical critiques of the status quo. The French-American contrast throws the social specificity of psychoanalysis into sharp relief. This specificity is not surprising given that psychoanalysis is not simply an intellectual theory, but is deeply intricated in social practice, first as a guide to forms of therapeutic intervention and second as a body of thought open to appropriation as social/political ideology. Psychoanalysis is socially embedded thought; a public's interest in it as an intellectual doctrine and as a social or therapeutic ideology opens up questions of a sociological nature. This essay asks and tries to answer some of these questions as it introduces the French psychoanalytic movement from a sociological perspective.

We begin our introduction to the French psychoanalytic movement with a brief overview of its history. From this history it is apparent that our story has a central character: the French psychoanalyst and theoretician Jacques Lacan. Indeed, although the French psychoanalytic movement is far from monolithic, Lacan's influence on all of French psychoanalysis makes some general characterizations possible. It is dominated by an interest in its status as a science, in epistemology, in linguistics, in mathematics, in aesthetics, poetics, and politics. These concerns are those of Lacan, and, although the postwar history of the French psychoanalytic movement is marked by a series of splits in which Lacan was the center of controversy, his ideas have influenced many of those who have left him no less than those who have remained loyal to him.

The question of "Why Lacan?" that is, why Lacan's particular brand of psychoanalytic thought had such an impact in France, is complex. In France today, Lacan personifies a conception of psychoanalysis as an enterprise whose goal is to find the truth of the subject; the notion of psychoanalysis as a technique of "cure," a quasi-medical technique, is rejected. Lacan has spent his career attacking the Americans, whom he sees as the worst offenders in this regard. For Lacan, being a psychoanalyst is a calling, a process of growth and discovery that has nothing to do with having a certain kind of academic degree, with belonging to the bureaucracy of an analytic institute, or with following a series of set rules about how to conduct analytic sessions. Lacan has institutionalized these beliefs in his own psychoanalytic school, the Ecole Freudienne de Paris, where there are not only no requirements for admission (such as an M. D. or a Ph. D.), but there is no set program for becoming an analyst. For Lacan, when it comes to analytic training or how to do analysis, the only rule is that there are no set rules.

For many analysts, Lacan has served as a bridge between political and psychoanalytic radicalism. Many French analysts seem to feel that Lacan and his work are offering them some respite if not relief from the "American dilemma" of analytic acceptability (what happens to psychoanalysis when it is no longer considered marginal or threatening, but rather is considered the "thing to do") by bringing them back to a vision of what is subversive in the analytic vision. Lacan attacks the idea that one can be true to the Freudian discovery by institutionalizing psychoanalysis in rigid training structures or by following a technique aimed at strengthening the ego. According to Lacan, psychoanalysis ceases to be psychoanalysis when it is routinized; and there is no coherent ego to be strengthened. Lacan demonstrates that the ego is formed by a composite of false and distorting introjections so that "I" and "Other" are inextricably confused in the language of the self; thus, any comforting, pleasant sense of the coherence of the "self" is purely illusory.

Lacan's central concern is with the status of human discourse in analysis, and, indeed, with the status of human discourse in general. For Lacan, the resolution of the Oedipus crisis is the entrance of the subject into the discourse of language and society, or what he refers to as the *Symbolique*. The central issue in psychoanalysis is the same as that for all discourse—that is, the problem of who is speaking. To question the status of discourse is to put into question the status of the subject. According to Lacan's reading of Freud, this was Freud's central concern. Lacan's structuralist psychoanalytic theory radically "decenters" the subject, subverting the ego both diachronically (in terms of its history) and synchronically (in terms of its underlying structural possibilities.)

Historically, for Lacan the ego is lost in the unconscious structure of desire, "fading" and slipping from its phantasm of an object (its mirror reflection) that was its illusory foundation.[1] When the child identifies itself in the mirror, he says, "That's me" and objectifies himself as what he sees. Only later will this "me" be brought gradually, but never completely, into line with subjective, with the "I." A second, permanent, structural distortion of the ego is that of its unconscious desire. For Lacan, like Hegel with his concept of desire as the "law of the heart," the ego's desire is an ungratifiable quest for the desire of the Other. In each ego demand, a specific need might be satisfied, but the *desire* that moves the ego toward its unattainable lost object can never be satisfied.

For Lacan, as for Lévi-Strauss, the self is decentered, man is the object of a Law that transcends him. Lévi-Strauss's Indians cannot recognize the rules governing the marriages between cousins, and since Freud wrote *The Interpretation of Dreams* it has been clear that man is inhabited by a Law that he doesn't constitute but that constitutes him. Man is inhabited by the Signifier; he didn't create it.

Lacan's Hegelianism (his emphasis on the "dialectics of desire") and his notion of the decentered self make his thought deeply resonant with the French intellectual currents of existential Marxism and structuralism. Indeed, intellectual historian H. Stuart Hughes remarked that the French were resistant to psychoanalysis until they had produced Lacan, their own "indigenous heretic" whose structuralism, formalism, and linguistic emphasis were resonant with the French Cartesian tradition.[2] It is certainly true that the new French psychoanalytic-structuralist hybrid is in harmony with major themes in the French philosophical tradition. However, it is very important to remember that the new infatuation with Freud in France is a *social* phenomenon. As such, it is not understandable if one looks only at the resonance of its particular forms with other elements of French intellectual life. The question of "why now?" of understanding why the long-standing French resistance to psychoanalysis has crumbled, remains as a challenge to the sociologist and historian. This question also challenges any analyst sensitive to the fact that both his legitimation as a privileged listener and his potential efficacy as a healer are dependent on his relationship to the social field within which he operates. When we look at the French shift from resistance to infatuation, we are looking at a part of what must be a more general inquiry: How do changes in social relations inform the kinds of therapeutic (and particularly psychotherapeutic) relationships that are conducted in a society; how do social institutions work for and against the development of different types of ideologies of healing; how do these ideologies of healing, in this case psychoanalytic ones, find roles in areas of social life outside of medicine—in politics, in education, in childrearing?

Thus, in this essay we do not focus on French psychoanalytic theory or on how Lacan's work is intellectually resonant with French intellectual traditions. Rather, after examining the history of the French psychoanalytic movement, we concentrate on the social world within which the French psychoanalytic movement has been able to grow into a French psychoanalytic culture. In Section II, we develop a theory about the timing of the French psychoanalytic explosion, relating it to recent social changes in France. In Section III, we describe a set of circumstances that came together to create a setting where psychoanalysis, although so slow to develop, could take a particularly powerful and politicized form in France beginning in the late 1960s. In Section IV we look at the same phenomena of psychoanalysis in the popular culture and in politics from a different point of view. We present an empirical study documenting how the French psychoanalytic culture has entered the public's consciousness and how the social image of psychoanalysis has changed since the mid-1950s.

I. Lacan and the History of
the French Psychoanalytic Movement

By 1926 a small group of analytic "pioneers," drawn largely from medical circles, had founded the first French psychoanalytic society, the Société Psychanalytique de Paris (SPP); but this group remained insignificant in size and influence until well after the Second World War.[3] The resistance of the French medical community to psychoanalysis was intense and prolonged; in France, the initial interest in psychoanalysis was in the artistic and literary communities, particularly among the surrealists. Before the Second World War psychoanalysis was rejected in France as a system of German inspiration; after the war it came to be seen somewhat disdainfully as yet another postwar commodity "imported from America" and tended to be associated with Dr. Spock and permissive childrearing. It subsequently underwent a major Gallicization via Jacques Lacan's structuralist reading of Freud.

Lacan's presence has marked the postwar history of the psychoanalytic movement by precipitating a series of schisms. The first schism, in 1953, was of the Société Psychanalytique de Paris. It grew out of a double-edge controversy. First, the Paris society was about to set up a special institute to train analysts, and many of its members (as well as its analytic candidates) objected to this "American-styled" formalization of psychoanalytic training. Second, by 1953, great controversy surrounded the "unorthodox" analytic practice of the Paris society's president, Dr.

Jacques Lacan. Lacan's practice had become commonly identified with "short" (often five-minute) analytic sessions. On June 2, 1953, a scientific meeting of the SPP confronted Lacan with the rumors about his high volume of patients and abbreviated sessions. On June 16, 1953, the society's administrative body asked for Lacan's resignation as president, causing an uproar, since many French analysts saw in Lacan the greatest psychoanalytic thinker since Freud. In the polarization of opinion that followed the motion asking for Lacan's resignation, supporting Lacan became tied up with opposing the idea of a training institute.

After the censure vote on Lacan, a group of analysts, among them Daniel Lagache, Françoise Dolto, and Juliette Favez-Boutonnier, resigned from the Société Psychanalytique de Paris and formed their own group, the new Société Française de Psychanalyse (SFP). They were soon joined by Lacan, several other analysts, and a group of candidates. Although many of the analysts who participated in this second French psychoanalytic society refer to their days in it as a kind of "golden age," the group was haunted by the specters of the very issues that precipitated its formation—the issues of "discipline" (Does psychoanalysis have "rules"?) and training (Should analytic training be codified?). The International Psychoanalytic Association (IPA) decided not to immediately recognize the new French psychoanalytic society on the grounds that it did not offer adequate training; but IPA did form a study group to further investigate the question. The study group's members interviewed French analysts and candidates and reported back to the International Association. Their decision went against the schismatics, who were excluded from membership in the International Psychoanalytic Association; the new Société Française de Psychanalyse was denied status as an accredited training institute. This first decision was handed down in something of a rush to judgment, but for the analysts who had followed Lagache and Lacan into the new venture the question was far from closed. The issue of "recognition"—or rather what to do about nonrecognition—continued to preoccupy the Société Française de Psychanalyse for all of its ten-year history.

Some members of the new analytic society continued to seek recognition by the International Psychoanalytic Association as a way of demonstrating their dissatisfaction with Lacan's practice. Many analysts had left the parent analytic society in 1953 not because they supported Lacan, but because they opposed the idea of having what they saw as an "American-styled" psychoanalytic training institute with courses and a curriculum.

Far from feeling any unconditional loyalty to Lacan, they resented his unorthodox practice which was keeping them out of the IPA. In 1963 the IPA agreed to recognize the second French psychoanalytic society, but only on the condition that Lacan and his close colleague Dolto be demoted from their status as training analysts. Once again French analysts had to take sides. This time they were being asked to choose between "official" status in the international psychoanalytic establishment and loyalty to Jacques Lacan. In 1963 the Société Française de Psychanalyse split in two. One group, among them Lagache, Favez-Boutonnier, and some of Lacan's closest students, including Jean Laplanche, J.-B. Pontalis, and Didier Anzieu, left Lacan and formed the Association Psychanalytique de France (APF), which was duly recognized by the IPA. A second group stayed with Lacan. Lacan founded his own school, the Ecole Freudienne de Paris, and they followed him into it. The analysts who joined the Ecole Freudienne in 1963 did so for a variety of reasons. For some, it was unthinkable to deny training status to an analyst widely considered to be France's leading theoretician. For some, long association and personal loyalty to Lacan made any other option impossible. For some, the International Association had shown itself to be hypocritical and politically motivated, and they wanted nothing more to do with it. Many of the founding members of the Ecole Freudienne had been analyzed by Lacan. The International Association had been willing to let them become training analysts although it denied that status to Lacan, their analyst. To many, the position seemed theoretically indefensible.

Although its traumatic birth imparted an initial spirit of solidarity to Lacan's Ecole Freudienne, it, like its predecessors, was to be torn apart by the issue of what constituted "responsible" training and practice. Most members of the school accepted Lacan's formulation that "L'analyste ne s'autorise que de lui-même" (Only the analyst can authorize himself to act as an analyst) as a statement about the impossibility of "routinizing" an analysand's decision that he is ready to see patients as an analyst.[4] However, even some staunch Lacan defenders felt uncomfortable as more and more young members of the Ecole Freudienne declared themselves Lacanian analysts and began to recruit patients on the Paris scene, where their welcome was warmed by their "affiliation" with Lacan's prestige and where their practice was made possible by the new burgeoning of interest in psychoanalysis in general and in Lacan in particular. If Lacan's defenders became uncomfortable, Lacan's critics became virulent at the exponential growth of Ecole Freudienne analysts; they characterized the training program at the Ecole Freudienne as the cheap manufacture of unqualified "little Lacanians" by assembly line.

Tension at the Ecole Freudienne mounted through the 1960s, and a group of members split off from it in 1969. The "official" reason for the split was disagreement about a procedure that Lacan calls *la passe*.[5] In *la passe* an analyst speaks about his experience of the didactic analysis to two "witnesses" (*témoins*). These witnesses are his *passeurs*, chosen from among the analysts in training with senior analysts (*analystes de l'école*) at the Ecole Freudienne. The analyst who is to *faire la passe* chooses his two *passeurs* by lot from a pool of *passeurs* who are selected by their analysts. Opposition to *la passe* (for example, because it violated analytic confidentiality or because being chosen as a *passeur* by one's analyst might disrupt an analysis) precipitated the 1969 split in the Ecole Freudienne, but it is clear that other tensions prepared the break long before *la passe* became a problem. An important source of contention was the pressure at the Ecole Freudienne for unanimity in support of Lacan's ideas. For example, *Scilicet*, the school's official publication, publishes all articles anonymously *except for those written by Lacan*. Analysts asked the question of whether the Lacanian "return to Freud" was compatible with their sense that the Ecole Freudienne was becoming a closed *chapelle* where Lacan's ideas took on the force of law and where his students often came to prefer his words to a serious reinterrogation of Freud's texts. The voting of the "proposition du 9 octobre 1967" on *la passe* led to the resignation of ten analysts from the Ecole Freudienne, among them Piera Castoriadis-Aulagnier, François Perrier, and Jean-Paul Valebrega. They formed France's fourth orthodox Freudian analytic society, known as the Quatrième Groupe. These "Lacanians without Lacan" hoped to create an analytic society that could follow some of Lacan's ideas (particularly regarding openness to other disciplines) without having to deal with Lacan's narcissism, his mercurial temperament, and his penchant for putting forward his preferences as a return to the "true Freud."

The French psychoanalytic community is caught up in the myths, images, and conflicts of this history, dominated by a series of relationships to Lacan. Thus, Lacan dominates the French psychoanalytic scene, either by his presence or by his absence from any given group. He tends to be a cherished object, a preoccupation, or an obsession. Few analysts are neutal about him. In my interviews with French psychoanalysts of all four analytic societies, the Société Psychanalytique de Paris, the Association Psychanalytique de France, the Ecole Freudienne, and the Quatrième Groupe, Lacan was often present as a fantasized audience, a third party to whom I was an imagined messenger. For members of the Ecole Freudienne communication with Lacan can be difficult; dialogue with a living *Maître* poses tremendous problems. For analysts outside the Ecole Freudienne, communication can be almost impossible. Lacan considers himself abandoned by three successive generations of students and colleagues, often left by just those people with whom he had worked most closely. The possibilities for dialogue have been shut down; the feelings run too high; the history is too charged.

Thus, although almost everyone's communication with Lacan is blocked, it remains almost everyone's preoccupation. Desire for some audience with Lacan seemed implied when French psychoanalysts would ask me, "Avez-vous déjà vu Lacan?" (Have you already seen Lacan?) In this almost invariable question the time marker of "déjà" (already) was always present. The question was, after all, "Have you already seen Lacan, or are you going to be seeing him; are you in a position to carry my message (of apology, of recrimination, or self-justification) or some resonance of my feelings to him?" Appreciating the force of feeling behind the fantasies that I would deliver such messages to Lacan offers some sense of how he preoccupies French psychoanalysts and influences the French psychoanalytic scene.

II. French Social Change and the Emergence of a Psychoanalytic Culture

Several researchers have tried to understand the initial and longstanding rejection of Freud by the French psychiatric community and public by looking at the fit, or rather the lack of fit, between psychoanalysis and a set of values thought to be widely held in French society. For example, Anne Parsons's study of the introduction of Freud in France finds that traditional French values were important influences on the negative reception given to Freud's ideas.[6] Parsons interprets the French rejection of Freud as a "moral" act and demonstrates that Freud's theory was deemed inacceptable more on value grounds than on scientific ones. French values of rational control, realism, and individualism based on a conscious manipulation of one's own talents seemed threatened by con-

cepts like id and unconscious which implied that one was not in control of
one's fate.

A 1967 study of Carol Ryser demonstrated that the French psychiatric literature through the mid-1960s maintained a pattern of values congruent with those that Ryser identified as general French cultural values.[7]
These values, shared by psychiatry and the society at large, were hostile
to any "psychological" (and by extension psychoanalytic) focus in treatment. Psychiatrists insisted that there was an irreconcilable distance between a basic shared personality and the environment created by modern
industrialism. Traditional patterns of French life were seen as being good
for people's emotional state. Based on her analysis of how values influenced the acceptance of different therapeutic ideologies, Ryser predicted
a gloomy future for psychoanalysis in France. In fact, things went very
much in the opposite direction, and the years immediately following Ryser's research were when psychoanalysis "took off" in popularity in
France. Analysts began to take larger roles in medical settings, in mental
health programs, in the school system, in the University, in the training of
a rapidly expanding number of psychologists and social workers, in the
media, and in the publishing industry, where book series specializing in
psychoanalytic writing have sprung up like mushrooms since 1968.
Clearly, by looking only at values, Ryser missed incipient changes. The
"motor" for the current French psychoanalytic "visibility" lies deeper,
rooted in underlying social variables.

In *The Triumph of the Therapeutic* Philip Rieff argues that the development of modern industrial societies has been accompanied by a process
of "deconversion" from the belief systems and symbols of traditional "positive communities" to those of "negative communities" sharing only the
symbols of science, where each individual must create his own personal
world of symbols and meaning.[8] In societies that are positive communities
or contain such communities within them, the culture itself can serve as
its own therapeutic order and offers a belief system through which its
members can interpret their experience. Rieff's discussion is not an historical one, but the development of a psychoanalytic culture in both France
and America can be traced to the development of social situations that
relate to the phenomenon of deconversion. Traditional French society
contained within itself important elements associated with positive communities. The traditional therapeutic order in this society did make use of
the forces of communal symbology; to a certain degree, traditional French

psychiatry's rational and moral language called upon the community and the community's values to cure. Psychoanalysis, on the other hand, is a morally neutral therapy in that it speaks of self-control, not of the social control that comes from belonging to a positive community of nation, church, or etiquette.

Psychoanalysis was welcomed in America in the early twentieth century at a point when America, particularly urban America, had to come to terms with restlessness, with geographic and social mobility from within and immigration from without.[9] America's affluence and lack of a coherent national culture helped psychoanalysis achieve a greater social role. Analytic absorption in the history of the individual helped to compensate for the absence of a collective past in the American nation of immigrants. By the time that Freud visited America in 1909, urbanization and increased affluence were developing simultaneously with a liberalization of religious practices and sexual conduct, whereas in France ancestors were still known by their names and habits, the past was secure, and the future began in it.

In America, the breakdown of community, the process of "deconversion," was well under way when psychoanalysis took root over a half century ago. Current American efforts to construct living collectives and new religious communities, the rebirth of fundamentalism, the Eastern sects and Jesus freaks, may be attempts to build new "artificial" positive communities as oases in a desert of pervasive individualism. In France it would seem that the moment of deconversion has but recently arrived, having had to wait for the end of the extraordinary synthesis of state, society, and individual that had marked France's Republican period.[10] The synthesis was attacked in the prewar period and began to be seriously damaged during the war and after. Politically, the bourgeois politics of *le juste milieu* was attacked by the Right and the Left. Economically, France's "aristocratic" values in business crumbled, and the fragmentation and mobility of industrialization and urbanization were forced upon her. The new sweep of rationalism, beginning with the First Plan at the end of World War II, but only fully implemented with the coming of De Gaulle and the end of the Algerian war, has profoundly shaken the traditional "stalemate society." The traditional French family business is giving way to new industries in the American corporate model, and the percentage of the population who work in agriculture and who live in rural villages has been dramatically reduced. A managerial revolution has led to the emergence of a new class of technocrats wherein hierarchy is based on skills, performance, and profit rather than on an aristocratic notion of prowess. The French family is less closed and no longer plays its formerly exclusive role in the socialization of the child.

Such changes in social circumstances seem to have made psychoanalytic theory and the therapies inspired by it more appropriate in France. At the same time, French psychoanalysis has developed under the influence of a social environment that has presented it with some culturally specific problems, particularly as concerns psychoanalysis and politics. In sum, France is now less like what Reiff called a positive "moral" community. The development of existentialism and the French "discovery" of psychoanalysis may represent two cultural expressions of recent processes of deconversion on many levels of the social experience. The events of May–June 1968 seem to mark a moment in that process and have a Janus-like quality: they are analogous to attempts to re-create community where it has disappeared and also seem to be an expression of a sense of community that is dying. A tradition of sociological literature on France has elevated the cliché "Plus ça change, plus c'est la même chose" into something of a paradigm, working out continuities through apparent changes and concentrating on the persistence of tradition in newer and "seemingly" less traditional settings. Here we stress two important discontinuities: French society has experienced some significant changes in recent years, and, at the same time, psychoanalysis (both as a treatment model and a social ideology) has achieved a dramatic prominence. A psychoanalytic language which tends to refer the visible back to the invisible, the manifest back to the latent, the public back to the private, has become part of the contemporary French discourse on the family, the school, the church. In France, the boundaries between the public and the private have traditionally been very rigid. The social appropriation of a psychoanalytic framework (which tends to blur the boundaries between public and private) for thinking about social problems is a sign that the boundary has been softened in recent years. Previously private concerns such as abortion, contraception, the question of whether there should be sexual education in the school system, have become the focus of public debate. Traditional political, moral, and religious categories proved insufficient to deal with the surfacing of these previously private issues into the public domain. Their consideration has brought the psychoanalysts, perceived as the experts of the private, into the public sphere, where they have offered people a language for thinking and talking more openly about these aspects of their lives. The language that we use to talk about a problem influences the way we think about the problem; thus, the psychoanalytic visibility has contributed to a revaluation of the private in France.

People respond to processes that touch on what Rieff has called "deconversion" (in many ways similar to what Max Weber called the "world's disenchantment") by developing real fascinations with the depth and mystery of an interior alchemy.[11] In the midst of rapid social change, the French, used to a fairly structured sense of the "rules of the game," are left with few social prescriptions. Family traditions and family rituals are no longer secure; once-coveted diplomas and titles no longer fulfill their promise of prestige or even employment; religious faith and religious institutions are in crisis. When the individual seeks "anchoring-points" for his life or help in dealing with distress, he may not find them in the experience of a community, in a set of established institutions, or in a faith. He must look to himself and his personal relationships. In this personal sphere psychoanalysis in both France and America has offered itself as a way of addressing new insecurities. It has also responded to the lack of norms by offering new experts for social problems that traditional formulas (religion for example) no longer seem able to handle. Thus psychoanalysis, in France as in America, has emerged as the "therapy of deconversion."

In a next section we shall describe some of the ways in which psychoanalysis has become involved in French social life. It will be apparent that in France, psychoanalysis and politics are now involved in a kind of dialectic where each is being transformed by its encounter with the other.

III. PSYCHOANALYSIS, SOCIETY, AND POLITICS

We have seen how social changes such as those associated with what Rieff terms "deconversion" can lay the groundwork for an interest in, even an enthusiasm for, psychoanalysis. In the French case, recent stresses on the family, on the educational system, and on traditional institutions such as the church have left a void that the psychoanalytic culture is in a position to fill.

The French family seems to be searching for a new definition of itself in terms of a psychological function. In recent years both popular and scholarly French writing on the family have come to stress the psychology of family life rather than the moral and economic role of the family in the life of the national "organism," as had traditionally been the case. The old emphasis on the *famille souche* has shifted to an emphasis on the family as a *lieu privilegié d'épanouissement*, that is, to the primacy of the psychological dimension of family life.

French traditional childrearing codes went relatively unquestioned through the mid-1960s. However, the French youth revolt of the late 1960s brought to the surface profound parental uncertainties about how they were raising their children. These anxieties about childrearing, relatively new in France, were well known on the American scene in the postwar era. As in the American case, uncertainty led parents to turn to new experts and opinion makers. In France, professionals and organizations with a psychoanalytic perspective have responded to parental demand. Psychiatrists and psychoanalysts testify to the change in the nature of the demands parents make on them since around 1968. One analyst who specializes in treating children characterized the desperation of the parents who come to him as reflecting "an almost total abdication of parental responsibility since 1968; parents are horribly afraid of hurting their children and feel that they know nothing, understand nothing. So they say: 'We need an expert.' Psychiatrists and psychoanalysts have been profiting from their deep malaise."

In the late 1960s advice columns and articles on a psychoanalytic approach to childrearing proliferated in a range of French magazines and newspapers. The increase in articles was simultaneous with an increase in the number of radio and television programs on this same subject. The demand by parents for "experts du psy," particularly in Paris, has created an economic climate in which the number of analysts being trained could proliferate and in which the number of psychologists group leaders and *animateurs* of all sorts could similarly explode. Psychoanalytically oriented institutions that could respond to the demand for expertise and for new norms have blossomed in the public sector, where they are often part of the national community mental health movement (known in France as the *sectorisation*), and in the private sector, where they are but one of the industries springing up around the troubled relationships between parents and their children.

Psychoanalytic expertise has also come into wider use in education in recent years. The school system uses psychologists (often under psychoanalytic supervision) for counseling and educational and professional orientation. Psychoanalysis has also become implicated in the educational system by a massive entrance into students' educational plans as a way of ensuring themselves of what the educational system cannot offer: a job. The explosion of psychoanalytic training in recent years, particularly in the unrestrictive Ecole Freudienne, and the explosion of students who are studying psychology in the hope that it may lead to the possibility of becoming an analyst, must be viewed in the context of students' desires to increase the domain of *emplois réservés*. Students cannot enlarge the numbers of doctors and lawyers or graduates of *grandes écoles* whom the state is willing to train, nor can they change the number of open posts for teachers. But they seem to feel that the fields of psychology and psychoanalysis open areas of employment that they can enlarge for themselves. Students perceive the domain of "le psy" as a growth sector that can accommodate students displaced from other work opportunities. Thus an interest in a career in this area is built on a confluence of "cultural infatuation" and economic realities. If psychoanalysis is talked about a lot in educational circles, it is in part because many people who a few years ago would have gone into education are now going into psychoanalysis.

Psychoanalysts are now intensely involved in the French university system. They control the education of French clinical psychologists and are major voices in departments of literature, linguistics, and philosophy. At Vincennes (the University of Paris VII) there is even a department of psychoanalysis.

The relations between the church and the psychoanalytic movement have traditionally been stormy, but faced with a decline of interest and confidence in their traditional roles and with changes in social life and religious participation that make their future roles unclear, some French religious leaders seem to be more receptive to redefining their function in terms of a counseling model, heavily influenced by psychoanalysis; they are starting to view the priesthood as yet another "profession du psy." Clergy participation in psychoanalytic training is increasing, particularly at the Ecole Freudienne, as is the amount of Catholic literature on psychoanalysis. This literature is aimed at reassuring Catholics that psychoanalytic thought and Catholic thought are compatible and even complementary.

These brushes of psychoanalytic expertise with French crises in family, church, and education have often been highly politicized, both in terms of the internal divisions in the psychoanalytic movement and of larger political issues as well. For example, the involvements of psychoanalysis in social institutions (what might be referred to as "psychoanalytic imperialism") often is a kind of colonization. That is, different social domains tend to be "colonized" by one or another of the different psychoanalytic schools, or else a given domain (the University, for example) will be broken up with different schools occupying ajoining "turfs." For example, the Ecole Freudienne "controls" the department of psychoanalysis at Vincennes; the Association Psychanalytique de France "controls" the education of clinical psychologists at Censier. In such settings, as in the state community mental health movement, the politics of the different psychoanalytic societies are played out on a social stage, marking the social situation with the clear traces of French "psychoanalytic politics" and sensitizing psychoanalysts to social concerns.

Psychoanalytic involvement with French social institutions has not always meant participation to bolster their traditional ways of functioning; in some cases it has involved a radical critique of their basic assumptions. Indeed, the politics of the different psychoanalytic societies (a politics internal to the psychoanalytic movement) do in fact have implications for a politics outside of them. In addition, the politics of educational and health institutions are deeply rooted in French radical politics as a whole, and thus the political sensitization of French psychoanalysis also grows out of its increasing involvement with the concerns of the French Left. This involvement has become deeper in recent years, particularly as an outgrowth of the events of May–June 1968. Here we shall give a flavor of what psychoanalytic politics looks like by indicating how it is played out in the sectors (catchment areas) of the French community mental health movement.

In the late 1960s, institutions that could respond to the new demands for therapy proliferated in the public sector as part of the community mental health program, which had become French national health policy after 1968. In the late 1960s parents rushed to these centers which in turn expanded and became a major source of employment for young analysts. Different centers came under the control of different branches of the psychoanalytic movement. Some of the centers that became controlled by the Lacanian group were used by the analysts as bases from which to challenge their medical and pedagogical ideologies. Indeed, the institutions became places in which to concretize Lacan's notions in an attack on the repressive role of the therapeutic institution in society. Centers under more traditional psychoanalytic tutelage, such as those under the direction of a member of the Société Psychanalytique de Paris, kept traditional "medical" orientations. Thus, the state health system was divided into psychoanalytic-political units with radically different kinds of functioning. These units developed an increasingly charged politics, both within the institution and in relation to the outside. These health centers first became the loci for psychoanalytic politics during the May–June 1968 events. In this way and in many others, the 1968 student uprising in France was a turning-point in the relationship between psychoanalysis and French politics.

In the 1950s the French Left and in particular the French Communist party strenuously attacked psychoanalysis as a bourgeois product and a potential instrument of bourgeois domination. In their own defense, analysts pleaded political "neutrality," tried to separate their lives as citizens from their analytic work, and often denied themselves the political arena altogether. Today the situation is transformed. The politics of education and health are the context for more open political interest and activity by psychoanalysts, some of whom are integrating their psychoanalytic and political activities, for example through participation in the highly politicized antipsychiatric movement. During the late 1960s in France an interest in the relationship between Freud and Marx was rekindled on the Left. Both the Communist and non-Communist (or *gauchiste*) Left have appropriated elements of a psychoanalytic discourse into their rhetoric.

The "classical" Communist position on psychoanalysis was best stated by Georges Politzer, one of the first French Marxists interested in psychoanalysis, although, as a Communist, he was highly critical of it. Politzer is a very important figure in the history of psychoanalysis and French Marxism because, unlike other Marxists of his generation, he did not see psychoanalysis as irrelevant, but only in error from the point of view of dialectical materialism. In 1924, Politzer, then twenty-one, both defended psychoanalysis ("cette science jeune et alerte") and affirmed that "tout le fondement théorique de la psychanalyse est à refaire."[12] Politzer's position, which combined a defense of Freud's scientific ambitions with a criticism of his individualism and lack of interest in history and economics, came to characterize the French Communist party position on Freud. For example, Politzerian "classicism" marks the June 1949 condemnation of psychoanalysis by eight Communist psychiatrists in *La Nouvelle Critique*, entitled "La Psychanalyse: Idéologie Réactionnaire."[13]

The French Communist position on psychoanalysis hardened through the 1950s in conjunction with the Russian emphasis on behaviorism in psychology and the hard line of criticism of psychoanalysis coming out of Moscow. However, in the mid-1960s French Communist interest in psychoanalysis was revived by the work of Louis Althusser; by 1973, Editions sociales (the French Communist party publishing house) published *Pour une critique marxiste de la théorie psychanalytique*, written by three Party members: the philosopher Lucien Sève and two younger philosophers who are members of the Ecole Freudienne, Catherine Backes-Clément and Pierre Bruno.[14] It was the first book officially published by the Communist press that "condones" psychoanalysis (although Communist party magazines, particularly those destined for the youth movement, have been giving psychoanalysis a "good press" since around 1970). The authors do not repudiate the Politzerian criticism of psychoanalysis, but simply link that criticism to one form of psychoanalysis which they alternatively describe as "psychological," "American," or "reactionary." In their view the Politzerian criticism does not apply to the psychoanalysis of Jacques Lacan, particularly as he is interpreted by Louis Althusser.[15] The contributions of Lacan and Althusser are presented as having changed the terms of the discussion from the time when Politzer wrote. Lacan's structuralist perspective permits Communist intellectuals to look at Freud and Marx not as social theorists with competing notions about the way in which the individual functions in society, but as scientifically homologous thinkers. Althusser made this point of contact between scientific socialism and scientific psychoanalysis explicit, stressing that Lacan's fundamental contribution has been his insistence on the specificity and irreducibility of the unconscious as the object of psychoanalysis, an object that constitutes psychoanalysis as a science.

The Freud-Marx rapprochement of the late 1960s made it easier for many young intellectuals to find a home in the Party, and Lacan's statement that the Soviet Union's rejection of psychoanalysis was understandable in terms of how the Americans had distorted it facilitated a Communist reconciliation with psychoanalysis via Lacan. In any case, by focusing on Lacan, the French Communist party emphasized that it was showing its interest in an indigenous psychoanalytic movement, altogether different from that of the Americans. The Communist interest in psychoanalysis has its own internal politics. The Party is a home both for those who, following Althusser's perspective, wish to explore the epistemological connections between psychoanalysis and Marxism and for those who feel that on the contrary, it is now most "strategic" in terms of the Party's constituency to use a medical model of the psychoanalytic enterprise and to put psychoanalysis to work "treating" the working class as it has been so long used for "treating" the bourgeoisie. Given what we have described as the Lacan criticism of the American "medicalization" of psychoanalysis, it is clear that this puts the "practical" side of the party at odds with the "theoretical," pro-Lacan side.

Like the Communists, the *gauchistes* came to their post-1968 interest in psychoanalysis from a position of relative hostility to psychoanalysis as reductionist and as a class-bound phenomenon. What is different is the relationship of their new interest in psychoanalysis to the May–June 1968 events. The Communists disparaged them; for the *gauchistes* they were a time during which a direct contact with psychoanalysis was made. In a certain sense, May 1968 gave psychoanalysis back to the surrealists. Once again, analytic "slogans" were put to utopian use: "Take your desires for reality . . . a policeman sleeps within you, kill him . . . liberate psychoanalysis." The student movement was seized in a curious love/hate relationship with Freud. The classical criticism of psychoanalytic theory as upper-class luxury seemed to pale in comparison with a phenomenal social expression of a desire for contact with psychoanalysis. Wilhelm Riech became a *maître de penser;* long nights of political debate were held in a Sorbonne lecture hall which was rechristened "L'amphithéâtre Che Guevara-Freud." Psychoanalysts responded to this demand in a variety of ways, ranging from full participation in the movement to immediately writing about it in a way that tended to "psychoanalyze away" its political content.

In general, the Lacanian analysts took the largest role in the May movement. The *gauchisme* of the Ecole Freudienne seems to have several roots. There is first the recruitment of Ecole Freudienne analysts from Marxist circles around Louis Althusser at the Ecole Normale Supérieure. Lacan held his seminar at the Ecole Normale from 1963 to 1968, when the dean asked him to leave for political reasons. Moreover, Lacan's son-in-law, Jacques Alain-Miller, a central figure at the Ecole Freudienne, was a Maoist for many years. The *gauchiste* Left has exempted Lacan from their general criticism of structuralism and seems to identify with his psychoanalytic vision of the alienated subject. In addition to identifying with Lacan's ideas, *gauchistes* also identify with his behavior in psychoanalytic politics: Lacan attacked the Americans, broke analytic "rules," challenged hierarchy. For the student movement in the throes of contesting the hierarchy and discipline of the French university system closed unto itself, the Lacanian analysts who had waged these battles within the psychoanalytic world seemed to be the *aficionados* of such struggles. Lacanian analysts had pioneered several experiments in anti-psychiatry, such as that of the Clinique de la Borde at Cour-Cheverny, whose use of "institutional psychoanalysis" was felt by many to be relevant to the May movement. And if the magic of the May days was to return psychoanalysis to the spirit of the surrealists, who but Lacan, friend of the surrealists, inspirer of Dali in his work on paranoia, could accept the gift?

The May–June 1968 events brought the question of the politics of speech into sharp focus for the Left. In May, *la prise de la parole*, "the taking of speech," was seen as a privileged form of social action. The cult of speech during May left a legacy: the issues that mobilize *gauchistes* since 1968 seem to revolve around groups defined by their languages, seen as languages of exclusion. Since 1968 *la parole privilégiée* belongs to the mad, to prisoners, and to children. Part of the new interest in the vicissitudes of speech is a kind of fallout from May 1968. In May 1968 *gauchistes* took the *autre scene* postulated by psychoanalysis, the world of fantasy, *le ludique,* as an important part of their political identities and ascribed special value to those aspects of experience usually excluded from Marxist discourse: dreams and "pure desire." When the political component of the action ended, what remained for many people was an interest in the form of the experience—the word. Reflections on the desire, language, and politics of the excluded are also a way for the Left to reflect on its own experiences of failure and marginality, a projection of its own speech onto groups that are conveniently silent. Much debate on the current French Left turns on the question of the status of language: can dialectical materialism be reconciled with a belief that words can change things? The concern with *la parole privilégiée* is the context for the current interest in psychoanalysis on the Left; the interest in psychoanalysis both manifests and supports this larger concern.

Thus the events of May–June 1968 marked the public appropriation of a psychoanalytic language even as they marked a moment in a process of profound social reassessment. Although there were few physical traces of the May days left in Paris even a few weeks after the outbreak, an important change did occur. The social upheaval brought with it important shifts in the ways in which French people think about themselves and their relationships, shifts in what we might call meaning systems and the symbols by which they are reflected and refracted. May began with the political mythology of community and collectivity; it ended by turning inward to psychoanalytic individualism. The idea that the experience of '68 had a "psychological" rather than political motor has become a kind of *idée réçue* in French life, common coin even among those who had been the most critical of the "reductionism" implicit in any examination of the events' psychological component. The social use of psychoanalytic images—psychoanalysis is after all a way of understanding and synthesizing experience—is particularly sensitive to social processes, and was highly sensitive to the particular mix of cultural festival and social revolt that characterized May–June 1968. In the final section of this essay we shall look at how the changing social and political involvements of psychoanalysis have expressed themselves as changes in the social image of psychoanalysis in France.

IV. The Changing Social Image of Psychoanalysis

We are able to document the changing social image of psychoanalysis in France over the past twenty years by comparing the current situation with data collected in the mid-1950s by social psychologist Serge Moscovici.[16] In light of changes in French society and of changes in the involvement of psychoanalysis in French social life, I conducted a study in Paris in 1974 designed both to document changes in the social image of psychoanalysis since the 1950s, and to explore possible new associations of psychoanalysis to political and social beliefs.[17] Although my study was based on a sample far smaller than Moscovici's and is not a definitive replication of his work, it does indicate the nature and the dimensions of the changes in the social image of psychoanalysis in France as psychoanalysis has "come of age" in this traditionally resistant environment.

In the past twenty years psychoanalysis has come to have a social image that is more positive, more concrete, and focused on the therapeutic. Today over three-quarters of the representative sample reports generally positive attitudes toward psychoanalysis.[18] Whereas in the 1950s people tended to give definitions of psychoanalysis that stressed its philosophical importance or its similarity to religion, in 1974 the definitions are more concrete: people describe what psychoanalysis can do as therapy or associate it with something else in their lives such as schools or childrearing. The current association of psychoanalysis and children is strong; even people who are not particularly interested in psychoanalysis feel that it has something to contribute to bringing up and educating children. This attitude may reflect the proliferation of psychoanalytically oriented childrearing information in the media and the presence of psychologists and psychoanalysts in the schools and in child-treatment centers.

The predominant image of the psychoanalyst has also become more positive and more concrete. When people today use images that seem stereotyped, or not based on their own experience, they seem to be using them in order to associate themselves with what is current in psychoanalytic popularization, of being *dans le bain*. The old stereotyped images of psychoanalysts which Moscovici encountered referred to generalities about the analyst's magnetism, authority, and physical attributes: "Barbu avec les lunettes." The 1974 stereotyped images are closer to being "injokes" about real psychoanalysts and their behavior, images disseminated by rumor and by the media: "Un farfaleu contestataire qui travaille dans un centre de l'enfance inadaptée."

The new data indicate that more people know more about psychoanalysis and have more contact with it than they did in the 1950s. Particularly among the groups that are the principal analytic "consumers"—liberal professionals, upper middle classes, and students—people have more information on the specificity of the psychoanalytic encounter as distinct from other forms of psychotherapy. Although the 1974 sample seems aware that psychoanalysis is a more intense form of treatment than other psychotherapies, they are not particularly reticent about approaching an analyst, although many of them made a clear distinction between seeing an analyst for "conversations" and going into analysis. These informed reflections find expression in a distinct drop in the percentages of subjects in all classes who say that they would go to an analyst for reasons of "curiosity" alone.[19]

The positive images of the analyst and positive attitudes toward psychoanalysis are strongly associated with class origin, with liberal professionals, upper-middle-class people, and students being the most favorable to psychoanalysis followed by lower-middle-class people and workers. Working-class people talk about their negative associations to psychoanalysis largely in terms of their experiences with therapists in institutional settings. These experiences also play a part in the high percentage of their members (31) with negative attitudes toward psychiatry. The middle-class sample shared some of the workers' hostility toward psychiatry (24 percent of this sample was hostile), and here too it seems to be a case of contact with institutional psychiatry breeding resentment. The liberal professional upper-middle classes, which tend to have little contact with institutional psychiatry, are more likely to be positive toward it. "Institutional psychoanalysis" seems to alienate people in very much the same way that institutional psychiatry does. The liberal professionals and upper-middle-class subjects who are most open to having their own children analyzed envisage a very different context for these sessions than do workers and lower-middle-class subjects who imagine their child with a therapist. While the liberal professional is imagining his child in a chic private consulting room, the worker is imagining a crowded public facility, a CMPP (Centre Medico-Psychopédagogique). Several of the working-class mothers with whom I spoke complained about the way they felt that their children or children of their acquaintances had been abused in these settings. Some spoke of long waiting lists and having to "explain yourself" to four or five people before being "assigned" someone. Others talked about the "crazy psychoanalysts" in the centers who refused to take care of their children and who wanted to put the whole family in psychoanalysis. One mother complained about a Lacanian analyst in her sector's CMPP who refused to see her son's learning disability as a problem for technical reeducation and who wanted to treat the child's emotional problems by putting his parents in psychotherapy.

In 1974, nearly 60 percent of the representative sample felt that knowing about psychoanalysis could have a positive effect on their lives, most of them looking to it to "make me a happier person," to "give me greater understanding of my children," or to "help me have a more harmonious family life." Thirty-six percent of the sample claimed to make some "use" of psychoanalysis in their daily lives, mostly to better understand themselves or their children. Different ideas about the "uses" of psychoanalysis are strongly associated with class. Students and liberal professionals see psychoanalysis as useful for their own internal conflicts, whereas workers and lower-middle-class people focus immediately on problems with children. The liberal professional and upper-middle-class person sees psychoanalysis in many contexts: as a potential therapy for himself or for his children, as a subject taught in the university, even as a

politically relevant ideology. His sense of how psychoanalysis is useful is
thus quite diffuse. A lower-middle-class person or a worker may have
come across someone whom he perceived as a psychoanalyst only once—
for example, in a consultation at the primary school about his child's reading difficulties—and psychoanalysis (and indeed all kinds of psychology)
become "fixed" as related to the problems of children. If the contact was
instead made in an institution related to mental health, psychoanalysis
could become "fixed" as related to the problem of madness.

The groups who are seen as potential analytic clients have changed
since the 1950s. Unlike during the 1950s, many subjects assumed that
most people today would like to be in analysis if they could and that the
answer to the question "Who uses analysis most?" should therefore be
given in terms of who would actually be able to afford it. Thus, an increased percentage of all groups see "the rich" as likely to be in analysis.
For example, one medical student from a *petit bourgeois* background
likened the "competition" to get into analysis to the competition in France
to get into medical school: "Everybody wants to get in, but it's mostly rich
people who make it." More people now see intellectuals as analytic
clients. They seem to infer this from the flood of books and articles that
intellectuals produce about psychoanalysis. One engineer said, "French
intellectuals bury themselves today with practically nothing else . . . I
suppose they all want to do it, that is, to be in analysis." The *petit
bourgeois* are seen as more likely to be analytic consumers than they were
twenty years ago, particularly by the worker sample, who have heard
enough about psychoanalysis to be interested in it, but feel that it is just
out of their reach, just "above them." Seeing *petit bourgeois* as analytic
patients brings analysis just a bit closer to them. Two new categories of
potential analytic clients which appeared in the 1974 survey are students
and *gens de gauche*. The prominence of the student response may reflect
the growing public awareness that young people are interested in psychoanalysis and that they are learning about it in the schools.[20] The addition
of *gens de gauche* seemed to express public awareness of the increased
association between psychoanalysis and the Left.

A final, very significant change in the image of psychoanalysis in
France in the past twenty years is that among most groups psychoanalysis
seems to have lost its reputation as a therapy "for women only," with
some dramatic increases in the percentages seeing men and women as
having equal use for psychoanalysis.[21] The student group has the highest

percentage (71 percent) of members who think that psychoanalysis is used equally by men and women, and the worker group was the only one that continued to see psychoanalysis as being overwhelmingly for women.

The percentage of the middle-class sample that reports psychoanalysis as a frequent subject of conversation is six times greater in 1974 than it was in the 1950s. During the 1950s middle-class people from thirty to forty-nine said that they spoke about psychoanalysis little or not at all. In 1974 this age group reported the most interest in and conversation about psychoanalysis of all groups. They are the people who have come to their maturity as psychoanalysis has come of age in France.

Although more people register psychoanalysis as a subject of conversation, within each group there is a greater polarization of responses between people who claim to speak of it a great deal and those who claim to speak of it not at all. Interviews suggested that in 1974 my question about the "presence" of psychoanalysis in daily conversation was taken quite literally. People are exposed to worlds where psychoanalysis is a preoccupation; the "standard" of measurement for the intensity of discussion of psychoanalysis is thus very high. The polarization is particularly pronounced among young people from ages fifteen to twenty-nine, an age group largely composed of students who give evidence of having become the group most knowledgeable about, favorable to, and personally implicated in psychoanalysis.[22] As in the case of polarized responses in the middle-class sample, the intensity of many of the "don't speak of psychoanalysis at all" response from young people indicated irritation at being "saturated" with psychoanalysis from "des copains et des enseignants," friends and teachers. A University student studying literature at Censier states his dissatisfaction in the following terms: "We try to talk about a text . . . the professor talks of nothing but Freud and Lacan. I am sick of it . . . I can't bear it any more. I don't want to hear a word about it at home."

Fewer people see psychoanalysis as having cognitive aims or aims related to adaptation than in the 1950s. The emphasis is now on self-knowledge and growth, with the shift most pronounced for those who are the best informed about psychoanalysis. It seems that enthusiasm for psychoanalysis in France today among the best educated is not related to ideas about its efficacy as a treatment that makes you "feel better." The groups of people who have the most contact with psychoanalysis are those (for example, the liberal professionals and the upper middle class) who express the most skepticism when asked if psychoanalysis is efficacious. In general, the groups who most believe that psychoanalysis is efficacious are those with the least contact with it—the lower-middle-class and worker samples.

One wonders if the lessening emphasis on adaptation and efficacy among the best educated reflects the political critiques of psychoanalysis made by the Left in France over the past twenty years, and in particular the current Lacanian/*gauchiste* criticism of any vision of psychoanalysis that stresses cure or adaptation to society. It is almost as though (for groups who are involved with the new literary-philosophical appreciation of Lacan) psychoanalysis is devalued when it is discussed in terms of the "benefit" of getting better.

Nearly 70 percent of the 1974 representative sample feels that psychoanalysis has grown in importance in France in recent years, most people attributing this change to individual needs and to insecurities related to social life. The emphasis on the United States as the "perpetrator" of psychoanalysis has dropped off from the 1950s. In the 1950s, novelty was not mentioned often enough to even be coded, but in a seeming paradox, it was heavily relied on twenty years later as people try to account for the growing influence of psychoanalysis. It would seem that for the French general public, psychoanalysis *is* new; they are experiencing it as a recent French discovery. In 1974 French people are often careful to distinguish the psychoanalysis they are talking about from the brand that they have so long and so negatively associated with the United States. Everyone seems to have a different reason for wanting to disassociate French and American psychoanalysis. Middle-class people are not favorable to the permissive childrearing that they associate with American psychoanalysis and Dr. Spock; the *intellectuels de gauche,* taking their cue from Lacan, criticize the "adaptationist tone" of American ego psychology. The aggregate effect of the French-American distinction is dramatic. Over half of the representative *sample* feels that there is an important difference between French and American psychoanalysis, claiming the French brand to be more "radical," more "intellectual," more "mature." The French media help maintain the image of psychoanalysis as a recent French invention. Magazines carry features on psychoanalysis under the rubric of "nouveautés" or, even more incredibly, of "nouveautés de Paris." During the 1950s people with unfavorable attitudes toward psychoanalysis tended to associate it with fashion, but today this relationship has been reversed.[23] More peo-

ple associate psychoanalysis with fashion, and these people are psychoanalytic "promotors," not detractors. People interested in psychoanalysis
seem proud that it is *la mode.* Looking at psychoanalysis as a part of fashion used to be a way of expressing at the very least a slur; today, seeing
psychoanalysis as fashion in France is simply facing a fact.

Popular attitudes toward the commercial diffusion of psychoanalysis
have shifted dramatically in the past twenty years. More people are now
relying on popularization as a source of information than in the 1950s,
when the group interested in psychoanalysis stuck mostly to their books as
a way of finding out about it. Popularization has become a topic of considerable controversy. During the 1950s about one-fifth of the liberal professional sample had no opinion on the popular diffusion of psychoanalysis.
There was little large-scale popularization in the 1950s—one could avoid
the issue. Now, the liberal professional group has almost no one without
an opinion on popularization. They are the people who are the most interested and involved in psychoanalysis, and they tend to be the ones who
are preoccupied with popularization, often expressing concern that they
are "losing" psychoanalysis to oversimplifications and distortions. In the
1950s the more educated people, the potential analytic consumers of their
time, held the most positive attitudes toward the popular diffusion of psychoanalysis.[24] The less educated tended to be indifferent. There is some
evidence that this pattern has reversed. Unambivalently positive feelings
about popularization now tend to decrease with education. It would seem
that during the 1950s privileged groups who had almost sole "custody" of
analytic knowledge in France were frustrated because it had not captured
the public imagination and played little role in public life. In short, their
knowledge gave them little power or prestige, and they desired increased
popularization. Now psychoanalysis is no longer "exclusive"—its recent
and widespread social diffusion has led to its leaving the exclusive control
of the elite who formerly produced and consumed it. Distressed by their
partial loss of control and fearing its extension, elite groups are reticent
about further popularization. The demand for "la vulgarisation de la
psychanalyse" comes from the formerly excluded who now see themselves
as potential consumers. Moscovici's data indicated that familiarity with
popularization once bred contempt for psychoanalysis. In the 1974 representative sample, however, two-thirds of the people who learned about
psychoanalysis from the popular media were positive toward it and

thought that popularization was a good thing. Most people seem to enjoy the media's treatment of psychoanalysis, even if they fear that it has gotten out of their control.

We have already discussed the dramatic changes in the political climate surrounding psychoanalysis in France, and in particular the changed relationship between psychoanalysis and the French Left. These changes are reflected in changed public attitudes about psychoanalysis and politics. Different views about the relationship of psychoanalysis and politics reflect differing intensities and kinds of exposure to the several varieties of "psychoanalytic politics" to be found on the current French scene. The students, the liberal professionals, and the worker samples have the highest percentage of members who see a relationship between psychoanalysis and politics. They are also the groups that have the majority of their members declaring their political preference to be on the Left. Members of these samples not only saw a relationship between psychoanalysis and politics, but thought that the political attitudes of an analyst would be a criterion for choosing one. The lower-middle-class sample is the only group where politics is not cited at all as a criterion for choice of analyst. This breakdown seems related to the political composition of the subpopulations. With the exception of the lower-middle-class group (which is made up largely of people on the political Center and Right), all of the other subpopulation samples are composed of more than a 28 percent membership of people on the Left, a milieu where psychoanalysis is now frequently discussed in relation to politics.

In the Moscovici study, believing that psychoanalysis and politics are compatible was associated with being on the political Right.[25] In the 1950s, because of the long tradition of Communist hostility to psychoanalysis, Communists tended to see psychoanalysis and politics in an adversary relationship. Today these relationships have completely disappeared: people on the Left are now the most rather than the least favorable toward psychoanalysis. Eighty-six percent of the non-Communist Left sample and 58 percent of the Communists express positive attitudes toward psychoanalysis, as opposed to only 37 percent of those on the Right. When the total sample is sorted by political preference, the strongest statement of the compatibility of psychoanalysis and politics comes from the Left, another reversal from the pattern of the 1950s. The percentage of students and liberal professionals who see a link between psychoanalysis and Marxism has more than doubled in the past twenty years. In the 1950s people on the Left were the most skeptical about the ability of psychoanalysis to influence personality change. Now this pattern too has completely reversed. The Left has started to develop an image as having a particular interest in psychoanalysis. For example, 37 percent of the middle-class sample and 54 percent of the student sample felt that *gens de gauche* were the most likely group to be in psychoanalysis, a response that did not appear at all in the 1950s study. Of the 54 percent of the representative sample who had heard of Lacan, 13 percent linked him with some kind of radical politics, referring to him, for example, as the "psychanalyste de la contestation."

People on the Left report the greatest change in attitude toward psychoanalysis in recent years, most of it occurring since 1968. The Communists, whose party has undergone the most dramatic about face in this regard, report more changed attitudes than any other political group. Ninety-one percent of the Communists say that their attitudes toward psychoanalysis have recently changed, a full 40 percentage points higher than the change reported by the Center/Right and more than twice the percentage of change reported by the politically noncommitted.

Nearly half of the 1974 representative sample reports that their attitudes toward psychoanalysis had changed in recent years, with more than 60 percent of those who reported changed attitudes dating these changes as occurring since 1968. The events of May–June were usually mentioned as an explicit "marker date" for these changed attitudes. Participation in the events is strongly associated with newly positive attitudes toward psychoanalysis: 87 percent of the subjects who participated in May–June 1968 have come to be more interested in psychoanalysis in recent years, more than twice the percentage of changed interest found among nonparticipant subjects.

Participation in the May–June events is associated with positive feelings about psychoanalysis, interest in psychoanalysis, and willingness to seek therapeutic help from a psychotherapist, usually described as "an analyst." In my sample, participants in the events claimed to "use" psychoanalysis in their lives more than three times as frequently as did nonparticipants. Most nonparticipants feel that any recent changes in their attitudes were due to the influence of their children and the media. On the other hand, participants in the events attribute their more massive changes in attitude to their firsthand experiences: knowing more people involved with or interested in psychoanalysis, a personal experience in therapy. Participation in the events is thus associated with "active" rather than "passive" trajectories into the psychoanalytic culture.

May 1968 was a festival of speech and desire, and to the students it seemed only natural to turn to psychoanalysts, perceived as the professionals of both. Psychoanalysis was asked "descendre dans la rue." Participation of the analysts in the events ripped apart the analytic societies. Each society had its own internal *contestation* movement as member analysts struggled with their role in the social movement as a whole. Participation was confusing for the analysts since they were alternatively denounced as legitimators of the status quo and cited in "revolutionary" slogans. The participation of analysts in the events did not go unnoticed. Over one-fifth of the representative sample felt that psychoanalysis and psychoanalysts played a significant role in May 1968. The greater the degree of participation in the events, the more positive the subject's testimony that psychoanalysis and psychoanalysts played an important role in 1968, a case both of having to be there to know and of May participants being predisposed to think of analysts as politically active.

May participants are more likely to see a relationship between psychoanalysis and political thought and action than are nonparticipants and those who participated little. They are more likely to associate psychoanalysis and sociology as being of similar *political* relevance, are more likely to know about the work of Jacques Lacan, and are more likely to associate Lacan's work with some kind of radical politics. They are less likely than others to associate psychoanalysis with its "old links" to surrealism, existentialism, and Christianity, the associations that dominated the 1950s study. Instead, participants tend to associate psychoanalysis with a new set of intellectual connections to Marxism and structuralism.

Thus in the past twenty years the social role and the social image of psychoanalysis have changed dramatically. Any French analyst over thirty-five has seen within his professional lifetime the transformation of psychoanalysis from an enterprise marginal to the public as well as to the medical, educational, and scientific communities into something of a privileged commodity in each of these worlds. French psychoanalysts have come to take larger social roles within a community that accepts them. They are perceived as experts in a variety of domains; their ideas are popularized and receive wide diffusion by the mass media. No longer marginal men, they are some of the best-known members of the French medical community on the one hand and the *vedettes* of radical chic on the other. Whereas in the 1950s psychoanalysis was little known except to a financially and culturally privileged elite, psychoanalytic popularization has now brought images of psychoanalysis into the lives of many French people. These images are now influencing the ways in which they think about themselves, their children, their relationships, and about their frustrations with their lives.

The media have transmitted psychoanalysis as a cultural product, and the French public has received it as a form of social knowledge that has captured their imaginations. French people now see psychoanalysis as a French product, a privileged therapeutic modality, and a politically relevant ideology. Whereas in the 1950s psychoanalysis was widely associated with religion and philosophy, it is now seen not as abstract knowledge but as an immediate vehicle for thinking about one's personal problems.

For French people, the May–June 1968 events seem to have served as a marker for their perception of important changes in their society. The events precipitated insecurities about how to raise children and how to live one's life. There were shared moments of social reappraisal and collective anguish as well as festival. The events had a particular, Janus-like quality, reflecting both nostalgia for a community that was gone and a desperate attempt to bolster a community the French sensed they were losing. It seems appropriate that the events also served as a "marker" for people's perception of a new *social* relationship to psychoanalysis. The events of 1968 were a moment of encounter of many of the currents, political, intellectual, and social, which define the uniqueness of the new "French Freud." They mark a moment in the process of deconversion which seems to underlie the emergence of psychoanalysis as a dominant psychological and therapeutic model.

NOTES

1. In Jacques Lacan, "The Mirror-phase as Formative of the Function of the I," in Jacque, Lacan, *Ecrits: A Selection*, trans. Alan Sheridan (New York: Norton, 1977). A good discussion in English of the implications of the mirror phase for the development of the psyche is to be found in Juliet Mitchell, *Psychoanalysis and Feminism* (New York: Random House, 1975). A good English introduction to Lacan is Anthony Wilden, *The Language of the Self* (Baltimore: Johns Hopkins University Press, 1968).

2. H. Stuart Hughes, *The Obstructed Path: French Social Thought in the Years of Desperation, 1936–1960* (New York: Harper and Row, 1966), p. 290.

3. For a more complete history of the history and current situation of the French psychoanalytic movement, see Sherry Turkle, "Contemporary French Psychoanalysis," *The Human Context* (Summer 1975), 7:333–42 and (Autumn 1975), 7:561–69.

4. The translation of the reflexive French verb *s'autoriser* as "to authorize oneself" is problematic; the English connotes a formal act whereas the French is referring to a personal step of self-acceptance.

5. In principle there is no hierarchy at the Ecole Freudienne, that is, there is no distinction between training analysts who can form other analysts and "regular" analysts who only see patients with no intention themselves to become analysts. There is however a distinction between different levels of theoretical ability, with the "analystes de l'école" at the top of the scale. Lacan first envisaged *la passe* as a way to do research about what happens in a training analysis. He then made it the mechanism by which an analyst at the Ecole Freudienne might "pass" into the ranks of the "analystes de l'école," that is to the ranks of analysts considered "apt" to do serious theoretical work.

6. Anne Parsons, "La Pénétration de la Psychanalyse en France et aux Etats-Unis: Une étude de psychologie sociale comparative," Thèse du doctorat, Faculté des Lettres, Paris, 1954.

7. Carol Pierson Ryser, "The Influence of Value Systems in the Practice of Psychiatry: The French Case," Ph. D. dissertation, Harvard University, 1967.

8. Philip Rieff, *The Triumph of the Therapeutic: The Uses of Faith After Freud* (New York: Harper and Row, 1968).

9. See Paul Roazen, "Freud and America," *Social Research* (Winter 1972), 29:720–32. This essay is a discussion of two books by Nathan Hale which are crucial to understanding the early development of "American Freud": *Freud and the Americans*, vol. 1 (New York: Oxford University Press, 1971) and *James Jackson Putnam and Psychoanalysis* (Cambridge, Mass.: Harvard University Press, 1971).

10. For a description of this synthesis, some of whose most salient features persisted through the 1960s, see Stanley Hoffmann, "Paradoxes of the French Political Community," in Stanley Hoffmann et al., *In Search of France* (New York: Harper Torchbooks, 1965), pp. 1–117.

11. Peter Berger, "Towards a Sociological Understanding of Psychoanalysis," *Social Research* (Spring 1965), vol. 32.

12. Georges Politzer, *Ecrits*, vol. 2, *Les Fondements de la psychologie* (Paris: Editions sociales, 1969), pp. 12, 18.

13. "La Psychanalyse: Idéologie réactionnaire," *La Nouvelle Critique* (June 1949). The eight authors of this declaration included Dr. Serge Lebovici, who since his days as a Communist and his denunciation of psychoanalysis became an architect of the psychoanalytically inspired French community health program and the first French president of the International Psychoanalytic Association.

14. Catharine Backes-Clément, Pierre Bruno, Lucien Sève, *Pour une critique marxiste de la théorie psychanalytique* (Paris: Editions sociales, 1973).

15. See Louis Althusser, "Freud et Lacan," *La Nouvelle Critique* (December–January 1964–65), pp. 88–108.

16. His results, based on data collected from 1951–55, are published in Serge Moscovici, *La Psychanalyse, son image et son public* (Paris: Presses Universitaires de France, 1960; a second, revised edition was published in 1976).

17. The 1974 study was based on a standard interview which took about three hours to complete. The author conducted 78 of the interviews; the remaining 104 were done by three research assistants. The instructions to the interviewers were to take down everything that the subject said verbatim, as one would do if giving a Rorschach. Thus, in coding the data the author had 182 full transcripts to work from. All coding was done by the author. Proceeding in the same manner as Moscovici had twenty years before, the subjects were quota-sampled

in order to assure a representative distribution by age, sex, and class. Moscovici's representative sample was made up of 402 subjects. These subjects were chosen by quota sampling by criteria of age, class, and sex to meet the specifications used by IFOP (Institut Français d'Opinion Publique) in their survey work with representative samples of the Paris population. My representative sample was made up of 103 subjects, chosen to match 1973 IFOP specifications for a representative sample of the Parisian population. This 1974 representative sample allows for comparisons with the responses of Moscovici's representative group. The other 79 subjects are members of the various subpopulations of the representative sample. These 79 respondents are added to the members of the respective subpopulations in the representative sample to constitute the five subpopulations analogous to those used by Moscovici. The subpopulation samples are liberal professions (N = 43), upper middle class (N = 34, referred to as Middle Class B or MC-B), worker (N = 32), and student (N = 32). The "Middle Class" (MC) sample is made up by pooling MC-A and MC-B and is the analogue to Moscovici's "Classes Moyens" group.

18. The general approval of psychoanalysis in the 1974 survey sets it apart from psychiatry and psychological testing, which received much more measured approval. Only 40 percent of the subjects in the representative sample expressed an unambivalently positive attitude toward psychiatry; 33 percent had strong reservations, and the rest were completely hostile. In the past, the French have shown hostility or lack of interest toward psychoanalysis but have been more positive toward psychological testing. Although the entrance of psychoanalysis in France may have been paved by the acceptance of the psychological test, my data indicate fairly strongly that this "classical" period is over. There is a clear disinfatuation with psychological tests; only 25 percent of the representative sample was in favor of them; 33 percent were completely hostile. The reasons for this hostility were frequently political or demonstrated the new preference for the therapeutic in France: "Tests don't help the child, they just categorize him . . . they help the school."

19. For example, 63 percent of Moscovici's student sample cited curiosity as the reason they would go to an analyst. In my sample, curiosity alone was mentioned by only 6 percent of the majority of whom now say they would go to an analyst for personal reasons.

20. When people referred to students and psychoanalysis, they often made reference to the student interest in psychoanalysis as expressed in May 1968. Several people mentioned that psychoanalysis was now more accessible to students because young Lacanian analysts who are just starting out will see them for very little money.

21. In the 1950 study, no one in the liberal professional or upper-class sample thought men and women used analysis equally. In 1974, 20 percent of the representative sample and 35 percent of the liberal professional sample felt that men and women made equal use of analysis.

22. Three-quarters of the students in my sample claim to speak of psychoanalysis a great deal.

23. All associations reported were significant to at least $p < .05$ using the chi square measure of association.

24. See Moscovici, *La psychanalyse, son image et son public*, p. 183.

25. *Ibid.*, pp. 205–8.

SECTION II
Psychoanalysis

❧ 3 ❧

Unconscious Inscription: Another Memory

SERGE LECLAIRE

RESPONDING TO a photograph of himself, taken at about the age of four, Cyril sees or recalls himself, in a limit memory, with a face he no longer knows: in full possession of his body, captured by the camera, fixed in his memory, in a moment of serene self-confidence. He is in a garden, at the foot of a tree; his gaze, his mouth, his hands, and even his hair, which is curly and blond, impel him toward an intent and happy game. At the edges, like a fringe, a smile is showing; in the center, unblinking, he faces, he sees . . . what?—that which impels him, or that toward which he goes, but which, in his memory, remains without name and without form, yet is there: just on the other side of the memory's image, so near the photo you would think the reflection of this other thing is fastened onto it. Cyril is not looking at the photographer and he no longer knows who it was. He remembers the place; that's all, in terms of the setting. What is being played out here takes place beyond; there surely are large white daisies, yellow anemones, shimmering silver grasses, a ball, and, present although not represented, his father. In this scene, on the other side of the memory, a festival of muscles, of fragrances, and of caresses is playing. Here, the actors' body parts, disguised as light, as leaves, as toys, and as insects, perform, like so many characters, a madcap and sumptuous

Translated from the French by Jacques F. Houis.

love story, filled with terrifying or delightful escapades, free from tragedy or dead end, as if desire had found the right words.

The practice of analysis forces us to recognize that *all* the recollections registered in what we commonly call memory always create, like Cyril's fragmentary representation, a limit or a screen, beyond which unfolds the scene of *another memory*. This, strictly speaking, is an unconscious memory whose engrams elude the representational instrumentation and the logical discursive organization of the conscious system.

From the beginning of his discovery, this became obvious to Freud, who only acknowledged memory insofar as it is unconscious, denying to consciousness even the capacity of memory: "Consciousness and memory are mutually exclusive." This affirmation, like all of psychoanalysis, runs counter to our thinking habits; the term "memory," in its common usage, designates something altogether different from what Freud had in mind when he recognized the determining force of unconscious inscriptions. Reserving the term "memory" to designate the connections that occur on the other side of the screen requires a preliminary critique of the conventional concept of memory. We must admit that this term has been invested with too much learning and too many conceptual connotations to allow for a correct approach to life forces whose paradoxical arrangement determines, with unparalleled power, the imperative constants of every life. We commonly conceive of memory as, at the same time, the inscription of traces and the capacity to summon them. As such, the term expresses such a clear conception that machines have been modeled on it; and, after all, these machines work quite well. They are faster and more reliable than the human brain. Magnetic tape is more convenient than the stone tablet, but the model remains the same: in each case there is an inscription of a trace on a material that ensures its conservation and that allows us constant access, in the present, to what has been inscribed or recorded. We should stress the fact that mnemic inscription is only very selectively related to the actual event, that the traces are only fragmentary reflections of the experience. What has been recorded (despite the illusion fostered by the "hi-fi" gadget) constitutes a kind of abstract, set forth in a few selected strokes. In a similar fashion, a caricature retains only a few singular features of the face depicted. Essentially, we can say that the relation of the memory trace to the reality of experience is homologous to the relation of a ballistics formula to the reality of the trajectory and the effect of the projectile. As an inscription, it is already an abstraction; in other words, it is an operation that, by fixing a trace, abstracts it from the actual event, leaving out the greater part. The least analysis worthy of the name conclusively shows that the photograph that corresponds to Cyril's "screen memory" fixes a reflection of his gaze and a crystallized image of his moving body: the rest of the scene, like the submerged mass of an iceberg, is simply not taken into account by the inscription process of memory.

As long as we are on the topic of the "abstract" character of the memory trace, it should be pointed out that the work on a memory, performed by psychoanalysis, is fundamentally work on a text: faced with the account of a memory, we are, as analysts, confronted with a literal inscription whose abstract and fragmentary nature, formulated in a quasi-algebraically articulated continuum, reinforces its enigmatic aspect.

So this is the nature of the material we analysts have to work with: not only do we have enigmas to discover; we also have to decipher them. How do we go about it?

Let's go back to Cyril's "screen memory." By working out the elements that make up this memory, we hope to decipher what the mnemic inscription is telling us, hardened as it is into the mute and ultimate nature of the screen, erected there like a limit. Like good obsessional neurotics, we try to extend the limits, even to force them; and, thanks to the investigative procedure Freud invented, which consists in being attentive to all that happens to be said in the patient's verbal associations, we advance, like the legendary Sherlock Holmes, holding a magnifying glass, attempting to collect newer traces, newer clues. It is upon this freely associated discourse that we exercise our sagacity. Thus we collect, like some precious essence, the ball, the yellow anemone, and the white daisy that Cyril brings up in his talk. But we shall also take into account all that he will offer us during the following session; such as that fragment of an image (memory or dream?) of a small indoor fountain topping an aquarium where shimmering goldfish glide past aquatic plants. As the first clue of a fruitful investigation we shall make a connection between the silvery *shimmering* of the grasses, which appeared from the start, in the botanical and agrestal series, and the shimmering of the small fishes who roam the aquarium. We should discard, at this point, any interference caused by our desire to understand, which remains the analyst's pet vice. We run

the risk of losing track of the enigma if we immediately paralyze the
progression of the telling by revealing to our patients the aired-out mysteries of our psychoanalytic science of symbolic representation. For instance: aquarium equals maternal womb; and shimmering or brilliance
equals tumescent penis. We have better things to do than waste time
yielding to the temptations that befall those bumblers, eternally ignorant
of psychoanalysis. A more subtle temptation, in that it is infinitely more
legitimate, involves considering the white daisy or the goldfish as leftovers
of the process of mnemic inscription—whereas both of them must be understood as a trace already inscribed but not yet noticed. We are closer,
on the other hand, to the leftovers of the mnemic process when the fragmentary and uncertain image of the fountain is evoked in the uncertainty
of its reality as a memory (a memory or a dream). Not that the elements
that constitute the image escape the status of memory trace; but because
each of the details that makes up the uncertain representation—such as
the basin's glazed ceramic relief, or the jade-green color of the spouting
dolphin's head—is evidently borrowed from a different context and assembled into the uncertain composite image of the fountain, as if to approach or grasp some event of great intensity—an event that retains its
strength and vigor precisely because it has managed to elude the process
of mnemic inscription. The event remains left over, and owes its retention
of a noninscribed, unbound force eluding all conscious mastery or grasp to
its fall into irrevocable oblivion.

Already, beginning with Cyril's screen memory, the evidence repeatedly insists that the marks of that memory were no more than the abstract
cipher of a scene infinitely greater and more complex, ever present, alive,
and active within him: something on the order of an instinctual play
wherein each piece of the body plays its part with the other human,
animal, mineral, or vegetal actors. As far back as we take the analysis, we
repeat the same process of shedding light on more or less archaic, fragmentary inscriptions that we shall be tempted to arrange together, in
order to construct a scene, a so-called true memory, as Freud did in his
analysis of the "wolf-man," reconstructing a "primal scene" to serve as a
pivotal point of reference for situating the patient's history. The only thing
that we must not forget, since it is the essential stage in the psychoanalytic process, is to challenge the validity of this reconstructed scene by
bringing the rediscovered memory traces into light and order. We know
that Freud himself completes this challenge by pointing out the impossi-

bility of settling and articulating the work of analysis in terms of a homogeneous entity: *Non Liquet*. We must be wary, here, of the passion that first led us into practicing the art of analysis, and threatens to lead us into becoming mere readers of a dead language; this is a passion quite close to the one that led Freud into his adventure, a passion yielding an imagistic if not phantasmic terminology: trailblazer, archaeologist, decipherer of enigmas. We must not forget that these enigmas are alive. The mnemic inscriptions that formulate them, like the features of a face and even its deepest lines, do not cease to maintain, with the passions (or the instincts) that animate them, an ever-present relationship, as troubling in its mobility as it is fascinating in its constancy.

Thus, as Freud claims, the only true memory is in the unconscious system. Our conscious system, on the other hand, strives to maintain a kind of register whose accounts stand for a necessarily false "official" memory, much as history textbooks are only an ideological and petrified version of ever-living History.

We come up against a paradox here, which our clinical experience forces us to take into consideration. This paradox is usually expressed in trenchant formulas that, while summary, nevertheless abruptly testify to an always recurring difficulty: on the one hand it is often said that analytical work consists in rendering conscious the unconscious; on the other, it is granted that the unconscious, as such, is irreducible, and that it eludes, by its very nature, any conscious grasp. To stick to the very Freudian metaphor of inscription that concerns us today, we might say that unconscious inscription is neither translatable nor transposable into any other than the unconscious system. Here, as so often in the analytical area, we encounter a terminological difficulty pregnant with practical consequences. The term "inscription," like any other word drawn from a conceptual register, whatever its claims to promoting the dignity of a pure concept, drags along with it a load of theory that cannot escape the phantasmic implication in which, to tell the truth, it originated. Thus the term "inscription" (*niederschrift*) does not differ greatly from that representation of the trace (*Spur*)—the memory trace (*Erinnerungsspur*). From this point on we are caught in the enclosure of a phantasmic system. He who says "inscription" will almost immediately think "trace" (trace of the pen on paper), and will implement an entire imaginary instrumentation, comprising at the very least a surface of inscription as an instrument for recording the trace. This imaginary instrumentation asserts itself with so much simplicity and clarity that memory machines have always been built, as we added earlier, to its specifications. But let one of these little machines, so prized by the students of today, take a leave of absence, and the disturbing shadow of the other memory will loom up ahead. Say, for instance, that you have a paper to prepare for just such a meeting as we are having today, and that you simply cannot be bothered to put pencil to paper and write out your contribution; so you get one of those cassette recorders, and, comfortably settled into your easy chair, with drink and cigarette in hand, you confide your inspired thoughts to the machine. Of course, if you happen to think of it, you make sure that the needle, witness to the recording, responds to your voice; and then you abandon yourself to inspiration. Once all has been said, you have a nightcap, just to heighten the satisfaction your conscience derives from the performance of duty. The next morning, in order to buttress your uncertain wakefulness, you decide to play back the tape. But, damn, deceptive needle! After a few scraps of your voice, there are only grotesque rumblings, a shrill whistle, and then, nothing. What is left of your inspired improvisation? Judging by the violence of your feelings at that very moment, infinitely more than if the machine had yielded the reflection of your own voice. It certainly isn't the same. A bit of advice: if you have the courage to do so at the time, pick up paper and pencil, and you'll see that what comes to you, under the influence of this loss, will be far better than what you had dictated the night before. It is as if your new text, strengthened by this loss, has rediscovered the unconscious sources of what we call creativity. And if this isn't enough, you need only lose your manuscript in the subway. The main thing is not to try to reproduce what has been lost, but to make use of this loss, confident that is in the imageless memory of the unconscious that the most authentic part of one's being expresses itself, timelessly.

It is enough that something of the imaginary instrumentation of props and traces be disconnected by fate, as in the tale of the faltering tape recorder, for the term "inscription" to come back to life outside of its phantasmic context, and for us to experience, if not understand, the existence of "unconscious memory" and to know that it forces us, against our habits, to stay as faithful as possible to ourselves. Here, props and traces become confused: inscription eludes the platitude of the footprint in the sand. But how, then, do we express it? What words can be found to convey its indescribable power?

The Freudian term most often used to designate what is written in indelible fashion in the unconscious, is *Vortellung* (translated in various contexts as either "idea" or "presentation" or the more general "representation"); he also uses "representative" (*Reprasentranz*). In French psychoanalytic circles, the term "signifier," borrowed from Saussure by J. Lacan, is trying to gain acceptance. As for myself, I have come to use the more Freudian term "unconscious memory trace." To tell the truth, each of these expressions lends itself to criticism. "Unconscious memory trace" retains the words "trace" and "memory," and therefore tends to maintain the imaginary instrumentation that structures the way we view memory. "Signifier," borrowed from linguistic terminology, has the advantage of emphasizing that the unconscious is structured like a system (that of language) which has its own logic (differing radically from the logic of discourse); but it has the weakness of never breaking away from the logic of meaning, which the Saussurian correlatives "signified" and "sign" imply. Perhaps it is, after all, the Freudian expression (instinctual) "unconscious representative" that least lends itself to criticism, although, when it comes to designating the elements that make up the unconscious system, "representative" is itself problematical.

We know that, in therapy, the patient is invited to say everything that comes to his mind during the course of the session, without voluntarily excluding anything and without having to construct a coherent discourse. Of course, regardless of good intentions, it is not possible to conform to this rule. From this fact alone, strange verbal juxtapositions and nonsequiturs will make themselves heard, punctuated by an occasional "it has nothing to do with . . ."—but, in fact, the relationship is there, manifest and undeniable in the very text of the verbal sequence. Thus there are breaks, lapses, or stammers that interrupt an outburst; sometimes there are unknown words, strangely concocted from a mixture of languages, which surface much as they do in dreams.

Thus, a patient—we shall call him Laurent—brings to my attention— as I am in the process of composing this text—a dream that involves a phrase manifesting itself. The phrase "Guet libus ombres," which scans as a hemistich, has *no meaning* in any known language. This hemistich, culled from the "royal road of dream," yields as faithful as possible a representation of a *text composed of unconscious inscriptions*. It sits there as if unveiled, and we have only to decipher it. Let's analyze, then, with Laurent, just what he is saying in this unknown language, so as to try and hear what it tells us about the unheard-of truth of unconscious elements.

First of all, a very free translation of the dream text occurs to Laurent; he hears "guet" as it would be said in "schwitzerduch" by a native of Zurich or a peasant of the Oberland, pronouncing the Germanic *gut* (good) with a marked dialectal accent. Then, despite the very Latin appearance of "libus," German asserts itself provisionally, as if by contagion, to produce *lieben* (to love). Finally, since we shouldn't think in terms of French and take "ombres" to be "shadow," Spanish replaces it, and "ombres" becomes *hombres* (men). Thus, our "translation" yields: "It is good to love men." But we shouldn't make haste to understand it, to establish this translation as the correct one, and to stop listening under the pretext that, knowledgeable as we are, we have picked up an admission of homosexual desire. Are not "men" rather shadows escaped from the kingdom of the dead? At any rate, Laurent doesn't stop there: "Libus" intrigues him, because *lieben* does not seem to have exhausted the meaning of the enigmatic libus. Now an Italian term surfaces: *busillis*. This word, he explains, has a curious history, in that it was discovered on a stele bearing a Latin inscription. It caused great bewilderment among the archaeologists, who, blindly and obstinately, sought the meaning of a busillum or busillus. Only after having noticed, on the top line, "inre," similarly inscribed at regular intervals between the letters, were they able to read, once the proper spaces and continuities had been restored: "in rebus illis." *Busillis* has nevertheless entered the Italian language to designate a difficulty or an obscure point: thus, "the busillis of the question" designates its stumbling-block. We are now in a better position to reevaluate the situation. From this point on, what interests Laurent is the actual scansion of the dream text. "Guet libus ombres": he hears one dactyl, one spondee, and only five feet. What remarkable terminology!, he adds, referring to that of versification, which speaks a festival of body parts: *finger* (dactyl), *libation* (spondee), *foot* especially, which is still understood in French today only in the expression *prendre son pied,* which means to take one's pleasure in a specifically sexual sense.

We notice, through free association according to the Freudian prescription, that through allowing the dream text "guet libus ombres" to express the contents of its unknown language, a series of elements appears that cannot be naturally transcribed into a meaningful formulation. It is rather a matter of lines of force, taking shape around terms that seem to elude the common sense to our conscious reasoning abilities. The first of these lines, "to love 'shadows,'" even if we are tempted to reduce it to a homosexual wish, remains open-ended and in motion around the signifier (or unconscious representative) "ombres," which, beyond "men" and "shadow," also contains the indeterminate thing "res" (already evoked by "in rebus illis"). The second line of force, "busillis," and the most eloquent in its concision, highlights very well the untranslatable nature of unconscious inscription and the stumbling-block that it puts in the way of ordering a conceptual expression. Finally, the series of metrical terms heightens the emphasis we had placed on the fact that what is said in the dream hemistich is on the order of a festivity where pieces of the body drink in tenderness and enjoy their relations.

This is how the unconscious appears in analysis—not only as *another system* radically different from those we elaborate consciously, but as another place, "another scene" ordered by neither time nor space. This other place is the most familiar, the most intimate we have. It is so *heimlich* that the rational exile into which we are drawn by civilization (*Kultur*) makes us feel it and live it as if it were *unheimlich,* strange and disturbing. What is being played out in this other place toward which analysis takes us back is the life of *desire* alone; the players are not characters from some play, seductive and imposing in their presence, in fine array and proferring ideological speeches. Rather they are each of the parts of our bodies: our fingers, our eyes. our skin, our mouths, divested of all imaginary clothing and speaking *among each other the forgotten language of love* where the words of desire agree with and modify each other. These parts of the body, actors of the unconscious scene, are not those dissected by the necrophiliac anatomist or the obsessive physiologist. Rather they are those the psychoanalyst has taught us to recognize: "erotogenic zones" (and they all are, in the body) which elude any fantasy of totality and distinguish themselves by *speaking* before ever having been taught to do so. They never cease to conjugate the "I," the "you," the "he" around all the verbs that bespeak "relations," in a language so profoundly forgotten (or repressed) that it seems unknown to us. It is *these words and especially these verbs that constitute unconscious discourse:* no metaphor, no translation, no transcription can give an account of it, because it has no account to settle. Least of all can it be represented; because the unconscious is, more than any other thing in the world, present, here, *hic et nunc,* in all the actions and utterances of our day-to-day lives, and this despite the screening of our rationality. This unconscious discourse is right here, immediately present in ourselves and in the world, like the heaven of the theologians—despite all the constructs and systems through which we incessantly account for the order of things, calling them "reality," even though order and reality are right here, unmediated, in desire (the very essence of man) which makes us live. Only poets and lovers still seem to realize it. And yet, every one of us has had at least the inkling, if not the certainty, of it, when we try, in the "sexual relation," to affirm for ourselves and for another the presence of the words of desire that constitute the unconscious. Psychoanalysts are not alone in their awareness of the usual deficiency, if not the outright poverty, of what we call, nostalgically, our "love life." The problem is that we are still, we men and women of this culture, "illiterates when it comes to love," as the protagonist says in I. Bergman's "Scenes from a Marriage."

Thus, we must learn to read, to understand, to write, and to speak the language of the unconscious; or, even better, to rediscover, despite all that our culture has inculcated, this unconscious language that was given us along with our lives as speaking beings.

We should allow ourselves to marvel, whatever our deafness and blindness, at the miracle of wisdom and the purity of desire that spring forth from the child during his very first days. He lives in the present of the world's memory, the real one, the other one, the unconscious one, the one that has neither to be inscribed nor erased. Of the sexual relationship that conceived him and brought him into the world, he gives us, to see, to touch, and to feel, that part which lives and is rediscovered within him like so many signs of desire: his gaze, his cries, his gestures, his smile. Without any words other than those played out between him and us, and between each part of his still-new body, it is—despite our having forgotten its unconscious language—desire that speaks through his every pore. Here, as in love, it babbles, and we understand it.

The memory of man, or his "history," the real one, is only voiced in the present, in an always original language. To rediscover it, we need only remember, as we do without knowing it when we are in love, that a gaze in the direction of the other, a bit of patience, and an increment of silence, are enough for the words of desire to "sing"—"live" and unrecorded.

❧ 4 ❧

On Death-Work
in Freud, in the Self, in Culture

J. B. PONTALIS

MY TITLE INDICATES an orientation of thought, a progressive movement, certainly not a program of study that could be completed within the
framework of this paper. I shall limit myself to a bit of trailblazing—
however rough and uncertain—in an area where the terrain may become
rather shaky underfoot.

The expression "death-work" evokes immediately, by analogy, some
familiar Freudian terms.

The first is *dream-work:* the whole of operations that transform very
diverse raw materials of the dream: bodily stimuli, dream thoughts, the
day's residues, so as to "manufacture" a product, a narrative sequence of
images in which almost indefinite chains of representations are intertwined into "nodal points."

Next is *work-of-mourning:* a complex process that operates no longer
on representations but rather on an *object* incorporated into the shell, the
container, of the ego; a process, therefore, that is intrapsychic in the
strongest sense, and whose teleological purpose has been said to be to
"kill the dead."

Lastly comes what will remain throughout the most general definition of *Trieb,* of drive or instinct: *a constant demand for work* imposed
upon a psychical apparatus, the complex modalities of its response to

Translated from the French by Susan D. Cohen. Copyright © 1978 J. B. Pontalis. All
rights reserved. Reprinted by permission.

whatever is a "foreign body" for it, but compels it to function, being the very object of the analysis.

In fact the relation of death-work to these three modes of psychical work is, as we shall see, more than analogous.

In the first place let us posit that death-work was at work *in* Freud, and that he was able to transcribe it theoretically—at the price of so many difficulties and contradictions—only because it never ceased being active in him.

In my view, the theme of death is as basic to Freudian psychoanalysis as is the theme of sexuality. I even believe that the latter has been widely put forward so as to cover up the former. Both will come out as transformed by Freud's work, by the *work of the theoretical apparatus*, as drives are by the work of the psychical apparatus.

Concerning Freud's attitude toward death—the attitude of the man and of the thinker being singularly linked, as ought to be the case for every psychoanalyst—one can differentiate, very schematically, three stages.

First stage: death felt by the body, the *soma* let's say, or, better, represented as a mute character in a picture.

Second stage: death thought about, or, better, represented like a drama in the multilevels of space of the psychical scene.

Third stage: death acted, or, better, acting in the depths of being, in what I'll call the "psychical body," like a repetition of elementary processes of an organic appearance.

As for the first stage (which unfolded itself roughly between the years 1890–95), in his book *Freud: Living and Dying*, Max Schur brings out some facts which are not all new but which, when put together, make a strong impression upon the reader because of their insistency in Freud's life.

What is Freud suffering from during these years? What does he complain of to Fliess—to his faraway friend, and ear-and-throat specialist, grandiose and slightly nutty theoritician of periodicity? The clinical picture is heterogeneous, but it is completely organized by the figure of Death (like in those pictures of "Vanities" where the mere gray presence-absence of a macabre shadow dulls the shine of the most precious and most coveted objects).

What is in this picture? A mixture of "psychical" symptoms—of the obsessive series—and of organic symptoms of the anxiety-neurosis type.

Some samples, rapidly:

—Freud proves to be very preoccupied by the date of his death, and always foresees it prematurely (this is a means of attempting to conjure it away: he wants it to come at his time and not at its own; a process that also indicates a desire for immortality, for nonirreversible time). He gives himself deadlines, and, to determine them, calculates according to the law of periodicity thought up by Fliess, which, let us note in passing, associates the determination of sexual cycles to that of illnesses. This idea of periodicity will reappear in Freud's work in the totally transposed form of repetition compulsion.

The first implicit answer to the question: "What are we lived by?"—a question for which Freud had various answers, all of which he sought in a transindividual reality—could be formulated thus: we are lived by death. The term "survivor" comes up repeatedly in his writings. Freud is a survivor; his place is in between two deaths.

Added to these preoccupations are superstitious fears concerning names and numbers: unnamable names, maleficent numbers, carriers of death. Fifty-one, for example, is a redoubtable number; his fifty-first birthday (twenty-eight plus twenty-three of the Fliessian cycles) remains a critical date for him for a long time until it is replaced by another. In short, it's a whole funereal bookkeeping (according to Michel de M'Uzan's expression), which takes possession of him.

These symptoms are not connected to each other, in an obsessional neurosis. In a way it's just the opposite. For in these superstitions, in these more or less obsessive preoccupations, it's the *body* that's directly concerned, attacked, threatened, the body in its different parts. Here, in the head. Conscious and even hyperconscious death anxiety, *Todesangst*, sets upon the body directly, with a minimal of psychical mediation, of transposition, of displacement, or of phantasmic elaborations.

Death doesn't talk, it acts.

Another part of the body, another organ struck: the *heart*. I will quote one letter among many others (that of April 18, 1896). "It was then," he writes, with a precipitation and an odd choice of words that cannot be rendered by translation, "that great cardiac disturbances occurred: violent arrythmia, perpetual rapid heartbeat, a heavy, oppressive feeling, a burning sensation in my left arm, a little dyspnoea—very slight and perhaps hinting at an organic cause. All this in fits, that is, happening two or three times a day, prolonging itself and accompanied by a psychical depression which is manifested by ideas of dead people and of farewells, and which replaces a normal hyperactivity."

The German word *Malereien* evokes painting, the painted picture, more than ideas. It isn't Freud who sees death; one can't look it in the face; he feels seen by it. If the right distance that permits vision is no longer maintained, he is thrown toward it (death), after each part of his body—and not the total body—has experienced its ascendancy.

Even his famous and persistent dependence on tobacco, a veritable addiction, has to be connected to death anxiety. When Freud speaks to Fliess of *abstinence,* we must understand not sexual abstinence (very easily endured by him as far as we know), but rather abstinence from tobacco. Forbidding him to smoke, as Fliess persists in doing, is the equivalent of forbidding him any intellectual activity! Not that the two are identical, but he finds more than a stimulant to this activity in his addiction: it is a necessary condition for it. On the one hand, the rising and quieting of excitation in the mouth and the respiratory tracts is coupled repeatedly in that zone, thus keeping it at one level; on the other hand, however, intellectual activity, which Freud defines as a "psychical complication," this activity that will become more and more his very life, interposes constantly renewed mediations between excitation and the return to point zero.

I don't wish to pursue an inventory of the ills of this period: recurrent migraines, fatigue, nasal suppurations, intestinal disorders. (Freud goes as far as giving a name to his intestine—Conrad). I'd just like to mention two points:

1. Freud's symptoms evoke something that was one of his principal nosographical, etiological, and theoretical interests: the *actual neuroses;* his interest in this remained lively even when he had the model of the *psychoneuroses* entirely at his disposal. A point that has not been stressed enough is the remarkable convergence of certain, particularly French, contemporary theories of the so-called psychosomatic affections— a theory that draws inferences from a firm distinction between conversion and somatization—and on the other hand, the "old" Freudian theory of the actual neuroses. The word "actual" connoted two things simultaneously, whence its importance: the existence in the present of the conflict and its actualization in the soma, its nonsymbolization, which implies the prevalence of economic factors.

2. The disorders Freud complains of are mostly inserted in his rela-

tionship with Fliess: he sends him "detailed reports of sickness," he calls him his "healer," his "supreme judge." He is ill with Fliess, by Fliess, for him, from him. Well, we all know the story. It is also known that he will disengage himself only with one and the same painful effort from his Other and be able to gain access to the unconscious meaning of his symptoms, of all symptoms.

Then, with the *Traumdeutung*, the second stage begins, the one the most familiar to us. Dreams that demand dramatization, the putting of sequences into figurative action, allow Freud to move about in a new, absolutely psychical space this time, that of a shadow show where he becomes at the same time the theater and the director. The rule of telling everything presupposes, if not the representation of everything, at least the ability to articulate everything, the decomposing into elements. To the work of unconscious representations bound and unbound in the flow of associations, corresponds the work of *interpretation* which connects and disconnects in another way, which uncovers or constructs the fantasy and the history of the subject.

Death ceases to have a direct grip on the body. It is internalized. It spreads out, it multiplies itself. In changing area it changes meanings. It is no longer met as an external menace that one could only try vainly to protect oneself against, but as a wish, as *Wunsch*, directed toward the possessor and the rival. A wish entirely caught up with the Oedipus structure. The present bite of conscious death anxiety changes into a repressed desire and into the unconscious guilt of the survivor.

It will be remembered that Freud was able to say about his book on dreams that it was a piece of his self-analysis, his reaction to the death of his father.

How can we avoid comparing this admission to another later and more intimate one? "Now that my mother is dead, I can die." An admission that might be understood in this way: how could I, the beloved son, bear having to announce my own death to my mother, single figure of the three Fates, in which she who begets, she who loves, and she who destroys are joined. There lay the meeting with the uncanny, in those "caskets" where the secret of Freud remains hidden.

For one can't but be struck by the fate reserved by Freud for death anxiety, at this high point of psychoanalysis, and from then on. At least on the theoretical plane (for in his life it's another story), he resolutely frees himself of it by effecting a total reversal.

It is now merely a mask, a form among others (weaning, separation) of castration anxiety, which he makes the pivot of every object loss and behind which "no deeper secret would be hidden." "In the unconscious there is nothing capable of giving content to our concept of destruction. I hold firmly to the idea that death anxiety should be conceived of as an analogon to castration anxiety."

These lines were written in 1925 (from *The Problem of Anxiety*), five years later, therefore, than *Beyond the Pleasure Principle*, where the idea of the death instinct made itself felt, and ten years after the essays on mourning and on narcissism, which hinted, however, that the most intense anxiety could be related to systems and oppositions other than those of castration and difference (ego-non ego, outside-inside, unity-fragmentation, the oceanic feeling-the feeling of annihilation, elated self-retracted self, repleteness-emptiness).

Two remarks here—his words "I hold firmly," etc., reveal Freud's wish: if only the whole affair could be taken care of by Oedipus, and by a *conquering* Oedipus—this while ignoring the attempt to murder Oedipus the child (Leclaire) and also forgetting that besides the parricide, Oedipus's and Jocasta's suicides are the price exacted by the transgression (Barande).

As for the assertion so often reiterated by Freud that "our unconscious can not imagine our own mortality," wouldn't this be a denial? A curious "oversight" or slip in any case for someone who was able to recognize the function of the double and to spot so many symbolic figurations of death in dreams or in tales, such as disappearance, muteness, the hidden, and Cordelia's pallor.

Unless the formula "the unconscious deos not know the negative" should be understood in this way: it doesn't know the negative because it *is* the negative, which is in opposition to the supposedly full positivity of life. And it is the negative to the extent that its very constitution, as a heterogeneous system, is correlative to the loss, absence, and negation of the object of satisfaction.

The fact remains that death, thus apparently dismissed, shows up again in his work, knocking off center an edifice the author nevertheless considered complete, and with what power does this reappearance take effect! In its double drive against nature and against law, in this inconceivable concept, unless we are conceived by it, the death instinct.

This is the third stage, which also seems to me to correspond to a specific dimension of our clinical experience. The first stage, as I've said:

actual neuroses, nonsymbolizable soma. The second stage, the one *par excellence* to which analytical models and methods can be applied: the so-called classical neuroses, when the psyche is the metaphor of the body, but of the body as nervous system, the network of representations of the *Traumdeutung* being substituted for the neuronal paths of the *Project for a Scientific Psychology*, the network of nerves, of rails, or of words. The introduction of the death instinct as referent or as primal myth confronts us with another problematic, which "narcissistic personalities" and "borderline cases" are making us more and more sensitive to. Here the psyche becomes body. From the question, "What does that mean?" we go on to, "What does that want?" Death is no longer localized in consciousness or in the unconscious; it is at the very root of the unconscious. It is no longer the property of one psychical agency; it is rather the principle of discord in every one of them. It is a-topia. It is no longer speech but silence, sound or fury. If Freud admits that "it is extremely difficult to form a more or less concrete idea of the death instinct," isn't this because he meets up with the most fundamental form of "work of the negative": on this side of or beyond the imaginable, the representable, should we say the analyzable? Yes, if analysis presupposes as its Greek etymology ἀναλυειν, the primary inscription of sense-giving and minutely localized elements.

Whatever the personal or collective motives (bereavements, the hecatomb of the World War—which didn't have a number yet, and which also makes a corpse of reason) that could have impelled Freud to put forth a principle beyond the couple of pleasure principle and reality principle, without decisive clinical proof, it is clear that these pages (the 1920 essay), so near in their movement, not in their style, to an associative discourse, are carried throughout by a demand of thought, a demand analogous to the desire that seeks irrepressibly to make its way into truth. "It's as though I'm obliged to believe in it."

This course was hardly pursued by his disciples of the time, or else it was diverted into another direction, in my opinion, by those who, like Melanie Klein, seemed to be profoundly committed to it but focus the death instinct on the object (external or internal), thus reducing it to a force aiming at destroying this object.

Everything about this notion is disturbing: its speculative air (recognized by Freud), the combination in one word (*Todestrieb*) of the terms "instinct" and "death." Instinct was until then associated with self-preservation, with life, above all with sexuality, but now it is associated with death—death, traditionally associated with the cessation of life and attributed to the expected but denied intervention of an external agent.[1] But what is concerned here? A desire for death or of the death of desire? And how can we tolerate the assertion that reiterates itself that "every being dies necessarily from internal causes"? (Was that a sideways message to psychoanalysis, that entity conceived, made, and kept alive by Freud, an admission of disillusionment as to the creative ability of its members, the very presentiment that the death instinct would turn against the edifice of psychoanalysis, against the Eros?)

The term "instinct" is also awkward here. Where would the source, the object, the aim of the death instinct be? What would be its delegates: what representations, what affects?

There lies perhaps the error committed by partisans of the idea of the death instinct as well as by those who reject it: to act as though it were a question of a particular form of instinct, and then to look for what *represents* it:

—Is it aggressive, destructive behavior (Freud was able to maintain that), especially self-destructive behavior, or else a state of apathy?
—Is it unleashed violence or else the temptation of nirvana (each generation discovering or rediscovering its own)?
—Is it an overabundance, an excess of excitation, demanding a devastating acting-out, or else a vacuum of excitation, this lack inducing a feeling of nonexistence, or a void of thought and of affect?
—Is it, for Narcissus, fascinated self-sufficiency or else an omnipotent and raging grip placed on the object?
—Is it zero or infinity?

So many possible, circumscribable *figures*, but which threaten to make us lose what is essential in the Freudian intuition: it is in its fundamental *process* of *unbinding*, of fragmentation, of breaking up, of separation, of bursting but also of enclosing—process that has no aim but its own accomplishment and whose repetitive nature brands it as instinctual—it is here that the death instinct operates. This is a process that no longer has anything to do with conscious death anxiety but that *mimics death* in the very kernel of being, and this brings Freud, in his metabiology, to insert it in the cell, kernel of the living organism. Then the psyche is no longer a substitutive representative of the body. It is body. The unconscious no longer delivers itself up to be read in its *forma-*

tions, in a mobile and articulable logic of "signifiers"; it is realized and immobilized in a logic of the psychical body. This process of functioning will
affect reality in a secondary way, inducing splittings in the object, in the
ego, in every group or individual agency that claims a vocation to an ever
increasingly embracing unity.

No psychopathological structure is exempt from this capacity of unbinding and of unleashing, which operates in the midst of a smaller and
more and more limited closed system, by a play of increasingly elementary oppositions, like an organism traversed by energies. One can only say
that the frequency of states at the limit of the analyzable has made analysts more receptive to its modes of operation and to its effects. But it is
found in the most certain, the most straightforward neurotic organizations, for example, in obsessional neurosis, in which mental activity is literally encapsulated. Freud had more than an inkling of this: I refer you to
his "Analysis Terminable and Interminable" and in particular to what he
says of "alterations of the ego" compared to "anachronistic institutions."

Every psychoanalysis talks about death insinuated into life. And if the
psychoanalyst's work has at its goal a psychical space that is not a mere
surface, but that has some consistency, some flesh to it, that becomes
body, and acquires freedom of movement and of playing, this implies that
he can not evade the antagonistic work of death, that he must meet it
halfway.

Time does not permit serious consideration of the third part of my
title: what in culture? Time and also some reluctance: psychoanalysts are
no more in a position to analyze society than anyone else, unless they
yield to the imperialism of applied interpretation.

One simple hypothesis, therefore: what the death instinct generates
as movements and as defenses has taken over the conflict between the
claims of desire conveyed by sexuality, and the forces of repression and
suppression. It is perhaps in the ways the death instinct is carried out, in
the types of anxiety and defensive responses mobilized by it, that clues to
civilization's present "discontent" can be found (the word "discontent"
having become weak and "civilization" being declined in the plural).

If the psychoanalyst seeks to designate the present social figures of
the death instinct, he has at first glance, rather than a "problem of forming a more or less concrete idea of it," the burden of choice! Our books,
our newspapers—if it were only just them—are full of it without however
succeeding in nullifying its power: the atomic threat, not so much as a

concrete menace but rather as a concrete metaphor of our own potential fragmentation as humans (return to the a-organic), the cycle of violence and counterviolence, pollution, servitude, and above all what La Boetie called voluntary servitude, in the flash of genius of his youth three centuries before we spoke of masochism. Even what appeared to be constructive forces in our history, life forces, are now presented as though undermined by the forces of death. The revolutionary alternative of socialism or barbarism is no longer posited; barbarism is discovered in socialist cells. The industrial world no longer dares extol its progress; it worries, instead, about its wastes and goes about wondering, like one of Ionesco's characters, "How can we get rid of it?"—and this should be understood as: how to get rid of men, all of whom are "waste" as regards the demands of any social machine that wants only to function and to regulate itself. Proclaimed sexual liberation is abolished in the *Eros Center* which already in its very principle is a *Thanatos Center*.

Examples of this are numerous: the anarchical proliferation of suburban complexes, which in fact create fragmentation; an ever-growing mass on information that cuts off the individual from any sensual reality or social communication, that robs him of his creativity; the increase in "cultural life"; closed lingos that no longer refer to anything but themselves: there is an exchange, but only with another which is the same as oneself—prevalence of endogamy.

But here as well—in the collectivity as in the individual—the effectiveness of the death instincts can be recognized less in the images we give to them than in their *process*, which negates any possible dialectic, every image being able to turn itself into its opposite. "Our real necropolises," writes Baudrillard, "are no longer cemeteries, hospitals, wars, hecatombs . . . they are the storerooms of computers, blank spaces purged of all human noise (the noise of Eros), a glass coffin." Well and good, I approve: let's break the computers! And I find myself a vandal, a possibility that a more perfected computer will not fail to insert in its next program. The more closed the system the more explosive the breaking out. Enclosing-unbinding this pair of opposites repeats itself unceasingly, a pair that seems destined to generate only its own repetition. Let us recall that Freud made turning something into its opposite and turning something against itself the primary mechanims of psychical functioning, as prior to repression of representations and to cultural sublimations.

It looks like the metaphors of *Beyond the Pleasure Principle* are, fifty years later, those which traverse our culture. We yell "Bring the imagination to power!" in a time of trauma that ruins the possibility of exercising it; we whine for the values of a "natural life" while the questions of "survival" plagues us. It is conceivable that bringing the self to the forefront is itself one effect of this process. What series of lost illusions does it not follow? That of a collective subject as agent of history, that of a personal subject as creator of meaning and, lastly, that of an interlocking of symbolic orders that structure enough to confer an identity upon us, were it only an "I" reduced to a grammatical fiction. Must we take as our new illusion an idolized space of the self, expanding and retracting alternately, from which all of culture could emerge again?

The analyst of today, grappling with narcissism, the narcissism of patients, of his colleagues, and his own, has the feeling that what reaches him from the great murmuring of this world, stopped up with cement and full of cracks, is but the echo of what he hears in his seemingly insulated office. "I am located," said Freud, "on the ground floor or in the basement of the building." We, with less confidence than he in the powers of the Architect, will say: at the frontier of death and of life, a constantly moving frontier, which is drawn only to be erased and carried elsewhere.

NOTES

1. One might consider that the modern philosophers of "being for death" (Kierkegaard, Heidegger, Camus) do not break with a humanist conception of the mastery of death as much as they think. As Jean Baudrillard rightly notes, in *L'Echange symbolique et la mort* (Paris: Gallimard, 1976), p. 229: "The terrorism of authenticity through death: another secondary process by which through dialectical acrobatics consciousness salvages its 'finiteness' as destiny. Anguish as the principle of reality and of freedom is still in the imaginary, *which in its contemporary phase has substituted the mirror of death for the mirror of immortality* [my italics]. . . . With Freud it is something else entirely. Sublimation, even tragic sublimation, and dialectics are no longer possible with the death instinct."

❧ 5 ❧

The Crane-Child

FRANÇOIS PÉRALDI

MICHEL IS A CRANE-CHILD.

He talks about only one thing: cranes. He draws only one thing, but with the accuracy of an industrial designer: cranes.

He imitates, on all sorts of semiotic levels (voice, gesture, noises as well as spoken language) only one thing: cranes.

Only cranes fascinate him, or move him, or frighten him, for some unknown reason.

Only cranes can bring the shadow of a smile to his lips or provoke the ecstasy of his body.

Michel has a mother, a poor woman, completely disoriented in a life and in a world she has never understood.

At the age of sixteen, she had been raped by some old drunkard. Michel is the child of this rape.

When Michel was a very small baby, his mother sometimes sat near the cot where he was lying, distressed and paralyzed "because, she said, Michel was not talking to her." She would sit in silence, waiting for some words to come out of the tiny mouth and, when she would bend over the body of her child, she presented him only with the marmorean mirror of her face—a mirror in which Michel could recognize himself as if he were of stone.

She did not know what a child was or could be or need. She did not know how to *hold* him, to *handle* him, *to present him with objects,* so she did almost nothing with him: "I never could teach him anything," she said, "I have never been able to teach him to be clean, even when I tried."

"*How* did you try?" I asked.

"Well," she said, "each time he shat in his bed I used to rub his nose into it and to slap him on the buns." She certainly noticed my surprise for she added: "I don't understand why it did not work, because it does with the kitten."

Through the curtainless window near the cot Michel could see the cranes working nearby, all day long.
He could see them waving at him. He could hear them talking to him, for they did not wait for him to speak first, they just were "talking," mixing *repetitive* gnashings, gratings, grindings with the orders shouted by invisible men: "Up! down! nearer! . . ."

He listened each morning, and waited for the return of the cranes, for the cranes to wake up and begin to talk.

This is the only language that Michel could learn, and the window was the only mirror in which Michel could read the repetitive signs of what he was.

Only cranes answered to what I would like to call without any further explanation his semiotic drives.

Many years later, when I was sitting in my office in the institution where I had met Michel, suddenly I heard a loud metallic racket outside and all sorts of voices, shouting, "Left, no, no . . . higher. . . ."

When I went to look through the window into the park, I could see nothing but a tall boy, all alone, rearranging with the movements of a crane a pile of logs. It was Michel and he was then seventeen years old.

The institution was a center for mentally handicapped children, most of them psychotic. But the organization as well as the functioning were unusual. Instead of constituting a yoked group in which they would have had specific roles according to their status and specific tasks to accomplish allotted them by "specialists," the educators had constituted an unyoked group: un *groupe-sujet*. By "unyoked-group" I mean a group that tries to master its own behavior, to discover its object, a group that has emerged from a petrified hierarchization and in which *speech* can circulate freely, a group attentive to all the manifestations of its unconscious desires, through the manifestations of language.

This unyoking of the group was worked out in the presence of three young psychoanalysts whose task was to *listen* to the unconscious desires; to listen not only with their own knowledge of the unconscious process, which is an inevitable mode of listening, but also to listen without any previous knowledge, to listen without knowing what they were going to hear, to listen to the *unheard of*. As Serge Leclaire, who insists on those two types of listening, puts it: the psychoanalyst, when he listens without knowing, must be ready for anything. For anything can happen to the person in analysis as well as to the analyst, even if, as Leclaire says, something rarely happens to the analyst.

If there had ever been any politics in this center we could speak of the *Politics of Desire*. And among the questions brought up by this Politics of Desire was the following: How can Michel ever have access to a human desire, how can he become a human child instead of a crane-child?

Michel was a very elaborate and a very articulate crane-adolescent when he arrived at the center, and he was able, as a crane, to establish all sorts of very complex relationships with others and to have very complex and diversified semiotic productions (rather than a language). But as a human being he had very few contacts with people except with a female educator to whom he was very much attached, but in the same way a young baby is supposed to be attached to his mother—something like what Margaret Mahler described as symbiosis. We (by "we" I mean *all* the staff of the center, for everybody was concerned by what was happening to everyone)—we decided to attempt the process of separation-individuation by letting at first the symbiotic relationship between Michel and his pseudo mama develop by means of the well-known surrogate-maternal techniques.

But in a way we were listening to Michel with the wrong ear, I mean with all our knowledge, for at that time we were very much impressed by the texts of Bruno Bettelheim or Maud Manoni, and much influenced by a certain psychoanalytic knowledge of certain techniques, certain forms of psychotherapy derived from psychoanalytic knowledge. I am *not* going to talk about them, for they may have nothing to do with the question I want to raise. But I want to stress that in the type of relationship established by Michel with his surrogate-mama and, through her, with the rest of the institution, there was, from the very beginning, something of a nonrecognized desire, a desire that has nothing to do with castration. This is why, perhaps, the question of Michel's desire, which was the question of our desire, was extremely complex.

If, as a man, I ask, "What does *she* desire? What does a woman desire?," I formulate the question of my desire as a man, as a man who has recognized the break central to the difference between sexes, a break that has something to do with castration; what do I formulate then when I ask: "What does a psychotic desire?"

In fact I don't know if the desire of a psychotic can be considered as *Le Désir de l'Autre*—the desire of the Other, as Jacques Lacan puts it, the desire that is linked to castration, the desire of the child to be the phallus when his mother desires it.

I would say, but don't ask me to prove it, that castration is foreclosed or *Verworft* by the psychotic. He forecloses the affirmation—*Bejahung*—of castration. But does that mean he has no desires or no human desires? I would not say so. I would rather say that his desires are absolutely indifferent to the difference between sexes and therefore to that difference comprehended in the light of castration.

We cannot think his desires in terms of what is missing; we have to think his desires in other terms, perhaps in terms of "desiring machines" as Deleuze and Guattari are trying to work out; or in terms of *branchements d'organes*—"plugging the organs into each other"; on in terms of *circulation* or *seriation* of desires, circulation in which even the opposition subject/object would not be pertinent; for such a circulation implies another system than the binary one we are accustomed to.

But if we have to think the desire of the psychotic in a different way, we also have to think his language in a completely different way, for it is through the manifestations of language (taken in a broad sense) that desires circulate. If we try to apply the Saussurian model—which is a binary one—to the study of the language of psychotics we fail, and we do so because we have been listening with the wrong ear, the ear of knowledge.

If we listen to the language of the psychotic with the other ear, the not-knowing ear, then we might discover that his language functions differently, that instead of having a binary structure, a *representative* function, and having an arbitrary relationship with the objects it represents, it has a ternary structure, it has a performative function, and is to be understood in terms of action on the object or in terms of an organic relationship with the body of the enunciator.

The semiotic functions of the psychotic are very close to the semiotics of C. S. Peirce, which, as more and more people are beginning to learn, have nothing to do with the general approach of linguistics today.

But let us come back to what we failed to achieve with Michel and to what happened to the institution when it began to listen to the desires of the psychotics with a not-knowing ear.

To be extremely brief, we tried to triangulate the symbiotic relationship between Michel and his surrogate-mama, by introducing the Law through the presence of a third person, referred to in the speech of the female-educator to Michel, as well as in his day-to-day life.

But as soon as Michel was told that a third person, a man, would interfere, he went to the cellar and, by opening a few valves, he made the furnace explode a few minutes later. No one was injured, but half of the buildings were destroyed by the explosion. There would be many ways to explain this reaction, among them the endless list of our technical errors in so-called psychotherapy. But something very special and unusual happened.

Instead of trying to *understand once again* what happened, instead of trying to discuss *once again* Michel's case or the color of his psychoses, instead of trying to elaborate better techniques to make him enter into the realm of Oedipus, we suddenly realized that we had not been listening to

Michel with the not-knowing ear, that we had refused to listen to the *singularity* of a desire that had nothing to do with ours.

But worst of all we began to realize that we did not even know why we had been trying to Oedipalize Michel and that in a way we had been unconscious agents of a power we did not master. And then we began to "analyze" our desire, to listen to it as it responded to the desire of the psychotic.

Something happened to the institution: a deep and unexpected revolution within its social structures.

With our questioning of the Oedipalization that we had taken for granted as being our task, the whole matter of *desire* was questioned, of a desire based, granted, *twisted* by castration which is nothing but a law, a social law. As we were questioning in this sense, we tended toward what I would like to call a *communistic* structure. And the institution transformed itself into a community into which everything, everyone, was, if I may say so, commonly available.

Married couples among the educators broke their marital ties; the difference between sexes was not pertinent in the circulation of desire; even language tended more and more toward its performative or its poetic functions.

The sense of property disappeared as well, in a certain sense, as the common form of individualism which was replaced by what I would call singularities.

In one sense we might say that what happened was a "schizophrenization" of the institution, but I would rather say that the institution had been the site of a real communist revolution.

I'll end my long question now by mentioning two phenomena that occurred while the "revolution," or if you prefer the "schizophrenization," of the institution was taking place.

First, all the psychotics began to evolve at a fantastic rate, but not toward normality, if such a name ever had any other meaning than conformity to the Law, but rather toward what I call a complexification of their relationship to their *Unwelt*, to their environment, to the others; and this through a multiplication and diversification of the semiotic levels and of the semiotic productions that are usually either refused or prohibited in normal communication.

In a way I would say that they did so because they found at last a place in the new structuring of the institution, a place from which their desire could be listened to.

A semiotic world was invented which I would qualify as *unheimlich* in painting, writing, sculpture, and so on.

At the same time there was a free circulation of desire according to the singularities of each individual rather than to the roles attributed on both sides of the line demarcating the difference between sexes.

All this I know should be detailed, examples should be given that would sound certainly weird, but all this speech is only a question.

The second phenomenon was a political struggle with the authorities. Repression came very quickly, as we expected, but we had established deep political ties with the communist unions of the area, and, at the first signs of repression, there was unexpected but total support from the unions.

My question has been asked, but I would like to add a final remark. We have learned that everyone grows up, but it is how they grow up that matters. And may I add: some people grow up bitterly out of their *green* years, and the best way to grow up is not necessarily in the verdure of the psychoanalytic society.

❧ 6 ❧

The Disconnected Self

ERNEST S. WOLF

I

"IT STILL STRIKES ME as strange that the case histories I write should read like novelettes and that, as one might say, they lack the serious stamp of science. I must console myself with the reflection that the nature of the subject is evidently responsible for this."[1] With these words Freud apologized that much as he might try to tear apart and analyze in the fashion of the scientific laboratory, his patients did not yield up their central continuity of character and development. Even the fragments of his case histories revealed coherent courses of events; indeed it was Freud's singular achievement to discern the developmental threads of his patients' lives and weave them into an understandable narrative web. In this sense Freud was perhaps the last novelist of our age. He could still write about *whole* people, people whose names and faces would transcend their anonymity. Who will ever forget Dora, the Rat-Man, the Wolf-Man, or Little Hans? To be sure, Freud's patients were seared by anxiety and torn by conflict, but they did not split apart. They always knew who they were, from whence they came, and where they were going, albeit that they might have to limp into bed or drag themselves to work.

Eighty years later the psychoneurotic patient of Freud's time has almost disappeared from the consulting room of today's psychoanalyst. Rarely nowadays do we see patients with the conversion symptoms of hys-

teria or who suffer the preoccupations and rituals of the obsessive-compul-
sive neurotic. Rather our analysands now come to us because they feel
depressed and desperately out of joint with themselves and with the
world. Character disorder or personality disorder has been the label that
we have attached to these sufferers from marital incompatibilities, from
work inhibitions, from delinquency and perversion, or from the scourges
of alcoholism and drug addiction. Though our therapeutic efforts are
usually quite ameliorative and of great value in improving the functioning
of our analysands, they still often leave us quite dissatisfied with our inability to effect the radical and analytic cures that had at one time been
the justified hope of Freud and his early followers. What has happened?
Some of our friendly critics tell us that modern man's suffering no longer
is mainly a matter of his inner psychological makeup, but is the result of
his being the victim of social forces; his salvation thus lies in the reform of
society. It has become the conventional wisdom to recognize in the convergence of capitalism, racism, and poverty the cause for the malaise of
our time, which has been labeled "alienation," a term that has almost replaced the former fascination with an equally modish and banal use of
"neurotic." Certainly, there are fragments of our population for whom
social conditions have become the overwhelmingly destructive trauma of
their lives. And, certainly, we all live in a social ambience that is in many
respects significantly different from Freud's time and to which we respond
on the psychological level with adaptations and distortions of our personalities. Until recently this aspect of the individual psychology of contemporary man was not well understood by psychologists—including psychoanalysts—though, with its usual prophetic perspicacity, the vision of modern
art was penetrating our psychological state long before we scientists became able to formulate the new insights.

My aim here is to focus your attention on new developments in psychoanalysis, on an emerging psychoanalytic psychology of the self which
appears to be of the greatest relevance to the individual suffering from the
malaise of our time. And I shall illustrate these newer concepts by referring to certain artistic creations of the first half of our century. At the same
time I want to disclaim any pretense of a comprehensive statement about
society, man, or art. Our therapeutic clientele is a selected group, not
unlike the novelist's readers and not representative of society as a whole.
The patients who come to a psychoanalyst today usually are not the vic-
tims of poverty and discrimination, nor are most of them torn by psycho-

neurotic conflicts caused by their unresolved Oedipal conflicts: by and large our analysands come to us today because they are no longer willing or able to bear the mortifications of crumbling self-esteem as their vulnerable selves fragment under the impact of the kind of trauma that we used to call narcissistic injury.

The concept "self" is an old one in psychoanalysis, but only recently has it become possible to study the self scientifically. The discovery of the narcissistic transferences by Heinz Kohut has made it possible systematically to investigate and successfully to treat with the methods of psychoanalysis the narcissistic personality disorders, or, to use a more felicitous designation, the disorders of the self. The discovery of the self-object transferences has ushered in the first significant post-Freudian expansion of psychoanalytic theory, and, at the same time, an analogous broadening in the scope of psychoanalytic treatment.

In the most general terms, patients who suffer from narcissistic personality disorders enter analytic treatment with a fragile or shattered self; that is, they experience tension and impaired functioning. In the course of treatment a relationship with the analyst may emerge in which the analyst is experienced as a binding force that strengthens the self into a cohesive structure; the analysand experiences a new calmness and feels "whole." This is the self-object transference, so called because it is a state where an object, the analyst, is experienced as a part of the self—therefore, the analyst is termed a self-object—and it is a transference because it repeats a psychic state of childhood when a parent was a self-object whose presence and responsiveness allowed the child to feel good with beneficial effects on further psychological development. The child's needs are for two kinds of parental self-objects, a mirroring self-object and an idealized self-object. The mirroring self-object confirms the child's valued self by an empathic responsiveness, such as a mother's warmly glowing look of appreciation even of the child's foibles. The idealized self-object is the parent who is available as a source of strength and values that the child can make its own by a psychological merger; a son or daughter, for example, may absorb an admired parent's moral strength by incorporating the admired values and ideals into his or her own character. Failure of the self-object during psychological development results in incompletely structured selves that remain even as adults grossly dependent on outside supplies of narcissistic gratification from self-objects in their environment. These fragile selves fragment when the self-object is unavailable or unresponsive. Among resulting symptoms, poor self-esteem regulation—that is, oscillations between depression and grandiosity—anxiety, hypochondriasis, sexual perversions, delinquency, and addiction are most prominent.

The recognition of the self-object transferences and of their vicissitudes in the psychoanalytic treatment of narcissistically vulnerable analysands has provided the data for conceptualizing a psychoanalytic psychology of the self.[2] Some of these concepts can be illustrated with the help of art as they reveal themselves in the form and contents of the artistic product; *pari passu*, artistic creation takes on new meanings when seen through the eyes of psychological insight.

Perhaps the most central recurring experience in the lives of narcissistically vulnerable people is the experience of unbearable emptiness that comes with loneliness—I mean here a psychological aloneness that may occur as easily in crowds as anywhere else in the *functional* absence of the self-object—a loneliness that almost immediately elicits some relieving action to restitute the crumbling self. Some sort of frenzied activity, often tinged with the excitements of sexuality or of aggression, is used to create a sense of aliveness, to banish the dreaded nothingness that comes with the loss of self. These restitutive actions in their protean forms have become, of course, the bread-and-butter of the psychiatric nosologist and of the novelist.

Without becoming too clinical, I shall just briefly mention neurosis and perversion as examples. If the disintegration of the self occurs during the time of the phase-appropriate flowering of the Oedipus complex, then the Oedipal constellation of family relationships will become the prominent fragment around which restitutive attempts are organized. The end result will be a classical psychoneurosis. However, if the self fragments earlier in the life of the child, pre-Oedipally, then restitutive reorganization of the self takes place around a core of dyadic relationships, for example around the struggle for autonomy, and the result will be a narcissistic personality disorder. If sexual fragments prominently participate in this reorganization, i.e., when the relationships have become sexualized, then perversion will be part of the symptom picture.

II

After this necessarily brief and sketchy introduction to the psychology of the self, I will now come to the self in the modern novel. I have mentioned the central experience of deadly loneliness of the disconnected self—disconnected from its needed self-object—at the core of narcissistic personality disorders. The same experience of disconnectedness, loneliness, and fragmentation informs the most significant of our modern novels.

An early and extremely graphic description of the utter sense of isolation, self-disgust, and worthlessness in modern literature is provided in Kafka's "Metamorphosis" (see also Kohut).[3] The suddenness of Gregor Samsa's transformation, his awkwardness and helplessness, his itches and pains, his cold shivers, and his inhuman birdlike voice are the indices of a crumbled self plagued by hypochondriacal fears. And whoever has been more estranged from the responsive warmth of a loving family? The words he utters are not understandable by them, although they seem clear enough to him. His father is hostile, his mother repelled, his sister unable to touch him; he is driven back into his room as if he were cattle. In his presence the three talk and act as if he were loathsome and unimportant. That these attitudes existed even before his catastrophic transformation we can discern from the life Gregor lived with his parents. He meant nothing to them but the benefits of convenience that they could derive from him. As one gets to know the Samsas one is not surprised that the story began with Gregor's awakening from a nightmare into a state of fragmentation.

For my next illustration I want to use Sartre's novel *Nausea*.[4] Roquentin, the novel's protagonist who reports his self-experience, uses the symptom of nausea as a label for his disorganized self, his fragmentation. Quite early he tells us the central fact of his existence when he says that he lives alone, entirely alone (p. 6) and even feels alone when in the midst of happy, reasonable voices (p. 8). Sartre's description of the experience of inner disorganization that comes with such utter aloneness is unsurpassed. First there is the sudden awkwardness of bodily movement, the loss of muscular coordination and of sensory perception: Roquentin feels strange, his hand seems changed in the way it picks up a pipe or fork or holds a doorhandle (p. 4). A familiar face suddenly looks unknown, and street noises become suspicious (p. 4). Life has become "jerky, incoherent" (p. 5), it seems that the fragmentation of his self is projected also on his perception of the world. The self has lost its sense of direction. Roquentin notices being paralyzed, unable to express himself, like being full of "lymph and milk" and of yet "feeling empty" (p. 5). No longer is it possible to tell "clear, plausible stories" (p. 7); in other words, meaning has been lost, boundaries of the self seem lost when "you plunge into stories without beginning or end" (p. 7).

Roquentin is obsessed by the life history of the Marquis de Rollebon, and we soon see that the Marquis's life also seems to have been subject to the kind of abrupt turns that elude Roquentin's self-understanding: the reports "do not contradict each other, neither do they agree with each other; they do not seem to be about the same person." Lacking is "firmness and consistency" (p. 13), or, as we might paraphrase, cohesion has been lost to fragmentation. We know that Roquentin is really talking about himself. When he looks into the mirror, his face is just a "gray thing," no longer having sense or direction. In fact, except for the beautiful red hair, his face is compared to a clod of earth or a block of stone; "obviously there are a nose, two eyes and a mouth, but none of it makes sense, there is not even a human expression" (p. 16).

Sartre even illustrates the causal sequence of the unexpected absence of the needed self-object followed by the regression of the self to a state of fragmentation. Roquentin has gone to the café expectantly, but when the waitress informs him that the *patronne* is out shopping he feels disagreeable tingling in his genitals; his vision is fogged by a colored mist and a whirlpool of lights, smoke, mirrors, so that he can no longer see and recognize people. He floats, dazed, becomes nauseous, can no longer move his head, which feels elastic and detached (pp. 18–19). No longer is the nausea within him; he is the one who is within it (p. 20). In other words, his self has lost its boundaries and he has become an incoherent collection of threatening experiences.

Sartre's diagnosis is straight to the point: "In order to exist, [people] also must consort with others" (p. 6). Otherwise they will, like Roquentin, experience a sudden estrangement from themselves in a somatophysiological manner: the nausea. The sudden loss of inner cohesion is experienced by him as a sudden senselessness of the world around him, a strange and disconcerting absurdity. The one place where sense remains, vaguely, for which he strives as the concluding hope of the novel, is the unity and intelligibility of a song. As Iris Murdoch states: "For Roquentin all *value* lies in the unattainable world of intelligible completeness."[5]

Kafka has given us an unparalleled dramatization of the self-disgust and Sartre an unsentimental description of the hypochondriasis that occur when the self has gone to pieces. We now turn to Virginia Woolf for the subtle ups and downs of a fragile self in its battle to remain cohesive.

Mrs. Dalloway starts with an act of self-assertion: ". . . she would buy the flowers herself."[6] The novel then makes the reader witness one day's experience of a delicate and sensitive self as it is exposed to the ordinary confirmations and rebuffs of an ordinary existence. Clarissa Dalloway never totally fragments, perhaps, because her "gift was knowing people almost by instinct" (p. 11), and thus, her talent as a hostess allows her continuously to re-create her self through the medium of giving a party. Here she is able to exercise a quasi-artistic creativity in bringing together disparate personalities *pari passu* with reestablishing connections to her own self. Let us observe Clarissa in the vicissitudes of her day and note how Virginia Woolf has used stream-of-consciousness techniques in rendering the inner experience of a struggling self.

The novel begins as Clarissa walks home through London. She feels alive in the hustle and bustle of the cars and the people: ". . . one loves it so, how one sees it so, making it up, building it round one, tumbling it, creating it every moment afresh; . . . life; London; this moment of June" (p. 6). Woolf goes on to tell us: ". . . loving it as she did with an absurd and faithful passion, being part of it, since her people were courtiers once in the time of the Georges, she, too, was going that very night to kindle and illuminate; to give her party" (p. 7).

We are in touch here with the self-experience of feeling strengthened by its merger with a lively environment, "being part of it," a merger that includes admired ancestors and being like the king and the queen and the lords of the palace, a merger that is reified in the act of giving a party.

As Clarissa walks on, her associations lead to Peter, who had wanted to be too close to her, ". . . everything had to be shared; everything gone into. It was intolerable" to her, and so he had called her "cold, heartless, a prude . . ." (p. 10) and married another woman. Recalling this, Clarissa stands still for a moment and Virginia Woolf describes a self that contemplates its shaky identity and uncertain boundaries: "She would not say of any one in the world now that they were this or were that. She felt very young; at the same time unspeakably aged. She sliced like a knife through everything; at the same time was outside, looking on . . . a perpetual sense . . . of being out, . . . and alone . . . very dangerous to live even one day, she knew nothing, no language, no history, . . . she would not say of herself, I am this, I am that" (p. 11).

She would have preferred to be large, stately, and dignified instead of this "sense of being herself invisible; unseen; unknown" (p. 13). One wonders whether Clarissa's special fascination with gloves alludes to her need to find a substitute for her missing psychic skin.

Somehow she is led to think of her daughter, Elizabeth, who has become inseparable from Miss Kilman; the thought stirs up the "brutal monster" of hate in Clarissa, a hatred that she recognizes, however, as "nothing but self-love" (p. 15).[7] Clarissa then regains her cohesion at the florist's, where she merges with the beauty of the flowers, "this beauty, this scent, this color, . . . were a wave which she let flow over her and surmount that hatred . . ." (p. 16).

The narration then switches to Septimus Warren Smith who, like Clarissa, suffers from a crumbling self, but who is not able to save himself and goes on to utter fragmentation, psychosis, and suicide. Virginia Woolf knows a great deal about the experience of regression to insanity, but we shall have to postpone discussion of that point. Instead let us follow the process of disintegration one more time when Clarissa Dalloway arrives home and gets the message of her husband's being out for lunch with Lady Bruton (p. 34).

It was a "shock" that made her "shiver" and "rock." Slowly she goes upstairs, "as if she had left a party, where now this friend now that had *flashed back* her face, her voice; had shut the door and gone out and stood *alone* . . . feeling herself suddenly shriveled, aged, breastless, . . . out of her body and brain which now failed, since Lady Bruton . . . had not asked *her*" [my italics].

She goes on: ". . . withdrawing . . . and emptiness about the heart of life . . ." (p. 35)—and after some musings on her sexual frigidity, "a virginity preserved through childbirth"—she states clearly: "She could see what she lacked. It was not beauty; it was not mind. It was something central which permeated" (p. 36). We need not follow here now the memories of attempts to make some contact, to break out of the loneliness and isolation by homosexual merger with Sally, an adolescent alter-ego with whom she had "meant to found a society" (p. 38).[8]

Instead let us follow Clarissa to the mirror where she goes "collecting the whole of her at one point" (p. 42). "That was her self when some effort, some call on her to be her self, drew the parts together, she alone knew how different, how incompatible and composed so for the world only into one center, one diamond, one woman . . ." (p. 42). Note that in the above paragraph Woolf, by separating her and self into two words, acknowledges a noun, the self, which stands for a subjective experience of togetherness.

It is a rich novel of self-experience, of integration through creativity and disintegration as a result of disconnectedness.

The formal qualities of this novel seem to me also to reflect the to-and-fro struggle between the fragmenting tension and the efforts to restore cohesion to the self. The text abruptly shifts from topic to topic, back and forth in time without transition, and, similarly abruptly, there are changes in location of the narrative. The impression is of a mosaic rather than of a watercolor. And yet, at the same time, there is a smooth continuity, a seamlessness that makes the novel an undoubted whole. No chapters break it up; the periodic strikes of Big Ben become the rhythmic linearity along which the narrative develops into a unity.[9] It is perhaps not an accident that the regularity of a clock imprints the unity and wholeness, because it is a regularity not unlike a pulse or heartbeat, reminiscent of the experience of secure wholeness of a baby held against its mother's breast. It is the same soothing and restoring quality that can be conveyed by musical rhythm while the fragmentation experienced finds its representation in the dissonance and rhythmical disruption of contemporary music. The art of our time illustrates the task of individuals in our time. In an age of increasing isolation and disconnectedness the fragmenting self must reconstitute itself through creative action.

III

Psychoanalytic theories relate introspective-empathic data (Kohut 1959) to other data—for example, behavioral observations, physiological symptoms, and biographical information. In other words, psychoanalytic theories attempt to bring the canons of science to the task of making sense of the psychological experience of man. Kohut's conceptualization of a psychoanalytic psychology of the self evolved from the psychoanalytic treatment of adult analysands in the classical Freudian psychoanalytic situation. In the preceding I have demonstrated that the concepts of the psychology of the self can be illustrated with vignettes from modern literature: the almost complete loss of self as experienced in psychoticlike regressions is graphically rendered in Kafka's Samsa; the experience of a nonpsychotic fragmentation of self following the loss of a self-object is exemplified by Sartre's Roquentin, especially the psychosomatic symptoms, hypochondriasis, paranoid suspiciousness, and feelings of emptiness that accompany the loss of a firm sense of self; finally, the experience of a fragile self as it endures the struggle to preserve its cohesion against the disintegrating stimuli of living through an ordinary day is portrayed by Woolf in *Mrs. Dalloway.* Samsa, Roquentin, and Clarissa illustrate Kohut's concepts of self, of self-object, of cohesion, and of fragmentation much as Jensen's Gradiva illustrated Freud's theories, particularly his concepts of dream formation.[10]

Dream interpretation, of course, had been an ancient art to which Freud brought a method, psychoanalysis, that for the first time made a scientific study of dreams possible and that led to certain psychological theories of dream formation. These theories, which had been constructed to make sense of clinical data, also found a measure of congruent support in the ease with which they could be illustrated by examples drawn from literary texts. Analogously, the vicissitudes of self-experience, the alienation and disintegration so familiar to twentieth-century man, have been a topic of artistic concern for decades. The psychoanalytic psychology of the self is enriched when the intuitive insights of great artists dovetail so smoothly into the matrix of its theories.

The concepts of the psychoanalytic psychology of the self are the result of prolonged and intensive introspective-empathic immersion into the lives of analysands by observers whose empathic perceptivity has been sharpened by training and experience. What is the significance for criticism that these same observers can discern in literary texts psychological constellations that serve as illustrations for the psychological constellations first observed in the clinical situation? Psychoanalysts would insist that critical insights are enriched through the contributions made by the observer who is trained and experienced in the perception and scientific integration of introspective-empathic data. Literary material evokes introspected experiences akin to those that are empathically perceived in clinical psychoanalytic situations. The hypotheses and interpretations that are derived when these introspected data are processed with appropriate biographical, behavioral, social, and other data become useful instruments to deepen insight into the meaning of artistic *oeuvres* in much the same way as they are useful in making sense out of the experiences of an analysand. The sensitive introspective-empathic perception of evoked mental states and not the application of theoretical systems is crucial for the emergence of psychoanalytic insights, whether the psychoanalytic method is applied clinically or to a work of art. Freud condemned the rote application of psychoanalytic theories as "wild analysis".[11] His warning should be heeded not only clinically but wherever psychoanalysis is applied. The specifically psychoanalytic nature of psychological interpretation is dependent on the incorporation of the introspective-empathic data. The rote application of psychoanalytic theory when it is torn out of its sustaining matrix of correlated data results in the reductionistic assault for which it has been justly criticized. Here psychoanalysts have sinned as much as other interpreters who have not had the benefit of psychoanalytic training. I hope in the interpretations in this essay to have avoided that *pons asinorum*.

SUMMARY

Contemporary society increasingly seems to produce people with fragile selves that fragment under the impact of ordinary life-stress. Psychoanalytic study, especially the work of Heinz Kohut, has conceptualized a developmental psychology of the self and proposed that normal self-development depends on the self-objects which appropriately confirm the developing self through empathic mirroring responses and through availability for idealization. The family in contemporary society appears to fail frequently in providing the sustaining ambience for the developing self; the latter subsequently remains fragile.

Modern novelists have vividly illustrated the burdensome tensions resulting in the fragmentation of these fragile selves. They seem also to say that the absence of self-objects in ordinary daily existence is experienced as the noxious trauma. Modern art thus echoes one major aspect of contemporary individual experience, namely, the vicissitudes of self-psychology.

Psychoanalytic interpretations, when grounded in the introspective-empathic data evoked by the artistic opus and its context, can make enriching contributions to the critical study of art.

NOTES

1. Sigmund Freud and Joseph Breuer (1893–1895), "Studies on Hysteria," *Standard Edition* (London: Hogarth Press, 1955), 2:160.

2. Heinz Kohut, "Forms and Transformations of Narcissism," *Journal of the American Psychoanalytic Association* (1966), 14:243–72; Kohut, "The Psychoanalytic Treatment of Narcissistic Personality Disorders," *The Psychoanalytic Study of the Child* (New York: International Universities Press, 1968), 23:86–113; Kohut, *The Analysis of the Self* (New York: International Universities Press, 1971), Kohut, "Thoughts on Narcissism and Narcissistic Rage," *The Psychoanalytic Study of the Child* (1972), 27:360–400; Kohut, "Psychoanalysis in a Troubled World," *The Annual of Psychoanalysis* (New York: International Universities Press, 1973), 1:3–25; Kohut, "The Future of Psychoanalysis," *The Annual of Psychoanalysis* (1975a), 3:325–340; Kohut, "The Psychoanalyst in the Community of Scholars," *The Annual of Psychoanalysis* (1975b), 3:341–70.

3. Heinz Kohut, *The Restoration of the Self* (New York: International Universities Press, 1977); Franz Kafka (1912), *The Metamorphosis* (New York: Schocken Books, 1946).

4. Jean-Paul Sartre (1938), *Nausea* (New York: New Directions, 1964).

5. Iris Murdoch (1953), *Sartre: Romantic Rationalist* (New Haven: Yale University Press, 1959), pp. 12–13.

6. Virginia Woolf (1925), *Mrs. Dalloway* (London: Hogarth Press, 1947).

7. See Kohut's discussion of narcissistic rage (1972).

8. See Wolf, Gedo, and Terman on the function of the adolescent's *academia*, the secret society, in the adolescent's effort to create an adult self. Ernest S. Wolf, John E. Gedo, and David M. Terman, "On the Adolescent Process as a Transformation of the Self," *Journal of Youth and Adolescence* (1972), 1:257–72.

9. Big Ben might also be interpreted as a clock that shatters disruptingly; however, the theme of a self striving for continuity and cohesion against fragmenting forces encompasses both interpretations.

10. Sigmund Freud (1907), "Delusions and Dreams in Jensen's *Gradiva*," *Standard Edition* (London: Hogarth Press, 1959), 9:7–95.

11. Sigmund Freud (1910), "Wild Psychoanalysis," *Standard Edition* (London: Hogarth Press, 1957), 11:221–27.

SECTION III
Creativity

❧ 7 ❧

(Nonsymbolic) Motion / (Symbolic) Action

KENNETH BURKE

THIS IS THE basic polarity (like the traditional pair, *res* and *verba*, things and the words for things).

It's at the root of such distinctions as mind-body, spirit-matter, super-structure-substructure, and Descartes' dualism, thought and extension.

I say "at the root of such distinctions," though no such terms quite match the motion-action pair.

Thus we can begin by logologically secularizing the theological (Thomistic) view of "matter" as the "principle of individuation."

The human body, in its nature as a sheerly physiological organism, would thus be in the realm of matter, for which our term is "motion."

In that respect it would be like a fish or a tree or one of B. F. Skinner's operationally conditioned pigeons.

But the use of such resources as a tribal language would be in the realm of "action."

Action, as so defined, would involve modes of behavior made possible by the acquiring of a conventional, arbitrary symbol system, a definition that would apply to modes of symbolicity as different as primitive speech, styles of music, painting, sculpture, dance, highly developed mathematical nomenclatures, traffic signals, road maps, or mere dreams (insofar as a dream is interpretable as "symbolic" of the dreamer's "psyche," or whatever such term a psychologist might prefer to work with).

Thus our use of language here is an example of symbolic action, in which we variously participate by use of "conventional, arbitrary symbol systems" (one language or another).

Since the overall topic is "Self and Culture," I take it that the term "Self" is meant to designate in some sense what has been referred to as the "principle of individuation."

I take it that, even if the "Self" were thought to merge into the "Culture" as a whole, each member of the "Culture" would be thought of as having in some way a "Self" different from each and every other member.

It would be grounded in the realm of nonsymbolic motion, and would mature into what one would call a "person" in the realm of symbolic action.

So far as is known at present, the only typically symbol-using animal existing on earth is man.

The intuitive signaling systems in such social creatures as bees and ants would not be classed as examples of symbolic action.

They are not conventional, arbitrary symbol systems such as human speech, which is not inborn, but has to be learned, depending upon where the child happens to be "thrown," an accident of birth that determines whether the child learns Chinese, or French, or whatever idiom may prevail in the given locality.

Symbol systems of that sort also differ from intuitive signaling systems in that they have a second-level (or "reflexive") aspect.

That is to say: They can talk about themselves.

Cicero could both orate and write a treatise on oratory. A dog can bark, but he can't bark a tract on barking.

If all typically symbol-using animals (that is, humans) were suddenly obliterated, their realm of symbolic action would be correspondingly obliterated.

The Earth would be but a realm of planetary, geologic, meteorological motion, including the motions of whatever nonhuman biologic organisms happened to survive.

The realm of nonsymbolic motion needs no realm of symbolic action; but there could be no symbolic action unless grounded in the realm of motion, the realm of motion having preceded the emergence of our symbol-using ancestors; and doubtless the time will come when motions go on after all our breed will have vanished.

With regard to the theory of evolution, obviously critical conditions for the emergence of culture arose at that stage in the prehistoric past when our anthropoid ancestors underwent a momentous mutation.

In their bodies (as physiological organisms in the realm of motion) there developed the ability to learn the kind of tribal idiom that is here meant by "symbolic action."

And thereby emerged what we might call a "mechanism" for the steps from nonsymbolic motion to symbolic action.

Descartes, in his speculations on a possible bridge between his polar realms of "thought" and "extension," proposed the possibility that a small gland in the brain, the pineal gland, might provide the medium.

But with regard to the materials for an intermediate step between the realms of "motion" and "action" we need not look for so recondite a locus.

The necessary materials are implicit in the physiological nature of sensation.

In his early essay on "Nature," Emerson described the process transcendentally, tender-mindedly thus:

Words are signs of natural facts. The use of natural history is to give us aid in supernatural history; the use of the outer creation, to give us language for the beings and changes of the inward creation. Every word which is used to express a moral or intellectual fact, if traced to its root, is found to be borrowed from some material appearance. *Right* means *straight; wrong* means *twisted; Spirit* primarily means *wind; transgression* the crossing of a *line; supercilious,* the *raising of the eyebrow.* We say the *heart* to express emotion, the *head* to denote thought; and *thought* and *emotion* are words borrowed from sensible things, and now appropriated to spiritual nature.

Jeremy Bentham would deal with considerations of this sort, perhaps not tough-mindedly, but at least matter-of-factly thus:

All our psychological ideas are derived from physical ones—all mental from corporeal ones. In no other manner can they be spoken of. . . . In the case where to the object thus spoken of, existence is actually an object of one of the five senses, and in particular of the sense of touch or feeling. . . . Here there is no fiction—as this man, this beast, this bird. . . . The object spoken of may be a real entity.

On the other hand in the case in which the object is not a tangible one, the object, the existence of which is thus asserted, not being a real existing one, the object, if it must be termed an entity—as on pain of universal and perpetual non-intercourse between man and man, it must be—it may, for distinction's sake, be termed a fictitious entity.

To every word that has an immaterial import there belongs, or at least did belong, a material one. In a word, our ideas coming, all of them, from our senses, . . . from what other source can our language come?

Though Bentham's theory of fictions involves many other aspects, for present purposes note that we are but applying the traditional scholastic formula, *Nihil in intellectu quod non prius in sensu,* which itself isn't the whole story, insofar as the grammar and syntax of a language can be thought of as adding a dimension not reducible to terms of sensation alone. (Leibnitz added this logological qualification in his metaphysical style thus: *nisi intellectus ipse.*)

Surely our basic consideration is clear enough; namely:

The sheer physiological *sensations* of the human organism are on the *motion* side of the motion-action polarity; they furnish material for the vocabulary of a language; and such vocabulary lends itself to figurative usages to which Bentham gave the name of "fictions."

Though the mutation that makes speech possible is itself inherited in our nature as physical bodies (in the realm of motion), the formation of a nomenclature referring to sensory experiences is on the side of symbolic action.

Even if language could have been kept within bounds of such strictly physicalist reference, its use would in effect have "transcended" motion and attained the rudiments of action.

With the wider use of physicalist terms as necessary "fictions" for reference to supposed nonphysical entities or processes, the realm of specifically symbolic action is strongly involved, and is completed with the formally stylistic use of metaphor, or equivocation generally.

The nature of language is such that it could not possibly be confined to strictly literal, univocal usage.

If words did not admit of loose application, you couldn't apply the same terms to a variety of objects, processes, circumstances.

For in its details, every situation is unique.

In his book entitled *Poetic Diction, a Study in Meanings,* Owen Barfield would want to deny that the step from terms for sensation to their use in referring to nonsensory "entities" is metaphorical.

He would hold that the material objects (to which such terms had literally referred) themselves contain such a range of what Emerson would call "supernatural" connotations.

To meet the minimum conditions of what is meant here by "symbolic action" all that is necessary is the inability of words to "stay put," as when even a proper name like "Caesar," referring to one particular person in history, gives birth to such words as "Kaiser" and "Czar."

The purely physiological aspect of the "Self" (its grounding in the realm of motion) is characterized by the centrality of the nervous system.

Its sensations are immediately its own, not thus felt by any other organism.

Like organisms presumably have similar pleasures and pains, etc., but these are *immediately* experienced only within the centrality of each one particular organism's nervous system, as individuated at parturition.

The "Self" as a "person," member of a community ("culture") characterized by motives in the realm of symbolic action, is not thus differentiated.

Whatever may be the genetic traits differentiating one individual from another, and whatever the distinct histories of individuals, the nature of symbolic action shapes the Self largely in modes of role, of sociality.

In this respect the Self becomes a product of the Culture.

Here figure the individual's relations to family, to groups, to ever-widening and partially conflicting organizations such as church, business, political party, nation, "global" tentatives. Here, in contrast with the *im-*

mediacies of the body, we confront for our overall "reality" an indeterminately interwoven complexity of symbols, reports about local, national, and international affairs, about history, psychology, geology, astronomy, expectations true or false, promissory or forbidding, etc., etc.

"Reality" (the "world"), as thus symbolically conceived, embraces a potential "universe of discourse" far beyond the realm of physiological sensation.

But the opportunities for such exercising (via resources in the realm of "symbolic action") depend wholly on the realm of physiological motion (the basic conditions that determine whether the individual organism lives or dies).

In sum, when to the principle of individuation (involving the underlying physiology of sheer motion) there is added an organism's ability to parallel the realm of sensations by learning to use *words* for them, the concept of "Self" must necessarily be defined in terms of a *polarity*.

In terms of nonsymbolic motion, the "Self" is a physiological organism, separated from all others of its kind at the moment of parturition.

In terms of symbolic action, it becomes a "person," by learning the language of its tribe, with corresponding identity and roles (beginning with the equivalent of a proper name, and expanding variously in keeping with the currently available resources of symbolism and the institutional structures reciprocally made possible by them), the three corresponding Dramatistic axioms being:

There can be motion without action (as the sea can go on thrashing about whether or not there are animals that have a word for it).

There can be no action without motion (as we animals could not have words for anything except for the motions of our nervous systems and the vibrations that carry our words from one of us to another through the air or that make words visible on the page).

But (and this is the primary axiom that differentiates Dramatism from Behaviorism) symbolic action is *not* reducible to terms of sheer motion. (Symbolicity involves not just a difference of *degree*, but a motivational difference in *kind*.)

Yet this difference in kind amounts to a primary DUPLICATION.

This is due to the fact that the nomenclature of symbolic placement is borrowed from the materials of sensory motion.

And the terms are of such a nature that they are "fictions" or analogical extensions, of their beginning in reference to physical processes and objects.

A Culture's symbolically conceived "World," or "universe of discourse," is thus built figuratively of terms originally grounded in reference to the nonsymbolic realm of motion.

Otherwise put: The realm of what are usually called "ideas" is constructed of symbolic materials usually called sensory "images."

The "Self," like its corresponding "Culture," thus has two sources of reference for its symbolic identity: Its nature as a physiological organism, its nature as a symbol-using animal responsive to the potentialities of symbolicity that have a nature of their own, not reducible to a sheerly physiological dimension.

Symbolicity itself being of a nature that can rise to higher levels of generalization until all is headed in some all-inclusive title, we can readily understand why psychologists like Jung are moved to talk of an overall oneness, as *Unus Mundus.*

Yet in the light of the critical Dramatistic distinction between the motives of a physiological organism as such and the motives of such a "Self" as *personalized* by participation in its particular Culture's modes of literal (univocal), equivocal, and analogical symbol using, we can at least glimpse (if not wholly understand) why Jung could be exercised by such a symbolically engendered "idea" or "ideal" of Ultimate Unity.

And by the same token we should see why the motion-action "Polarity" is unbridgeable in the sense that although, in every tribal idiom however rudimentary, there is a wholly reliable basic correspondence between a thing and its name, never the twain shall meet.

That might seem quite obvious, as regards the kind of "polarity" that prevails with the correspondence between a tree and the *word* "tree."

But look how far afield from such obviousness you get when the distinction shifts from the realm of sheer motion (as with the physicality of a tree) to the corresponding word (which is in the realm of symbolic action), and you confront what Dramatism would view as inaccurate equivalents, such as "matter" and "spirit," "matter" and "mind," or even "brain" and "mind."

There could be no total unity between the realms except along the lines of orthodox religion's promise to the faithful that their bodies will be restored to them in Heaven.

An unchartable complexity of behavings among the cells of the body may add up, for instance, to an overall "unitary" sense of feeling good; but no sheer term for an ideal unity (such as Jung's expression, *Unus Mundus*) can match that purely physiological kind of "attitude."

Keats, dying, modified a passage in Shakespeare to state it thus: "Banish money—Banish sofas—Banish Wine—Banish Music; but right Jack Health, true Jack Health—Banish Health and banish all the world."

Though any attitude, even in purely theoretic matters, has a summarizing, unifying aspect, it must prevail only insofar as in some way it is grounded in purely physiological behavior (as per William James's charming and often-quoted statement that we're sad because we cry).

In his chapter on "Attitudes" (*The Principles of Literary Criticism*), I. A. Richards was presumably speculating on a behavioristic parallellism of this sort when he wrote:

Every perception probably includes a response in the form of incipient action. We constantly overlook the extent to which all the while we are making preliminary adjustments, getting ready to act in one way or another. Reading Captain Slocum's account of the centipede which bit him on the head when alone in the middle of the Atlantic, the writer has been caused to leap right out of his chair by a leaf which fell upon his face from a tree.

Whatever the implications of an ATTITUDE, as a kind of incipient or future action, it must be by some means grounded in the set of the body now; and thus, though an *attitude* of kindness may be but the *preparation* for the doing of a kind *act* (a subsequent mode of behavior), it is already "behaving" physiologically in ways of its own (as a dog's implicit way of "conjugating the verb 'to eat' " is to begin by salivating, a bodily motion that in effect implies the future tense, "I will eat," the present tense of the verb being bodily conjugated by eating; and "I have eaten" is also in its way a *now*, as the dog curls up for a comfortable, satisfied snooze).

But whatever the correspondence between purely symbolic attitudinizing and the kind of immediacy that poor Keats with his dying body confronted, his very efforts, to endow his poetic attitudes with sensuous immediacy made him all the more cruelly aware of the respects in which the poet's modes of symbolic action were comparatively (to use his own word for his own poetry) "abstract."

His "Ode on a Grecian Urn" symbolically enacts the "transcending" of the body.

But that letter he wrote to Fanny Brawne while nearing death was concerned with a situation in which the sheer nonsymbolic realm of motion (the plight of his diseased body) was taking over; for such in essence is the unbridgeable "polarity" between the social realm of "symbolic action" and motion's "principle of individuation" whereby the symptoms of *his* disease were the *immediate* sensations of *himself* and none other.

All told, in our "Selves" sheerly as physiological organisms, our World is made of what Santayana would describe as but a single line drawn through an infinity of possible "essences."

But all of them are experienced *immediately,* as yours and no one else's, though you doubtless rightly assume that others of your kind experience similar immediate sensations.

Beyond that, in polar distinction, is the vast symbolic realm of tribal sociality, or orientation, as shaped by the influences that you encounter by reason of your being a symbol-using animal, whose "reality," at every stage, is determined by such terms.

In Santayana's *Realms of Being,* his *Realm of Matter* would correspond to what is here called the realm of Nonsymbolic MOTION (for which his word is sometimes "flux," sometimes "action," though I must here employ a different usage).

His passionate *Realm of Spirit* would be much what I mean by "symbolic action."

And his *Realm of Essence* would deal with "sensation" as the bridge between the realms of "matter" and "spirit," though his term "intuitions" here would ambivalently include both bodily sensations (such as color) and purely symbolic fictions (such as the character of Hamlet).

The "Self" as a "person," beyond the individual's identity as a strictly physiological organism, confronts with varying degrees of comprehensiveness and profoundness the interrelationships among the manifold details of "reality" (whatever that "orientation" may be) as known and interpreted in terms of the symbolic lore current in the Culture of that time.

Necessarily, any individual's formal or informal version of such lore is selective, in keeping with the limitations and engrossments besetting that individual (as both person and physiological organism).

The interrelationships among such a conglomerate will be related consistently (this *therefore* that), antithetically (this *however* that), adventitiously (this *and* that).

When such an aggregate is felt to fall together "holistically," the gratification of such purely symbolic symmetry can rise to an ecstasy of conviction that we call "mystical."

The fall from such a state (whereby the fullness, *pleroma*, of purely symbolic exercising gives way to a sense of its underlying emptiness as tested by a similarly structured physiological counterpart) is called "accidie," *acedia*, sloth, torpor, drought.

Or the sense of such a confluence among motives can also have the Allness of a pandemonium, a Pandora's box let loose, a Walpurgis Night, a jangling conflict of all the pieces with one another, the very fullness being felt as a drought.

In the state of contemporary "Culture," I take it, the corresponding "Self" is likely to manifest "in principle" fragmentary aspects of all three such symbolically engendered "fulfillments."

The fragmentary delight is in putting anything together. The drought is usually met by purchasing some form of entertainment.

The variant of pandemoniac entanglement can even be attenuatively transformed into a bit of research on the problem itself.

Hart Crane is a notably pathetic example of a poet whose mode of mysticism terminated in a corresponding drought.

While he was writing portions of *The Bridge,* there were times when everything seemed to fall ecstatically into place, its many disjunctions inspirited by one transcendent principle of unity.

But the very strength of his hopes for the work as a wholly *organic* solution for his problems as a personal Self set the conditions for the drought that was necessarily implicit in his reliance upon symbolicity alone.

There may be drought, not as a comedown from the mystic exaltation of "holistic" symbolizing, but as a kind of sloth implicit in the sheer failure to take delight in the wonders of purely symbolistic enterprise.

For such a condition there are direct (nonsymbolic) resources available to the Self—and they are widely resorted to.

I refer to the many drugs that act directly upon the Self as a physiological organism (in the realm of motion), though there are attendant difficulties due to the fact that each such physical means of gratifying the organism also happens to tax the health of that organism; and even if it didn't, there is the problem that the very directness and efficiency of its appeal to the body robs the individual Self of the human gratifications resulting from engrossment with the manifold manifestations of purely symbolistic enterprise.

But surely, above all, in confronting the tangle of "Global" problems that beset the current state of affairs, we should pay wan appreciative tribute to the remarkable symbolic resources whereby "pandemonium" can become "attenuatively transformed."

All about us (as with us assembled in this hall, to the ends of interaction among our individual modes of symbolic action) there are our various Selves each to varying degrees tracking down the implications of his particular nomenclature.

For I take it that, just as each good poet speaks an idiom of his own, so it is with each symbol-using animal—and there is a kind of reciprocating relationship whereby the Self selects its key words, and they in turn become formative, to shape further developments of the Self, along with countless such unchartable interactions, including reactions back upon the behavior of the Self's sheer physiology.

The reference to physiology enters here in connection with the concept of "psychogenic illness," which refers to a reverse relationship whereby, just as drugs can produce physical effects recorded as a corresponding "attitude" or "state of mind," so such attitudes or states of mind can function suggestively to induce corresponding physiological behavior (in the sense that, if you received some information you believed in, and the information was highly disturbing, it would affect your bodily behavior, your blood pressure, respiration, pulsebeat, and the like, quite as were the situation actually so, though the information happened to be in error).

In this sense there is the "polar" relationship whereby an individual's mode of symbolic action (his investment in a particular kind of literary style, for instance) might attain an organic replica in a kind of physical behavior that happened to be a kind of disease.

In cases of that sort there could be a mutually reinforcing relationship (a "feedback"?) between the author's symbolic prowess and corresponding processes of his body whereby the development of his skill at his particular mode of symbolic action would be making him sick and keeping him sick, as his symbolic exercising was reinforced by the effects of his physiological "misbehavior."

Our attitudes toward past or future (remembrances or expectations) are products of our symbolicity.

But their behavioral counterparts in the realm of physiological motion must be in the immediate present.

For the only way a body can possibly behave is from one present moment to the next.

In the realm of symbolicity, there are two totally different notions of sequence: the temporally prior (yesterday/today/tomorrow) and the logically (nontemporally) prior (as with the syllogism, first premise/second premise/conclusion).

Myth, being narrative, features the modes of temporal priority (as discussed in the section on "The First Three Chapters of Genesis," in my *Rhetoric of Religion*).

The same work deals "logologically" with respects in which even *temporal* terms can be treated as in nontemporal relationship to one another (as per my "Cycle of Terms Implicit in the Idea of 'Order' ").

The strategic intermediate term here is IMPLICATIONS.

Thus the terms "order" and "disorder" are nontemporally related in the sense that, being "polar," each implies the other, regardless of whether we go *from* the idea of "order" *to* the idea of "disorder," or *vice versa*.

But narrative (myth) can set up a temporal sequence whereby the story goes *irreversibly* "from" one "to" the other.

Insofar as IMPLICATIONS all fall harmoniously into place, any given exercise in symbolic action approaches the feel of mystic unity.

Insofar as they add up to a jangle (and though "polar" terms such as "order" and "disorder" imply each other without strife, they imply much conflict when reduced to terms of irreversible story), the Implications are under the sign of pandemonium.

Insofar as, of a sudden, all such symbolic enterprise seems vacuous in comparison with the immediacies of physiological sensation (in the realm of motion), we are on the slope of sloth, of drought, for which the alternative "remedies" are either physical "dissipation" (as with direct recourse to drugs) or further study (as thus fittingly when on the subject of sloth, Dante sums up for us the entire rationale of the *Purgatorio*, in this very canto where we are assured that, though rational (*d'animo*) love may err, "the natural" (*lo natural*) is always *senza errore*).

Gershom Scholem's engrossing studies of the Kabbalists enable us to glimpse a further marvel with regard to the vibrancy of IMPLICATIONS among terms.

We see hermeneutic ways whereby, though the teacher would not so much as modify a single letter of the Torah, while honoring the text as the very signature of JHVH Himself, and considering the Law so basic to Creation that it was propounded *before* Creation (*there's* a "priority" for you), the disciple was taught modes of transformation that enabled him to see all such literalnesses double, in terms of esoteric IMPLICATIONS.

And thus some of us *goyim* can glimpse how St. Paul was doing exactly that, long before the Kabbalists, when scrupulously leaving the O.T. letter of the Law intact, he but introduced N.T. interpretations (as with the shift from a strictly *physiological* behavior of circumcision, which obviously had its symbolic aspects, he improvised a new symbolism, "circumcision of the heart").

Much of our engrossment with all such interpretations and reinterpretations (as exemplified, for instance, in the various schools of psychoanalysis) stems from the vibrancy of interrelated IMPLICATIONS that thus suggest themselves for the spinning.

And "case histories" are, as it were, the translation of such logically, doctrinally interrelated terms into the corresponding parables of narrative (the "mythic" parallel).

Thus the catalogues, or "inventories," of Whitman's poetry are unfoldings of terms that IMPLY one another, their associative interrelationship being revealed in a succession of tiny plots.

Since the principle of Duplication begins in the polarity of our dual nature as symbol-using animals, the split across the two realms of non-symbolic motion and symbolic action will necessarily manifest itself in endless variations on the theme of duplication.

For it is the combination of bodily sensation with symbolic counterparts and corresponding analogical extensions that "keeps body and soul together" until the last time.

And neither realm can be complete without the other, nor can they be identical.

Thus ultimately, when properly discounted along "logological" lines (whereby his "archetypes" are seen as *quasi-temporal* terms for terms *logically prior*), Plato's version of IMITATION, as a species of DUPLICATION, will be seen to go much deeper than Aristotle's.

Aristotle's is good common sense, inasmuch as there is a notable difference between real victimage (as with a Roman gladiatorial contest) and the mere IMITATION of suffering (as with the *pathos* of a Greek tragedy).

But Plato was digging into the IMPLICATION that, once we turn from the realm of motion to the realm of symbolicity, and try to envision everything in terms of that ideal symbolic universe, then all actual things in nature become in effect but *partial* exemplars of what they are *in essence,* as no single object can fit the exact description of the countless other and different objects classifiable under that same head.

Possibly the motion-action distinction, as conceptualized in this statement, implies that the line of demarcation between "conscious" and "unconscious" should be moved farther to the side of sheer motion.

That is, dreams would not be on the side of the "unconscious" insofar as dreams, like the most mature works of science, philosophy, literature, or the arts generally, admit of analysis as modes of symbolicity.

The Unconscious would be relegated to such processes as digestion, metabolism, the healing of a wound, even if we study the physiology of such behavior.

DUPLICATION is so basic to the relation between motion and symbolicity, nothing of moment seems quite complete unless we have rounded things out by translating it into symbols of some sort, either scientific or aesthetic, practical or ritualistic.

Sex is not complete without love lyrics, porn, and tracts on sexology.

The nonsymbolic motions of springtime are completed in the symbolic action of a springsong.

But let's stop there since further comments on that aspect of Duplication could readily lead into many comments along sociological and anthropological lines, in connection with what happens when the "mythman," adept at fitting ritualistic symbols to the season, can get things turned backwards (as indicated in the story of the missionary who wore a raincoat when it rained, hence, during a drought, was asked by the tribesmen to put on his raincoat, for the obvious reason that raincoat and rain went together). The Implications of DUPLICATION include a vast lore of ways in which the doublings get turned backwards, often with puzzling shifts in views on the nature of causality. I shall, however, add two items in an Appendix. The first will deal with an article by William Willeford, "Jung's Polaristic Thought in Its Historical Setting." Comments on it help sum up the burden of this message. The second applies the terministic lineup to some poetic texts.

"Jung's Polaristic Thought in Its Historical Setting"[1]

(Comments on selected passages, to point up matters treated in my article, "(Nonsymbolic) Motion/(Symbolic) Action.")

Willeford: "The historical trends that Jung rejected in Freud's thought can be summed up under the names mechanism—seen, for example, in Freud's use of the expression 'psychic apparatus'—and positivism, the belief extolled by A. Comte, H. Spencer, and others, that culture was destined to pass through an evolutionary development from magic through religion to science. Although Jung was profoundly committed to the values of empirical science, he regarded the positivistic program as an illusion, because the religious impulse was for him a permanent reality of the human mind, not a stage of culture that would yield to Progress."

Comment: Obviously the Dramatistic Perspective would be on Jung's side insofar as terms like "psychic apparatus" implied a reduction of "symbolic action" to "nonsymbolic motion." But as compared with Behavioristic psychologies, Freud is far from any such reductionism. . . . In the Dramatistic ("logological") Perspective represented by the present article on the Motion-Action pair, regardless of the truth or falsity of Religion, Buber's "I-Thou" relation is here viewed as in its way the "perfect" expression of the form basic to the sentence: speaker/speech/spoken-to. One here directly addresses the most distinguished audience conceivable; and in prayer (petition, in effect saying "Please") there is most grandly enacted the attitude of submissiveness to an all-powerful magistrate. Magic by comparison "commands." Applied science does neither, it but "contrives" (hence, fittingly, our word "mechanism" is etymologically related to Greek words for means, expedient, contrivance, remedy.)

Willeford: "I will focus upon Jung's tendency to conceive the world as basically consisting of polarities of various kinds. Day and night, sun and moon, heaven and earth, right and left, such mythical twins as the *Dioscuri* (born of a single egg) and *Romulus* and *Remus,* the double-headed *Janus,* such ornaments and cult objects as the double spiral, twining snakes, the double-headed axe, the double-headed eagle, pairs of horns; the wealth, antiquity, and wide distribution of such symbols suggest an archetypal basis. I will be concerned not with these but with the attempts of certain thinkers to give their subjective sense of polarity a philosophical form."

Comments: Though language does talk a lot, the very essence of its genius is in its nature as *abbreviation.* A sentence such as "The man walks down the street" is in effect a kind of *title* that sums up an unchartable complexity of details involved in any particular situation to which such words might be applied. (The issue is discussed at some length in my essay, "What Are the Signs of What? A Theory of 'Entitlement,'" reprinted in my *Language as Symbolic Action.*) And what more "perfect" abbreviations are possible than the replies, Yes or No? In fact, the choice is ideally so perfect, except with the kind of questions artificially set up for examination papers, we usually have to settle for a mere Maybe as the answer. Most voting says Yes or No to a decision that is at best a Maybe. All antitheses embodied in polarities of the sort listed by Willeford are by comparison but weak attenuations of this "ideal" form. (An aspect of "Logological" theory is the stress upon what it calls an "entelechial" principle underlying the trends intrinsic to the nature of symbolicity as a realm of motives considered in its own right. Any strictly *psychological* manifestation would be classed as but a special case of such symbolic resources in general.) . . . But prior to such polarities of antithesis within the nature of symbolicity there is the incentive to DUPLICATION inherent in the unresolvable polar relationship between symbolicity and the non-symbolic realm of motion.

Willeford: For Jung "consciousness is always subject to the unconscious background; and the ego, no matter what pride it takes in its powers, is always subordinate to the self, the purposes of which the ego cannot appropriate except by the difficult way of individuation."

Comment: To quote the presumably persuasive TV commercial on the principle of individuation's grounding in the strictly physiological (the realm of motion), It's "my" acid indigestion, and "my" gas, for which I (my ego) takes this medical *material.* But my ego is an aspect of my self, which is developed through modes of sociality (culture) made possible by the resources of symbolism. I shall reserve until later a discussion of the "logological" equivalents for the relation between "consciousness" and the "unconscious."

Willeford: "Polaristic thinking is even present in Kant, whom Goethe (in a letter to Schweigger in 1814) acknowledged as the authority for his own tendency to think in polarities. . . . In the *Farbenlehre (The Theory of Colors)* he says that, no matter how one tries to think about a phenomenon, one cannot escape seeing that it implies an original division capable of unity, or of an original unity capable of division, and he claims that to divide what is united, to unite what is divided, is the life of nature."

Comment: Yes, here is a basic correspondence between the realms of motion and action. We can put *things* together and take *things* apart. And as Socrates says in the *Phaedrus,* the dialectician is skilled in the use of *words* that can perform similarly in the realm of ideas. Bergson has astutely shown how this very nature of words leads to "pseudo-problems," as theorists speculate on how to "resolve" antitheses in nature that were already "resolved" because they didn't exist in the first place, and were but the result of symbolism's failure to formally recognize its limitations as a medium for the discussion of wholly nonsymbolic processes (in the realm of motion). Psychologically, we encounter naivetés of this sort: According to primitive belief, there were ceremonies in which a sacred animal could be torn into bits, with each member of the tribe eating a portion. Here certainly was the principle of division, separation (in early

Greek ceremonies called *sparagmós*). But it was matched by a principle of *merger* inasmuch as all members of the tribe were felt to be made consubstantial by eating of this same numinous substance. The difference between a "logological" treatment of such matters and the views too closely wedded to mythological origins of human thinking resides in the fact that stress upon the *mythic* would tend to derive the sheerly dialectical principles from their operation in such primitive rites, whereas Logology would view the primitive rites as a special case of the more general dialectical principles. A similar risk is to be seen in some Freudian thinking, with regard to the processes of "condensation" and "displacement" in the symbolism of dreams. Symbolism in its most general sense permits of these two processes, which thus are not derivable from such manifestations of them in dreams, which are but special cases of symbolicity's resources. I bring up this point to illustrate what I have in mind when saying that Logology can go along wholly with Psychology insofar as Psychology is viewed as a subdivision of symbolic processes, rather than as the revelation of their source. True, there is a sense in which the human ability to talk at all could be analyzed as a kind of "built-in alienation," separating us from our "natural condition'" as an earthworm presumably is not. But considerations of that sort involve philosophic ironies not strictly reducible to psychological terms, though such quandaries obviously would have profound psychological IMPLICATIONS (there's that word again!).

Willeford: "These examples from Nietzsche, Jung, Goethe, and Schiller illustrate a tendency, extremely pronounced in the early part of the nineteenth century, to conceive difference as the result of division, which is finally the expression of universal antagonistic principles. The antagonism of these principles, and a contrary tendency to resolve it give rise to the forms and energies of nature (Goethe), of the human mind (Hegel, Fichte, Schelling), of art generally (Schelling), and of poetry specifically (Schiller). Indeed, the influence of this polaristic thinking is strongly present in all of the major forms of depth psychology, but it is in some ways especially pronounced in Jung."

Comment: Add Heraclitus (as Willeford does later), and the list would have its perfect top. Apparently in his scheme, all was strife; and the strife added up to perfect harmony. The theory of the U.S. Constitution viewed a *conflict* of powers as a *balance* of powers.

Willeford: "The first source of this polaristic thinking is the nature of the human mind. . . . Polaristic thought has an archetypal basis in that the human mind is disposed to structure its experience by making distinctions between what something is and what it is not, between a thing of one kind and a thing of another. This may be seen in binomial properties of language—the tendency to pair words and concepts in various ways."

Comment: Logologically, the stress would be not upon "the human mind," but upon the nature of *symbolism*. High among my reasons for this statement of the case is my belief that we should not take on more obligations than necessary. Why haggle with Behaviorists when you don't need to? They can't deny that our kind of animal behaves by a lot of verbalizing. So let's account for as much as we can in such terms. To my thinking, in carrying out the implications of that one shift of locus, we completely invalidate Skinner's attacks upon the concept of what he calls "autonomous man" (which I interpret as his own addition of a straw man).

Willeford: "The individuation process described by Jung is governed by the self which is a principle of unity and purpose in the unfolding of the personality."

Comment: Though I have already "translated" Jung's nomenclature into "logologese" on this point, one further qualification is here suggested. In the realm of sheer motion, the individual organism is motivated by such obvious "purposes" as the need for food. But once you turn from the need for food to the ways of buying food by money, you're in a realm where "purpose" involves modes of authority, enterprise, and the like not even remotely reducible to the sheerly physiological needs of living. And, incidentally, the concern with a principle of individuation is itself a notable step in the right direction. Since, in the last analysis, each thing is but a part of everything, there is far too much tendency to overstress this principle of merger at the expense of concerns with a *principium individuationis* (such as the centrality of the nervous system so obviously supplies).

Willeford: "The 'Panlogism' of Heraclitus, the idea that all things partake of the *logos*, which reconciles the opposites."

Comment: Logologically, all things partake of the Word in the sense that all discussion of them is by the same token in the "universe of discourse" (the Greek word *logos* encompassing a range of meanings, such as "basic principle," that favor such an extension). We have already noted the modes of stylization whereby competition can be a form of cooperation (as competing teams on the ballfield in effect cooperate to make a good expert game).

Willieford: "Schelling was influenced by Boehme's idea of the *Ungrund* as part of God."
Comment: Ultimate "polarity" in symbolism is made possible by the fact that any term of highest generalization, such as "ground" or "being," can have the grammatical addition of a negative, as "unground" or "nonbeing," for such are the resources "natural" to dialectic. Thus, in Kant's dialectic (explicitly so named) his overall term for the phenomenal, empirical world of the "conditioned" set up the purely terministic condition for the term "unconditioned" as applied to the noumenal "ground" of this world's conditions. Whether it means anything or not, any synonym for "everything" can still have verbally as its ultimate "context," some synonym for "nothing." Hegel was quite clear on that point.

Willeford: "The first stage, then, in the development of mythology is one of relative 'monotheism,' a monotheism that includes the possibility of polytheistic development."
Comment: In my essay, "Myth, Poetry, and Philosophy" (*Language as Symbolic Action,* pp. 406–9) I discuss the sheerly terministic aspects of this question. Suffice it here to say that any concepts of *priority* with regard to mythic thinking center in an ambiguity whereby the "logically prior" becomes confused with the "temporally prior," since myth is by its nature a vocabulary that states theoretic "principles" in *narrative* terms. Thus the issue becomes somewhat like trying to decide whether the "divinity" of godhead in general is "prior" to some one god's nature as a particular "person." One even encounters paradoxes whereby a monotheistic religion can become "a-theistic" in comparison with polytheism. For instance, many institutions that monotheism treats in purely *secular* terms (such as *Finance* or *Agriculture*) would merit in primitive paganism special temples to their corresponding deities. Logology holds that, regardless of whether one believes or disbelieves in religious nomenclature, one should study theology for the light that "words about God" throw upon "words about words."

Willeford: "Jung came to regard the archetype as 'psychoid,' as transcending the psyche, and as occupying an indeterminate position between *Geist* and *Stoff*, between spirit and matter."

Comment: That would be translated into "logologese" thus: Since the archetypes all have a notable *imagistic* feature, they relate to the role that sensation plays in providing the material for symbolic action's nomenclatures. And by the same token they are in an "intermediate position" between the realms of "matter" (nonsymbolic motion) and "spirit" (symbolicity in its full development, via the fictions of analogical extension). Their "psychoid" identity would reside in the fact that their role, as an *aspect* of nomenclature could not be treated as encompassing the full development of a human being in response to those manifold resources and influences of sociality we sum up as "culture."

Willeford: "Jung's attempt to solve the problem of the opposites is concerned with the archetype of the *unus mundus,* the unity of the cosmos. . . . Jung writes that 'While the concept of the *unus mundus* is a metaphysical speculation, the unconscious can be indirectly experienced via its manifestation. . . . The contents of the unconscious . . . are mutually contaminated to such a degree that they cannot be distinguished from one another and can therefore easily take one another's place, as can be seen most in dreams. The indistinguishableness of its contents gives one the impression that everything is connected with everything else, and therefore, despite their multifarious modes of manifestation, that they are at bottom a unity. . . . The psychoid nature of the archetype contains very much more than can be included in a psychological explanation. It points to the sphere of the *unus mundus,* toward which the psychologist and the atomic physicist are converging along separate paths, producing independently of one another certain analogous auxiliary concepts.' The concept of the *unus mundus* is, then, at the furthest reaches of Jung's thought. And though he has tried to remove the concept from the realm of metaphysics to that of empirical science, we should not overlook the analogy between Jung's *unus mundus,* which he sometimes treats as equivalent to the self, and Schelling's absolute monotheism."

Comment: Unus isn't so clearly an "archetypal" term as images can be. It figures thus among the *transcendentales,* terms or properties which the medieval scholastics said go with all things of whatever sorts: *Res, Ens,*

Verum, Bonum, Aliquid, Unum. In that sense anything we look at is a *one.* And the obviously *summarizing* nature of a title is implicit in Jung's usage, as with our wishful title, "United States." And quite as "God" is the overall title of titles in theology, so logology looks upon any expression like *unus mundus* as high up in the scale of "god-terms," if but in the technical sense of what Korzybski would have called a high level of generalization. For think of how vastly much is encompassed by your title, "One World" if, when you say "I am talking about everything," you feel that you are talking about everything. . . . Since Jung equates the One World with the self, he is in effect trying to deny by idealistic fiat the polarity of *Geist* and *Stoff* that he begins with. . . . The concept of the "collective unconscious" would seem logologically to involve these possible sources: our responses to the sheer physiology of our bodies, in their metabolistic processes wholly outside our awareness except for the sensations, pleasures, pains that we experience as a kind of summarizing titles for such goings-on within us, and many of which function as signs that help us find our way about (thereby to that extent becoming "conscious"); the vast social lore that becomes part of us, though most of it does not explicitly engage our attention; the portions of this which, although they explicitly engage us, involve many implications not tracked down as when we do develop thought and conduct in some particular channel; the implications even here, when they but begin to emerge and exercise us greatly until we have brought them into order; the irresolutions involving each of us differently by reason of his own particular history; and above and behind and within all the goads to DUPLICATION that are intrinsic to the unbridgeable polarity between the realms of motion and action embedded in the physiological developments whereby the physical organism became genetically endowed with ways to build this unbridgeable gulf.

Through Freud's stress upon the formative effects of the individual's early history (the period when the physiological organism is but *beginning* to acquire the symbolic rudiments of a Self), we are introduced to a different aspect of the Duplication principle, namely, the paradox whereby the process of temporal *pro*gression can by the same token set the conditions for a later corresponding kind of *re*gression. Logologically, the situation would be characterized thus: Since words are a major factor in sharpening the nature of attention, the very paucity of a child's emergent vocabulary causes many experiences to escape the clarity that makes for the kind of observation most conducive to *explicit* remembrance. Never-theless, the child's experiences with intimate family relationships serve in effect to surround it with a "cast of characters" and corresponding "plot." These roles (by reason of their temporal priority in the individual's his-tory) become as it were "essential," and thus "dramatically creative" in setting up a pattern of relationships which the individual later DUPLI-CATES by unknowingly imputing similar roles in situations that, as a mat-ter of fact, are but remotely analogical.

Later at the NPAP-NYU conference in which I presented the sub-stance of this article, Professor Norman Holland discussed his thesis that psychoanalysis is now in a third stage. After having first stressed the Un-conscious, next the Ego, it is now in an "Identity Phase." His statement was particularly impressive because he used the same poem, Words-worth's two "Lucy" quatrains beginning "A slumber did my spirit seal," to illustrate the changes of approach.

The choice was a most happy one for my purposes, since it was al-most as though deliberately designed to illustrate my notions about the "polar" relationship between the realms of (nonsymbolic) motion and (symbolic) action. I have situated the principle of individuation, with regard to the Self-Culture pair, in the physiological realm of motion, as circumscribed by the "centrality of the nervous system" (whereby the given human individual, as a biological organism, "immediately" experi-ences only its own sensations, as distinct from the sensations that any other organism, each in its way, immediately and exclusively experi-ences). The realm of symbolic action, in contrast, is characterized by kinds of behavior (with corresponding modes of identification) that are made possible, for example, by social relations highly dependent on "arbitrary, conventional" symbol systems, of which a tribal language would be the prime specimen.

I had said that the only transcending of the permanent "split" be-tween the two realms (of symbol and nonsymbol) would be as in some ul-timate condition like that which orthodox Western religions imagine, in promising that the virtuous dead will regain their "purified" bodies in Heaven. Wordsworth's poem suggests a different "solution," as per the second quatrain:

> No motion has she now, no force;
> She neither hears nor sees;
> Roll'd round in earth's diurnal course,
> With rocks, and stones, and trees.

Lucy now has "no motion" in the sense of her motions as an *individual* biologic organism, a state she has "transcended" by merging wholly with the motions of rocks and stones and trees as they move in earth's diurnal course. And the merger with "symbolic action" is embedded in the very constitution of the poetic medium that celebrates her oneness with nature as the ground of all physiologic bodies.

Our art-heavens such as Keats's "Ode on a Grecian Urn" and Yeats's "Sailing to Byzantium" bridge the gap by aesthetic conceits, each in its way inviting the realm of symbolic action to take over, in terms of *images* that stand for *things* (materials) that are *symbolic*. Thus, Yeats:

> Once out of nature I shall never take
> My bodily form from any natural thing,
> But such a form as Grecian goldsmiths make
> Of hammered gold and gold enamelling
> To keep a drowsy Emperor awake. . . .

And Keats's Urn is a viaticum, with its transcendent destiny already imaged in its nature as a symbol-saturated object.

In sum, in his nature as the typically symbol-using animal, man would make an *unus mundas* by making everything symbolic, as with Baudelaire's great sonnet *Correspondances*, celebrating Nature as a "temple" where man passes *à travers des forêts de symboles*. The special poignancy of Yeats's poem is his (essentially hysterical?) gallantry in affirming his aesthetic "solution" in the very midst of recognizing the tyranny of the sheerly physiological dimension:

> An aged man is but a paltry thing,
> A tattered coat upon a stick, unless
> Soul clap its hands and sing.

In his "Intimations of Immortality," Wordsworth seems to "solve" the problem by interpreting his confused wonder-tinged memories of presymbolic infancy as remembrances of a still further past (a principle I have called the "temporizing of essence" whereby the *narrative* way of trying to say how things *truly are* is to say how they *originally were*). This symbolic pressure explains why Freud felt it necessary to postulate a placement for his "Oedipus Complex" in "prehistory," whatever that is.

To sum up: The dialectical relationship between Self and Culture centers in a nonsymbolic principle of individuation or rudimentary physiological identity which becomes matched (or countered, or extended) in the full (social) sense by symbolic identifications with both personal and impersonal aspects of the Non-Self.

An obvious example of personal identification would be the relationships involved in primitive kinship systems, membership in secular or religious social bodies, citizenship, occupational status, and the like. The clearest example of impersonal sources would be terminologies developed as per the "inborn psychology" of the individual body's responses to physical processes, conditions, objects, locations by the analogical use of words like "sunny" and "stormy," or "distant" and "intimate," as "fictions" for referring not to climate or *extensio* (Descartes' term), but to a "person" (a word that itself originally referred to a *thing*, the material mask worn by an actor). In this sense, as Bentham and Emerson agreed, despite their widely different ways of getting there, all terms for "psychological" or "ethical" subject-matter (quite like the believer's words for the realm of Heaven) can be traced back etymologically to an origin in sheerly physicalist reference.

There is a kind of "synchronic" relationship between the realm of "symbolic action" and its grounding in the sensations made possible by the physiology of nonsymbolic motion. Such would seem to be at the roots of Jung's concern (almost nostalgic concern?) with the "polar" problem inherent in his ideal of an overall nomenclature to be formed in the name of *unus mundus*.

Freud's concern with the temporally prior would be on the "diachronic" side, having to do with the fact that the human animal develops from speechlessness (nonsymbolic *infancy*) through successive stages in the ways of symbolicity (plus corresponding difficulties in the acquisition of such aptitudes, difficulties that cannot be wholly surmounted, if only because the problems do not lend themselves to a wholly adequate solution in symbolic terms, since our empirical problems of life and death are ultimately grounded in physiology, not symbolism).

In any case, both of such concerns (Jung's and Freud's) require us to track down the ultimate implications of what it is to be the kind of animal whose relation between its Self (as an individual) and its Culture (its society) is infused ("inspirited") with the genius (for better or worse) of its symbol systems, which it learns to manipulate and by which it gets correspondingly manipulated.

But this particular paper should end on at least a paragraph or two, listing if only at random some of the many cultural forms which, whatever their nature in their own right, can be glimpsed as responding (in various and even quite contradictory ways) to the principle of DUPLICATION implicit in the motion-action alignment:

Most obvious are the traditional metaphysical or theological distinctions between body and mind (matter and spirit). Others: the microcosm-macrocosm pair, "eternal recurrence," variations on a theme, double plot, cults of the body (attempts to *will* that all be reduced to the immediacy of physiological sensation), transcendence (attempts like Jung's to have the "polarity" encompassed by an ideal unity), theories of "imitation" (such as Plato's and Aristotle's), bisymmetry, delegation of authority, antecedent and consequent in musical phrasing, identification by association, ritual (which symbolically reenacts some supposedly literal event). In a case of psychogenic illness, is not the body behaving (misbehaving?) in problematical ways of a repetitive nature? Are not the symptoms that characterize its illness contriving in spontaneously uncharted ways to duplicate in terms of physiologic motion certain distresses that are exercising an individual socialized Self that happens to be entangled in unresolved *symbolically* engendered vexations? And is not the *physical* disease in effect a disastrously "literal" translation of the victim's predicament? Indeed, may not the symptoms be so radical a physical counterpart that they in effect serve to reinforce the *symbolic* burden to which they were originally but a response?

I dare but ask that. However, I would end for sure on this family of DUPLICATIONS:

Quid pro quo, lex talionis, Golden Rule, categorical imperative, guilty suspicion (whereby, if Mr. A has malicious designs on Mr. B, he will suspect Mr. B of having malicious designs on him). In brief, projection. And in brief, over all, JUSTICE, PROPRIETY. If you're to be wholly human, no springtime (motion) is wholly complete without the (symbolic) action of a springsong. Man has solved that one, beautifully. But as for the REVERSE DUPLICATION, completing a springsong by bringing about its seasonal counterpart, the human symbol-using animal hasn't yet quite solved that one. But indications are that we keep on working at it! Indeed, topmost among Transcendent Duplications is the symbolism of Utopia—a Platonist Idea, to be imitated largely in the realm of Motion.

NOTE

1. William Willeford, "Jung's Polaristic Thought in Its Historical Setting," *Analytische Psychologie* (1975), vol. 6.

❦ 8 ❧

The Unconscious and Creativity

─────◆•◆─────

ALBERT ROTHENBERG

CONSIDER the meaning of the now very familiar word, "unconscious"; it is the negative of "conscious," literally equivalent to "not conscious." From a conceptual viewpoint, such negating or negation produces broad and extensive categories. Describing someone as "not tall" or something as "not hot" merely eliminates a characteristic and introduces a good deal of nonspecificity rather than necessarily sharpening or clarifying the description. Although we often tend to use and understand negations as though they designated polarities and oppositions, "not tall" is not synonymous with "short," nor is "not hot" equivalent to "cold." The negatives of "tall" and "hot" include a very large range of height and temperature. Straightforward as this point may seem, the failure to recognize the difference between negation or negative form and polarity or an opposite form has caused many problems in various types of theories. In psychology and philosophy, such a problem has developed with respect to the designation "unconscious." The term has been used to designate a polarity or an opposite of consciousness, and it or the anachronistic term "subconscious" have been used as a negation or a negative form roughly equivalent to "nonconscious." This latter type of use potentially applies, and it has been applied, to a wide and extensive range of phenomena.

My purpose is to address both these usages in relation to creativity. With respect to the use of the term "unconscious" as the opposite of "con-

I am grateful to the estate of Gladys B. Ficke (Ralph F. Colin, executor) for support of this research.

scious," I shall clarify some implications and try to correct some wide-spread misconceptions. With respect to the use of "unconscious" as a negative form and its application to creativity, I hope to narrow down some of the extensiveness and nonspecificity. I intend, if you will, to whittle down the vastness of this great negative unconscious. In so doing, I hope to reduce some current intellectual polarity, real polarity, about the role of the unconscious in creativity and also to present some findings from my own creativity research.

Invoking unconscious processes as explanations for creative activity is common among thinkers in diverse intellectual fields. This has come about because of inferences derived from descriptions of creative activities, and from some qualities of creations. The groundwork for these inferences about creativity, interestingly enough, was laid by Plato. This is not to say that Plato formulated a concept of an unconscious, nor that he considered the roots of creativity to lie in some particular aspect of the human mind. On the contrary, he considered creativity to be supernatural or divine in origin and the creative artist's performance to be the result of possession or madness; creativity thus arose from a divine madness.[1] In the dialogue *Ion,* the Rhapsodist protagonist Ion was convinced by Socrates that it was not his art or skill that accounted for his ability to recite Homeric verse and that, therefore, there was some other source of the creative power.[2] When performing creatively, the artist's own senses were not directly responsible for the product, and consequently the creative process was a matter of being out of one's mind and bereft of one's senses. This emphasis on being out of one's senses and on the seemingly possessed, inspiratory, "bolt from the blue" aspect of creative activity has been the basis for a long tradition emphasizing external sources for creativity such as the Muse, a tradition that has culminated in a modern psychological emphasis on the unconscious aspect of the mind. The modern emphasis on unconscious factors in creativity derives from a focus on dramatic events seeming to come from outside the creator's awareness; rather than attributing them to a source outside the creator himself, they are located within the creator as another aspect of his mind.

The specific concept of the Unconscious is, of couse, associated with psychoanalysis and Sigmund Freud. Although Freud did not originate the concept—others such as Eduard von Hartmann proposed it earlier[3]—he was the first to develop a full and systematic theoretical account. Although Jung's concept of an unconscious, specifically a Collective Unconscious, has had a prominent place in some modern theories of creativity, I shall not here embark on a thorough recounting and assessment of the differences between Freud's and Jung's theories of unconscious functioning. As the major thrust of the matter is similar for both, I shall focus on the Freudian Unconscious and merely touch on similarities and differences from the Jungian where indicated.

Freud and other psychoanalysts have considered the Unconscious to play a significant role in creativity. Turning to great works of art in order to corroborate the findings about psychological processes derived from work with patients, psychoanalysts have long been interested in what appeared to be manifestations of the Unconscious in works of literature and of visual art. Indeed, Freud referred to Shakespeare's great play *Hamlet* in his initial presentation of the very important concept of the Oedipus complex (and of course derived the term from the myth elaborated in Sophocles' play). Citing Hamlet's inability to act against his uncle-stepfather and the intense relationship between Hamlet and his mother Gertrude, Freud proposed that unconscious incestuous feelings toward Gertrude and unconscious murderous feelings toward the real father could explain Hamlet's plight.[4] Since that time, numerous other psychoanalysts, as well as Freud himself, have described myriad instances of apparent manifestations of unconscious phenomena in works of art. Because of the seeming ubiquity of such manifestations, psychoanalysts have reasoned that artistic creators are particularly sensitive to their own unconscious processes, and, further, that unconscious processes themselves play an important role in artistic creation. Artists' own testimonies that their creations frequently result from dramatic, seemingly automatic, types of inspirations have also strengthened the psychoanalytic belief that phenomena coming from out of awareness play a critical role in creativity. Artists repeatedly report that they cannot trace the steps in their achievement of outstanding ideas, and that such ideas seem to intrude into their awareness without warning or preparation. Or, in many cases, important ideas have been said to arise when the artist is not directly working on his creative task, when he is relaxing or occupied with something else. Thus, the Platonic idea of possession by an external factor has been transposed to constitute a factor that is external to awareness but, nevertheless, resides within the human psyche itself.

The inferences so far would seem to point to a merely negative factor, that is, a factor that is not conscious or is outside of awareness. The

Freudian Unconscious, however, is much more specific than this. Intrinsic to Freud's psychodynamic point of view is a definitely formulated and therefore positively defined Unconscious, an Unconscious that is antithetical to the Conscious. The Freudian Unconscious consists of elements derived from the individual's past that are kept out of awareness for a reason. These elements, designated as drives, wishes, memories, and affects, remain unconscious to the individual himself because they are either personally or socially unacceptable and cannot therefore be tolerated in consciousness. They are kept unconscious by the active process or barrier of repression. Moreover—and with respect to creativity this is the more important issue—elements in the Unconscious have a diffuse and controlling effect on behavior and on consciousness by virtue of being kept out of awareness. It is precisely because the element is unconscious that it exerts a consistent and potentially ubiquitous effect on conscious thought and behavior. Once the element becomes conscious, once its form, substance, and permutations are known, then it can be changed and modified by will and intentional control. Repression keeps unacceptable personal memories, affects, and so on out of awareness, but these elements nevertheless continue to exert an effect. And the more strongly they are kept from awareness, the more diffuse is their effect. Strongly repressed unconscious drives, for instance, tend to influence all conscious thought and behavior. Although the matter is somewhat different with respect to the Jungian Collective Unconscious, the contents and themes of this type of Unconscious are also derived from the past and also exert a controlling effect on individual consciousness.

What are the consequences of such unconscious functioning for a theory of creativity? For one thing, if this type of Unconsciousness and the controlling force of past events were entirely responsible for creative activity, a severe restriction of our definition and conception of creativity would be required. Newness or novelty resulting from a radical discontinuity with the past, an intrinsic quality of creativity emphasized by such modern philosophers as Bergson, Peirce, Morgan, Croce, Collingwood, and Hausman,[5] would not be a characteristic of the creative process or of creations. Creations would not be unprecedented and intrinsically unpredictable because they would be derived from antecedent conditions. As Hausman has quite cogently argued, the characteristic of the unprecedented and unpredicted is crucial to the recognition that creativity has occurred.[6]

A second consequence is that the unacceptable and banal provides the basis for great works of art and other important human achievements. While this proposition is not as inherently offensive to me as it is to some, it produces serious conceptual difficulties. As great works of art are not themselves offensive or unacceptable or banal, some type of transformation must occur and *the transformation factor thereby becomes, if not the specific agent or vehicle of creativity, at least a necessary element in the production of art*. On the other hand, the postulated presence of hidden banal factors in art satisfies certain requirements of aesthetic theory. The universal appeal of certain artistic works and the immediate and inexplicable stirring of feelings and emotions suggests the touching of banal and universal memories such as the Oedipal phenomenon and the evocation or reduction of anxiety associated with unacceptable wishes and longings.

Most problematical of all the effects of this type of unconscious functioning is the diffuse controlling effect on consciousness. For, although this diffuse control could plausibly produce a permeation of unconscious factors in the content of a work of art, *it could not be the basis for aesthetic form*. This effect is the basis for limited and problematic psychological approaches to art that focus predominantly on content and motivation, and very little on form.[7] Strictly formal operations are included in the Freudian conception of the Unconscious, but these are intrinsically incapable of dictating aesthetic form because their function is primarily to *conceal* unconscious content. These operations, called condensation and displacement, or particular psychological defenses such as reaction formation, projection, and so on, serve to alter and distort unconscious material so that it is not recognizable in consciousness. Such formal operations do not appear in consciousness and are themselves unconscious. They do not dictate aesthetic forms because of the intrinsic nature of unconscious functioning and because aesthetic forms are luminous rather than opaque. Other factors that have both fixed and independent relationships to unconscious material are required in order to account for aesthetic structures and forms. A fixed type of relationship between the psychological processes responsible for form and unconscious material is necessary because unconscious material cannot determine its own shape. Independence from unconscious control of the processes responsible for form is necessary in order to produce luminosity, including the revelation and overt appearance of certain types of unconscious material in art. Finally, a diffusely controlling unconscious force could not produce organic unity, but rather would produce monotony or disunity, *because the Unconscious is intrinsically disunified.*

Although Jung's Collective Unconscious is unlike the Freudian Unconscious in that it is not necessarily a repository of unacceptable affects, drives, and memories, similar theoretical problems are raised. A transformation factor is required to account for the numerous permutations in art of such Collective Unconscious themes as "the wise old man," "the great uroboric or unisexual mother," "the birth of the hero."[8] The themes of the Collective Unconscious are transmitted throughout history and they are embedded in the past of the human race as well as of particular racial and cultural groups. According to Jung, the artist uses his autonomous complexes to transform these themes into art.[9] Thus, there is only a tautological resolution available, as follows: autonomous unconscious factors produce autonomous form and content in art.

Despite these problems, there are important reasons to insist that these positively defined types of unconscious functioning play a role in the production of created objects, especially in art. Ordinary conscious productive thinking is too stepwise and oriented to means-end relationships, too free of affect and emotion, and too much focused on ordinary temporal sequences in the natural world and on things as they are, to provide the kind of remote and unusual connections and penetrating affectual experiences characteristic of art. To some extent, the distorting, affect-laden operations of the Freudian Unconscious which link childhood, adult, and immediate transitory thoughts and experiences together without regard to ordinary temporal sequences or physical characteristics, and which also produce constant shifts in thinking without regard to manifest goals, play important roles in various phases of the creative process. Visual thinking, so important in the arts, seems to have some special connections with affect and with childhood modes of organizing experience. Moreover, there is little doubt that an artist's unconscious conflicts (or the contents of the Collective Unconscious) determine his preoccupation and recurrent use of particular themes. Artists return over and over again to themes having the basic structure of some unconscious element, be it the Oedipus complex, bisexuality, castration, reunification with a mothering or fathering figure, or the themes of the Collective Unconscious. With respect to the Oedipus complex, not only Sophocles and Shakespeare but more recent writers such as Hawthorne, Melville, O'Neill, Poe, Butler, Dostoevsky, Miller, Williams, Pinter, Albee, and Beckett show definite preoccupation with permutations of this theme, and other types of artists do so as well.[10]

Critical aspects of creative processes do not arise from these positively defined types of unconscious functioning, however, nor are they conscious in the sense that the creator is totally aware of them. There are special forms of thinking involved in creativity that do not follow the patterns of ordinary productive thought. My own researches on creativity have been based on extensive and intensive research interviews (over 1,600 hours) with some of the leading American poets, novelists, and playwrights as well as Nobel Laureates in science. Also included have been special statistical and psychological analyses of literary manuscripts in progress and extensive psychological experiments with large numbers of creative subjects and controls. These studies have been empirically focused on the creative process in distinction to critical or theoretical analyses of completed works of art or of fully developed scientific discoveries.[11] In these investigations, two specific cognitive processes, which I call Janusian thinking and Homospatial thinking, have been found to play an important role in creativity. It is the structure of these two processes that accounts in part for the seemingly nonconscious aspect of creative thought. Janusian thinking consists in actively conceiving two or more opposite, contradictory, or antithetical concepts, ideas, or images *simultaneously*. Homospatial thinking consists in actively conceiving two or more discrete entities occupying the same space, a conception leading to the articulation of new identities.

The term "Janusian thinking" is based on the Roman god, Janus, who faces opposite directions at the same time. The simultaneous conception of two (not necessarily dual or binary) opposite, contradictory, or antithetical concepts, ideas, or images is an active intentional process in which opposites, antitheses, and contradictions are visualized or posited as existing side by side and/or as equally operative and equally true. In an apparent defiance of logic or matters of physical impossibility, the creative person formulates two or more opposites or antitheses coexisting and simultaneously operating, a formulation that leads to integrated concepts, images, and creations. This form of thinking, either unique or very highly developed in creative people, plays a constant role in diverse types of creative processes. It operates during the creation of a poem, a novel, or a play, very likely during creation of a painting or a sculpture, and it also operates during the creation of a new scientific theory or in the creative leaps of thought frequently connected to important scientific discoveries. Occurring at crucial moments during the process of creating, usually at the moment of inspiration, its effects are not always directly manifest in the final product. The Janusian formulation, in other words, is often a crucial step or way station that later undergoes a good deal of alteration and revision.

Before describing the revisions and alterations as well as the functions of Janusian thinking, it is important to note that many unaltered Janusian formulations are manifest in some of the great creations of the world. There is, for instance, the Yin and Yang formulation of the Oriental Taoist religion: two opposite and universal forces or principles operating together as a single force. Also, Nirvana and Samsara are the two dominant, simultaneous, and unified principles in Buddhist theology; Nirvana, the end of the cycle of rebirth, is opposed to Samsara, the endless series of incarnations and reincarnations of living things. In the Middle East, the major religion up to modern times of the vast Persian Empire, Zoroastrianism, had as its basic tenet the simultaneous presence, from the inception of all things, of the twin but opposite gods, Ormuzd, the god of light and goodness, and Ahriman, the god of darkness. And the precepts and descriptions of the simultaneous operation of God and the Devil in various aspects of Western theology, insofar as they are creations of the human mind, are also direct manifestations of Janusian formulations.

In philosophy, simultaneous opposition and antithesis is manifest in the pre-Socratic conceptions pertaining to being and becoming, Nietzsche's Dionysian and Apollonian principles, and Sartre's representation of being and nothingness. And in psychology, there are Freud's formulations of the Conscious operating together with the Unconscious and the opposing but coexisting basic instincts or drives of sex and aggression. But nowhere is the direct manifestation of simultaneous opposition more apparent than in the poetry produced by great creators throughout the world and throughout the ages. Many poets and critics, including William Blake, Samuel Taylor Coleridge, Cleanth Brooks, Robert Penn Warren, Allen Tate, and John Crowe Ransom,[12] have emphasized that poetry is based on the element of paradox, a close relation to simultaneous opposition and antithesis.

All these examples suggest the workings of Janusian thinking in diverse types of creations, but my critical evidence does not come from a

consideration of these final created products. It is based rather on research observations of the constant use of this type of thinking in the
achievement of creative ideas as well as on controlled experiments geared
toward eliciting cognitive patterns of creative persons. A playwright, for
instance, conceived the idea for one of his greatest dramas in the following
way: plagued all his life by the suicide of a roommate in his youth, a
suicide apparently precipitated by the roommate's wife's infidelity, the
playwright came to realize that the suicide was also motivated by guilt—
the man had wanted his wife to be unfaithful. The formulation resulting
from this realization, the idea that his former roommate had both wanted
and not wanted his wife to be unfaithful, instigated the writing of the play
and directly influenced its central theme, its metaphorical and tragic
structure, and numerous elements of its substance. Another playwright,
deciding to write a comedy shortly after his father's death, structured this
highly successful play around characters who were living and dead at the
same time; they were not merely to be represented as ghosts but as lost
persons struggling to survive and to understand what had happened to
them.[13] A novelist, during an early phase of thinking about the plot of a
novel, conceived of a revolutionary hero as being responsible for the
deaths of hundreds of people but only killing one person with his own
hand; this person was someone who was kind to him and whom he loved.
Much of the subsequent novel became an elaboration of this early idea.
To return to poetry, a poet conceived the central image of a poem when
he thought of horses as both human and beasts simultaneously, that is, he
realized that horses were beasts but that they also lived human lives.
Another poet, walking on a beach, came upon some rocks and thought:
the rocks are heavy, they are weapons of violence but, at the same time,
they feel like human skin. This inspiration led to the construction of a
poem concerning the relationship between sex and violence. That sex and
violence had much in common was an immediate formulation at the time
of perceiving the antithetical qualities of the rocks.[14] And in painting, I
have shown that a careful analysis of the successive stages of Picasso's creation of the great mural, *Guernica*, leads to the clear conclusion that his
earliest conception, visually formulated, was of a woman (holding a torch
in the completed mural) both looking inside a room and outside onto a
courtyard at the same time.[15]

The cognitive process I am describing is not the same as that reported by other investigators. It is not merely a manifestation of Guilford's

"divergent thinking,"[16] Koestler's "bisociation,"[17] DeBono's "lateral thinking,"[18] or Mednick's bringing together of remote associates.[19] It is a directed thought process involving active formulation rather than association or bisociation. Moreover, it involves active and simultaneous conception of specifically antithetical or oppositional entities rather than some undefined connecting or generating of such broad and diffuse categories as "divergent," or "lateral," or unrelated or unusual, or remote. Nor is Janusian thinking an illogical or prelogical process. In distinction to schizophrenic thinking or the thinking in dreams, for instance, it is a logical postulating of what, on the surface, seems illogical. The creative person is fully aware that the elements of his thought are, in a particular context, antithetical, but he engages in what may be called a "translogical" leap of thought, a type of thinking that transcends ordinary logic.

The term for the second of two cognitive processes operating in the process of creation, "Homospatial thinking," derives from the Greek *homo* (same). In conceiving two or more discrete entities occupying the same space, concrete entities such as rivers, houses, human faces, as well as sound patterns and written words, are superimposed, fused, or otherwise brought together in the mind and totally fill its perceptual space—the subjective or imaginary space experienced in consciousness. Loosely, we describe this space as that in the "mind's eye," but to be accurate we would include such unusual terms as the "mind's ear," etc., because entities perceived in any of the sensory modalities may be involved: visual, auditory, tactile, kinaesthetic, olfactory, and gustatory. The Homospatial process is therefore a matter of abstraction from concrete reality; it is a conceptual experience and a process of spatial abstracting. For it is only through the abstracting capacity of the mind that discrete entities can be made to occupy the same space; only through abstraction (rather than literal or concrete modes of thinking) can such identities and unities be produced and experienced.

The Homospatial conception of discrete entities occupying the same space is, of necessity, always a diffuse, rapid, and fleeting one. Discrete entities cannot remain fused or superimposed for very long, even in the mind, and the diffuse initial conception soon leads to a sharpening and separating out of various components. But, the important thing is that the components separated out of a Homospatial conception are new ones, they are not simply aspects of the original discrete entities considered independently in some stepwise or dialectical or analogical fashion prior to the Homospatial conception. Take, for instance, the poetic metaphor, "the road was a rocket of sunlight." Most people, when asked how they think this particular metaphor was conceived, will say—I know, I have many times asked both sophisticated and unsophisticated people—the poet was standing above a road on a very bright sunny day, or he was imagining standing above such a road, and he *noticed* (or imagined) that the sun made the road look like the trail of a rocket. Or else they say: the poet was driving his car on a sunny road, or imagining it, and he *felt* like he, the car, or the road, was a glistening, blazing rocket. Or, they speculate about some experience combining the two types of circumstances. Or, they vary the details. As another example, take the metaphor, "the branches were handles of stars." When asked how this metaphor was created, people invariably say: the poet was walking in the country (or a park) at night, and, when he looked up at the trees, he *noticed* that the branches of the trees looked like they connected with the stars shining through them.

Now, the Homospatial conception does not occur in that way, and Homospatial thinking is a prime factor in the production of poetic metaphors. The common view of metaphor creation, the one most people hypothesize and propose, is one that is based on their own experience of the impact of the metaphors when heard or read. In other words, when hearing or reading both "the road was a rocket of sunlight" and "the branches were handles of stars," we tend to think of the ways that branches look like handles and to conjure up scenes in which sunlight on a road makes the road or the sunlight look or feel like a rocket. We tend to compare branches and handles, rockets and roads, or rockets and sunlight, and we experience awareness of their similarities as newly perceived insights, an experience that is part of our aesthetic reaction. But the poet did not create these metaphors in such a fashion at all; he did not merely notice similarities between disparate entities that were previously unnoticed, nor did he merely have unusual associations nor engage in systematic searches for comparisons and analogies to something he perceived. He actively produced these metaphors through the Homospatial process as follows: attracted to the words "handle" and "branch" because of their similar sound qualities—the assonance—as well as the similar shape of the physical entities denoted, the poet superimposed and fused them in his mind's eye—he brought them together because he felt they *ought* to be together; in a fleeting moment, he then had a concomitant thought and an experience—he thought to himself, "when in reality are they the same?," and experienced a vivid impression of the letter "a" overlapping in the two words. Then, only then, he conceived of the connecting idea of stars and the full metaphor. No prior idea of stars, nor of a country scene at night, generated the image or the metaphor; "stars" was precipitated and separated out from the Homospatial conception and provided both the plausible factor in experience and the sound qualities that unified the words and their meanings. Similarly, "road" and "rocket" were brought together in the poet's mind because of alliteration and of some resemblance in shape; then he thought, "when does a road look or feel like a rocket?" and the answer came (the terminal alliteration), "in sunlight." In both cases, he visualized a vague scene as well as found the answer in words. And later, he too visualized more fully developed and vivid scenes similar to the ones experienced (as above) by a reader or audience. But the fully visualized scene did not produce the metaphor; it merely added to the poet's feeling of the aptness of his creation.

I have used these two examples of metaphors because they are clear and can be discussed outside the context of a particular poem. Such independent and extractable metaphors are rather a rarity in poetry nowadays, since most modern poets tend to create metaphors as the central image or statement of an entire poem or a segment of it. Tracing the process of development of such central metaphors would be quite complex and a digression from the main topic here, but I must emphasize that the general procedure of development described in the examples I cited remains the same. Discrete entities may be brought together for many other reasons beside, or in addition to, similarities in their shape or in the sound of words; in each case, the metaphor is produced from a conception in which the discrete entities occupy the same space.

Many factors derived from the context of a poem or literary work in progress may influence the particular entities chosen. Rhythmic connections, verbal overtones and associations, emotional relationships, and conceptual formulations may stimulate the Homospatial process. For example, in the instance, previously cited, of a research subject of mine whose initial idea for a poem was the Janusian formulation of a horse as both human and beast simultaneously, this formulation was subsequently integrated into a central metaphor by a Homospatial conception. A horse and human being were conceived as occupying the same space and this conception led to the construction of a central poetic image or metaphor in which a horse and a rider were virtually fused:

> One spring twilight, during a lull in the war,
> At Shoup's farm south of Troy, I last rode horseback.
> Stillnesses were swarming inward from the evening star
> Or outward from the buoyant sorrel mare
> Who moved as if not displeased by the weight upon her.
> Meadows received us, heady with unseen lilac.
> Brief, polyphonic lives abounded everywhere.
> With one accord we circled the small lake.[20]

Notice that the resulting image was not of a centaur nor was it some other combination of horse and man. The Homospatial conception leads to integration, an essential feature of metaphor, not merely combination.

Metaphorization is a prime element in poetic creation and a crucial aspect of other types of creation as well, both artistic and scientific. Metaphors occupy a central place in the creations of painters, novelists, composers, sculptors, architects, other types of artists, and applied and theoretical scientists. Homospatial thinking is important in the creative process because it produces metaphors and also because it functions in other significant ways. Characteristically, Homospatial thinking operates together with Janusian thinking; it functions to integrate a Janusian formulation, producing metaphors as well as other unifications. But Janusian and Homospatial thinking also function independently. In literary creation, Homospatial thinking characteristically operates in the development of literary characters. Novelists, playwrights, and poets as well, actively fuse and superimpose images of persons they have known, images of themselves, and the developing image of the character they are creating. They do not, as is commonly supposed, merely combine various characteristics in some stepwise fashion, consciously or unconsciously. Also, the Homospatial process functions to produce effective literary double meanings, rhymes, assonances, and alliterations. For the painter and composer, Homospatial thinking brings aspects of figure and ground (as defined by Gestalt psychology), in the visual and auditory sphere respectively, into the same spatial plane, superimposed or fused with one another. This leads to integrations and unifications of visual and musical patterns. For the sculptor, the following description by Henry Moore—one of the leading modern figures in that field—emphasizes the crucial role of what is clearly a Homospatial process in the creation of sculptural works of art: "This is what the sculptor must do. He must strive continually to think of, and use, form in its full spatial completeness. He gets the solid shape, as it were, inside his head—he thinks of it, whatever its size, as if he were holding it completely enclosed in the hollow of his hand. He mentally visualizes a complex form from all round itself; he knows while he looks at one side what the other side is like. . . ."[21]

In both the arts and in science, the relationship between the two processes is broadly as follows: Janusian thinking serves to bring together specific and interrelated elements out of the relatively diffuse substratum of experience and knowledge; elements that are opposite or antithetical, rather than merely different and unrelated, are crystallized and juxtaposed. "Tall," for instance, is opposite and highly related to "short" as a designation of height. Once juxtaposed and brought together, e.g., tall-short, these opposites and antitheses continue to be in conflict to some degree and to generate a sense of tension—a tension that is unresolved in art but leads to problem solving and elaboration in science. The Homospatial process, when operating in conjunction with the Janusian one, serves at first to blur the contours of the specific interrelated elements in the Janusian formulation by placing them in the same space. Out of this blurred and somewhat diffused conception a truly fused or unified creation is produced. Both when Homospatial thinking operates together with Janusian thinking and when it operates independently, the resulting product is an integration, a unity in which the discrete elements still interact and are discernible.

Returning now to the matter of the role of the Unconscious in creativity, the structure of these two cognitive processes, as I have said, accounts for the seemingly nonconscious aspect of creative thought. In the use of either or both of these processes, the creator only becomes consciously aware of the products of his thinking. He is unaware of the structural attributes of these processes but is only conscious of the resulting metaphor, characterization, plot idea, visual image, or theoretical formulation. As he is not aware (and does not need to be aware) of the structure of his thinking, and characteristically he does not retrace the detailed thought sequences leading to creative ideas, the ideas seem to result from factors out of his control. Because creators have never focused on or been aware of the specific structure of their thinking, they have not been able to describe these processes in their own writings and testimonies about creativity. Only through extensive and painstaking interviewing, observation, and experimentation was I able to identify these forms of cognition. Moreover, the structural attributes of these processes account in part for the creator's experiential sense of something coming from out of awareness. In the case of Janusian thinking, there is a leap of thought in which two or more opposites or antitheses are brought together at once. The coming together of the widely disparate opposites or antitheses produces an experiential sense of something coming out of nowhere. An idea, image, or proposition traditionally considered valid or reflective of reality is juxtaposed with its antithesis or opposite. As such opposites and antitheses are generally at the periphery of a body of knowledge, visual field, or propositional sequence, they are also generally at the periphery of consciousness. Bringing them together with a central idea produces a leap in which remote and exclusive cases are considered to be operative simultaneously. Thinking about the characteristics of motion, for instance, the artistic or scientific creator thinks of various attributes such as speed and rhythm, or else he thinks of the laws of motion, or of particular moving objects. Rest, the opposite of motion, is only considered as the discriminating or limiting condition at the fringes of the case, when suddenly the creator comes to the realization that motion and rest are the same, or that they operate simultaneously. This is precisely what occurred in Einstein's crucial initial formulation of the general theory of relativity, as I have extensively reported and documented elsewhere.[22] The experiential sense of extreme disparity, the turning around of what was previously believed to be totally untrue or contradictory, is part of what accounts for the feeling of strangeness and of external influence. The opposite or polar case is as close to nowhere as is realizable in human finite thought.

Creative thinking is nonconscious in this respect primarily. The creator is not aware of the specific structural features of the unusual modes of thought that he uses in producing creations. These types of cognitions occur, however, when he is fully aware, serious, and rational.[23] He is not dreaming nor in a special altered state of consciousness in which so-called unconscious processes become readily available as is postulated by such famous psychoanalytic explanations of creativity as "regression in the service of the ego."[24] However, just as all conscious thought is influenced by unconscious processes, the particular creative cognitive processes I have described are themselves subject to some degree of unconscious influence and control. For instance, there are often unconscious factors influencing the creator's focus on a particular task, his interest in a particular set of opposites, or his choice of particular discrete entities fused in the Homospatial conception. At times, the particular elements in these cognitions represent derivatives of unconscious conflict. But the relationship of these cognitive processes to unconscious material is both fixed and independent. Because of the structure and psychodynamic function of Janusian and Homospatial thinking, unconscious material is only indirectly represented in artistic creations. With Janusian thinking there is a fixed and indirect pathway between unconscious material and consciousness and with Homospatial thinking independent and autonomous psychic dynamisms are generated.[25] With both types of thinking, unconscious elements are molded by the independent functioning of the processes in relation to the aesthetic or conceptual requirements of the object or theory being developed.

Both types of thinking play a crucial role in delineating the formal or structural attributes of creations, especially artistic ones. As must be deduced from the definitions and descriptions, both types of thinking are consonant with broad and intrinsic characteristics of aesthetic form. Janusian thinking provides the basis for the intrinsic tension and conflict in aesthetic objects, and, as can be inferred from the concatenation of opposites and antitheses, it is particularly generative of the tragic mode and form. Homospatial thinking provides the basis for the structure of artistic metaphors, and, on a broader scale, it provides for fusion and organic unity. Though their functions in scientific creativity are primarily to facilitate innovative and productive conceptualizing, they also operate in a structural mode to help produce the symmetry (Janusian thinking) and unity (Homospatial thinking) characteristic of outstanding scientific theories.

To come full circle, the Platonic diatribe with Ion was essentially correct. Only Plato's conclusions and the tradition derived from them or related to them, the tradition emphasizing a source of creativity completely external to consciousness, are found wanting. The creator is not aware of the specific factors accounting for his skill or his art. He does not think of the particular structural qualities of the thought processes he uses in producing his creations. They are part of that diffusely negative nonconscious or unconscious aspect of his thinking, and, to some degree, they are derived from the specific and positive Unconscious defined by Freud and perhaps in some ways the Unconscious described by Jung as well. The creator is, however, neither out of his mind nor bereft of his senses. He is a more sensitive and flexible thinker than the rest of us and is capable of using thought processes and blending modes of thought in unusual and highly valuable ways.

NOTES

1. Plato, *Phaedrus*, Reginald Hackforth, trans., in Edith Hamilton and Huntington Cairns, eds., *Plato: The Collected Dialogues* (New York: Bollingen Foundation, 1961), pp. 475–525.

2. Plato, *The Ion*, Lane Cooper, trans., in Hamilton and Cairns, *Plato: The Collected Dialogues*, pp. 218–21.

3. Eduard von Hartmann, *Philosophie des Unbewussten* (Berlin, 1869).

4. Sigmund Freud, "The Interpretation of Dreams (1900–1901)," in James Strachey et al., eds., *The Standard Edition of the Complete Psychological Works of Sigmund Freud* (London: Hogarth Press, 1953), 4:264–66.

5. For selected readings presenting these views as well as commentary and further references to the work of these thinkers, see ch. 5, "Alternate Approaches," in Albert Rothenberg and Carl R. Hausman, *The Creativity Question* (Durham, N.C.: Duke University Press, 1976).

6. Carl R. Hausman, *A Discourse on Novelty and Creation* (The Hague: Martinus Nijhoff, 1975).

7. Many psychoanalysts and psychoanalytic literary critics have used such an approach extensively. See Frederic Crews, *Out of My System* (New York: Oxford University Press, 1975) for a cogent critique of this type of approach to literary criticism.

8. Carl G. Jung, *Psychological Types* (New York: Harcourt Brace, 1946). See also Erich Neumann, *Art and the Creative Unconscious*, R. Manheim, trans. (New York: Pantheon Books, 1959).

9. See Carl G. Jung, "On the Relation of Analytical Psychology to Poetic Art," in H. Read et al., eds., *The Collected Works of C. G. Jung* (Princeton, N.J.: Princeton University Press, Bollingen Series XX, 1966), 15:84–108.

10. See extensive references to psychoanalytic studies of these writers in Albert Rothenberg and Bette Greenberg, *The Index of Scientific Writings on Creativity: Creative Men and Women* (Hamden, Conn.: Archon Books, 1974).

11. See detailed descriptions of my research methodology in Albert Rothenberg, "The Iceman Changeth: Toward an Empirical Approach to Creativity," *Journal of the American Psychoanalytic Association* (April 1969), 17:549–607; Rothenberg, "The Process of Janusian Thinking in Creativity," *Archives of General Psychiatry* (1971), 24:195–205; Rothenberg, "Poetry and Psychotherapy: Kinships and Contrasts," in J. Leedy, ed., *Poetry the Healer* (Philadelphia: Lippincott, 1973), pp. 91–126; Rothenberg, "Homospatial Thinking in Creativity," *Archives of General Psychiatry* (1976), 33:17–26; Rothenberg, "Janusian Thinking and Creativity," in W. Muensterberger, ed., *The Psychoanalytic Study of Society* (New Haven, Conn.: Yale University Press, 1976), pp. 1–30; Rothenberg, "Word Association and Creativity," *Psychological Reports* (1973), 33:3–12; Rothenberg, "Opposite Responding as a Measure of Creativity," *Psychological Reports* (1973), 33:15–18; Rothenberg, *The Emerging Goddess: The Creative Process in Art, Science, and Other Fields*, forthcoming.

12. See especially Cleanth Brooks, "The Language of Paradox," in A. Tate, ed., *The Language of Poetry* (Princeton, N.J.: Princeton University Press, 1942), pp. 37–61.

13. These examples of the creative process in playwrighting are taken from reconstructions derived by a special technique of manuscript draft analysis combined with intensive interviews of surviving close members of the playwright's family (e.g., Carlotta M. O'Neill). For the first example, which is Eugene O'Neill's writing of the play *The Iceman Cometh*, the technique and reconstruction are described in Rothenberg, "The Iceman Changeth."

For the second example, Maxwell Anderson's writing of the play, *High Tor*, a description of the technique and report of the results are contained in Rothenberg, *The Emerging Goddess*.

14. The examples of the creative process in literature in this section are derived from the interview studies described above. Both writers are Pulitzer Prize winners whose names are withheld at their request.

15. *Ibid.* The analysis cited is based on Picasso sketches presented in Rudolph Arnheim, *Picasso's Guernica: The Genesis of a Painting* (Berkeley and Los Angeles: University of California Press, 1962). Arnheim's work is an excellent presentation of successive sketches leading to the final painting of the mural and an interesting reconstruction of some phases of the creative process. The conclusion I have presented here, however, is mine.

16. J. P. Guilford, *The Nature of Human Intelligence* (New York: McGraw-Hill, 1967).

17. Arthur Koestler, *The Act of Creation* (New York: MacMillan, 1964).

18. Edward DeBono, *Lateral Thinking: A Textbook of Creativity* (London: Ward Lock Educational, 1970).

19. Sarnoff Mednick, "The Associative Basis of the Creative Process," *Psychological Review* (1962), 69:220–32.

20. Title, author, and publication not cited at the author's request.

21. Henry Moore, "Notes on Sculpture," *Listener* (1937), 18:449.

22. Rothenberg, "Janusian Thinking and Creativity," pp. 20–24. Also see Albert Rothenberg, "Einstein's General Relativity: The Creative Leap," *American Journal of Psychiatry*, in press.

23. In stressing awareness, seriousness, and rationality here, I am drawing a distinction to dreams and jokes which, as Freud pointed out, often derive from the equivalence of opposites in the Unconscious. See Sigmund Freud, "The Interpretation of Dreams," and "Jokes and Their Relation to the Unconscious (1905a)," in James Strachey et al., eds., *The Standard Edition of the Complete Psychological Works of Sigmund Freud* (London: Hogarth Press, 1960), vol. 8. Janusian thinking is not a manifestation of the unconscious primary-process thinking responsible for dreams; it is a function of conscious processes and "translogical" secondary-process thinking. Nor is it a manifestation of "Doublethink," the propagandistic distortion of truth described by George Orwell in his novel *1984*. Homospatial thinking is also not a form of primary-process thinking. Both forms of cognition resemble aspects of primary-process thinking, but there are marked distinctions. See Rothenberg, "Homospatial Thinking in Creativity."

24. See especially Ernst Kris, "On Preconscious Mental Processes," in *Psychoanalytic Explorations in Art* (New York: International Universities Press, 1952), pp. 302–20.

25. For an explication of the overcoming of repression through negation in Janusian thinking, see Rothenberg, "Janusian Thinking and Creativity." For an explication of drive fusion, neutralization, and release of adaptive energy for autonomous creative functioning, see Rothenberg, "Homospatial Thinking in Creativity."

❧ 9 ❧

Creativity as the Central Concept in the Psychology of Otto Rank

ESTHER MENAKER

IT IS UNFORTUNATE, yet probably inevitable, that Otto Rank, to the extent that he is known at all, is known primarily as a dissenter from Freudian psychoanalysis, and that his name is associated chiefly with his much misunderstood book, *The Trauma of Birth*. While it is true that he was first a disciple and then a dissenter, it would be a mistake to view Rank's divergencies from Freudian theory and from a Freudian way of thinking as just another splinter from the main stem of psychoanalytic doctrine. For if we study Rank's life and his works from early on, from a time before his meeting with Freud, we find present a profoundly unique personality struggling, against great environmental odds, to give it adequate and appropriate expression. Without going into the biographical facts of his life in detail, it is important to know that he came from an economically, culturally, and emotionally deprived situation, that originally his advanced education was of a purely technical nature, and that the breadth and depth of his knowledge of culture was acquired through his own efforts. It was in fact his avid reading in many fields which brought him in contact with Freud's writings, and which resulted in his own application of Freud's ideas in a book called *Der Künstler* (*The Artist*) which he wrote in his early twenties and which was instrumental in bringing him, through the intervention of Alfred Adler, to the attention of

Reprinted from *Journal of the Otto Rank Association* (1976–77), vol. 11.

Freud. Freud was so impressed with the young man's book that he not only helped him to publish it, but furthered his education and gave him a special place in the psychoanalytic movement.

The importance of these facts lies not in an explanation of how Rank became an analyst—which I view as a phase in his life—but in the way in which they delineate the creative thrust of his personality. Jessie Taft[1] in her biography of Rank has expressed it as follows: "It has been my aim to present throughout something about Rank as a genius, an artist in his own right, not as a disciple of Freud but in terms of his own self-development. . . ."

It is Rank's creative striving to form and unfold his own personality which is responsible for his interest in the artist and his concern with the issue of creativity as it is expressed in all aspects of life. For undoubtedly Rank, in the early aloneness of his introspection and of his self-education, perceived his own creative will—a term which he coined much later. To my mind, it was this awareness which led him to focus on creativity in its broadest meaning as the central concept in his understanding of man.

The role of subjectivity in the choice of question which a scientist, psychologist, or philosopher will ask is a generally accepted fact. Freud, who was much more embedded in the culture and *Weltanschauung* of his time than was Rank, and whose education and professional life was geared to medical practice, asked, in his attempt to understand human personality, "How is it put together? Of what does it consist? How does it function? How do the parts interact? What interferes with its normal functioning? What is the nature of its pathology?" These questions grew out of his subjective interest in and astute perception of what I should like to call anomalous phenomena: hysteria initially, and then other forms of neurosis, dreams, and parapraxes. As a result of the observation of these phenomena within the framework of the particular questions which he posed, Freud created a system of psychology whose central concepts can be described as mechanistic, materialistic, atomistic, and deterministic.

Rank, on the other hand, perceiving growth, change, striving, and the creation of the new as part of his own experience, turned his attention to the artist, as the exemplar of the creative experience. His questions then were: "Wherein does the creative urge reside; how is it expressed; what is its function, for the individual and for society; how does it contribute to an explanation of the development and functioning of personality?" He did not wish to "explain" the artist or his work in causal psychological terms; rather did he wish to apply his perception of the operation of the creative process as he observed it in the artist, to the understanding of human psychology in general, in fact to life as a whole. He says explicitly:[2] "Creativeness lies equally at the root of artistic production and of life experience."

Even in his first work, *Der Künstler*,[3] in which he was strongly under the influence of his reading of Freud, Rank thinks in interactional terms. He is concerned with the movement and progression to higher levels of conscious awareness of the individual and of the culture in which he lives as the creative forces existing in both are expressed and mutually influence each other. Speaking in Freudian terminology, he refers to the sublimated work of the individual as not only expressing his own creative need, but also that of society.

One might, therefore, describe Rank in philosophical terms as a process thinker, wherein a progressive, creative process underlines all the phenomena of life. Both in individual and collective terms life processes are in evolution, spurred on by a creative impulse which is released by the need to resolve conflicts caused by certain inevitable dualities in life itself, and which is expressed in the functioning of the will.

This philosophical position of Rank's in which creativity is a central dynamism has profound consequences for a psychology of personality, as well as for the treatment of its anomalies. For Rank holds that a purely *individual* psychology cannot explain personality, nor, indeed, man as such. And since the genius, i.e. the productive personality at its maximum, is the most characteristically individual, the "psychology of personality has helped little or not at all" in understanding it; and "moreover, that it probably never will contribute anything, since ultimately we are dealing with dynamic factors that remain incomprehensible in their *specific* expression in the *individual personality*. This implies that they can be neither predetermined nor wholly explained even ex post facto."[4]

What a blow to a deterministic theory of personality! What respect for the uniqueness of the individual; for the emphasis in Rank's perception of creativity as it expresses itself either in the *work* of the productive personality, or in the creation of personality itself, is on the *specificity* of this expression in the *individual personality*. Certainly we can arrive at some psychological generalizations as Rank himself does. But his awareness of the almost infinite variability and diversity of individual persons is an indication of his sensitivity to the creative aspect of the evolutionary life

process. This diversity is manifested first in the biological process of evolution through the chance rearrangement of chromosomes when, in fertil-
ization in a specific instance the paternal and maternal chromosomes
are paired. In the human—"the chance against two individuals having
exactly the same pattern of combination of chromosomes is almost
300,000,000,000,000 to 1. So we see why no two people in the world (except identical twins) are exactly alike genetically, and these innate differences are accentuated by the diverse cultural influences to which they
respond."[5]

The uniqueness of individuals, especially when they are creatively
productive, results in an individual expression of creative will which can
be neither predetermined nor predicted in its specific detail. It can only
be accepted as a manifestation of a certain life process.

But just as life itself in the biological sense struggles to emerge, persist, and reproduce in the face of the disintegrating forces of entropy in
the universe, so in the creation of personality and in the creation of the
products of personality—artistic, literary, philosophic, scientific—various
forms of duality are responsible for analogous struggles.

There is in man precisely because he is a self-conscious, sensate creature and is therefore able to create his unique personality, an urge to
eternalize it. Thus the duality between his individual mortality and his
wish for immortality[6] becomes an inevitable aspect of human life. The
wish for immortality is expressed in the artistic creation of the individual
as well as in the creation of religious forms and other social institutions.
The latter is a communal immortality, the former an individual one. Thus
out of the mortality-immortality conflict of the individual, a new duality
arises, especially for the creative artist, that between individuality and
collectivity.

It is in his book *Art and Artist*, especially in the chapter entitled
"Creative Urge & Personality Development," that Rank spells out in detail the nature and consequences of the mortality-immortality conflict in
relation to other dualities to which it gives rise. Rank uses the artist as an
example of the operation of creativity while realizing that his insights
apply to all forms of creative expression, not least to the creation of the
self.

The individual artist is born into a specific culture within a given
epoch. This sociohistorical situation which is an outgrowth of the cumula-
tive effects of sociocultural evolution provides him with its characteristic

art form or style, with a given cultural ideology, with its store of scientific knowledge. To express something personal, i.e., to satisfy his need for immortality, he uses the given cultural form, but in so doing also adds or alters something so that his product differs sufficiently from the cultural cliché as to be his own individual creation. Ultimately the expression of his individuality and that of many creative individuals acts upon the whole cultural ideology so as to alter it. This interplay between creative personality and cultural form, ideology and institutions advances sociocultural evolution. For the individual creative personality, however, it represents the conflict between the dualism of individuality and collectivity. For just as the growing child must create his personality out of a synthesis of individual experience with the sociohistorical reality into which he is born, so the artist must wrest his uniqueness from the collectivity in which he finds himself and yet create a product which is in harmony with his culture.

Rank was profoundly sensitive to the conflict aroused by this duality. At a much later date, with no awareness of Rank's earlier contribution to an understanding of the creation of personality via the exploration of the artist's struggle to synthesize his individual expression within the context of his historical setting, Erik Erikson, writing about the formation of ego identity, says: "The growing child must derive a vitalizing sense of reality from the awareness that his individual way of mastering experience (his ego synthesis) is a successful variant of a group identity and is *in accord* with its space-time and life plan." [7] However, as I have remarked in another connection, [8] "For psychological and sociocultural evolution to take place, for there to be any 'gains' which can then be consolidated into socially usable and transmissible form, the individual ego, or at least the egos of a sufficient number of individuals within a culture, must advance *beyond* what could be regarded as a 'successful variant' within the group to a higher degree of individuation, thus forming foci from which the diffusion of higher levels of organization into the group as a whole can take place." Through his emphasis on creativity, Rank had already pointed out that increasing individualization as it interacts with collectivity alters the whole cultural ideology and therefore art with it.

There is another aspect of the dualism of individual and community which brings into sharp relief the nature of the creative impulse; that is the dualism in psychological form between self-assertion and self-renunciation. According to Rank the creative urge is self-assertive; the experience of aesthetic pleasure is its opposite, i.e., self-renunciation, in that the individual loses himself in the enjoyment of a communally affirmed creation. While such renunciation of self may be an *aspect* of the psychology of the aesthetic experience, it would scarcely serve as a total description of that experience in the eyes of philosophers of aesthetics. For example, Flaccus sees within the aesthetic experience a sort of secondary creating in response to the artist's creative work: "The artist gives himself in his work; he offers a personal interpretation—we who respond to what the artist gives, read it whether we will or no in psychic terms. A few patches of color and strokes, a few sequences of sounds, a few words is all that we need to set us off on this enriching. We must see to it, however, that we are always in harmony with what of psychic value the artist has built into his picture, his poem, his symphony." (Perhaps this aspect of the act of aesthetic experiencing corresponds to what Rank refers to as self-renunciation.) "The double process, then, of creating and moving within a world of semblance, and of enriching the images and shapes of that world with our psychic wealth yields the meaning of the aesthetic experience." [9] In art the dualism of individual and community is reflected in the uniqueness of expression of the artist, on the one hand, and the collectively dictated style of an epoch, on the other.

In relation to creativity Rank points out another duality, a seemingly paradoxical one, namely, between life and creation. He does not mean that life lacks creativity, quite the contrary. But in discussing this duality, for the artist especially, he attempts to differentiate the artist's life of actuality, his transient experience, that which is ephemeral, from the sought-after eternalization in his creative product. The artist tries to protect himself from the transiency of experience by creating in some form a concretization of his personality, thereby immortalizing his mortal life. For the average man such immortalization is achieved through participation in or identification with the creative cultural ideology of his time, be it religious, political, scientific, or artistic.

The conflictful relationship between the immediate and the eternal, between the ephemeral and the enduring, between experience and artistic creation can never be totally resolved. In fact, it is in the nature of the life process itself, in growth, in change and creation, to battle continuously with this duality. It is the creative urge, expressed through the individual will, that at one and the same time produces the conflict and attempts its resolution through all the manifestations of creativity.

The dualities which Rank sees as crucial in the life of man—that between mortality and immortality, between individuality and collectivity, between transient experience and artistic creation—lead to a psychology of personality quite different from that of Freud. It is a psychology essentially existential in character, in which the inevitable conditions of life itself impinge upon the formation of personality and in which the creative urge expresses itself volitionally both in the structuring of personality and in its creative products. It is a psychology of the self, and the dualities and the conflicts which they precipitate are those from which the self must emerge. The self is propelled into such emergence essentially by the life impulse, which is creative. Freud perceived the duality of impulse and inhibition; of conscious and unconscious, and later of ego and id. That which propelled the individual toward maturation and toward the formation of ego was basically the need for the reduction of energic tension—in Freud's terms, the pleasure principle. True, the instinctual drives which dominated the life of the individual could be tamed, their gratification postponed, their aims diverted. Sublimation of libidinal drives was held to be the source of creativity and therefore of its products. For Freud the drives were primary; for Rank creativity was primary, deriving from the life impulse and serving the individual will. Rank felt that Freud's explanation of the impulse to artistic productivity as deriving from the sex impulse failed to bridge the gap between the sex act and the art work. How is one produced from the other? And how do we account for the creation in the art work of something different, higher, symbolical, and above all uniquely individual? To bridge this gap, to account for individuation in the created product, Rank introduced the concept of the creative will. The creative will operates first in *self*-creation, for the first work of the productive individual is the creation of his own artistic personality. Here Rank describes a most interesting phenomenon—the appointment of the artist by himself as artist. This is a spontaneous manifestation of the creative impulse. It is as if the first creative endeavor of the artist were a self-definition, a statement of his self-conception. It is a self-conception which is a glorification of his personality, unlike the neurotic who is either overly self-critical or over-idealizing and who is overly dependent for his self-image on others. The ability to appoint oneself is an act which reflects one's individuation, one's emergence from the matrix of childhood dependency. It is the precondition in the average individual for the creation of a mature, separate personality, and for the creative artistic personality it is the first productive work since subsequent works are in part repeated expressions of this primal creation and in part justifications of it through the dynamism of work.

The problem of justification for the creative individual brings his self-appointment into juxtaposition with the values and ideology of the society in which he lives and creates. For his self-appointment can only succeed in a society which recognizes and values his individual creation; or as Rank would phrase it, a society which has an ideology of genius, an appreciation of individualism in contrast to collectivism, or at least of some individualism within a predominantly collectivist framework. Today we have a striking example of this interaction between the artist and his social justification in the case of Solzehenitsyn, whose self-appointment was not valued, was in fact denounced and persecuted, in the Soviet Union. The tremendous strength of his individuality made it possible for him to create even in the face of active social opposition, but he had ultimately to seek a milieu which was congenial to his conception of himself as a creative artist—a milieu in which he could justify himself and his work. For while an artist's work rests on the precondition of the glorification of his individual personality, he is called upon within his own psychic life to justify his individual creation through work and ever-higher achievement. This aspect of individuation, which Rank has understood so profoundly, leads us to the issue of guilt, the inevitable accompaniment of all manifestations of creativity and therefore an inevitable fact of existence. For creation implies separation, which for the human creature is always achieved at the expense of "the other." The resultant guilt must be expiated, and the creative artist can do this through social justification of his work. However, a further concern with the issue of guilt is beyond the scope of this discourse.

Rank is critical of psychological attempts to "explain" the artist's work by an interpretation of his experience. It is not experience but the reaction to experience which is crucial. Only the creative impulse, i.e., the will to create interacting with the social milieu, can explain the inner dynamism through which the creative work is born. However, since personality itself is the product of a creative endeavor, we would assume that Rank, unlike Freud, would place the emphasis when interpreting the nature of individual personalities not so much upon experiences but upon the strength of creative will which is accessible to each individual in the task of assimilating experience.

The impulse to create originates in an inherent striving, in Rank's terms, toward totality—toward what we would call ever-higher and more complex levels of integration. This tendency is no less characteristic of the psychic life of man than of living matter in general. It is a process which takes place in the conflictful context of a duality between a surrender to life and an urge toward a creative reorganization of experience as it is concretized by the artist in his individual product. For the artist, unlike the neurotic, the traumas of childhood, which in Freudian theory are viewed as causal in the anomalies of personality, are overcome through *"the volitional affirmation of the obligatory."* This is the creative act which the neurotic is unable to perform. Rank views the neurotic as an individual inhibited in the exercise of the positive will to create. His therapy, therefore, would focus primarily, not on a causal understanding of early experience and the implementation of insight gained thereby, but would address itself to a reexperiencing of the anxiety and guilt which stunted the creative will of the individual and through affirmation of this will in the therapeutic interaction would seek to free it to function positively and creatively. It is thus creativity which stands in the center of Rank's theory and therapy and which ultimately serves man in the resolution of conflict.

Let us leave the highly theoretical formulation of Rank's central concept of creativity to explore its applicability to the actual psychotherapeutic treatment of patients.

Two cases occur to me, in which the approach of the final sessions before the interruption of treatment for the summer vacation produced so much anxiety that some of the deepest levels of the problem of separation and individuation came to the fore. One is the case of a young woman about whom I have already written [10] and whom, for convenience, we will now call Jeanne. I shall review briefly the situation which pertained in the early phases of her treatment. At the time of my original report of her, she was in her thirties, unmarried, and a writer by profession. She came to treatment primarily because of depression—a condition which had been lifelong, but which had become exacerbated by an unhappy love affair. Despite her high degree of intelligence, her imaginativeness, her integrity of character, and her personable outward appearance, she thought poorly of herself. Her low self-esteem was reflected periodically in moodiness, depressive withdrawal and resentment, and a shy awkwardness in her interaction with people.

The fact that her therapy took place over an extended period of time gave me an opportunity to see the repetition and recurrence of the deepest problem of her psychic life, to identify it as an inhibition in the autonomous functioning of her will, resulting in a stifling of her creative capacities, to experience her stubborn resistance to change, and to see the limitations of insight and understanding in the therapeutic process.

Very early in Jeanne's life she became aware of her mother's need to make a battleground of every personal encounter and to be triumphant and dominant in every human relationship. Out of an intuitive perception of her mother's fragile self-esteem which these needs reflected, coupled with her own normal wish for love and affection and her fear of separation from her mother, she protected her mother's need to dominate by sacrificing her own autonomy. To avoid the anxiety of separation, she allowed her mother to triumph over her in the name of upholding her bond to her.

In a session in which she was reminiscing about her childhood and about the nature of her interaction with her mother, I interpreted to her this fear of separation from her mother, connecting it with her willingness to assert her own will in relation to her mother's in order to maintain the symbiotic bond. Furthermore, I pointed out that the giving up of the natural impulse toward individuation was responsible in large measure for her low self-esteem. Jeanne reacted with momentary relief and exclaimed: "You have put me in touch with my will."

But the positive effects of this insight were short-lived. The patient reacted with anxiety which did not become manifest as such, but was immediately converted into disappointment, anger, depression, and rage. She began to justify her anger by projecting blame for the frustrations and deprivations in her life upon the therapist. At the moment of insight into her symbiotic mother relationship with all its crippling consequences upon her self-image and her freedom to function as a separate self, she had a choice: to remain, figuratively speaking, with her mother, or to change her former conception of self, to become individuated, to grow and live according to her own lights through the exercise of what she herself would "will." According to Rank, it is the first choice—the fear of growth and change—that is neurotic; it is the second, the affirmation of growth and change, of the very life process itself, which is creative. We shall return to the issue of choice and to the question of what factors either inhibit or free the individual to make a creative choice, presently. For the moment there is more to be said about Jeanne.

In a very recent session, Jeanne reported the experience of another emotion, namely, shame, which she unconsciously used to uphold the neurotic tie to her mother and to dampen the creative assertion of her own personality. Fortunately, her daily work life did not always suffer from her neurotic fixations. But just as she had reacted in the past with fear and anger to insight into her own personality structure in its interaction with her mother, so her successes at work often had paradoxical consequences. In the session to which I refer, shame appeared after particular success on the preceding evening. She had been teaching a class in English literature. Her lecture had gone extremely well, she had been articulate in her expression of her own views and opinions; and the class response had been very positive. Instead of enjoying her successful performance, she was overwhelmed by a feeling of shame—the same shame which still reverberated in her therapy session on the following day. It was manifest in her tentative bearing, in a certain shy awkwardness, and in her halting speech. She spoke of the repetitive nature of this reaction, and despite the frequency with which we had spoken of some of its origins, she was unable to overcome it. In terms of a Freudian interpretation, one could see in the shame response to a successful "performance" a compensatory reaction to exhibitionistic wishes which were charged with guilt. And, indeed, her frequent dreams about situations which involved her in a theater, either as performer or viewer, would seem to confirm such an interpretation. But this rather neat insight was of no help to her therapeutically. The guilt came from a deeper level of experience in the interaction with her mother. In this session she recalled early scenes of being humiliated by her mother with the words: "Look at you! Look at the mess you've made of yourself!" It is not hard to imagine the besmeared little girl who defied her mother's fastidious admonitions and either enjoyed the messy eating of her ice cream cone, or her mud-pie play. But the price of the enjoyed act was too high. Her mother's indignation and anger which in this instance were expressed in the need to humiliate her, were only one of the many situations in which she failed to affirm the child's growth, to understand her phase-appropriate activities and pleasures, and to permit her to be separate. For Jeanne what I shall call the willed and willful "mud-pie act" became symbolic for all future autonomous acts which, if they were pleasurable and successful, were not permissible—were, in fact, shameful. As she spoke about her feeling of shame, she recalled the childhood rhyme with which children often taunt each other: "Shame, shame—everybody knows your name!" In this context "name" stands for the independent or deviant act of which the group disapproves, and for which it seeks to punish the offending child by humiliation. However, the child's rebellious act of which the group is critical, and in the case of Jeanne, of which her mother disapproved, is not only an expression of negative will, of defiance or contrariness, but is positive in terms of its *function*, for it is indeed a *positive act of willing* even though its content may be negative, oppositional, and contrary. In this sense it is an expression of individuation and is therefore creative. An act, which in human life is most often the expression of conscious willing, only becomes negative because it stands in opposition to the will of another—originally that of the mother. At best the task for each individual of emerging as a separately created self from the maternal matrix is attended with fear and guilt; guilt, because the function of willing cuts its milk teeth, as it were, on the bone of contention; fear, because the aloneness that derives from an act that connotes separation, is more than the actually dependent child can bear.

When, in the course of the child's development, insufficient permission is granted for separation, when the mother says in effect: "You dare not be yourself; you have not the ability to be yourself; you need me to exist," the fear and guilt become deeply imprinted. The child believes the mother to be right because of his or her inevitable physical and emotional dependency. Thus, every normal manifestation of growth and development is feared since it symbolizes separation; every positive autonomous act is accompanied by fear, guilt, and sometimes shame. Jeanne's reaction to success with fear, depression, and shame, because it spelled the creation of an autonomous self which had been forbidden to her, parallels the fearful child's response to growth. In spite of much hard-won understanding which she acquired over a long period of time in her treatment, the reality of separation from me because of summer vacation precipitated anew these old fears.

It seems to me that the mystery of what Freud called the negative therapeutic reaction, i.e., the patient's worsened condition during analysis as a result of a better understanding of his unconscious impulses, is explicable in Rankian terms as the individual's fear of his own growth, maturation, and change because these represent individuation and are to be understood as the inability to affirm the life process, the creative structuring of his own separate personality. Having originally been denied the permission to exist autonomously, he awaits permission. But more, because of a bottomless anxiety he hopes that the permission itself will magically produce his autonomy and will absolve him of the inevitable responsibility of creating it himself.

Another patient, whom I shall call Ruth, and whose fears were also triggered by the approaching vacation, reacted more violently, more dramatically, but perhaps more creatively. She is a young woman who came to treatment because her relationships with people, especially men, were unsatisfactory and because she was having great difficulty completing her dissertation for a doctorate in psychology. It is important to know that on the day on which the explosive event, which I am about to describe, occurred she had just turned in the first draft of her dissertation.

It was the next to the last session before vacation. She stormed into my office in a rage because I had kept her waiting for a few minutes. This was not the first time that she had been angered by having to wait, but, although she was aware that I have often generously given her more than her allotted time, this fact did not dispel her paranoid-compulsive feeling that I do this intentionally to demean her. She experienced having to wait as a sign of my disrespect and inconsiderateness. Finally, she confessed that she had long thought of leaving her therapy because of this. I pointed out the displacement of her rage at being abandoned (the vacation) onto the issue of time, and made clear that whenever she interprets an event as abandonment, she leaves first, before being left. This has been a pattern in her life. When things don't go her way, she leaves—her friends, her boyfriend, her colleagues. In this instance, my casualness about time was not to her liking. She abusively demanded that I change, or she threatened to leave.

What begins to emerge is the struggle of wills. The therapeutic situation which by its very nature I am empowered to set up, i.e., the time of vacation, the time for the beginning of her session, is one to which she is afraid to yield because it connotes both separation and merging. She fights for her autonomy with counter-will. Her words were: "I am at your mercy." My answer was that, while I possibly was too casual about time, I certainly had no intention of demeaning her, and that she would have to take me as I am if she wanted to continue working with me. But I said more: I remarked that my time was valuable, that I had counted on her continuing treatment in the fall, had reserved time for her, and that it was unfair of her to let me know at this late date that she wished to discontinue. It is not my wont to speak this way to a patient, i.e., to use the value of my time to create separation between us, and I might not have done so on this occasion had it not really happened a few hours before that I had had to turn someone away who was eager to come into treatment with me, for lack of time. But what I had done without forethought, as a result of my spontaneous emotion of annoyance and anger, had an electrifying effect on my patient, which became manifest in the following and final session of the season which occurred two days later.

My patient came in, in a much calmer state, saying: "It clicked, when I thought it over; the key word was 'unfair.' I realize that the unfair thing was that I felt no gratitude for all your help with the dissertation." I had not had this particular meaning of "unfair" in mind; but I let it stand, because intuitively I realized that she was struggling to give up an old pattern, to effect change in her own attitudes, and to use the conflict between us creatively.

What had happened, to my mind, was that in Ruth's case, the word "unfair" had put the distance essential for individuation between us. She was able to perceive me, my needs, my reactions as separate and different from hers, and to realize the inappropriateness of her emotions relative to my having helped her to succeed in the very thing for which she had come for help—the finishing of the dissertation. But it was precisely this accomplishment, as well as my leaving on vacation, which precipitated the fear that in turn produced the angry chaotic and neurotic reactions of the previous session. For the dissertation in its symbolic meaning is an "end," a statement of self. It represents a leaving of dependency and of childhood. As Ruth spoke of these feelings she suddenly recalled that June had always been for her a time of depression and anxiety. Throughout her childhood it had meant separation—especially separation from school, which she loved and which was a refuge for her from a stormy familial environment. Suddenly it occurred to her that June was the time of her younger brother's birth, when her mother had left her to go to the hospital for the delivery, had become seriously ill after the baby's birth, and had remained in the hospital for three months. Ruth, who was three years old at the time, was being cared for by a neighbor into whose large family of children she was absorbed. When her mother returned she resisted returning to her parents' home. Out of the feeling of having been abandoned, she rejected her mother emotionally, yet subsequently sought the ancient symbiosis in every relationship. My upcoming vacation, the all-but completed dissertation, and her brother's birthday converged to press upon her the unconscious memory of an unresolved separation conflict. Up to this point in her life she had attempted to resolve it by a revengeful, angry act of "leaving," an act in which, because she actively took the initiative, gave her the illusion of functioning independently. She took the act of counter-will as one of positive willing.

While it is true that in the two sessions which I have described she relived with great affect the inappropriate displacement onto the therapist of the rage which she felt as a small child when her mother left her, physically, to give birth to her brother, and emotionally, through her concerns for another child (the phenomenon referred to in Freudian analysis as transference); and that she arrived at an understanding of the meaning and implication of the memories of these experiences and their connections with her current life, I doubt that all this in itself would have had sufficient therapeutic impact to effect a change in her. The "therapeutic moment" came when, in the stark realization of our distinct and separate individualities, she responded to the possibility within her own personality of a new, a changed reaction. She took the responsibility for a "volitional affirmation of the obligatory," in which the "obligatory" is the inevitable fact of our difference, and the "volitional affirmation" is a positive, rather than negative and reactive, act of creative will which uses the "inevitable" to promote growth and maturation, in fact, to structure an increasingly individuated self.

The felicitous outcome of these sessions does not, however, answer the question of what enabled Ruth to use the experience creatively; for it does not necessarily follow, even if the therapist, inspired by Rank, is oriented to the mobilization of the patient's responsibility for the creative development of his own autonomy, that the patient will be able to make this choice. The ability to choose growth and change creatively rather than to persist in the repetition of neurotic patterns depends on so many factors as well as on their complex interactions, that we can never know with certainty which elements are crucial. First, there is the enormous variability in the initial constitutional endowment of individuals. Ruth, for example, had tremendous vitality and energy from the first, and was readily able to find satisfaction—sometimes with a slight touch of grandiosity— in her own competent functioning in the external world. Her defensive reactions to anxiety were largely, though not entirely, projections of blame upon other individuals. Jeanne, on the other hand, was more internalized, given to self-hatred and depression. Her deep-seated defensive investment in a masochistic, denigrated self-image as a way of avoiding separation anxiety would inevitably make it more difficult for her to affirm the forward movement of growth and change, since these would involve a fundamental change in self-conception.

Yet, despite inherent differences, despite widely divergent life experiences, with consequent variations in ways of adapting, the ability of a patient to choose growth, i.e., to affirm the direction of the life stream, and to take responsibility for change and the fulfillment of his own capacities, will depend greatly on the therapist's belief in the human capacity to creatively structure and restructure personality, and on his ability to convey this, as well as permission to do so, to the patient. Just as in the course of development, a child's growth is enhanced by the mother's belief in and affirmation of it, so for the patient who has generally lacked such affirmation in childhood, the experience of the therapist's belief in and respect for his separate and distinct individuality creates the atmosphere of trust in which the patient can dare to will change. It is initially to Rank that we owe this insight into the development and function of the will, and its creative use in the structuring of personality.

NOTES

1. Jessie Taft, *Otto Rank* (New York: Julian Press, 1958), p. 18.

2. Otto Rank, *Art and the Artist* (New York: Knopf, 1932), p. 38.

3. Otto Rank, *Der Kunstler* (Vienna: Psa.V., 1925) 1:50, 52–53.

4. Rank, *Art and the Artist*, p. 25.

5. C. J. Herrick, *The Evolution of Human Nature* (Austin: University of Texas Press, 1956), p. 115.

6. Note here that Rank's emphasis on the positive life force, the creative urge, leads him, in contrast to Freud, to posit a *wish* for immortality rather than an instinctual impulse toward death. (*Todestrieb-Thanatos*).

7. Erik H. Erikson, "Identity and the Life Cycle," *Psychological Issues* (New York: International Universities Press, 1959), 1:22.

8. Esther and William Menaker, *Ego in Evolution* (New York: Grove Press, 1965), p. 72.

9. L. W. Flaccus, *The Spirit and Substance of Art* (New York: F. S. Crofts, 1926), pp. 65–66.

10. Esther Menaker, "Will and the Problem of Masochism," *Journal of Contemporary Psychotherapy* (Winter 1969), 1:66–67.

❧ 10 ❧

The Creation of Plays: With a Specimen Analysis

MARGARET BRENMAN-GIBSON

The whole man must . . . move at once.
—RALPH WALDO EMERSON

1. THE BACKGROUND AND PROBLEMS OF METHOD

I HOPE YOU will not find it merely personal that I preface what I have
to say about the creation of a play,[1] any play, with a history of how I came
to this undertaking. It is in the spirit of a mode on inquiry and of thought,
which seeks to accumulate psychohistorical evidence for any proposition,
that I tell you a portion of this background. In a field of study where "disciplined subjectivity" is the prime available research tool, the investigator's relation to the segment of experience he is studying becomes an indispensable part of the data (Erikson 1968a).[2] To be sure, to paraphrase

This material was presented in rough draft at the Stockbridge end of the Wellfleet-
Stockbridge axis at a meeting on November 6, 1971. Participants were Margaret Brenman-
Gibson, Joan Mowat Erikson, Erik H. Erikson, Leo Garel, William Gibson, Ann Birstein
Kazin, Alfred Kazin, Bessie Boris Klein, Rachel Klein, Betty Jean Lifton, Robert Jay Lifton,
Inge Morath Miller, Arthur Miller, Peggy Mowrer Penn, Arthur Penn, Virginia Rowe, Hell-
mut Wohl. It issues from a long-range inquiry into the nature of the creative process sup-
ported in part by the Austen Riggs Center, Foundations' Fund for Research in Psychiatry,
National Endowment for the Humanities, the Guggenheim Foundation, the Grant Foundation, Foundation for Research in Psychoanalysis, the Whitney Foundation, the American Association of University Women, the Rockefeller Foundation, and the Lederer Foundation.

Polanyi, not only *can* we "know more than we can tell," we usually do[3] (1966). We psychoanalysts are not, alas, in the enviable position of contemporary physicists whose accounts of the relation of "the observer and the observed" can remain manifestly impersonal (Holton 1970).[4] This makes things more difficult for us. Nonetheless, it is occasionally possible to describe in broad outline the interactions between the observer of what we loosely call "creative processes" and the practicing artist. All of which is by way of explanation for the detailed account which follows.

In late July of 1963, in a period of renewed Hope that the nuclear test-ban treaty had given all of us—and our children—an unexpected reprieve from the forces of Evil, I was on vacation, and busy reading in manuscript a colleague's book about two personages whose relationship on the stage of history had for some time engaged, moved, and mystified the entire world. I had followed, for many years, with fascination the painstaking gathering of information on the lives of these two men by my colleague and had—on the basis of the internal consistency of his raw data and before reading this manuscript—come to the conclusion not only that Alger Hiss had not been guilty even of perjury, but that my colleague was about to deliver himself of the finest "psychoanalytic double-biography," as he called it, that had ever been written.

Now as I was trying, at his request, to be a friendly critic of his soon-to-be published manuscript on Hiss and Chambers, I found myself troubled—in the face of what appeared to me to be his somewhat "Freudian-fundamentalist" and ahistorical modes of thought about the unfolding drama of these two intertwined lives. Whereas I had found the raw data of both life histories—unearthed in detail by him with all the patience, wit, and resourcefulness of a detective—to be stunning, it now was disconcertingly clear that even we two psychoanalysts did not quite share a systematic view of the organizing principles whereby to order the data of these lives and to discern their critical turning points, nor of the dynamics of their motivation, let alone a conception of the relation of individual pathologies and ideologies to the trajectories of ongoing history and *its* recurrent crises.

In the midst of this task, there arrived from California a small package from playwright Clifford Odets. This proved to be another biography (already published), this time not by a psychiatrist but by an earnest and intelligent professor of drama, who in his small volume, documented the thesis that Odets in 1935, not quite thirty years old, had, in less than twelve months "cut a swath in American theatre such as few are able to cut in a lifetime." He argued that his historic stature as an American playwright did not rest on the manifest "social protest" of his work, and that, in any case the best of Odets' work was yet to come. With a handful of biographical facts, he had gone on to write a life history plus analyses of Odets' eleven full length plays and four one-acters, conscientiously attempting to demonstrate their origins in his life. As in all such biographies, a commonsense psychology informed his interpretations and conclusions.

This was the second time in twenty-four hours I felt oppressed by the complexities of conceptualizing the story of any life, let alone how to relate a life history to its works in such a way as to illuminate the problems of so-called psychoanalytic or psychohistorical biography without repeating the reductionist errors of so many such studies. I had been struggling for years with this problem in the day-to-day clinical work of the hospital where I am employed, and it had long been evident that the chasm between the language used to describe a patient's "case history" and that to tell a neighbor's life story was wide. This had always seemed to some of us, not only conceptually but clinically, pernicious. Accordingly, we had begun systematically to explore the problem of how to conceive *any* life story in a way that would most comprehensively and harmoniously integrate the grid of available "facts," individual and historical.

It has become increasingly evident as this work has progressed that we are barely beginning to establish "rules of inference" for the naturalistic and clinical research models: that is to say, we do not yet have verbalizable criteria for the particulars of statements that seem strongly effective, and those that seem weakly effective, in respect to establishing a consensus of "meaning" either of states of consciousness or of behaviors. The remarkable thing is how far we have nonetheless come in building psychohistorical bridges between the internal vicissitudes of *any* human being (not merely of the highly gifted) and those of the society into which he is born (Brenman-Gibson 1976; Erikson 1950).[5]

Lest the reader think these difficulties stem only from the fact that our clinical research is in the "soft" science of psychology, hear this from a "hard" scientist:

Time and again the question of evidence and inference in experimental physics has been used as a starting point for the discussion of scientific method. I shall discuss the question in a rather personal way, for in my own work I have been puzzled at times by the striking degree to which an experimenter's preconceived image of the process which he is investigating determines the outcome of his observations. The image to which I refer is the symbolic anthropomorphic representation of the basically inconceivable atomic processes.

Modern microphysics deals with phenomena on a scale on which there are no human sense organs to permit a direct perception of the phenomena investigated. . . . The human imagination, including the creative scientific imagination, can ultimately function only by evoking potential or imagined sense impressions. I cannot prove that the statement I have just made is absolutely true, but I have never met a physicist, at least not an experimental physicist, who does not think of the hydrogen atom by evoking a visual image of what he would see if the particular atomic model with which he is working existed literally on a scale accessible to sense impressions.[6] (Deutsch 1958, p. 88)

Much later, I retrieved from Odets' files a note I wrote him on this day: I spoke first of my unclarified dissatisfactions with the Hiss-Chambers "double-biography," saying I should have undertaken it myself, adding then, of the little book he had sent about *himself*: ". . . what a testament to the juiceless, academic thought-process is this little volume . . . you must admit it is quite a feat to deal with a guy like you and somehow turn it into a bland exercise, . . ." casually adding that his biography, too, was a book I would "maybe write some day." A few days later, there came a note from Odets: "I am on the way to the doctor just now for xrays. There are some gastric troubles and we don't know what it is. . . ." I wondered why he made no reference to my letter with its careless and —so far as I knew, idle—offer "some day" to tell *his* life story. Two weeks later, at the Cedars of Lebanon hospital in Los Angeles, he was dead, the autopsy revealing a massively metastasized cancer of the stomach.

For good reasons—which are not strictly personal, but also generational—I found myself inconsolable and now determined first to reconstruct and then to try to understand the life and the works of this representative American playwright who had been for me, along with so many of my generation, a culture hero long before we had become friends. A clue to the meaning this death held for me, and for many, appeared in my inability for days—as I considered writing this biography—to rid my thoughts of a line from Gerard Manley Hopkins: "It is Margaret you mourn for." This subjective note offers a datum for the nature of a *collective identity* shared by the playwright with his audience. Alfred Kazin, in

his account of his first experience of Odets, has expressed better than anyone the nature of the transaction:

. . . watching my mother and father and uncles and aunts occupying the
stage in *Awake and Sing!* by as much right as if they were Hamlet and
Lear, I understood at last. It was all one, as I had always known. Art and
truth and hope could yet come together—if a real writer was their meeting place . . . I had never seen actors on the stage and an audience in the
theater come together with such a happy shock. The excitement in the
theater was instant proof that if a *writer* occupied it, the audience *felt joy
as a rush of power.* (1965, p. 82)[7]

Odets had helped *those of us who felt we did not belong* in our country—
by no means only the unemployed children of immigrants—feel "like
Somebody": less estranged, more at home, more real, and, assuredly,
more hopeful that we could yet collectively take our places in a larger,
more unified, and freer design than our individual lives promised. As we
sat in the dark, intent on the framed, lit space of the proscenium stage,
we, in astonishment, *recognized ourselves and knew we were at last being
recognized.* Kazin, in a revelatory sentence on the very nature of the
playwright-audience bond, adds: "The unmistakable and surging march of
history might yet pass through me. There seemed to be no division between my effort at personal liberation and the apparent effort of humanity
to deliver itself" (p. 83).

The "moral contagion" of this time against the Forces of Darkness extended to Odets' bride, the large-eyed, wistful Luise Rainer from Vienna,
who played on the screen an oppressed and starving Chinese peasant. We
adolescents, hungry for an ideology, were in love with her, too, and determined to lift her oppression along with that of the American worker.
These were the mid-1930s, and the planet was beginning to be locked in
combat. We yearned for voices and faces that promised liberation inside
and out. We would yet be "home free" in the United States of America.

Now, three decades later, I found myself involuntarily committed to
the resurrection on paper of this life that had so moved and enlivened us.
I knew there existed only one conceptual edifice sufficiently comprehensive even to approach this undertaking and hoped I would not do violence
in my account of an entire life span to this quantum jump in psychological
theory, a formidable model of human developmental and of generational
sequence whose growing body of integrated psychosocial principles is still

regarded with suspicion in some quarters of the psychoanalytic establishment.

I had come upon the beginnings of this psychological Reformation in 1937, in a paper published in the *Psychoanalytic Quarterly*, entitled "Configurations in Play—Clinical Notes." Written by a then-unknown young child analyst arrived in Boston from Vienna barely a year before the liquidation of psychoanalysis in Germany, it is the only paper that has remained clear in my memory of my junior year in college. Later, the same writer—in the context of constructing his view of the human life cycle—described the extremes of "play": at one end, he said, there stood the "microsphere" of the child's small world of manageable toys . . . (a harbor to return to when he needs privately to overhaul his ego)" and at the other end, the productions of the artist. I never forgot this first paper of Erik Erikson's on play-configurations nor his discussion a decade later which closed with a sentence from William Blake: "The child's toys and the old man's reasons are the fruits of the two seasons" (Erikson 1950, 1977).[8] I took it that Blake, too, perceived a core-connection between the child's necessity to relive, correct, and re-create past experiences while preparing for future "visions" (and for his own roles in these) and the adult's need, whether as a theory builder or a theater writer, to accomplish—on another level of integration—similar ends.[9]

The words "theory" and "theater," interestingly enough, derive from words which mean "to look at" (*theorein*) or "to see, to view" (*theasthai*). Both derive from a root "referring to a *visualized* sphere which arouses fascination, belief or wonder"[10] and which was termed "a beholding, a spectacle." One branch became *theater*, where we watch the enactment by players of an unfolding *make-believe* reality, an order or a form created by the playwright; the other became *theory*, where we "look at" ("speculate" upon) a body of facts to determine what "is" the already-existing order governing their relations to one another. In both theater and theory, thus, the form is initially *created* by the visionary, be he theater-man, theologian-prophet, or theoretician. Indeed, the prefix, "theo" ("thea" is the feminine form) is defined as "a combining form meaning God." Clearly, here—with vision as the early prime integrator—is something at the heart of both the "creative" and the "religious" impulse.

Erikson (1977) continues with the early development of our visionary propensity: "I would postulate that the infant's *scanning* search with his eyes and his recognition of what is continuously lost and found again, is the first *significant interplay* (just consider its later dramatization in peek-aboo)." For my purpose here, this first dramatization in the game of peekaboo, this *interplay*, is the paradigm for the transaction between playwright and audience.

Situated as I was with one foot (by marriage) in the American theater and the other in this conceptually critical development of psychological theory, a development comparable both in scope and in form to Bohr's in physics, I came to the conclusion—during this period of mourning—that I was uniquely cast in the role of Odets' biographer; and, less uniquely (as part of a long-term investment in the study of states of consciousness) in that of an investigator of creative processes, particularly those of the playwright. Moreover, it was time, with our last child off to school, to get back to the labor of generating ideas.

I commenced with some exhilaration to gather Odets' mountainous correspondence, notes, and files, to interview dozens of people, and to reread all of Erikson's illusorily impressionistic books and papers, beginning only now—a quarter of a century after that first paper on "play-constructions"—to grasp the systematic complexity of the still-evolving conceptual edifice. In it, wide-ranging discussions not only of children's language and their play, but also of the life cycle, of overturners in history, of artmakers, of dream analysis, of ritualization, and of ontology itself, take their places, and (one is tempted to say) play their indispensable parts.

Were it not so ugly a stretch of hyphens, one should, strictly speaking, describe Erikson's approach as an inventory of complementary configurations made up of "biologico-psycho-socio-historical" factors. We have settled, for the moment, on the shorter adjective, "psychohistorical" when discussing the cogwheeling crises of the individual life history with those of history and taking it for granted that rock bottom existential issues, usually discussed within the realms of philosophy and religion, are naturally included.

For our purpose here, it is important to keep sharply in focus the view that historical processes are vitally related to the demand for identity in each new generation and that psychosocial identity must be studied from the point of view of a complementarity of life history and history[11] (Erikson 1968b). More specifically, as Erikson puts it, "some historians probably begin to suspect that they, too, are practitioners of a restorative art which transforms the fragmentation of the past and the peculiarities of those who make history into such wholeness of meaning as mankind seeks" (1968b, p. 69).

It began to dawn on me that I had committed myself to the most exacting piece of research of my life, and I feared I was indeed venturing on ground where, as Leon Edel (1959) had put it in his stern warning to psychoanalyst-poachers, not only do angels properly fear to tread but where psychoanalysts had already left many "large muddy footprints": "Possessing," he had written, "neither the discipline of criticism nor the methods of biography, they import the atmosphere of the clinic and the consulting room into the library. . . ." To be sure, shaking an equally admonishing finger at his own literary colleagues, he had added: "The other side of the picture has been inevitably the venture, on the part of critics and biographers, upon psycho-analytic ground, where they have been no less inexpert than the psychoanalysts on our ground. The use of the psychoanalytic tool involves high skills."[12]

Edel had concluded thus with a territorial division whereby the species psychoanalyst, by definition, could treat only of "what's wrong with the artist's mental health" while the biographer, holding a monopoly on "reading the same pattern in the larger picture of the human condition," would seek to show "how the negatives were converted into positives: how, for example, Proust translated his allergies and his withdrawals from the pain of experience into the whole world of Combray. . . ." Clearly this was a treaty I could not sign. It was precisely the "larger picture of the human condition," and not a narrow pathology, which had become illumined by the Freudian revolution and by Erikson's body of work, an illumination as sorely needed by those of us to whom fractured people were turning for help as by those who were writing biographies.

As long ago as the mid-1930s, Freud's celebrated statement that before the mysteries of the artist "psychoanalysis must lay down its arms" had become the defensive preface of the few biographies then being written by psychoanalysts about gifted persons. In each case, the biography would, nonetheless, proceed to reduce wondrously created aesthetic forms to the banality that the artmaker shares with the rest of us an out-of-time oral fixation or Oedipus complex, that he suffered from "ambivalence" in his "object-relations," or from his bisexuality; or that he personified one or another antique diagnostic category: his violent mood-swings were "explained" by the fact he suffered from a "manic-depressive psychosis," his prodigal overflow of metaphor and dream image derived from his being an "ambulatory schizophrenic" eager to make restitutions or his terminal despair pigeonholed as "involutional melancholia." Playwright Saroyan's comment, "The surprise of art is not shock but wonder" could find no place in such biographies.

The first groundbreaking model to appear was, of course, Erikson's *Young Man Luther* (1958).[13] In that volume which tackled only a circumscribed portion of a life cycle, Erikson described Luther's resolution of his own crisis of identity as roughly filling a "political and psychological vacuum which history had created in a significant portion of Western christendom." He argued further that "such coincidence, if further coinciding with the deployment of personal gifts makes for historical 'greatness.' " This discovery, drawn not from the life of an artist but from that of a religious overturner and originator, provided, it seemed to me, a means for studying great, or even "representative," originators of *any sort,* whether of action on the macrostages of history (like Luther), of theories about the natural universe, or of plays on the microstage of the theater. But a blazed path is not yet an easily traversed trail, and "only when the relation of historical forces to the basic functions and stages of the mind has been jointly charted and understood" can we begin to erect meaning structures that makes contemporary sense (pp. 20–21). In any event, the corollary emerged that if an attempted resolution of a conflict, or of a growth crisis, in the playwright is synchronous with the existential state of a segment of his society, this cogwheeling will facilitate the creative use of his personal gifts.

Neither the vast literature on the philosophy of aesthetics nor the more recent work on the psychology of creativity has begun to unravel the riddle of what constellation of complementary psychological and social forces releases or inhibits creative work. Despite the fact that in the first half of the twentieth century the number of contributions to this problem was more than twice as many as all previous contributions put together, we have just begun to pose the relevant questions. The building of bridges between the internal vicissitudes of a creative human being and those of the society which molds him is one of the prime necessities if we are to establish paths for a meaningful exploration of creativity, and of its fecund and its sterile phases. The absolute distinctions between the "psychology" and the "sociology" of creativity have been, in my opinion, misleading. The thirties—in certain ways an historic time analogous to the sixties and early seventies—are unthinkable as an era without the image of Odets. Odets had scribbled, "I will reveal America to itself by revealing myself to myself." He proposed to do this in his plays, and I now proposed to extend this revelation by a study of those plays in the context of his life story and of history itself. Taking the monumental pile of data I had by now collected about Odets' ancestry, infancy, childhood, adolescence, and adulthood, a serious "joint charting" of these with the prevailing historical forces appeared a sufficiently arduous integration. When I confronted, however, the additional task of considering in microscopic detail how all of these data "hang together" with his plays, I understood first, why most clinicians restrict themselves to traditional case histories; and secondly, why biographers who bravely title their life histories, "The Life and Times of . . ." are usually reduced to parallel statements of a life, a time, and a body of work. A *genuine* integration of a life, a piece of history, and the fruits thereof—as Hamlet says, the "very age and body of the time, its form and pressure"—requires a methodological sophistication and a set of psychosocial concepts only lately emerging[14] (Brenman-Gibson 1976).

I now felt apologetic toward my colleague—who had, by this time, been severely drubbed by psychoanalysts, historians, and literary critics, in concert, for his "double-biography" of Hiss and Chambers—and toward the drama professor whose short biography of Odets had been largely ignored. It was by no means so clear to me as it had been on that summer day in 1963 that a serious and detailed "joint charting" of a life, a time, and a body of work was to be accomplished by the method of "disciplined subjectivity" in a single lifetime, if at all. By now, however, it was too late to back off from this mammoth four-dimensional jigsaw puzzle, whose fluid and complementary systems were in steady and rapid motion.

I reminded myself that when Henry Murray was asked at a Harvard graduate seminar some two decades ago where he thought the "facts of personality," were, he replied they were to be found *only* in the life cycles of "whole human beings." He had come from research on the embryology of chicks whose orderly and awesome transformations he had watched through a microscope set at a tiny window cut in the eggshell. This was the research model for his subsequent statement that the study of life histories, set in history, are "the granite blocks on which to build a science of human nature."

I took further comfort from Fred Wyatt, who, in a remarkable paper,

"The Reconstruction of the Individual and Collective Past," had concluded:

The job of reconstruction, if it aims to transform subjective experience into insight relevant for others, must therefore begin with the checks and cautions through which rationality raises itself into science. It must accustom itself also to dwelling on the sharp edge of paradox by striving for what appears at that moment the most comprehensive context, while knowing at the same time that it will, of necessity, soon be transcended. (1964)[15]

It began to appear possible—at least, theoretically—to construct a playwright's line of development which starts as with all of us, with "the first significant interplay," that is to say: the infant's scanning and filtering of the "buzzing, blooming confusions" both within and without, and which moves on hopefully from the gestalt of his mother's face to efforts—in dramatic, enacted childhood play—to construct his future while reconstructing his past.[16] (Erikson 1977). Finally, blessed—as are all artists—with a gift for *symbolic* play-construction (playing with thoughts and with states of consciousness) and provided his guilt at such play with the fires of creation is not disabling, he will—by way of Form—create a vision which will evoke a *communal* response from an audience. In this regard, a play is assuredly first cousin to a ritual. A contemporary playwright, however, lacking the support of a communal tradition, must succeed in creating, by way of symbols, an *immediate interplay* with his audience, as he has little leeway for recovery.[17] Odets understood the entire process very well indeed: "As for the playwright, by the image of the *symbolic realization* shall you know the person and his life!" (1954).[18]

Whereas the theoretician in science, the historian, or the prophet asks us to use *his* created model as a lens through which to behold the wondrous spectacle of an already ordered wholeness (or holiness) *preexisting* in the universe—and which he conceives as "given" by Nature, or by God, and only discovered by him—the playwright marks off a play space and time within which he frankly *creates* a whole universe which director Peter Brook tells us becomes, at best, not simply a make-believe world, but a "holy" spectacle (1968).[19] The charismatic political leader, in what has been called the "theater of reality," manages to "produce" *his* visions with a large involuntary cast on the stage of history, to be played, not just as make believe, but for keeps, as in a "theater of war," what Bentham calls "deep play." Gandhi's famous stagings of such confrontations were a major spiritual and political strategy.

All these creators of "visions," be they discoverers, artmakers, or charismatic leaders, are not after all engaged in *essentially* distinct pursuits. I say this with an awareness of the danger in labeling so wide a range of human function "play." One set of visionaries, to be sure, restricts its constructed models of experience to the experimental detours to action we call *thought* or symbolic representation. These are theoreticians, theologians, yes, even theater people (Brenman-Gibson 1976).[20] Among these, some are on the one hand logically cognitive, verbal, voluntary, and "linear"; and others spontaneously intuitive, physically playful, spatial, and "nonlinear." Moreover, an individual originator may have one foot in the arena of "real" action, the other in harmless scientific theory or artmaking, which is "make-believe" action.

Even in the hard science of physics, as Holton has brilliantly shown, a theory—that is, a created vision of experience—may necessitate not only experimental action but also an account *of the interaction* between the system under observation and the agency used to make the observations[21] (1970). What used to appear a clear line between what is "inside the mind" and what is "outside in the real world"—clear to all, that is, except to poets, farsighted philosophers, and writers of scripture—now blurs.

A given culture sometimes separates, sometimes unites the drama of its entertainment, its religion, its healing, and its social change. A "dancesing" held in the African bush for healing purposes integrates most of these,[22] (Katz 1976), whereas Abbie Hoffman's radical dramaturgy, addressed primarily to social change, did not integrate but made a muddy mix.

In a time such as our own of massive breakdown of a communally shared vision of life experience: of what went before, and what is now, and what is yet to come, the widespread individual and collective identity confusion (even chaos) is projected in a range of outer forms. "Theatre," Odets wrote, "in a certain sense, is the outward play of inner play" (1953).[23] One can say the same of theory and of theology.

The chronological narrative of Odets' life history appeared to be proceeding satisfactorily enough until the time came to make complementary sense of it and the plays in the context of history: starting with his crude work-beginnings and going on to the published and produced plays. I knew only that unless I used as context the theoretical web of that unique life stage in youth during which a psychosocial identity jells (I believe with some degree of irreversibility), I could say little different about the emerging continuity of "meanings" of Odets' crude juvenile efforts with the eleven full-length and four one-act plays than had the critics, drama professors, or Ph.D. candidates with whom I had been so impatient.

For the first time now, I appreciated Erikson's wry comment, "Identity is a term used in our day with faddish ease; at this point I can only indicate how very complicated the real article is" (Erikson 1962).[24] The "real article" depends on the *complementary* relation between a synthesis achieved *within* the person and his role in his society (Erikson 1968b).[25] For our purposes, so to describe a playwright's relation to his audience is significantly different from falling into the "expressive" fallacy decried by literary critics who maintain a literary work must be "understandable" without reference to its origins. It seemed to me to be the task of a psychoanalyst, who is trying to make another kind of sense of a life and its creative fruits to explore not only such origins but also the bridges attempted by the playwright between his own state of being and that of the audience of his time. In the face of such snowballing complexities, it became evident that I was in urgent need of a navigator's map if I intended to make meanings which would join a playwright, his language, his plays, and his era.

Recalling, after many false starts, that in 1949 Erikson had proposed a new and systematic "Outline of Dream-Analysis" (Erikson 1954; Freud 1900)[26] I decided to restudy it with a view to adapting it for the microscopic analysis of plays. To be sure, there are significant differences between the creative and the dream states. They share, however, that necessary transcendence (of everyday conscious thought) which unbinds energies for the mastery of experience, to the end of integrating and liberating the dreamer or the creator. They have in common also the uses of imagery, metaphor, metonymy, irony, condensation, ambiguity—in short, the language of the primary process.

The perspectives supplied by this new approach to dream analysis opened the way for the development of two basic hypotheses regarding the process of playwriting—perhaps shared by all creative activity. First, that *whatever latent meanings can be found in a work, primary among them will be found the author's conscious and unconscious views of the very nature of his own creative processes*. These may include his celebrant sense of generativity and whatever conflicts may thereto be attached, be it the sense of hubris attendant on being an originator, or on failing to become as pure a creator as his calling dictates. A play analysis may decode the anxiety at integrating dualities, sexual or otherwise; or *au fond*, the existential terror of losing a sense of "what is really real" as the fictionmaker who *acts* in the spectacle of life while standing to one side of it as "witness,"[27] frequently with guilt at his detachment.

Secondly, that in any body of work subconfigurations of the playwright's identity structure, composed of "identity elements," appear as the various casts of characters. They are the playwright's distribution of himself, and are, psychologically speaking, interchangeable from play to play, and functionally similar to the dramatis personae of Erikson's "dream-population." This is consistent with the Lacanian view of the dream as a "first-person drama."

It begins to emerge with an astonishing thematic consistency that each one of the internal "gallery of characters" occupies its own psychological territory within a given playwright's identity structure, and that equivalences can be discerned from play to play even as these internal and external casts evolve with the unfolding cycle of the life of the playwright in the context of the history of his society. The recurring struggles among these identity elements—externalized as the play's warring characters—their crises, and resolutions—become then the central latent themes of all plays. Thus, in the case of Odets, a tyrannical mother in one play may represent the same identity element expressed as a film magnate in another; or, again, a delicate young pianist may occupy the same psychological territory in one play as that held by a young secretary in another. When we are able to decode the play (and this is very close to decoding a dream), we see the specificity and the constancy of these identity elements.

To be sure, it has long been part of our commonsense understanding of a play—or of any work—that in some amorphous way it "expresses" its author, or, put with more sophistication, that he "projects" himself into his work. What is new here is supplied by Erikson's concept, "identity element." This allows for a microscopic play analysis, quite different from the biographer's usual links between the dramatis personae of his actual life (his family, friends) and his plays.

In the absence of the live dreamer's—or in this case, the writer's—"associations" to his works, other kinds of collateral life data are clearly needed, if stratified meanings are to be extracted from these creations. This necessity leads straight back to the biographical material in its historical context.

Just as the child demonstrates in his play "the infantile form of the human ability to deal with experience by creating model situations and to master reality by experiment and planning," thus redeeming his failures and strengthening his hopes, and the adult dreamer is likewise driven to the accomplishment of the "deed that cannot be left undone" (Erikson 1977),[28] it now begins to appear that the playwright is doing all of this and something more. As he activates or "moves" himself, revealing himself to himself, bringing about not simply revelation but also renewal—called, in other areas, "enlivening," "healing," "holy inspiration," or "re-creation"— so is his audience revealed to itself, restoratively "reached," "touched," "moved," and (at best) integrated and thus liberated, at least for a time. We think of motion and evolution as the essence of life. Thus, we are grateful to the playwright who manages to leap the abyss separating him from us and in so doing *to bring us to new life* by "moving" us.

Like a child's play-construction or a dream, the play is ingeniously transposed, and far more cunning than either. Not only does it use all of the primary thought processes of the dream: displacing, condensing, reversing, and substituting; it captures within the basic communicative container we call Form (Sennett 1972)[29] a means to state the primary duality (conflict) and its resolution in a manner which is sufficiently universal to take it out of the privacy of the dream and into the realm of the collective.

It is one of the tasks of this presentation to ask whether *even* formal properties can be discussed psychologically; this is as yet fairly virgin territory. For this purpose, it is perhaps more instructive to analyze the meanings of a play like *Rocket to the Moon* in which there are *formally* harmful illogicalities—than one which is structurally more sound. In this play specimen, there occurs a structural confusion which, like the diagnostician's dye, while revealing the play's difficulties, makes visible not only its flaws but its underlying psychological anatomy.

To pursue *specifically* the configurations and subconfigurations of the identity elements, their conflicts, and accordingly, the larger meanings of *any* play, it becomes clear we must study *the fourfold complementarity of the writer's history, his present stage of life, the present state of his society, and the history of that society* (Erikson, unpublished ms.). It is the playwright's gift that permits him—out of these four interacting coordinates *within himself*—to create a total visible Reality of such authenticity that he transcends first his own boundaries, and, in communicating this created Reality to his audience, enables them to feel more unified, real, and free than before they came to his play.[30]

2. A BIOGRAPHIC SKETCH OF CLIFFORD ODETS

[This capsule account is drawn from a biography of Clifford Odets to be published in part in 1978.]

Just before the turn of the century, two sisters came to America: the younger, aged eight—a decade later to bear her first child, Clifford Odets—was named Pearl Geisinger; she was timid, sad, delicate, and, as it turned out, tubercular. From an early age she had loved the study of languages. When her sixteen-year-old, rough, bold, and illiterate sister Esther decided to flee their Rumanian ghetto for America, she went along to Philadelphia, a city designed—the historians tell us—first and foremost as a sanctuary where "men and women were free to come into their full fruitfulness" (Burt 1945).[31] This was step one in the unfolding of the American Dream. The struggle for survival in the stocking factory which employed them both was not quite the Garden of Eden, however, they had pictured. Pearl—always obsessional and afraid to take chances—had reluctantly left her mother (already dying of tuberculosis), hoping in America to pursue her study of languages. As it slowly dawned on her that this would not be possible, she became visibly depressed and quiet.

There had come also in this third (Eastern European) wave of Jews to Philadelphia two young men: one, a somewhat daffy, trigger-tempered, and proudly defiant Russian Jew with red hair and green eyes "like a Cossack," a man whose innocent being would supply the manifest form for Noah in *The Flowering Peach*, Odets' last play, a man he regarded as "the single most eloquent human being I've ever met." So pure was his singing voice that he aspired to become an artist, a cantor "like Yosele Rosenblatt." Instead, he had become—with a horse and wagon—a fruit peddler who sang out the quality of his onions. This Israel Russman, lonely and "disconnected" because the rest of his family had already wandered away to Boston to become "Richmans and Rosses," asked the elder sister Esther to marry him. She agreed she would if he would accept, as part of the bargain, her sister Pearl. All three now moved into a sunless red-bricked row house with a "storefront" in the Jewish neighborhood, all working from seven in the morning until six at night.

When the inhibited, quiet Pearl was in her teens, there came into this household the second young man, also a Russian Jew, named Lou Odets. Stocky and powerfully built, he was flashy, charming, and self-assured; he was perceived by Esther to be an "operator," a *macher* (doer), and totally self-absorbed. "Lou loved Lou at all times," she said.

He was interested in Pearl, now seventeen, and ingratiated himself with his "gift of gab," his imitations, his impressive amateur boxing, his "snappy clothes," and his mastery of the latest American dancesteps. Talking mostly "in exclamations," his English, all were agreed, was like "a born American," and he looked with undisguised contempt at the rest of the "greenhorns" around him. From the beginning, it was clear he had the tastes of a sybarite and his eye on the "Big Time."

To the straightforward Esther, who recognized Lou Odets' consuming vanity and his relentless drive, he was a "hypocrite, a liar, a phoney show-off and a bull-shitter, too particular about the crease of his pants." He pretended to have been born in Philadelphia, not Russia, and would not reveal his original family name. He was determined soon to have his own printing business and to become an "important Jewish Elk." Obtuse, "elephant-skinned," said Esther, he boasted that at six, he had had a governess and at nine was selling newspapers on the streets of Philadelphia. He often repeated that like his mother before him he had always nonetheless managed to "keep up appearances." Certainly he was a man who early learned about French soaps and "how to talk to a head-waiter." There was little observable in him of his gentle father, a Hebraic scholar and a spiritual man for whom learning and "the family" were sacrosanct.

Both still in their teens, Pearl and Lou had their first child in 1906, "the year," Odets was later fond of saying, "in which both Cezanne and Ibsen died," adding that, "no nightingales fell out of the trees" at his arrival. He meant, I believe, to suggest with some seriousness he had been brought into the world by his mother to fill the empty place either of the great painter or the playwright.

He was born prematurely, weighing in at three and one-half pounds, and Lou Odets decided he liked the elegant sound of the name "Clifford," like the names "Genevieve" and "Florence," later bestowed on his two daughters. Although Esther loathed Lou's fraudulence and his empty piety ("with the help of the good Lord"), she was glad he "always knew how to put his hands on a dollar." Lou, himself, was convinced that for a man of his ability, charm, and magnetism the sole obstacles to his becoming "a big man, number one" were his Jewishness and the fact he was married to this gentle, sad, "overly sincere," and "incompetent" Pearl, who, as he put it, "wouldn't go anywhere and couldn't talk to people." He had no such difficulty and was by now flagrantly "stepping out with the ladies," and driving Odets' mother (called "nunlike" by neighbors) still deeper into her quiet and chronic despair. Her best friend thought Pearl Odets was too timid, "put up with too much," and that "it must have been a spiritual crucifixion [sic] for her to live with Lou Odets." For his part, Lou felt himself to be a lonely man in a loveless marriage, held back from achievement by his graceless wife.

Pearl often stared out of the window at the cemetery, saying to her young son, "how peaceful it looks." She was unusually close with him until the crippling by polio of her next child, the girl they called Genevieve. Now, according to the neighbors, she abruptly shifted her time and attention to this crippled child who thus "won out," displacing Clifford *by reason of being crippled*. This abandonment of him by his mother for a maimed person would become a central theme in Odets' life and in his work.

Pearl rarely became openly angry, accepting her burdens with "something like the knowledge that suffering is the badge of the human race." Now and then she said to her son, "I think I will lose my mind." Her pervasive low mood—along with her verbal facility—was doubtless conveyed to him. As soon as she had had Clifford, Pearl confided to her sister she felt herself to be a lifetime prisoner, as the inviolability of "the family"—a central and steadily conflicted theme in Odets' plays—was a foundation stone neither she nor her husband questioned. Odets would come to be the Jewish-American playwright of "the family," celebrating and mourning both it and its passing—as a hearth and a jail.

To Clifford, his father appeared by turns seductive and charming, or as a crushing and invincible behemoth who could as easily abandon or destroy as protect him. He saw his frightened, depressed, undemonstrative mother as "full of integrity, but helpless and incompetent," and, above all, as oddly innocent, submerged, and vulnerable. He always wanted to crawl on her lap, saying, as all the family recalled, "lay my head on your chesh" [*sic*]. His mother had permitted him this luxury only until his younger sister's illness.

As a child, Odets impressed everyone with his radiant physical beauty, his enormous blue-gray eyes, which "took everything in," his verbal brightness, his pleasure in public "performing," and—until he went to school—his obedience: his father called him "Putty," and would steadily ridicule his passivity and seeming helplessness, saying he took after his mother. Odets wrote in a letter to the author:

I realized that when I was four or five, from then on I had a running battle with my mother. (She was 22 when I was five, you hear?) And from her side, too the battle was joined. She wanted to be consoled, appeased and comforted; and she begrudgingly would do none of these things for me; she was, after all, a child herself, in an unhappy marriage and, actually, was thinking about giving me away to a Pennsylvania farmer and his wife. This battle of who was the aggrieved, of WHO WAS THE POET, went on until she died, when I was 28 (I squirmed plenty over these years but never gave in and was glad (and sorry and sick-sad, too) when my father made pain for her!) And, you know, it is not over yet. Any autumn will come any dusk, and when I am one hundred and one, my heart will hurt that when the streets were cold and dark that, entering the house, my mother did not take me in her arms. (She had in her arms, of course, my sister crippled by polio.) No, till the day my mother died, she would say things like, "You'll forget me. You won't take care of me," etc., etc. And I, foolish child, wanted to be taken care of!

Before long, Lou Odets, by now called "LJ," (the "J" a relative said, "stood for nothing, just 'class' "), had established not only his own print shop, but an advertising agency. He aspired to writing his own "copy," but failing this, he hired copywriters, often pretending to have authored their work. Soon, he became highly successful, being what he called "a merchandising counsellor." His steadily rising income permitted him at long last to buy a Maxwell car, silk shirts, and to live in the first apartment house in the Bronx with an elevator. He enjoyed playing cards and "going out on the town" with three gangsters, to become notorious. Consciously, his son repudiated the passionate business ambitions of his father. Nonetheless, the central struggle of Clifford's life would be with becoming "a Big Man, Number One."

The wound of the father's life—until his only son was almost thirty—lay in the fact that, although he himself had acquired, like that classic

American salesman, Willy Loman, "the counterfeits of dignity and the false coinage embodied in his idea of success," he had not fulfilled his wish to write his own "copy." Moreover, his son was a humiliating failure, having dropped out of high school and being unable, even in the affluent twenties, to hold a job, except, on occasion, as a mediocre actor.

After a materially comfortable, but psychologically endangered adolescence and early adulthood during which he was chronically bored, sleepy, "submerged," depressed, "extruded," and "half-dead," Clifford had made—before the age of twenty-five—two suicide attempts, one of them in 1929 at the height of American prosperity. Only as the economic depression deepened and he became, during the summer of 1931, an actor-member of a group of then equally superfluous theatrical brethren, who (like him) combined a sense of aesthetic alienation and integrity with a loose and romantic ideological allegiance to Marxism and a bond with the suffering working class, did he have the conversion experience which became the turning-point of his young life and provided the bridge to his audience. Although he was considered second-from-the last in his acting ability, he had finally been "let in" to a family that did not ridicule him (as did his father), and that he hoped, might one day "bring out the best in me," even come to need him. His long-extended moratorium was coming to a close. Within the next year, filled with fidelity for his Group Theatre brethren, he wrote for them the full-length play which would soon establish for him a bond with a significant segment of his society whose voice he became, and who consequently affirmed him as the "playwright of the Thirties." Each Depression child who felt extruded by his world, experienced—on seeing this play—relief and gratitude that as Kazin had put it, ". . . there seemed to be no division between my effort at personal liberation and the apparent effort of humanity to deliver itself."

The subtleties of the psychohistorical transactions between playwright and audience are well illustrated by the fact that Odets (to become in the depressed thirties internationally known as the voice of the *economically* disinherited) experienced himself already in the twenties as *psychologically* "disinherited," at a time when his booming society was accommodating almost everyone in its productive system, and his own family was affluent. His favorite book at this time was *Les Misérables.* His sense of himself as orphaned, extruded, deprived, abandoned, unjustly treated was clearly *not* related to material deprivation. Yet, he could give voice to a significant segment of a Depression society because he understood—in the most profound way—the emotional meaning of such "disinheritance."

The play, to become a classic, begun in private despair, was first called *I Got the Blues*. Now, sharing with a collective their "wild hopes for the future," both for himself and for the suffering world, he retitled it, *Awake and Sing!* [32] Indication of Odets' radical transformation is in the following extravagant statement, taken from the Group Theatre Diary in July 1931:

I am done! done with chasing my febrile self down the nights and days. From ashes the phoenix! The clamoring hatred of Life has been hushed to less than a whisper! On the pivotal point of a quarter of a century of living (sweet Jesus, twenty five years old this month!) I have begun to eat the flesh and blood of "The Group." I partake of these consecrated wafers with a clean heart and brain; and I believe—as I have wanted to believe for almost ten years—in some person, idea, thing outside of myself. The insistent love of self has died with strangulation in the night. The stubborn stupid lugubrious pride that one develops somewhere between the ages of ten and twenty has dissolved with some minor weeping. I who cried from my inverted wilderness for strong roots with which to fasten to the swarming sustaining earth have found them at last in "The Group." I am passionate about this thing!!! [33]

At last he had found roots. This bright, unwanted son of an ambitious Russian-Jewish immigrant, this high school dropout and indifferent actor, long held in contempt by his businessman father, now felt his individual wandering in an "inverted wilderness" to be at an end. His romantic statement of rebirth is not simply of finding a professional affiliation but of a quasi-religious conversion, akin to the primal Christians, to a spiritual collective, a brotherhood whose "flesh and blood" he eats. It is the reorganization so frequently seen in sensitive youths in quest of a world view which, transcending their private identity struggles, supplies a renewed sense of wholeness and of trust, indeed, a faith in the life process itself.

Four years after this "conversion," he became not only a leading spokesman for the American Left, but even, in the opinion of "bourgeois" critics, the "White Hope of the American Drama." During the year 1935, at twenty-nine, six of his plays—including the hastily written runaway hit, *Waiting for Lefty*—were produced. All these early plays (for which Odets is best known) take as their manifest premise that man's (collective) suffering, his enslavement, stems from his material deprivation. His characters find deliverance in a *collective joining together* to the end of overcoming

the enemy—be he corrupt union official, capitalist, Nazi, or landlord—
and wresting from him economic or political power. A universal, joined
humanity would thus emerge, as in the lyrics of the theme song of the international communist movement.[34] Thus, he expressed the deepest longings of a significant segment of his cultural society. The plight itself, and
its solution, was stated in economic terms, and the *conflict* manifestly
seen simply as between groups with opposed material interests (workers
versus bosses, tenants versus landlords, peasants against feudal gentry). In
these early works it is clear that what stymies the fulfillment of one's creative potential is economic injustice.

After the full-length *Awake and Sing!*, however, in 1935, not only the
economic-political message, but also the manifestly Jewish-American
identity of the characters progressively recedes. In his *Paradise Lost*,
(which still holds to the collective identity: "No man fights alone," says the
protagonist), as Odets strained to become an "accepted American playwright like Robert Sherwood," he consciously tried to make his characters
neutrally American, with names like Gordon instead of Berger. Despite
his attempt to leave his immigrant family behind, and to universalize his
internal gallery of characters, drama critics all over the world continued to
refer, however, to his characters as "Odets' Jewish-Americans." Although
drama historians have been amused by this "error" on the part of critics, it
is clear that so systematic a mistake issues from the unconscious perception that indeed the collective identity successfully put onstage by
Odets—and, accordingly, the audience which was moved by his work—is
not so much that of the left-wing worker as the second-generation American immigrant—or even the radicalized American intellectual—who wants
"to belong."

Despite the continuing economic depression, his father, at forty-
nine, retired on a generous monthly stipend from his son, and took a trip
around the world. It is rare one sees so dramatic a reversal between a father and son when both are so young as now took place. Lou Odets, while
continuing to offer steady advice on business, on his son's conduct of his
life as well as on the structure of his plays, was doing so with apology,
fawning upon him and calling him "a genius." The son was now carrying
both his father and the Group Theatre on his creative and financial back.

In 1937—after a brief and well-paid sojourn in Hollywood—Odets
wrote the well-known *Golden Boy*, a work that emerges as transitional between the manifestly economic-political and what we can call

"the psychological" play wherein the conflict begins to be perceived as essentially internal. In the year following, Odets wrote what I have selected as our specimen play, *Rocket to the Moon.*

After many affairs—most of them compulsive, often pleasureless and dehumanized—he married for the first time. His wife was the European (part-Jewish) film star, Luise Rainer. It was an embattled and competitive relationship from the beginning on many counts, not the least of which was his fear that this marriage threatened his creative powers. The breakup of this marriage provided the complementary set of circumstances for the creation of *Rocket to the Moon.* History, as we shall see, was already providing the rest.

3. A SPECIMEN PLAY ANALYSIS: *Rocket to the Moon*

We must not lose sight of the fact that the creative process is not finally consummated until the artist's experience—given form on paper, on canvas, or in stone—has reached an audience. Most particularly, the dramatist, that most topical of artists, must feel that he has succeeded in obliterating boundaries and established a union with the group assembled to watch his play.[35] Proceeding from this assumption, the position of *Rocket to the Moon* in 1938—in Odets' personal history as well as in the history of American drama—is pivotal. While, to be sure, even in so manifestly agitational a play as his early and slight strike play, *Waiting for Lefty,* Odets' characters and dialogue are already characteristically vivacious, electric, and original, the shift from the emotional currency of economics and politics to that of psychology first becomes evident in *Rocket to the Moon.* This cogwheeling of an artist's personal themes with those of his society determines (aside from the size of his gift) his success or failure in his lifetime. It is not unusual that there is a lag in either direction.

The manifest spine of the play *Rocket* is no longer politically messianic: unlike Odets' early plays, addressed to the oppressed international proletariat, pleading with them to "awake and sing" in economic liberation; the appeal is, rather, for creative liberation. Odets told director Harold Clurman it was about "love and marriage." On the one hand, this shift clearly reflects Odets' own struggles with the crisis of intimacy. But that is not all. The cogwheeling turn of history was changing his audience: those who in 1935 had looked for ultimate salvation in the theory of Marx, the activities of the "working class," and the model of the Soviet Union were becoming progressively cynical and wary. The peaceloving Russian comrades—hitherto embraced by idealistic Americans as apostles of the realization of individual potential and dignity—had lately made a pact of mutual defense with "imperialist" France, and, worse, had begun the systematic extermination of their own domestic enemies. The barbarous Moscow trials of these "enemies" were leaving an increasingly bitter taste, straining the loyalty of even the most devoted of American fellow travelers. In short, there no longer existed so credulous an audience as the one that had risen in joyous unison at the close of *Waiting for Lefty* to shout, "Strike!"

The major critics dimly understood Odets' shift away from the manifestly political as a "landmark in his growth." Those writing for the communist press—missing entirely the point of the play: a plea for the liberation of creativity—mourned that he had given over his "magnificent flair for character study and dialogue" to such bourgeois concerns as "love and marriage." Of the first-line critics, only the sagacious Joseph Wood Krutch, writing for *The Nation*, understood the nature of Odets' evolution as a playwright and the resultant shifts within himself, and, accordingly, the nature of his transactions with an equally changing audience:

The tendency still persists to make of Clifford Odets and his plays a political issue. That, I think, is a pity from any point of view now that the facts are becoming increasingly clear. Whatever his opinions may have been or, for that matter, may still be, those opinions are shared by many, while Mr. Odets reveals a gift for characterization and a gift for incisive dialogue unapproached by any of his Marxian fellows and hardly equaled by any other American playwright.[36]

Another central point made by Krutch was that Odets—and correspondingly his audience—had gradually shifted from the manifestly political to the psychological arena.

Keeping in mind as scaffolding Erikson's new perspectives on the dream as well as his fourfold complementarity (that is, the writer's history and his present stage of life plus the present state of his society and *its* history), I proceed to our play specimen.

Odets' first jottings for *Rocket to the Moon*, made in 1937 when he was thirty-one, outline a play whose sensory quality and affective atmosphere are immediately reflected in its wasteland setting: in sharp contrast to the play's title, the space is tightly, even suffocatingly, bounded. People and flowers alike thirst, are dead, constricted, manifestly allowing little room for locomotion, "play," or growth. With fewer characters than ever before, he gives these again neutral "American" names of indeterminate national origins.

His earliest scribbled notes indicate Odets' conscious intention to create as the protagonist of *Rocket to the Moon,* a frightened, ineffectual, submerged little dentist named Ben Stark, a man in a "mid-life crisis," torn between his controlling, sterile wife and his juicy, aspiring secretary, and bitterly disappointed in his creative aspirations. Initially, it appeared the central *action* of the play would be his. The fourth, and perhaps the richest character is his wife's father, Judah Prince, a man of the world, determined to "have love" before he dies. A man who prides himself on knowing "how to talk to a head-waiter," he is the dentist's rival for the girl. The idea for this play had come to him, Odets said, when he was sitting in a dentist's chair looking at the equipment and the water cooler, and wondering what kinds of emotional life were concealed behind the numb routines of this office and behind the constricted face of the meek little dentist himself. Early notes, written by Odets at a time when he began to be in conscious conflict over his marriage, indicate the central theme would be *"about love and marriage in America."*

By way of this specimen play analysis, I will provide data which illustrate the two major hypotheses: first, *that a play always deals at some level with the playwright's view, conscious and unconscious, of the nature of the creative process itself,* and secondly, *that the playwright's distribution of himself (of his identity elements), constitute the cast of characters,*[37] their conflicts and resolutions reflecting the playwright's effort via Form to bring these dualities into harmony, restoring wholeness where there was conflict.

Over a year had elapsed after his first notes for *Rocket,* at the end of which time Odets' own efforts at a faithful intimacy were reaching a bitter climax in the crumbling of his marriage. In response to his coldly detached reply to her telegraphed announcement from Hollywood that she was pregnant, his wife had aborted their first and only child. Odets had fled with the company of *Golden Boy* from New York to London, and in the fall of 1938, now thirty-two, he drove alone to Canada, carrying with him, in addition to the few notes written the year before the "dentist play," the manuscript of his labor play, as well as the play about the Cuban revolution. It is evident his necessity is to work, preferably on material manifestly tied to the ongoing historic upheavals. In his "General Notes," from 1938, he had written:

The invasion of Prague, from news dispatches. Crowds of thousands stood, weeping silently, and then spontaneously broke into their national anthem! A policeman outside the city hall tried desperately to direct traffic but was too blinded by his tears. Many of the Czechs covered their faces with their hands and turned away at the first sight of the German troops. Well, can a writer write in the face of these things? Yes, he *must* write in the face of these things! [38]

It troubled him, however, that a formal vessel by means of which he might explicitly unite these large and somber historic events to his own emotional urgencies continued to elude him. Finally, he stopped work on the manifestly "social-historical" plays—all of which took as their theme the beginning of the end of the American Dream—and concentrated instead on what appeared to be the strictly "personal" struggles of three ordinary and lonely people, with Ben Stark, the passive, submerged dentist, trying to find sufficient courage to "take life by the throat" by having an affair with his childlike, attractive, and aspiring secretary, Cleo Singer.[39] It is implied that his stifled growth—his generativity—will thereby be given new impetus and he will escape the feeling he has "blown it."

In the playwright's original outline, written only a few weeks after his wedding, and during the first of many separations, the dentist's secretary succeeds in detaching Stark from his wife. After a year of intense emotional negotiation, Odets' own marriage all but finished, he found as he was rewriting this play that the character, Cleo, had begun to take center stage away from Ben and to evolve as the "identity element" by now familiar to me from his earliest juvenile writing: the aspiring, unformed, even damaged, artist, or—as he liked to call her—"the moral idealist," whose growth is in steady jeopardy of becoming fraudulent, or crippled by a premature restriction of options, manipulated by the seductive and worldly American businessman whose own innocence and idealism, like that of America, has long since disappeared.

The dentist, Stark, a "second-class professional," is a man who reads Shakespeare, but who would—according to Odets' notes—be frightened even to get a passport and who "plays it safe" in his own work. He is in competition for this girl Cleo (that is, for the identity element we can call Odets' Muse) with his father-in-law, who decisively proclaims, with no trace of his son-in-law's shame and doubt, *"I want what I want!"* This is the polarity between that aspect of Odets' identity structure which (like his mother's) is deadened by a fearful, proper, and obsessional paralysis, and his insistence on a full, joyful, and maximal experience of life which would "exclude nothing," and which he thought would therefore be "disobedient" and "evil."

Advising the meek Ben Stark he is an iceberg, half-dead, who excludes so much from awareness and action that there is no "play" in him, the older man recommends to the younger that he regain elbow room, leeway, and, thus, vitality before it's too late: "You'll be dead soon enough." Judah Prince concludes with an extraordinarily bold, locomotive proposal which in 1938 was synonymous with saying, "Undertake the visionary, the impossible." He says to the only half-alive dentist, "Explode, take a rocket to the moon!" supplying here the title for the play eagerly awaited by director Harold Clurman and then-actor, Elia Kazan.

The other pole of Odets' conflict is jotted in a "production note" in the margin: "Motto: 'You don't easily give up a home if you have been an orphan' ".[40] This caution issues from a person terrified to make a great leap lest he fall into an abyss.

So delighted were the Group Theatre actors that Odets had finally brought his new play that they swallowed their disappointment that he had completed only two acts. All agreed the three major characters were among his best and most mature yet. Director Clurman found himself, however, unsettled by what appeared from these two acts to be a significant shift away from the original plan of the play about a constricted man who stops "playing it safe" and who bursts *his* bonds by a union with a liberating young *anima*, the girl Cleo. "Awakened" by his love for this girl, Odets had said, he would undergo a ravaging depth of experience which, despite the girl's childish self-absorption, would increase his stature as a man and propel the growth hitherto blocked. As Clurman now listened to Odets read his first two acts, it appeared to him that subtly, the play's center—without sufficient psychological justification in Odets' development of her character—had shifted to the girl Cleo and that the play's focus had radically changed from that of a man torn between two women to a girl freeing herself from two men.

Moreover, with a new prominence for the worldly Prince (a man who recommends himself as someone who "don't look foolish before authority"), quite a different triangle had been created, with the aspiring girl instead of the frightened dentist at its apex. The play's theme had originally centered on the question of whether the timid and dependently vulnerable man could break through the enveloping, dead wasteland of his static and submerged existence by an explosive and creative thrust (a "rocket to the moon") toward a fresh, young (amorphously talented), girl in quest of both love and of self-expression. It had been conceived as the man's play, and the struggle was to be his. Now, the theme appeared to have moved from him to the girl even as Odets had moved from his failed struggle for intimacy with his wife to the broader issues of his own creativity or generativity: Carrying the responsibility for the recent destruction of his first unborn *biological* child, he deeply feared that his stagnation would extend to his "brain-children" as well. The characterer, Cleo, his Muse, now bore the burden of reestablishing his generativity. It was disquietingly clear to director Clurman that something significant in Odets' emotional life had intervened between the first outline of this play and the present two acts, throwing out of kilter the formal dramatic structure. He devoutly hoped the still unwritten third act would dispel his fear that the character, Cleo, had run away with the play, confusing its formal structure sufficiently to sabotage both its aesthetic unity and its commercial success.

An interesting question for study here is: how had an experienced playwright of great skill begun with one play and ended with another? [41]

For over a year, Odets had been seriously blocked in his work, had had a dismaying *sense of loss of emotional connection to his wife and of creative connection to the growing crisis in the immediate events of world history.* He sensed only dimly that the deeper connection in his current work to the unfolding of history lay in its reflection of an increasingly urgent conflict between the values of salesmanship and an innocent creativity. His notes suggest he was seeing both his wife and his father as "the enemy," while finding it increasingly difficult to identify "the enemy" as a simple, political-economic order with which he could do battle as he had in the past. The references in *Rocket* to the villainy of the economic system are perfunctory and hollow.

Now that his marriage was coming to an end, it must have appeared to him that, despite his loneliness and shame at this failure, he had a second chance, a fresh start in his *primary*—his most "real"—self-identity as an honest artist, if not as a husband or father. His *anima* (Cleo) says, "*It's getting late to play at life: I want to live it . . . something has to feel real.*"

It is as if Odets falls back to an earlier stage in his development and hopes this time for a firmer resolution at least of his work identity and for a renewal of his generativity as playwright. He will find the "real reality" in his brain-children, a safer fatherhood, he felt, than of a flesh-and-blood baby.

In *Rocket to the Moon,* for the first time in his life, Odets was writing a play which does not culminate in some kind of crippling or catastrophe: injury to his creative "hands," suicide, or death. A key tragedy of his childhood, it will be recalled, was the "abandonment" of him by his mother in favor of his crippled sister. It is this personal sense of disinheritance which had cogwheeled with the collective sense of disinheritance in the Depression era. *Rocket* is a desperate turn to a psychological instead of an economic deliverance. It is an adumbration of the reach in American cultural history—three decades later—toward self-actualizing (inner) values. In *Golden Boy,* written by Odets the year before, Joe Bonaparte, who has irrevocably lost himself as a violinist by crippling his hands in a prizefight, cries out in a climactic, locomotor defiance of gravity, "We're off the earth!" and—while the "money-men" are dividing shares of him—the speeding automobile incinerates Joe and his girl in Babylon, Long Island. It is the paradigm of the price paid for the machines and the worldly values inherent in the American dream.

Here, while there recurs the image of an escape from the constricting pull of a "Mother Earth," it is in a rocket, a machine even more powerful than an automobile and this time with the intrepid thrust of a confident citizen of a virile, technological world-power. The emotional tone of the rocket image is not suicidal but freely adventurous and open; of a man still on an explosive American frontier. With the impulsive surge of personal liberation from the constrictions of immigrant terror, the image is of a twentieth-century American conquistador planting his flag in unmapped territory (the feminine moon). Wholly different from the apocalyptic locomotor image which closes *Golden Boy,* or even from that of a businesslike astronaut, a "rocket to the moon" is filled with hope, initiative, and even a promise of a peak experience of freedom.

I wish there were space to discuss *Rocket to the Moon* "beat by beat." Only by following each of its dramatic moves in microscopic detail is it possible to see the specificity with which the data support the two working hypotheses I propose. I will try here to state the essentials.

With a pace and a focus of intent rare in dramatic literature, Odets manages in the first distilled "beat" of the very first scene to get into the heart of the play's conflict and its *apparent* theme: there is an immediate confrontation between the frightened, isolated dentist, Ben Stark and his scolding wife, Belle.[42] Their conflict commences in a sensory web of heat and claustrophobic *imprisonment*. He wants to "specialize," to grow, and she, like Odets' father, gives practical reasons against it, reasons which stifle his growth. By a most economic exchange, the playwright ends the first round, with the controlling wife, Belle, the victor. Indeed, she has won even before the play opens and when she concludes the opening beat with, "Any day now I'm expecting to have to powder and diaper you," she has established herself as the parent, the boss, the *obstacle* in the path of the aspiring Ben Stark's creative growth. As the play opens the conflict between these two—husband and wife—appears to be its theme.

The connective tissue of the play, as in a musical fugue, derives from fragments of this announced theme: Belle says her husband must not simply agree to *do* as she says; he must also "see that I am right," play it safe, and not try to expand his practice and creative work. He, who was once a "pioneer with Gladstone in orthodontia" (in making straight and whole that which is crooked) has already lowered his creative sights to tooth pulling and to cultivating petunias in a flower box, and his income to one-tenth of what "men with half my brains and talent are making." "If he had to go get a passport, it would become a terrific event in his life."[43] The fact that he is a dentist, not a doctor, is already a comedown in the "good prototypes" of Jewish middle-class life. But Belle does not approve his creative collaboration with Gladstone in dentistry, any more than did Odets' father approve of Harry Kemp or his wife Luise Rainer approve his association with Clurman in the Group Theatre. Even Ben's last-ditch attempts to nurture (to generate) his sadly drooping little flowers which his secretary calls his "orphan babies" are immediately revealed in the first few minutes as fumbling and inept:

STARK: I wanted to do something . . . what was it? not a drink . . . Oh, the flowers! (He fills a paper cup, puts his pipe between his teeth and tries without success, one hand full to fill a second cup.)

BELLE: Try one at a time, dear.

STARK: (Coolly) One at a time is a good idea. (At the window, right, he pours the water on a window box of drooping petunias. As he turns for more water he faces Belle who has brought him a second cupful.) Thanks.

BELLE: (Smiling) Any day now I'm expecting to have to powder and diaper you.[44]

In these few lines between the initial major player and counterplayer, the husband and wife, there stands a distilled illustration of the way a playwright juggles and adjusts the conflicts and the "moves" of his internal "gallery of characters"—that is, of his own identity elements and fragments—to the external masks of the people in his past and present worlds.

In this short exchange much is reflected: Odets' conviction at that time that his wife—like his father—chronically wished to criticize, denigrate, and control him and his work (Ben's petunias), as well as to convert, reform, and direct him. There are reflected other paradigms as well. Odets has condensed in the dentist's relation to his controlling, depressed wife not only his own responses to his father's tyranny, but also to the mood of his melancholy mother and the steady (internalized) combat between his parents. Were it not for the fact of Odets' own struggle between his longing to surrender, abdicating all autonomy, initiative, and responsibility (as he had long ago sat obediently for hours on his little chair, waiting), and his impulse to "explode," there would be no conflict and no play. In his production notes, Odets wrote of Stark, "He is a man who suffers because he can't make important decisions easily . . . fears scenes and fights. . . . If he feels it is a matter of principle, he can stand up, otherwise, he may cave in. . . . Principle is a shield where the self can be forgotten."

Ben Stark's physical ineptitude, his indecisiveness, an expression of Odets' own sense of incompetence, like his mother's, takes its contemporary external shape, however, from Clurman's clumsiness in practical undertakings. It was a steady source of banter in the Group Theatre that Clurman—like Ben Stark—could scarcely open a package of cigarettes, was unable to use a can-opener, and would say "Hello" without picking up the telephone receiver. Odets often said, "Gadg Kazan is Harold's muscle and his legs."

Odets, himself, consciously thought of Ben Stark's meek obedience to his wife's disdainful will ("You win, you win," he says to her wearily) as simply a literal copy of Clurman's compliance with the powerful Stella Adler. Not so. These characters are all configurations and subconfigurations of identity elements with Odets' own self, organized long before he met Clurman or Stella Adler. Such are the complexities of joining an inner gallery of characters with the playwright's actual contemporaries from whom he is said to have "taken" his cast of characters.

This is a good example of how misleading it is to make a one-to-one biographic correlation between the playwright as protagonist, and the people in his life as "supporting cast." To be sure, those in the playwright's life space, most especially members of a family, or even of a gifted acting company like the Group Theatre, call out his own internal "gallery," providing the masks for the characters who people his play. It is no accident, for example, that actor Morris Carnovsky always played the "spiritual" parts in Odets' plays, while Kazan was usually cast, as Odets put it, as the "original getahead boy." Odets regularly used each of the Group Theatre members as a mask for his own warring identity elements and fragments, and was actually helped to create whole persons (lovingly and fully) by reason of the independent existence of these excellent actors.

As the play moves on through this first act, with the playwright keeping the polyphonic conflicts alive while offering expository material, minor characters, crackling dialogue, and lovely jokes, we see reverberations not only of Odets' struggles with his wife and of his grief about their aborted child, but also of his own earlier trail of dead or aborted children, creative as well as biological. This is a play in which the people steadily reveal themselves. Belle Prince Stark, ironically calling herself "your terrible wife," as Odets' wife, in fact, often had—says, in Luise Rainer's actual words, "You have to love me all the time . . . a woman wants to live *with* a man, not next to him," adding she has been "blue all morning," thinking of their dead baby.

Throughout this first act of *Rocket to the Moon,* it is evident that the playwright initially intended the central question to be: Will this frightened individual summon the courage to break his bondage and fulfill his life by a love affair or will he play it safe, abdicate his growth, and be like the enslaved immigrant who continues to the end (in the words of Bob Dylan, born Robert Zimmerman) to "passionately hate his life and likewise fear his death?"

After the initial victory in the first scene of the wife (Belle) over the husband (Ben), the girl (Cleo) enters, and the play appears ready again to move forward. We are forewarned, however, of the increasing imbalance in the play's structure by the fact that the protagonist (Ben Stark) is, from the beginning, the least interesting character. He is the quiet observer, the static center, and, if the playwright had maintained him as the central character, the play would never have moved forward. Moreover, we have seen early hints that the new triangle is building, with the two men competing for the girl. While it is difficult to care what will happen between Ben and the sexy, stockingless Cleo Singer,[45] dressed in "angel-skin satin," the interchange between the passionate old man and this girl is from the outset arresting, enlivening, and involving. Clearly it is in *their* relationship that the playwright sees the formidable threat to the American artist: in the struggle between worldly and creative values. To the extent that it was difficult for the audience to see Cleo as a symbol of creativity, to that extent was the play a failure.

Obviously unsuited to her job and as inefficient in it as Odets in his youth had been in all of his, Cleo is like him, an insecure name-dropper and fabricator; she lies that her mother was an opera *singer* (her surname) in Europe and that "I come from a well-to-do family . . . I really don't need this job." Later, Ben says to her, "Everyone tells little fables, Cleo. Sometimes to themselves, sometimes to others. Life is so full of brutal facts . . . we all try to soften them by making believe." Cleo, the storyteller—the artist—becomes now (psychologically) *the central identity element in the play, though not yet the central character in its formal structure.* The fables she tells are the effort to make life bearable by "making believe." Precisely this is the work of a playwright: to make himself and other people believe in a reality he creates. Manifestly, however, at this early stage of the game, Cleo appears to be no more than a shallow rival to the oppressive Belle Prince Stark who is simultaneously patrolling many beats, strengthening her hand not only against the girl in this first triangle but on all those who are making her husband's office "inefficient." She is calling everyone to heel and trying to hold her barren fort in a status-quo position. As she leaves the office, we are introduced to the play's third major character, Mr. Judah Prince. Odets describes him in terms clearly recognizable as belonging to his father, L. J. Odets, yet with more affection and empathy than usual. Consciously, he thought he had modeled this character after Stella Adler's father, tragedian Jacob Adler, attorney Max Steuer, and the Yiddish actor, Tomashevsky:

He is near sixty, wears an old panama hat, a fine Palm Beach suit of twenty years ago and a malacca cane. There is about him the dignity and elegant portliness of a Jewish actor, a sort of aristocratic air. He is an extremely self-confident man with a strong sense of humor which, however, is often veiled. He is very alive in the eyes and mouth, the rest of him relaxed and heavy. (p. 339)[46]

His daughter no longer speaks to him because of the dreadful life he had given her dead mother, a punitive silence to be meted out much later by Odets to his own father. "I am the American King Lear," says Mr. Prince, whose dreams of self-realization—like the secret aspiration of the senior Odets to be a writer—have come to nothing: "In our youth we collect materials to build a bridge to the moon," Stark comments, "but in our old age we use the materials to build a shack."

The charged excitement between the sensual, worldly old man and the aspiring young person (read, artist)—as so often in an Odets play—is immediate and unmistakable; as it was between the equivalent characters of Moe and Hennie in *Awake and Sing!* or gangster Eddie Fuseli and fighter-musician Joe Bonaparte in *Golden Boy*. Structurally, it is clear something new is starting here: The old man tells the girl he likes her honesty and that "everything that's healthy is personal." He adds (as Odets' father often said of himself and his son) that he and she are identical. She aspires to being a dancer and he, *"without marriage"* could have been, he thinks, "a great actor." He was also once, he tells her, an idealist. In all of this, the old man is clearly making a move toward the girl. Structurally, by dint of this move, the play has shifted ground: alongside the original triangle of husband, wife, and aspirant girl there stands now a new one: that of husband, aspirant girl, and father-in-law. Prince, like Odets' father, announces he has been made to "play safe" by *his* wife even as Belle (his daughter) now urges Ben, her husband to do. ("A housewife rules your destiny," says Prince to Stark, adding he had "disappeared in the corner with the dust, under the rug" and lives a dull life "where every day is Monday.")

Although Judah Prince boasts that he still earns money, he bitterly asks to whom shall he leave it all, "to Jascha Heifetz?" Addressing himself, and simultaneously his son-in-law, he asks, "Is this the life you dreamed?" The answer is no, he thinks, for both of them and the path to salvation is clear:

PRINCE: (Suddenly turning, hand on door knob, pointing his cane at Stark and lowering his voice to a near whisper) Iceberg, listen . . . why don't you come up and see the world, the sea gulls and the ships to Europe? (Coming back into the room) When did you look at another woman last? The year they put the buffalo nickel on the market? Why don't you suddenly ride away, an airplane, a boat! Take a rocket to the moon! Explode!

> What holds you back? You don't want to hurt Belle's feelings?
> You'll die soon enough. . . .

STARK: I'll just have to laugh at that!

PRINCE: Laugh . . . but make a motto for yourself: "Out of the coffin by
Labor Day!" Have an affair with—with—this girl . . . this Miss
Cleo. She'll make you a living man again. (p. 350)[47]

By making himself one flesh with an innocent, growing girl, Prince
assures Ben he will be creatively activated by sex, a formula often alter-
nated by Odets, in his own frenzied life, with sexual abstinence. It is as if
(some of the time) he regarded the feminine aspect of himself as the
source of his generativity which would be brought to life by sexual union.
This element is in conflict with that of the worldly American businessman
who, though magnetic, is ruthless, exploitative, senses-bound, self-centered, lonely and fundamentally out of touch with his own creativity, with
the "play" in himself. By reason of his richness, this character, Judah
Prince, threatens to "run away" with *Rocket to the Moon*, as does his
equivalent character in so many of Odets' plays.

Act One closes with the inhibited Ben Stark looking out at the "Hotel
Algiers," modeled after the seamy Columbus Circle Hotel of Odets's
youth (a symbol to him of sexual vitality and forbidden freedom). At the
windows of this teeming place, he used literally to peep at "real life," in
order, he reasoned, to gather material for his plays.

As Cleo leaves, she reminds Ben of his dreary coffin of an existence:
"Your wife expects you home at seven." It is not these routines Odets
fears, rather it is that in the "real" intimacy of marriage he will disappear
as an artist. ("A man falls asleep in marriage," says Ben.) Thus Odets, on
some level, is convinced that a continuing intimacy with a woman
threatens his creativity.

The second act of *Rocket to the Moon* opens in sharp contrast to the
first: the girl, Cleo is offering Ben cool water to comfort him in the hellish
heat of this summer.[48] Unlike his wife, who wants him to play life safe,
she does not deprive him, fight him, seek to reform, and ultimately to
possess and control, him as though he were her lost baby. Indeed, Cleo
expresses her own reassuring determination never to marry: "It's too sordid," she says.

By now, it is becoming apparent to Mr. Prince that his obsessive son-
in-law—whose mentor for a fuller life he has tried to be—will not leave

his wife, nor even seek to renew himself by having an affair with Cleo. Accordingly, he makes his own dramatic "move," and, in a richly ornamented (indeed brilliant) scene of power and restraint, he is on the seductive attack. Like Odets himself, he is a "student of the human insect," flirting, teasing, and promising. He tells her she is "talking to a man with a body like silk" who "possesses the original teeth, every one" (*he* has no need for a dentist!), and "in all the multitudes of your acquaintanceship you won't find a man with younger ideas than your present speaker." True, he wears high-heeled shoes because "I don't like to be so small," but if she will put herself in his hands, he will help her to learn and to grow.

Just as in *Awake and Sing!*, where the powerful racketeer Moe Axelrod offers Havana on a silver platter to the girl Hennie, or in *Golden Boy* where gangster Eddie Fuseli promises fame and fortune to the violinist-fighter Joe, and the gangster Kewpie, a soft life to Libby in *Paradise Lost,* so now does Mr. Prince offer Cleo not only his money but his deep understanding of her needs ("My girl, I studied you like a scientist"). This same identity element would assume the form of the Hollywood film executive in Odets' later play, *The Big Knife*. The price, in each play, for material power (that is, attachment to the senses, not to money) is surrender of one's integrity and freedom.

Cleo, like an identity element of Odets himself, is naive, quick to take offense, frightened, fragile, and unsupported. She fears ridicule for her yearning to become a dancer (a clear echo of L. J. Odets' taunts to his son when he aspired to being an actor) and is convinced no one loves her : "Millions of people moving around the city and nobody cares if you live or die." She will, in revenge (as Odets had often, in fact, contemplated) "fall down on them all," from a high building.

It takes courage, says the girl, a courage she is not sure the dentist has, "to go out to things, to new experiences," to seek an expansion, an intensification of life: of one's consciousness and expression ("Don't you think," she says, "life is to live all you can and experience everything?" Shouldn't a wife help a man do that? . . . your wife broke up your courage.") Cleo clearly speaks Odets' struggle to establish himself as the "center of awareness in a universe of experience," unfettered by arbitrary inner and outer restriction. It is an innocent expression of Erikson's description of the very nature of "I-ness." [49]

A minor character cries, "Diphtheria gets more respect than me . . .

why can't they fit me in, a man of my talents?" The nineteen-year-old Cleo replies, "Just because you're sad you can't make me sad. No one can. I have too much in me! . . . I have a throat to sing with, a heart to love with! Why don't you love me Dr. Stark?" Ben, like Odets, smiles when he can't meet a situation. As this first scene in Act Two ends, Cleo announces that not Stark "or any other man" deserves her. This statement turns the central theme of the play from an inhibited dentist's struggle over whether to have an affair, to the aspiration of a young, unfulfilled artist. Taking this initiative, her answer to the question "how should one live?"—boldly or timidly—is unmistakable:

CLEO: (Shyly) I'll call you Benny in a minute! (after a throb of hesitation) Ben! Benny! . . . (They are standing off from each other, poised on needles) Don't be afraid. . . .
STARK: . . . No? . . .
CLEO: Love me. . . . Love me, Ben.
STARK: . . . Can't do that. . . .
CLEO: (Moving forward a step) Put your arms up and around me.
STARK: Cleo. . . . (Now they move in on each other. Everything else gone, they are together in a full, fierce embrace, together in a swelter of heat, misunderstanding, loneliness, and simple sex.) (pp. 379–80).[50]

The initiative *must* come from the girl; had Odets left it to the paralyzed identity element represented by the character of Stark, nothing would happen. Cleo, like Odets, always afraid of repudiation, is for the moment confirmed, and Ben Stark is breaking his long sleep to give rein to his impulse, with this girl. Perhaps, he dreams, it will restore his "power for accomplishment" lost through "unhappy marriage." A man who "don't get much personal satisfaction out of his work . . . is a lost man."

Another minor character who functions psychologically as a negative identity fragment in the play "glistens with arrogance." He, too, is trying to seduce Cleo, whose "jingling body" is a magnet. She is impressed by this man whose very name suggests a smooth, shiny surface: Willy Wax. "A man who gets his name in the paper so often," she says, "must be important to some people" (p. 382). Willy Wax is a caricature of the sexual predator who is at the same time a Spurious Artist. This is Odets' unconscious fear of what he could become were he to accede to the worst of his father within himself. Group Theatre actor Sanford Meisner, cast in this

part, recalled him with utter distaste, a man "with no redeeming feature."
"Movies," says Wax, "started me off on my path of painless perversion"
(p. 386). Director Clurman told the cast about this character, *He plays
with his talents.* His adjustment is a constant perversion of himself," and
Odets has added in the margin of the production notes, "He likes to as-
tound and impress . . . actually he is worn out, alienated." Not yet
thirty-three, Odets' terrified vision of his future lay tucked into this dis-
tasteful minor character.

It is not accidental that the play's motion has been taken from the
middle-aged, imprisoned dentist, Ben, and given to the nineteen-year-old
anima, Cleo. Odets finds himself at this time in a new edition of his central—essentially unresolved—adolescent identity crisis: whether to play
life safe and to become the kind of stereotyped householder his father
wanted him to be, obediently writing advertising copy for the Odets
Company, and rearing a family; or in the style of a priest (or a romantic
artist) giving first priority, before everything else, to the creation and
communication of *his* vision of life. This was, of course, not a conscious,
voluntary decision when he was nineteen, nor is it now at thirty-two. Art
deals not in a deliberate choice among a number of possibilities, only in
necessities. The "necessity" in *this* play is reflected first in the creation of
the submerged dentist as the central character. He is a man who has
abandoned his creativity. But, it emerges, Odets could not emotionally
"afford" to open up this static man and risk a violent confrontation with
the powerful Mr. Prince.

In the discussion which followed the original presentation of this material, playwright Arthur Miller said:

. . . *there is a terror underneath* (this play), *which stopped it from being
written* . . . my own feeling about the play (is that) there is a phantomlike
quality about it, which was one of the things that always drew me to
Odets. I could never understand how he was equated with realism, naturalism, or even social drama, after *Waiting for Lefty.* I think he is dealing
with phantoms. . . . In this play, he is raising conflicts which he never
engages in. There is a projection of myself into this, but that's the way it
is. . . . This play is a measurement—not in a moral sense, but in another
sense—of values, life values . . . and it seems to me that the showdown,
the climax, the unveiling which he is always promising, will have to
engage a real knockdown fight, between the dentist and that old man.
. . . Now there is a conceivable end to his play where the *Life Force* escapes all of them, and they are left in effect with no Force. Cleo, ridi-

culed, with her make believe and lying, a fairly pathetic creature, walks
out and with her walks out (ironically enough) all their lives, because she
somehow embodied their aspirations. There is a fear which is probably
very complicated, of just the conflict he proposed . . . which is a very
common thing in playwrights.

Miller continued: "It would involve some disaster which is too great a
price to pay, and consequently the conflict is aborted before it got started.
Of course, he can let her [Cleo] be free because her struggle is not a
menace to him, that's a free-flowing thing—he can create enough distance
towards it to allow it to happen. But these other two—he has too much of
an investment in, and they would really knock him to pieces if he would
allow them to come to blows, and *there would be nothing left of him.*
[Italics mine.] That's the kind of terror that casts a pall over the vivid-
ness."[51] The biographic data of Odets' life support Miller's impression of
an overload of anxiety attached to the *unconscious aspects* of Odets' conflict among the identity elements, experienced as the "corrupt" materialist
(Prince), the innocent "idealist" (Cleo), and the obsessively blocked intellectual (Stark).

Faced with this emotional dilemma, Odets tried thus in midstream to
find a safe *structural* solution by placing the heart of the play into the
hands of the identity element, Artist, trapped in a family where they
laugh at her wish to be a dancer. Here, he runs no risk of an unmanage-
able confrontation. However, it is precisely in this shift of focus that the
play's structure becomes confused, and for most critics (representing most
audiences), difficult to follow. The playwright does not quite succeed in
persuading his audience that Cleo is the identity element representing
their unconscious longing for creative fulfillment. The audience has not
been sufficiently prepared for so large a responsibility to be put on the
shoulders of a stockingless girl who wears "angel-skin satin."

With the Aspiring Artist Cleo at the center of the action, she is
wooed by all the men in the play: Odets' Muse is torn between the
sybarite Mr. Prince (Artist Manqué), the safe Ben—who has sacrificed
creativity for security—and the Corrupt Artist Willy Wax who warns her
she is "living in the city of the dreadful night" wherein a "man is coarse or
he doesn't survive." As for Cleo, ". . . even her breasts stand at attention. Alas, she is not yet wise in the ways of the world" (p. 384).

When the dentist's controlling wife—who counsels security—suddenly appears in his office, Ben is touched—as Odets had often been by

his own wife—by her loneliness and by her efforts to stir his jealousy. But her offer to *replace* Cleo as his assistant is an intolerable invasion, exactly like Odets' experience of his wife's efforts "to help" him in his work and to make a mutual career of their marriage. ("A man's office is his castle," says the dentist.)

His compassion and his tolerance come to an end as she states her suspicions. Finally he blazes out:

"Will you stop that stuff for a change! It's about time you began to realize there are two ends to a rope. I have needs, too! This one-way street has to end! I'm not going to stay under water like an iceberg the rest of my life. You've got me licked—I must admit it. All right, I'm sleeping, I don't love you enough. But what do *you* give? What do you know about my *needs?*" (p. 393)

Now, in a duplication of many such dialogues Odets had had with his wife, Ben continues: "It's like we're enemies. We're like two exposed nerves! . . . These scenes go on . . . we're always worried. We're two machines counting up the petty cash. Something about me cheats you—I'm not the man to help you be the best woman it's in you to be" (p. 395). The internal subconfiguration here is the struggle between the passive, deadened, and demobilized identity element of Ben Stark—which oppressed Odets' mother and does now him—and his Muse, Cleo Singer, the "radium girl" who gives off heat, light, and creative energy. The inner war is between the playwright's wish to be a "safe" householder and an adventurous Creator.

The second act closes with the dentist making a declaration of love to Cleo; he is now desperately jealous of both his rivals: the urbane Prince as well as the Spurious Artist, Willy Wax. He says, "You're more important to me than anything I know Cleo, dear," and her closing plea is, "Don't let me be alone in the world, Ben . . . don't let me be alone" (p. 397). The girl is using all power at her disposal to force the relationship with the dentist into an overt sexual affair. Here again these externalized relationships mirror the internal struggle.

If this exchange is understood solely on its manifest level—as it was by the critics in 1938—it is baffling what it is that has moved the dentist to the conviction that this storytelling, naive child who is steadily "making believe" has become "more important than anything I know" in Ben's life. If, however, we assume the identity element of the innocent Cleo to be Odets' *anima,* the Aspiring Artist, rather than simply the "jingling body" of a lovely girl, his capitulation to her makes sense. The confusion of these two levels of meaning has issued in many baffled discussions in drama textbooks.

The third act opens with the dentist and his wife silent, "each one revolving in his own tight little world." She is ready in her desperation to "forget" his affair with the girl if he will agree "it was only a thing of the moment." Impulsively ("anything to blot out this pale ghost before him") he cries, "Yes, yes!" but immediately finds himself twisting and saying, "It can't be settled in a minute, Belle. . . . I have a *responsibility*." He cannot agree to his wife's scream, "Your first responsibility's to me! You hear that?" Again, unless we seek a meaning beyond the manifest level, Ben's statement is baffling.

The key to this mysterious exchange lies in the word "responsibility." On the surface, it makes no sense that a man uses this word to his wife to describe his duty to a nineteen-year-old paramour. If, however, we ask what is the latent meaning—the underlying structure—of the word "responsibility" here, it begins to hang together. It refers to Odets' *allegiance to his own talent* ("Talent must be respected," he said). Their heated exchange sums up the position of an artist battling for his creative life. The struggle is only manifestly with his wife's demand that he give up the girl.[52]

Unaware that his underlying dilemmas in the play issue in part from his own current struggles with intimacy and generativity, Odets has his protagonist, the dentist (who is almost forty and yet "feels like a boy"), ponder what people get out of life "anyway" when he asks Frenchy, a bachelor chiropodist,[53] if he does not want marriage and children. In their ensuing dialogue on the nature of love and the difficulty of discovering it "in this day of stresses," this "nervous time," Frenchy declares happy marriages are rare "like the dodo bird" and sternly advises his friend to be practical, "leave the morals out. . . . Never mind the shame and guilt":

FRENCHY: (With extreme seriousness) Love? Depends on what you mean by love. Love, for most people, is a curious sensation below the equator. . . .
STARK: You're that good, you think?
FRENCHY: (correcting him): That *bad*, Doc! She'll have to be the good one. This is why: Love is a beginning, a jumping-off place. It's like what heat is at the forge—makes metal easy to handle and shape. *But love and the grace to use it!*—To develop, expand it, variate it!—Oh, dearie me, that's the problem, as the poet said!

Frenchy now offers a definition of love singularly close to Erikson's view of the developmental achievement of intimacy:

FRENCHY: Who can do that today? Who's got the time and place for "love and the grace to use it"? Is it something apart, love? A good book you go to in a spare hour? An entertainment? Christ, no! it's a synthesis of good and bad, economics, work, play, all contacts . . . it's not a Sunday suit for special occasions. That's why Broadway songs are phony, Doc!—Love is no solution of life! *Au contraire*, as the Frenchman says—the opposite. You have to bring a whole balanced normal life to love if you want it to go!

What Odets called his "slow exhaustion, this shame" over his failed marriage and his fear of precisely the kind of intimacy he has just described is promptly retracted in Frenchy's next words, which would be a pleasure to any member of a contemporary women's liberation front:

FRENCHY: In this day of stresses I don't see much normal life, myself included. The woman's not a wife. She's the dependent of a salesman who can't make sales and is ashamed to tell her so. . . . (p. 404)

Odets thus tries to understand his marital failure, his isolation, and the nature of his creative struggles in terms of the "stresses of the time." He is, of course, both right and wrong.

As the cynical chiropodist leaves this scene with the injunction that the dentist must choose between the girl and his wife—reviving the manifest conflict which opened the play—the latent meaning is once again underscored: the playwright must choose between his own development as an artist and the demands of a "normal, married life." His (partly unconscious) dilemma lies in whether he is wedded to the "real" world of relationships with other living humans or to a constructed world, peopled by the characters into whom *he* breathes life, who are, of course, the distribution of *himself*. It is a world he hopes to control. When Belle, his wife, pushes him to make this choice, it is more on the basis of a moral obligation than a mutually nurturant relationship. Moreover, real children, unlike brain-children, "break too easy," he says, and become (in Bacon's words) "hostages to fortune."

At this point, the other major threat to Odets' creativity reappears: Carrying an umbrella with a "fancily carved dog's head of ivory" for a handle ("A quiet dog always bites," he says, smiling smoothly), Mr. Prince, calling himself "King Midas," [54] confidently announces *his* intention to marry "Miss Cleo." Having dreamed the "secret of the world," namely, that "It is not good for Man to live alone," he is determined to capture his prize by offering her "maturity and experience in every-thing—love, what to eat, where, what to wear, and where to buy it—an eye turned *out* to the world!" Translation: The identity element which is flooded with desire for sensual and material fulfillment and power com-petes now with creative aspiration: *the eye turned in.*

When the dentist says, "And you dare to think you'll buy that girl? You're a damned smiling villain!," Judah Prince replies with a remarkable and passionate speech which signaled the by-now bewildered critics that the play's theme was "man's search for love":

PRINCE: Listen, a man in the fullness of his life speaks to you. I didn't come here to make you unhappy. I came here to make *myself happy!* You don't like it—I can understand that. Circumstances insulted me enough in my life. But *your* insults I don't need! And I don't apologize to no man because I try to take happiness by the throat! Remember, Dr. Benny, I want what I want! There are seven fundamental words in life, and one of these is love, and I didn't have it! And another one is love, and I don't have it! *And the third of these is love, and I shall have it!* (Beat-ing the furniture with his umbrella.) *De Corpso* you think! I'm dead and buried you think! I'll sit in the long winter night with a shawl on my shoulders? Now you see my face, Dr. Benny. Now you know your father-in-law, that damned smiling villain! I'll fight you to the last ditch—you'll get mowed down like a train.[55] I want that girl. I'll wait downstairs. When she returns I'll come right up, in five minutes. I'll test *your* sanity!—*You*, you Nobel prize winner! (He stops, exhausted, wipes his face with a large silk handkerchief, does the same to the umbrella head and then slowly exits). (p. 408)

The identity element embodied in Mr. Prince is not simply the nega-tive aspect of Odets' partial identification with his salesman father. In-deed, when this many-faceted character protests he *will* have love, it is Odets' own passionate statement that he cannot live a life without human intimacy. ("I love your needs!" Prince says to Cleo.) But this longing for intimacy wars with his wish to be a self-sufficient artist responsible only for what he generates on the stage, and not for a flesh-and-blood wife or their children. Just as Prince is more interesting than Ben Stark precisely because he harbors many strong polarities, so is *Rocket to the Moon* a more interesting play than the "political" *Waiting for Lefty*, where one end of a conflict is ploughed under, leaving a cast of simple characters in a simple play, all on one note.

There occurs now a short interlude between the dentist and the Spurious Artist, Willy Wax. The latter, just come from his own unsuccessful attempt to seduce the girl, says, "Your little Neon light spluttered right in my face," adding she is old-fashioned and "belongs somewhere in the last century."[56] This is Odets speaking not so much of a sexpot as of the virtues of integrity and of creative conscience. Ben Stark pleads with Wax, here representing artistic prostitution, not to corrupt the aspiring girl, to "keep away from her," as she is "young, extremely naive. . . . You might warp her for life. . . . She's a mere mechanism to you." This sentence expresses Odets' steady fear that his own identity fragment (Spurious Artist) could seduce him into an abdication of his gift, and into the film industry. Cleo, however, turns in a fury on this would-be seducer, Wax, saying; "Mr. Wax, we don't want you around this office. You make love very small and dirty. I understand your type very well now. No man can take a bite out of me, like an apple and throw it away. Now go away, and we won't miss you" (p. 411).

When she turns back to the helpless dentist, a man as "mixed up as the 20th Century," she finds him evasive, collapsed, on the point of tears, and unable to leave either his wife or the "prison office" of his life. He can say to her only, "Help me."[57] Only the small voice of that fragment of himself represented by the chiropodist, Frenchy, asks the opposite question, "What can I do for the girl, Cleo? What will she be in ten years *with my help?*"

The indomitable old man makes one last strong bid for the girl. She, in turn, asks the dentist if he will leave his barren wife, and he—consumed with fear and guilt—can say nothing at all. He is chained and sterile. The dentist's "decision" occurs by default; it is helplessly passive, not active. With the character of Stark having clearly gone beyond his emotional depth, and unable to handle the "mistake" of his intimacy with the girl, he is inarticulate. When Cleo asks, "What do you say, Ben?" Odets writes, "Stark (lost): Nothing. . . . I can't say. . . . . . nothing."

Here is a good example of the reflection in the play's overburdened structure of the playwright's inner fractures. Given the premises of the opening of the play (a man who will be forced to a choice between a wife and a mistress), the closing climax *should* be Ben choosing between Belle

and Cleo. But, as we have seen, there slowly emerged on this initial triangle a superimposed one, among Ben, Prince, and Cleo, and the play took
on the fuzziness of a double exposure, with the playwright emotionally
unable fully to loose the players and counterplayers into the struggle in either triangle. Thus, with Ben (the character originally at the play's center)
immobilized, it falls to the characters of Cleo and Prince to propel the
play to its end. Prince says of Stark, "He won't leave her. That needs
courage, strength, and he's not strong."

Cleo makes a last stab at passing the initiative back to the evasive,
lost Ben. His response is soft and defeated: "Listen, Cleo . . . think.
What can I give you? All I can offer you is a second-hand life, dedicated to
trifles and troubles . . . and they go on forever. This isn't self-justification
. . . but facts are stubborn things, Cleo; I've wrestled with myself for
weeks. This is how it must end" (p. 415).

When Judah Prince asks Cleo what she'd have to lose by a union
with *him*, she replies, "Everything that's me." The underlying meaning
here is Odets' conviction that the core of his identity lay in resisting his father's bids to surrender to him and to his values (arising from power hunger and sense satisfaction), and to become instead an honest artmaker.

As in the closing of Odets' earlier play, *Awake and Sing!* (equally
confusing to the critics), the powerful older man, identity element of
Odets' father, moves in, making a real "pitch" for the girl: "And I offer
you a vitalizing relationship: a father, counselor, lover, a friend!" In
Awake and Sing! the "equivalent" girl Hennie—mother of an illegitimate
child and subsequently married by a weak man called Sam Feinschreiber
(fine writer)[58]—succumbs and runs off with another old sybarite called
Moe (roughly the equivalent of Judah Prince).

In *Rocket to the Moon*, however, the Aspiring Artist (Cleo) makes the
final *active* statement of the play. Manifestly, she is "looking for love," but
Prince sees beyond this: he tells her she will never get what she is looking
for, namely a life with the purity of an aesthetic creation: "You want a life
like Heifetz' music—up from the roots, perfect, clean, every note in
place. But that, my girl, is music!" (p. 416).

In other words, says the playwright, only in that transcendent dis-
tillation of experience we call Art can there be found the precision, the intensity, the confident joy and serenity, and above all, the integrated and
liberating wholeness she seeks.

When Prince says to her, "You'll go down the road alone—like Charlie Chaplin?" Cleo's response and Prince's rejoinder finally clinch the hypothesis that this girl represents for Odets the identity element, Aspiring Artist:

CLEO: Yes, if there's roads, I'll take them. I'll go up all those roads till I find what I want. I want a love that uses me, that needs me. Don't you think there's a world of joyful men and women? Must all men live afraid to laugh and sing? Can't we sing at work and love our work? It's getting late to play at life; I want to *live* it. Something has to feel real to me, more than both of you. You see? I don't ask for much. . . ."
PRINCE: *She's an artist.* [Italics mine] (p. 416)

Whereas Odets' initial, conscious intention had been for the character of Ben to emerge with greater stature and confidence from the overwhelming experience of his love for this girl, it is now in fact Cleo who announces such growth: "Experience gives more confidence, you know. I have more confidence than when I came here. Button my coat, Ben" (p. 417). It is *she* who escapes the airless constriction of the dental office, not he. It is clear he will *not* return to "creative orthodontia," whereas her future is open-ended.

Prince says, "Yes, you love her. But now my iceberg boy, we have both disappeared."

In these two short sentences, there stands distilled a pardox filled with grief. On the one hand, the identity element I have called Aspiring Artist determinedly walks away, free alike from the vacillating, timid dentist lacking self-esteem, *and* from the sensual, worldly predator, *both of whom have abandoned their creativity.* Manifestly, Prince is saying both men have lost their chance for "love" (". . . we have both disappeared"). Beneath the surface, however, Odets is saying that he stands now in mortal dread that if this Muse escapes him—as Cleo does in the play—he will be left only with the internal war between the elements of a weak, constricted, and guilt-ridden indecisiveness and a strong, aggressive, and commanding sensuality. In their actual lives, *both Odets and his father* consciously felt themselves to the end of their days to be artists manqués, from whom their creativity had somehow slipped away.

Stark, in a desperate postscript, eyes flooded with tears, says, "I insist this is a beginning. Do you hear?—I insist."

"For years I sat here, taking things for granted, my wife, everything. Then just for an hour my life was in a spotlight. . . . I saw myself clearly, realized who and what I was. Isn't that a beginning? Isn't it? . . .

And this is strange! . . . For the first time in years I don't feel guilty. . . . But I'll never take things for granted again. You see? Do you see, Poppa?" (p. 418)

The play closes with Stark "almost laughing," confessing his ignorance of life: "Sonofagun! What I don't know would fill a book!" The final image is of an empty room, lit only by the lights of a hotel (where real—forbidden—life is lived) the locale of so much of Odets' actual peeping and listening: "Prince exits heavily. Stark turns out the last light, then exits, closing the door behind him. The room is dark, except for red neon lights of the Hotel Algiers and a spill of light from the hall . . . Slow curtain" (p. 418).

This last stage direction distills Odets' sense of the playwright as "witness," the man who, like all artists, cannot help distancing himself and watching his life's experience—and transposing it by way of Form—even while he lives it.

In making art one is free from inhibition and masking of emotions and fear of encounter. One ranges freely, taking *painlessly* all sides. Inactive, incapacitated, passive, arid and sterile, aware but unable and helpless—in art one becomes freely a man of action and all is possible!

In this world, one may always be the hero—loved, pitied, magnanimous, stern, strong, successful against men, women and dragons; one may forgive and even pity others—it is something god-like and absolute that the artist becomes with the exercise of what is usually his only talent. . . ."[59]

Although there is evident strain and self-doubt in Ben Stark's triumphant announcement that his identity has been significantly illumined and integrated by the play's events (". . . for an hour my life was in a spotlight. . .") it does affirm that aspect of Odets which *takes nothing for granted* (a creator). Ben declares, moreover, that "For the first time in years I don't feel guilty." While neither of these affirmations of enlightenment and freedom is persuasively buttressed in the play, we can decode the playwright's latent wish: he is saying (defensively) for the first time in any of his plays that he is determined not to surrender his creativity to the other pulls within him: the identity element of his Muse (Cleo) rejects not only the weak identity element which has fearfully abdicated creative powers (Ben), but also those which have "sold out" to the vulgarizations of

Art (Willy Wax) and to worldly fulfillment (Judah Prince). Moreover, he is here liberated from the guilt evident in all his work (even in an adolescent novel wherein the career of a promising young pianist is "cut short by an accident to his hand") and later in all his plays, wherein the moral idealists—after compromising themselves in their creativity—commit suicide, are murdered, or meet violent death.

Odets was always plagued by a lack of "aesthetic inevitability" in this play, and wondered if his wife had been correct that the seeker, Cleo, should after all surrender to the rich old sybarite, as Hennie had done in his *Awake and Sing!* Displacing his creative discontent, he would remain forever resentful on several counts: that director Clurman was so "full of ideas as to what my play was about" and had never raised the production money; that he had no leeway in which to rework the play, that he was always under emergency pressure to provide the Group Theatre with a brain-child which they would immediately gobble up; and finally, that he could not even protect his newborn progeny by directing the play himself. Almost three decades later, the memory of this time and his anger toward Clurman still fresh, he provided rich data illuminating the creative process:

He finally got to think that I was kind of like a cow who dropped a calf, didn't know anything about it. I think he still thinks that. He still thinks that when I write a play I have no idea what's in it. That I'm some kind of mad genius who just sort of drops a calf. Because this is what happened in the Group Theatre and I was very resentful of it. I dropped this calf and some people would rush up and grab it, wipe it off and take it away, and I would be left there bellowing. And while they were hustling this calf around you'd think that I had no relationship to it. I let them, too. I would let them do it, but with a great deal of resentment. I never would have let any private producer do anything of this sort. They'd go to work on it, and this one would be assisting Clurman. All the time I wanted to direct the play myself. But in order to direct the play I would have to have at least some decent distance between myself and the play. Well, that never happened. They had to have those veal chops on the table. For the next week or so everybody would go hungry. So in a certain way this gifted calf that I'm talking about, that I dropped, was also veal chops for everybody to eat.[60]

It was Odets' conviction that Clurman, together with his "sturdy crutch" Elia Kazan and the Group business manager, "ran everything, had all the fun, all the excitement and I would just stand there on my legs, like a bellowing mother cow who couldn't locate that calf I just dropped."

If this playwright's image of himself as a "bellowing mother cow," unable to locate her newborn child—the metaphor of pregnancy and an anxious delivery—were an isolated instance, or peculiar to Odets, we could not make much of it. However, the image of creation as a birth followed by the eating of "the child" (or of the forbidden fruit) occurs over and over not only in Odets' writings, but in those of a variety of creators as well as in folk legends, myths, and holy scriptures.[61]

This image appears to be one of the archetypes of the general argument I have been setting forth: this is the way a new "wholeness" emerges: by integrating the contrarieties, including feminine and masculine identity elements. Thus is a new organism created (be it a theory, a scripture, or a play), an organism that simultaneously "feeds" its originator and its audience.[62]

This originator is not far from the image of a Lord of Creation who gives manifest, concrete form to the eternal, the boundless, who breathes life into an Adam and creates an Eve from a fragment of him, who in turn instigates the eating of the forbidden fruit from the Tree of Knowledge or, as it is sometimes called, "The Tree of Life." That this player and counterplayer are then together banished from the innocent joy of trusting, unashamed celebrant children playing in Paradise, to the suffering toil of self-conscious Man—whose "plays" are now "works"—reflects a writer's witness to the vicissitudes, the joys, and the penalties of his own creativity.

4. SUMMARY AND CONCLUSIONS

I commenced with a discussion of the difficulties of the method used here; namely, that of "disciplined subjectivity" as described by Erik H. Erikson. Subscribing to the principle that this method dictates at least a general account of the investigator's relation to the segment of experience being examined, I touched on my share in that *collective identity* to which playwright Clifford Odets gave voice in the thirties. Transcending the boundaries of his own being, Odets, like all artists, draws on his inner gallery of conflicted characters—Erikson calls them identity elements—breathes authentic life into them, and tries by means of his gift to resolve their dualities. Repeating Odets' own words, "Theatre, in a certain sense, is the outward play of inner play!"

Two basic hypotheses are offered for the nature of playwriting: first, *that whatever else a play—or I would add, any piece of writing—seems to be "about," it regularly deals at some level of consciousness with the writer's deepest feelings about his own creativity;* and secondly, that *in every play the cast of characters represents a projection of the playwright's identity elements and fragments, a distribution of the self and its conflicts.* The playwright seeks, as he moves the play forward, to bring such resolution to the struggles of these identity elements as will enhance his own experience of integrated wholeness and freedom.

By way of a viable structure, a form, he finds a psychohistorical bridge to an audience who collectively then share his conflicts, his liberation, and his renewal of an inner cohesion. Of necessity, the bridge is hierarchically structured on archetypal, representative, and idiosyncratic levels. This evolutionary quest for unity and freedom is probably the universal function of *all* creative processes, be they expressed by an artmaker—like a playwright—or by a scientist, a charismatic political leader, or a prophet. Whosoever of these offers us the experience of sharing in *his* achieved wholeness, *his* freedom of movement (we call it the "play" in a system), to him do we offer our devotion, whether as playgoer, student, voter, or disciple.

NOTES

1. Although the basic thread of the argument can be followed without previously reading the specimen play under discussion, Clifford Odets' *Rocket to the Moon*, the specifics in the detailed analysis will be easier to follow if the play is read in advance.

2. Erik Erikson, "The Nature of Psycho-Historical Evidence: In Search of Gandhi," *Daedalus* (Summer 1968), 97:695–730.

3. Michael Polyanyi, *The Tacit Dimension* (Garden City, N.Y.: Doubleday, 1966).

4. Gerald Holton, "Roots of Complementarity," *Daedalus* (Fall 1970), 99:1015–55.

5. Margaret Brenman-Gibson, "Anatomy of a Play: With Specimen Play-Analysis," typescript, 1971; Erik Erikson, *Childhood and Society* (New York: Norton, 1950), p. 195.

6. Martin Deutsch, "Evidence and Inference in Nuclear Research," *Daedalus* (1958), 87:88.

7. Alfred Kazin, *Starting Out in the Thirties* (New York: Atlantic-Little, Brown, 1965).

8. To my pleasure, Erikson decided, after reading this paper in rough draft, to expand his view of the ontogeny of child's play, world views, and creative products. This essay has now appeared under the title, *Toys and Reasons* (1977). Its import reaches far beyond the circumscribed topics of children's play and its adult development. It reaches into the heart of the creative process in everyone: those we officially label "Artist" as well as the rest of mankind. It involves the universal effort to master experience in a manner that will be simul-

taneously unifying and freeing. Erik Erikson, *Toys and Reasons: Stages in the Ritualization of Experience* (New York: Norton, 1977); Erikson, *Childhood and Society* (New York: Norton, 1950).

9. After writing this, on a visit to the incomparable Blake collection in London's Tate Gallery, I learned from their catalogue that indeed Blake had seen the "fall of Man" not in original sin, but in his loss of an innocent sense of wholeness rent by successive subdivisions into a battleground for warring identity elements. It becomes the task of all of us to re-synthesize these into a unified whole by whatever means are available to us.

10. Further confirmation of this fact is Webster's listing of the words "miracle" (*mirar* means "to look") and "wonder" as synonyms. Like the word "theater," both of these are direct descendants of words referring to that earliest zone of intake (besides the mouth), the eyes.

11. Erik Erikson, "Psychosocial Identity," *International Encyclopedia of the Social Sciences* (New York: Crowell-Collier, 1968).

12. Leon Edel, *Literary Biography* (New York: Doubleday, 1959).

13. Erik Erikson, *Young Man Luther—A Study in Psychoanalysis and History* (New York: Norton, 1958), pp. 20–21.

14. Margaret Brenman-Gibson, "Notes on the Study of the Creative Process," in *Psychology versus Metapsychology: Psychoanalytic Essays in Memory of George Klein* (New York: International Universities Press, 1976), pp. 326–57.

15. Frederick Wyatt, "The Reconstruction of the Individual and the Collective Past," in *The Study of Lives: Essays on Personality in Honor of Henry A. Murray* (New York: Atherton Press, 1964), p. 320.

16. Erik Erikson, *Toys and Reasons*.

17. The late Theodore Goodman, professor of English at the City College of New York, said, "In a novel as in a car, you can stop and explore side-roads or look at the scenery; a play, however, is like being in a plane. If you stop, you're dead."

18. Clifford Odets, Personal Notes, "X," 1954 (unpublished).

19. Peter Brook, *The Empty Space* (New York: Atheneum, 1968).

20. Margaret Brenman-Gibson, "Notes on the Study of the Creative Process."

21. Gerald Holton, "Roots of Complementarity," *Daedalus* (Fall 1970) 99:1015–55.

22. Richard Katz, "On the Nature of a Healing Culture" (Read at Austen Riggs Seminar, 1976).

23. Clifford Odets, Personal Notes, "X," 1953 (unpublished).

24. Erik Erikson, "Youth: Fidelity and Diversity," *Daedalus* (Winter 1962), 91:5–27.

25. Erik Erikson, "Psychosocial Identity."

26. Erik Erikson, "The Dream Specimen of Psychoanalysis," in Robert P. Knight and Cyrus R. Friedman, eds., *Psychoanalytic Psychiatry and Psychology:* Clinical and Theoretical Papers, Austen Riggs Center, 1954), 1:133; Sigmund Freud, "The Interpretation of Dreams" (1900), *Standard Edition,* (London: Hogarth Press, 1953), vols. 4 and 5.

27. Clear examples of these universal unconscious preoccupations can be seen with equal clarity in contemporary films and in a variety of holy scriptures, all written, after all, by writers. William Gibson discusses Vedic thought from this point of view in *A Season in Heaven* (1974).

28. Erik Erikson, *Toys and Reasons*.

29. Richard Sennett, Wellfleet Meeting, August 1972.

30. It is Erikson's impression that before he has achieved this impact on another human being, the artist, in his isolation, feels himself to be less than anyone; but afterward, far more (personal communication). ("I am subhuman or superhuman," said Odets.)

31. Maxwell S. Burt, *Philadelphia, Holy Experiment* (New York: Doubleday Doran, 1945).

32. The title is from Isaiah 26:19: "Awake and sing, ye that dwell in dust and the earth shall cast out the dead."

33. All of Odets' life, he wrote as his father spoke, punctuated by multiple exclamation marks. Clifford Odets, Group Theatre "Brookfield Diary," July 1931 (unpublished).

34. "Arise, ye prisoners of starvation / Arise ye wretched of the earth / For Justice thunders condemnation / A better world's in birth / No more tradition's chains shall bind us / Arise ye slaves, no more in thrall / The earth shall rise on new foundations / We have been naught, we shall be all / 'Tis the final conflict / Let each stand in his place / The international Soviet shall be the human race."

35. In the contemporary theater, where alienation has for some time been the guiding theme, the improvisers (or writers) express on the surface their indifference—even their contempt—for the audience. But even here, the acting group is bitterly disappointed when no audience—from whom they can estrange themselves—appears in their theater, "closing down" their "play."

36. Joseph Wood Krutch, "Review of *Rocket to the Moon*," *The Nation*, December 3, 1938, pp. 600–1.

37. Margaret Brenman-Gibson, "Notes on the Study of the Creative Process."

38. Clifford Odets, Personal Notes, "General," March 15, 1938 (unpublished).

39. In the character of the pathetically aspiring Cleo Singer, there is distilled the symbol of the exhausted American artist, still yearning to realize her creative potential and steadily—like L. J. Odets—verging on fraudulence: she lies pretentiously and is tempted by the fame and fortune held under her nose by the minor character, Willy Wax. The beginning of the dissolution of the Group Theatre was already now evident as only one of the many casualties of the end of the American Dream. Three decades later (a wink in history), the protagonist of the film *Easy Rider* would cry out in despair, "We blew it." On his deathbed, Odets had pleaded with singer Edie Adams, "Don't blow it as I did." Given the fact that all civilizations have a "dream" which rises and falls, it is important for us as observer to note that this playwright conceives this play at a time when his own creative "descent" is more or less in "synch" with that of his culture.

40. Clifford Odets, Personal Notes, "General."

41. In the discussion which followed my presentation of this paper, both playwrights present (Arthur Miller and William Gibson) agreed that such a "distribution of the author" as I am hypothesizing here, in the form of identity elements, does indeed exist in every play. They agreed also that during the writing of the play these elements are seen only dimly, if at all, by the playwright. Miller commented, "When I'm writing the thing, it's as if somebody else is writing those notes. And I think that balance is crucial . . . because if you *know* something, something you *really* solve, then writing the whole play becomes unnecessary" (Brenman-Gibson 1971). The restorative function of the creative act is evident in this observation.

42. These names reflect a variety of identity fragments and elements: Odets took the name, Ben, from his lively Tante Esther's "ordinary" son, a man whose life was indeed in Odets' view "a long forgetting." The word "Stark," according to Webster's, means "desolate, bleak, unadorned or rigid, as in death." The wife's maiden name "Belle Prince"—as with Bessie Berger in Odets' *Awake and Sing!*—condenses the word "belle" (beauty) with the name of actress Stella Adler (Odets had scribbled "Stella, Bella, Belle, Bessie" when making notes); she was seen as a Jewish princess in a long succession of actors in the royal Adler family, and like Ben's wife, a powerful, even tyrannical figure. The conflict, as in a dream, is densely

overdetermined: it is simultaneously between a controlling parent (or wife) and a child (or husband).

43. Clifford Odets, *Rocket to the Moon* Production notes, October 26, 1938 (unpublished).

44. Clifford Odets, *Six Plays of Clifford Odets* (New York: Modern Library, 1939).

45. Her name, Cleo Singer, combines that of a sexually irresistible young "Queen of Sheba" (Cleopatra) for whom men would well lose worlds, and Odets' image, steadily drawn from music, of the artist (a *singer* like his Uncle Israel). "Clio" is also the name of the Muse of poetry and history. Odets says, "Whitman is half songbird, half alligator," and the gitka, a mouse, in Odets' last play, *The Flowering Peach*, has a high, sweet singing voice, but having no mate, commits suicide. Also *Cleo* = Cl. Odets: Odets had, in adolescence, often put an "L" in his signature as a middle initial, doubtless after his father's name, "Louis." Again, the products of creative transcendence, akin to dreams.

46. Clifford Odets, *Rocket to the Moon*, Production notes.

47. Clifford Odets, *Six Plays of Clifford Odets*.

48. Cf. Kenneth Burke on Odets in his classic essay, "Ice, Fire, and Decay," in *Philosophy of Literary Form* (New York: Vintage Books, 1941).

49. Erik Erikson, "The Nature of Psycho-Historical Evidence. . ."

50. Clifford Odets, *Six Plays of Clifford Odets*.

51. Margaret Brenman-Gibson, "Anatomy of a Play: With Specimen Play-Analysis."

52. Dynamically, this is identical with Elena's position in Gorky's *Country People*. She, a wife-mother, is however tolerant of her husband's sexual affairs in order, she says, "not to put obstacles in the path of his beautiful inner life." In Gorky's play, thus, the "affairs" are more obviously the artist's journeys into himself. In Pinter's *The Homecoming*, the wife's otherwise mystifying role is similarly illuminated if again we see her as the playwright's creative *anima* in danger of becoming a whore.

53. All his life, Odets had steady trouble with his feet, his hair, and his teeth. Continually seeking help for these difficulties, he came to see them as representing his steady sense of disintegration.

54. This appellation serves to highlight the struggle throughout between material and spiritual values.

55. This is a playwright's gift for eccentric metaphor: the content of Prince's threat reflects Odets' unconscious fear and guilt in competing with this powerful father.

56. In a play he would never finish, *An Old-Fashioned Man*, Odets expressed his yearning for the traditional values in art and in life that his world was steadily losing. Erikson has observed that the steady identity confusion in American life gives it chronically a somewhat adolescent quality (personal communication).

57. Profound issues of the polarities of activity and passivity as well as initiative and guilt are here condensed. Compare this with Odets' later play, *The Big Knife*, which closes with a despairing repetition of the word, "Help!"

58. This image expresses Odets' fear that *all* his creative children are "illegitimate."

59. Clifford Odets, Personal Notes, "Romantics," October 1957 (unpublished).

60. Arthur Wagner, "Interview with Clifford Odets,"

61. I have presented in another place data from this rich vein of investigation to illustrate the archetypal level of meaning which exists alongside the idiosyncratic and the representative (historical) levels. (Brenman-Gibson 1976). See also William Gibson's *A Season in Heaven* (1974)

62. William Gibson, *The Seesaw Log* (New York: Knopf, 1959); Gibson, *A Season in Heaven*. (New York: Atheneum, 1974).

SECTION IV
Psychoanalysis
and
Literature

❧ 11 ❧

Literary Interpretation and
Three Phases of Psychoanalysis

NORMAN N. HOLLAND

I AM STARTING from an historical view, namely, that psychoanalysis, and, with it, psychoanalytic literary criticism have (in their now eight decades of existence) gone through three distinct phases. All focus inward on Freud's original discoveries, but each successive phase moves outward toward a larger, more general human psychology. I would like to illustrate my point with a patient, but, since literary critics and psychoanalysts are both creatures of language, I will substitute for a lengthy patient a short poem. The patient as text, the text as patient, the patient text—

> A slumber did my spirit seal;
>   I had no human fears
> She seemed a thing that could not feel
>   The touch of earthly years.
> No motion has she now, no force;
>   She neither hears nor sees;
> Rolled round in earth's diurnal course,
>   With rocks, and stones, and trees.

An earlier version of this essay was the inaugural lecture of the Kanzer Fund for Psychoanalytic Studies in the Humanities, February 22, 1975. The fund, which will provide a forum for interdisciplinary work in psychology, psychiatry, and the humanities at Yale University, was established by Mark Kanzer, M.D.

It is a poem that has meant differently to me at different times in my life.

Once upon a time, so devout a new critic was I, I could scarcely relate to the poem at all. It seemed too simple to admit the critical exegesis I admired and needed. Now, I find it so apposite to the psychological criticism I advocate, it came unbidden to my mind like a free association.

Once I could contemplate the death the poem describes as a comfortable pantheistic abstraction. Indeed, I can still achieve that comfortable denial in the first two lines: a soothing slumber; "I had no human fears." Now, however, I bring to the poem more experience of the losses and deteriorations of middle age. Now the phrase, "She seemed a thing," shocks me, particularly as it follows on "spirit" or "human." I can argue to myself that that inhuman "thing" serves here simply for a pronoun, as if Wordsworth had written, "She seemed a being" or "She seemed something" that could not feel. But he didn't—he called her a "thing," and the word jars. One way, I get from it a reassuring escape from human fears and the erosions of earthly time, for it gives the "she" of the poem the sureties and certainties of an inanimate object. At the same time, however, I find myself recalling platonic phrases like "a thing enskied" (from *Measure for Measure*), and I realize I am contrasting "thing" to "earthly" in the next line. Calling her a "thing" makes her something less than human for me in one sense—an object—but something more than human in another: she is safely pedestaled above any earthly touch—with all the ambiguity and ambivalence pedestals confer.

Thus, I find in the first stanza a double denial: by giving up human touch and feeling and warmth, I escape human fear and the loss earthly time causes. Sneakily, for my own emotional well-being, I dehumanize another person. Yet, I want to say, *I* don't do this—the "I" of the poem does. Why should *I* feel guilty? Partly, I think, because I *do* tend to dehumanize people through systems and theories. Partly, I think, because I feel punished by the second stanza.

The first stanza was mild. Everything was past. A simple "slumber" rid me of fears. To some extent, I imagine those reassurances of the first stanza continuing in the second, but I feel they have been exaggerated to an extreme and painfully mortal form. "She" is not just protected from the touch of years; she is completely obliterated:

> No motion has she now, no force;
> She neither hears nor sees.

The first line in particular gives me a dreadul feeling of helplessness when I pause after "now" and when the limp phrase "no force" fails to balance out the line. When then I hear the repeated "earth," I contrast a maiden who could not feel the earthly touch of years at all to the body rolled round with rocks and stones and trees, now helplessly bombarded with touch and earth. To be sure, I can find some pantheistic comfort in her being part of a recurring, cyclic nature, but mostly I feel that my attempts at denial in the first stanza have been turned round into a monstrous universal indifference by the second. And throughout I feel, if I am being punished this way—retaliated upon—why then I must have been guilty of something.

If I try to bring the poem together around a unifying idea, as I like to do, I find its central feature its two-stanza structure, the second heightening and intensifying the first. The first was past—the second is now. The first was close-up—the second is long shot. The first spoke of states of mind—the second gives facts only. A somewhat lifeless "I" leads to a far more lifeless "she," as in the very ambiguity of that "she" which could refer to a loved woman or to the abstraction, "my spirit."

I imagine "she" polarized into subhuman thing and superhuman angel, but then converted wholly into thing, whence she seems all the more intensely felt as human. What I could not perceive when it was here, I feel when it is gone. The distant becomes the close. The vanished becomes the present. And through it all, I sense *retaliation,* paying me back in kind. The denier denied. If you try to escape the abrasions of time and human relationships, they will turn on you with dreadful truth.

I feel that retaliation directed toward me. Throughout, I feel, *if* I am being punished this way—retaliated upon—why then I must have been guilty of something. As a theorist of personality, I have been guilty of just such dehumanizings as those the "I" of the poem finds in himself and continues in scientistic words like "motion," "force," or "diurnal." As a formalist critic, I have protested the psychoanalysis of literary characters as though they were human beings. Is this why this so intensely simple and human poem came so insistently to me as *the* poem for *this* occasion? Is that even a question to be asked? I think I have come too abruptly to my subject. Let me start over.

Let me start with my general thesis: that psychoanalysis has gone through three phases. It has been a psychology first of the unconscious,

second a psychology of the ego, and today, I believe, a psychology of the
self.

Yet behind all these phases (or faces), psychoanalysis has always been
par excellence the science of human uniqueness—if there can be a science
of uniqueness. That is psychoanalysis has always existed in the tension between the uniqueness of the individual experience and the aspiration for
general, scientific laws. The datum Freud found himself working with was
the unique and individual consciousness, yet he had, as it were, taken the
Helmoltzian pledge: to explain behavior by means of "physical chemical
forces inherent in matter, reducible to the force of attraction and repulsion." In effect, he wanted to study people as if they were rocks or stones
or trees: but then a patient like Bertha Pappenheim (Anna O.) would give
radically new meaning to those forces of attraction and repulsion by falling
in love with her doctor!

To a surprising extent, the modern American literary critic (and more
recently the European) has sought the same impersonal, generalizable
kind of quasi-scientific knowledge. We Anglophones reacted against the
overindulgence in subjectivity by Victorian and Georgian critics. We also
reacted against the uncritical use of extra-literary knowledge, connections
that were often aimless and unconvincing between literary works and
their authors' biographies or literary periods. We sought instead an analytical rigor, at first by searching out the organic unity of particular literary
works, then by extending the methods of close reading we develped that
way to the total works of an author, to myths and the popular arts, to the
language of everyday life, and even to such artifacts as Volkswagens,
supermarkets, and political candidates.

We created an intellectual rigor and generality that has made literary
criticism an exiciting thing to do for the last twenty or thirty years—but
with an odd result. This objectivism has reached its natural goal in South
Carolina where, as part of a project in content analysis, a computer is
being programmed to read *Paradise Lost,* looking for recurring images,
metaphors, and structures. Thus, we Americans are fulfilling Dr. John-
son's famous comment on that epic: "Its perusal is a duty rather than a
pleasure."

We are also revealing the essential inhumanity of that kind of criticism. When critics are being "objective," they set the literary work in
marmoreal isolation, apart from other kinds of experience; and they cast
themselves as dispassionate observers (like scientists or computers) of a

process located outside the self and in the text. The more intricate the process, the better the critic can perform. Thus, we formalists became more able to talk about the complexities of a Donne or Eliot than the direct statements of an Olson or a Creeley or the simplicities of a Lucy poem. We prized irony and a certain hard-edged quality over the immediate, the intuitive, and the interior. I have to admit that this externalizing and complicating was for me—and perhaps for many others—reassuring. I did not have to feel I was putting myself on the line—my real self—only my mind. I had, so to speak, no human fears.

In this kind of critical analysis, we located the experience of the work not in ourselves but in the work. We said things like, "This poem is an experience of great intensity and depth," or, in general, "A poem is . . . a patterned, organic unit of significant experience,"[1] as though there were a kind of experience embodied in these eight lines without any particular experiencers. But there are experiencers, and the great gaping question for this kind of formalistic criticism is, Why do their experinces differ so, even for so straightforward a poem as this? For example, most critics assume that the "she" of the poem is the Lucy of this and four apparently related poems from the second edition of *Lyrical Ballads*.[2] But others point out that Lucy is never named in this poem, so "she" must refer to "my spirit"—which makes this quite a different poem indeed. And still a third group of critics argue for compromise: both Lucy *and* spirit.[3] As Paul de Man says, "The 'she' in the poem is in fact large enough to encompass Wordsworth as well." Or perhaps "she" is still Lucy alone but not as a woman, as a symbol of Wordsworth's relation to the external, in Geoffrey Hartman's elegant phrasing, "an elision of the purely human."[4]

The critics differ this much about the subject of the poem; they differ even more about its theme. Some, like F. W. Bateson, find in it a "pantheistic magnificence." "Lucy is actually more alive now that she is dead, because she is now a part of the life of Nature. . . ."[5] Others (among them, F. R. Leavis) see just the opposite: "the brutal finality of the fact," "the dead woman within the dead globe."[6] And still others find a median position: "The motionless girl has become part of the living motion of the earth . . . death-within-life."[7] In effect, the critics have arrived at three of the four logical possibilities: death within life; death within death; life within life. Given such differences, what do we mean when we say that the poem somehow controls or delimits the response?

Consider just a single word—"diurnal." How much does *it* define response? Hugh Kenner calls it an "abstract, technical term," and F. R. Leavis says the word has a "scientific nakedness" but also "evokes the vast inexorable regularity of the planetary motions."[8] By contrast, Cleanth Brooks finds in it a "violent but imposed motion," a "whirl."[9] F. W. Bateson calls it a "solemn Latinism" which contrasts with the other, simpler words, to set off "the invulnerable Ariel-like creature" against her present "lifeless and immobile" state.[10] Elizabeth Drew finds this "one long formal word in the poem" not lifeless at all, but contributing to "a majestic affirmation."[11] Robin Skelton finds in it a fear that, if the poet unites his soul with nature, he will be turned daily like the earth, selfless and unthinking. Skelton also finds a "subconscious effect of the syllable 'di,' which to the ear suggests that a word having reference to division, to the dichotomy of the world, is about to be spoken."[12] To whose ear? And yet I hasten to admit, I hear in "diurnal" the word "urn" as saying another way the whole earth has been made Lucy's funerary vessel.

The basic difficulty in this effort to put criticism on an objective or quasi-scientific footing is that different readers take the same text differently. And not just naive readers: we have been consulting some of the most distinguished critics in the last quarter-century of Anglo-American formalism, two of them poets of note. I have not found any satisfactory way of accounting for this divergence within my tradition of formalism. Nor have I been more successful with the great efflorescence of European literary theory in the last two decades. Neither seems able to account for the great variations in our personal experiences of literary works.

There is one salient exception to this general pattern, Georges Poulet and the so-called school of Geneva, which should perhaps be called the school of Geneva and New Haven. Studies of various writers or critics by, for example, Poulet or Hillis Miller, do indeed represent ways of talking about individuals with great precision. They correspond closely to what I call the third phase of psychoanalysis, but before getting to that third, I want to linger a bit on the first and second.

I see psychoanalysis as moving through three successive polarities. The first, the earliest stage, grew out of Freud's discoveries of latent and manifest content in a variety of settings: dreams, neurotic symptoms, jokes, forgetting, and slips of all kinds. As he realized this polarity applied in so many different spheres of mental activity, he understood that he had arrived at a general psychological principle, the polarity between conscious and unconscious, thought of as systems or even as places.

A literary critic bringing this first phase of psychoanalysis to a poem will use the early psychoanalytic vocabulary of the Oedipus complex and the phallic and anal stages. Typically, he will rely very heavily on Freud's lists of symbols in the 1914 additions to *The Interpretation of Dreams* or the first set of *Introductory Lectures* in 1915–17. In literary circles much of what passes for psychoanalysis or psychoanalytic criticism comes from this earliest stage, the search for a latent content.

Looked at this way, the latent content of "I had no human fears" is that I did not fear human losses—the loss of a person or the loss of a body part. In the early phase of psychoanalysis, the body model for loss was castration, so that the key word for the first stanza would become "she." She, being feminine, is invulnerable to that prototypical loss. In the same way, the "I" of the poem is "sealed," that is, closed up—there is no opening: he cannot be penetrated as a woman is penetrated. He, too, need have no human fears. And if the word "spirit" (as in Shakespearean English) carries a phallic meaning, again, a slumber sealing it provides another dimension of protection. The whole first stanza, then, as it applies to the speaker and to the maid, has the unconscious content: the two of us were safe because we were untouched.

In the second stanza, that earlier reassurance fails. The maid is invulnerable, yes, but inert. Untouched because she is unable to touch. The earthy rocks and stones would, in this first phase, symbolize dirt or, in the body sense, feces. She has become lifeless and worthless—like excrement. The trees and rocks might also symbolize a phallus. In effect, she has not lost a phallus—she has become one. Yet, at the same time, she has become completely impotent, without motion, force, vision, or hearing—she can neither penetrate nor be penetrated. It is as though, being separated, she *is* the castrated phallus, completely vital but completely dead.

That is a primitive reading by today's standards (perhaps by any standards). As long ago as 1936, Anna Freud defined the limits of this kind of symbolic decoding: "The technique of translating symbols is a . . . way of plunging from the highest strata of consciousness to the lowest strata of the unconscious without pausing at the intermediate strata of former ego-activities which may in time past have forced a particular id-content to assume a specific ego-form."[13] Applied by a literary critic, this kind of symbolic decoding hurls us from poetry to anatomy, from the words-on-the-page to the depths of the unconsious. Further, these symbolic equations being fixed, they give us no way to account for the considerable variation in individual response—even the variation in symbolic decodings by different psychoanalytic critics.

Miss Freud directs us to the ego processes that intervene between the depths and the surface and thus to the second phase of psychoanalysis as a science. We can date it from Freud's positing a superego, an ego, and an id in 1923. We can identify its basic polarity as between ego and nonego, that is, between the mind's snythesizing functions and external reality or some other internal psychic structure. Where therapy in the first phase tried to make the unconscious conscious, therapy in the second aimed at enlarging and strenghtening the ego. Indeed, one can no longer speak of "the" unconscious as a noun, only as an adjective.

Looking at a poem in this second phase, a literary critic would try to find ego strategies as they are apparently embodied in the language of a poem.[14] Here, I would ask how an unconscious fantasy about castration or turning into a disembodied phallus could become a conscious theme about pantheism, or cosmic indifference, or death as death-within-life. Between these two levels, ego strategies transform the one into the other, and a literary critic using psychoanalysis in its ego-psychology phase would concentrate his attention on those strategies.

The first stanza seems to embody the ego strategy (or defense or adaptation) of denial, that is, blocking a thought or feeling from being perceived.

> A slumber did my spirit seal;
> I had no human fears.

And she was likewise immune, because she could not feel the touch of earthly years. The speaker avoids dangers of loss by giving up something in advance, as it were, his awareness of his lover as a human, mortal being in danger.

In the second stanza, the denial becomes more severe. Where in the first it only seemed she could not feel, now she has neither motion nor force nor sight nor hearing. Something of the aggressive, nullifying feeling behind denial comes through: she has been made into a nothing, or a mere rock, stone, or tree. Literally, something other than the speaker has done this to her, yet in the poem, words like "now" or the transition from past to present, the repetition of the word "earth," and all the similarity of content between the two stanzas together suggest that the second stanza is a punishment for the first. *Now* the speaker *will* suffer human fears and the maiden who could not feel a touch will be rolled round thousands of miles with rock, stone, and tree.

By looking at the ego defenses between the unconscious body fantasy and the larger conscious theme, we can talk psychoanalytically about form. For example, we can talk about sound; we can understand the tonguey *s*'s of the first line as soothing soporifics in the service of denial. Similarly the *n*'s of lines five and six—we hear five successive n-plus-vowel sounds, *no, nah, now, no, nigh*. They help act out negations or omissions. So does the lost rhyme of line six: instead of saying she neither "sees nor hears," and so continuing the *-ears* rhymes of the first stanza, Wordsworth reverses the verbs. Again I have the sense of an omission: something has been denied.

For me, the feeling is strongest in line five. I sense a strong pause after "now," which stands for an *and* deleted from the deep structure, followed by a limp and inadequate feeling "no force." "No motion has she now, no force." Compare that to the closest possibility: "No motion has she now nor force." At the surface level, I find Wordsworth has omitted much more: "No motion has she now; no force has she now," with the second "has she now" omitted. Again, omissions in the form correspond to denials in defense.

Finally, in the *r*'s of the last two lines as one sounds them in one's mouth—"Rolled round in earth's diurnal course / With rocks. . . ." I find my mouth grinding and growling in a verbal version of the anger hidden in this brief tale of the death of the maiden.

Bringing the second phase of psychoanalysis to literary criticism results in a considerable improvement over the first. It is less bizarre. It relates to other ways of thinking and reading. We are able to integrate an unconscious content for the poem—some of which is available to us through the translation methods of the first phase—with conscious themes and the poem's repertoire of formal devices as discovered by regular literary criticism. In fact, literary analysis wearing the second face of psychoanalysis is very like regular formalist reading.

Yet, like regular formalist reading, it leaves us with unsolved problems. First, like criticism based in the first phase, it fails to account for the differences in people's reading experiences. We have not yet given the personal a voice alongside a hypothetical collective. "I" has dropped out in favor of "we" or "it." Second, I have had to talk about the poem as if it were a mini-mind—as if it had mental processes embodied in it, independent of any real minds like its author's or my own. Both these difficulties arise because I am talking about the poem as an external being, as something "out there" disconnected from whatever happens "in here" in relation to it.

When I begin to ask questions about what is "out there" and its relation to what is "in here," I am addressing the third face of psychoanalysis. In the first, the basic polarity for explaining human phenomena was "the" unconscious as against "the" conscious. In the second, it was ego as opposed to nonego. In the third, it is self versus nonself. One can relate the three phases by the parts of speech they make the word "unconscious" into. In the first phase, it could be a noun, referring to a thing, a system, or even a place. In the second phase, when Freud announced that "unconscious" was only descriptive, the word became only an adjective, as in a phrase like "unconscious ego." Now, Roy Schafer has ingeniously suggested that the word has become an adverb—we should think in terms of a whole person doing this or that unconsciously.[15]

At any rate, as early as 1930, in the first chapter of *Civilization and Its Discontents*, Freud had entered this third phase. He had, in effect, recognized that for at least the beginning of an individual's life span, the wholly *intra*psychic model of the first two phases had to give way to an *inter*psychic model, one that included both the individual mind and its surround. "Originally the ego includes everything; later it separates off an external world from itself." This is a monumental change in psychoanalytic theory, and Freud was not overstating it when he compared the discovery of this early developmental phase to the unearthing of Minoan and Mycenean civilization beneath classical and archaic Greece.

Once Freud accepted the idea of the ego as a permeable interface between self and outer world at the beginning, there has been a steadily increasing body of evidence that that is true all through life. Freud himself said our egos lose their boundaries when we fall in love or when we have mystical experiences. I have suggested that the same thing happens when we become "absorbed" in literary or artistic works. But long before I came along, Lacan had suggested his *stade du miroir* and D. W. Winnicott had developed his even more powerful concept of a transitional space between self and other in which *all* cultural experience takes place. Erik Erikson's large concepts of adaptation, mutuality, and psychosocial development draw on an interpersonal model of the mind. So does

Charles Rycroft when he updates the old-fashioned symbolic decoding to treat psychoanalytic symbolism as an active way of relating oneself to the world. So, too, does Roy Schafer in developing an "action language" of self and other that will get psychoanalysis beyond the second-phase constructs of id, ego, and superego. So do many other psychoanalysts (too many to mention individually) build on a polarity between self and other rather than between ego and nonego.

"Identity" is the key term. Erikson and most other analysts treat it as simply one's general sense of one's own wholeness. More precise and more relevant to literature is Heinz Lichtenstein. He shows that, from all the infinite choices that manifest a personality, an external observer can trace a single style running through them all. We can understand another person as a continuing sameness within change, while we understand change itself as change only by presupposing an underlying sameness. In effect, we can read one another like music, hearing ourselves play our lives like variations on a melody, an identity theme, which is, quite simply, our very essence.

This process of abstraction into an identity theme and variations quite resembles what a formalist literary critic does when he brings all the separate details of a poem together around a centering theme. Approaching people this way, I find myself describing them by themes like those for literary works: "being the essence of another"; "closing gaps with signs"; "managing great unknowns by means of small knowns"; "controlling the reversals caused by entrances and exits." In effect, I can speak about a person as about a poem, achieving rigor but retaining uniqueness. I can talk fully and rigorously about the individual—person or poem—provided I remember that *I* am talking.

Thus, this concept of identity adds a new dimension to all our games. Not only do we perceive, we also perceive ourselves perceiving. We become able to understand how our perceptions are themselves acts that express our identity themes. So too interpretation, so that when I read and comment on Wordsworth's lyric, I know that two seemingly inconsistent things are going on at once.

On the one hand, I am bringing my skills as a reader to bear, my knowledge of Wordsworth, English romanticism, and what others have written about them, but most important my own commitment to an honest search for a "valid" interpretation, one that will command assent from others besides myself. We call this being "objective." Yet at the same time I know I can only do this in a way which is wholly authentic for me—"subjective."

These are only seemingly inconsistent, however. All my acts, perceptions, and relationships are functions of my identity, including my relation to this lyric, for that is what identity is: my thematic sameness plus my variations on it. My relation to the poem includes *both* my emotions *and* my characteristic use of the critic's discipline. In fact, skills and feelings about skills and what the skills are being applied to are always inextricably interinanimated (in Donne's word). It is precisely because I feel emotion toward the poem that I can reimagine it in my own characteristic way, yet by tactics and commitments I share with other critics.

Identity theory enables me to understand that interaction of firm critical hypotheses with exciting, shimmering fields of personal knowledge. This third phase is not a retreat to subjectivity. It is giving up the illusion that I can only understand reality (or a text) by keeping myself out.

Thus, the third face of psychoanalysis looks toward the main current of twentieth-century scientific thought in a way that ego psychology never did. Even the hardest of sciences today acknowledge the role of the subject. The most obvious examples are the role of the observer in relativity or Gödel's theorem setting limits to impersonal mathematical axiomatization. In quantum mechanics, the physicist holds up solid reality as a magician would rub a coin between his fingers until he opens his hand and there is—nothing, nothing, anyway, but insubstantial clusters of complementary differential equations.

The experimental psychologists have set up shop as the guardians of Helmholtzian values and the methods of nineteenth-century science. Other social scientists, differently adaptable, have accepted and drawn on the observer, particularly the cultural anthropologists but even more spectacularly the psychologists of cognition and perception. They have shown over and over again in a variety of contexts that perception is a constructive act. We perceive, not in some one-way alley of cause-and-effect, stimulus-and-response, but as we bring hypotheses from within ourselves to bear against external reality. Similarly, post-Chomskyan linguistics takes us away from the sinple analysis of the surface behavior of speakers or the facile *signifiant-signifié, langue-parole* distinctions of the early twentieth century. Now, we understand both listening and performance as situations in which we generate grammatical hypotheses, deep structures, or protosentences, to compare them with surface sounds.[16]

The sciences, in short, seem to be taking us to a philosophical position like that of Husserl. The human being becomes a freely emitting center of meanings. We confer meaning on events instead of letting the world shove its meanings down on us. And indeed, when twentieth-century historians like Thomas Kuhn trace back the history of science, they show discovery is not a matter of logic and experiment alone or even the discoverer's passion. Discovery depends crucially on the capacity of scientists as people to take new perceptions into the paradigms they already have in their heads. Even theory building is an act in which a human being replicates his identity.

Third-phase psychoanalysis, then, is itself a scientific paradigm, but it is also the science that describes how people get such paradigms in their heads. It is not just a hermeneutic to get us from a manifest content to latent, as in the first phase. It is a hermeneutic of hermeneutics. It tells you not only what I said but how it came to be me who said it. Why, for example, did this poem come to me as *the* poem for this subject? Why did I find in it a retaliation on the speaker, something stronger than the learning other critics have described?

These are some things I have written about myself (before writing on this poem). "For me, the need to see and understand is very strong." "I feel a real conflict in me between scientific impulses and literary ones." I have "a passionate desire to know about the insides of things with an equally strong feeling that one is, finally, safer on the outside." For that reason, "I *like* examining the verbal surface of a text, looking particularly for an 'organic unity' in the way the parts all come together." "My identity theme [has] to do with preserving a sense of self and securing self-esteem by gaining power over relations between things, in particular, mastering them by knowing or seeing them from outside rather than being actually in the relationships."

In this poem, the first stanza of not touching moves to a stanza of still greater distance. For me, that very distance leads to still greater intensity. No wonder I feel the poem as a retaliation in kind. As Robert Duncan once said, "The poem is a protection that dares the thing it protects you from." As I put it, "If you try escape the abrasions of time and human relationships, they will turn on you with dreadful truth." Yet there is a more positive side. The poem says to me—or I say through it—that to be close to another person, you must unseal yourself in a world of perhaps indifference or perhaps intrusion. Either way, you must risk yourself, but it is worth it, because you can gain both intimacy and the safety of a larger being.

What, then, about the three faces of psychoanalysis? Here, too, I find myself moving from the center of psychoanalytic insight outward to greater and greater generality. From the original polarity of conscious as against unconscious to the intrapsychic model of ego and nonego, finally to the largest but most close way of confronting individuality, one's own and others, identity, which involves both intimacy and distance.

So far as reading is concerned, I find I have performed a similar expansion: from the decoding of particular symbols to the study of ego strategies. Yet my last move—which you will share with me, I hope—makes criticism into an act of personal discovery. We use our critical commitment to interpret not only the text but also what we say about the text. By combining the two dimensions, we use literary knowledge to gain self-knowledge. We express and re-create ourselves in our interpretations—that we have always done—but now we can do it understandingly.

What does that mean in practice? What does the interpretation through the third face of psychoanalysis look like? It could look like what I said at the outset about this poem, a conscious in-mixing of the features of the poem with my own feelings of guilt and punishment, my personal achievement of generality *and* intimacy. It could look like that but it need not. There can be as many readings as there are readers to write them. Can be and should be. For criticism from the third phase of psychoanalysis risks intimacy in order to restore individuality. The best interpreters will speak from self-knowledge as well as from the knowledge of literature. How to do this? That, the third phase tells us, we each will have to find for ourselves.

NOTES

1. Wright Thomas and Stuart Gerry Brown, *Reading Poems: An Introduction to Critical Study* (New York: Oxford University Press, 1941), p. 642; M. L. Rosenthal and A. J. M. Smith, *Exploring Poetry* (New York: Macmillan, 1955), p. 89.

2. Gene W. Ruoff, "Another New Poem by Wordsworth," *Essays in Criticism* (1966) 16: 359–60; Rosenthal and Smith, *Exploring Poetry*. See also Cleanth Brooks, "Irony and 'Ironic' Poetry," in Morton D. Zabel, ed., *Literary Opinion in America,* rev. ed. (New York: Harper, 1950) and F. R. Leavis, " 'Thought and Emotional Quality," *Scrutiny* (1945).

3. Jonathan Wordsworth, "A New Poem by Wordsworth?" *Essays in Criticism* (1966), 16:122–23; David Ferry, *The Limits of Mortality* (Middletown, Conn.: Wesleyan University Press, 1959), pp. 79–81.

4. Paul de Man, "The Rhetoric of Temporality," in Charles S. Singleton, ed., *Interpretation* (Baltimore: Johns Hopkins University Press, 1969), pp. 205–6; Geoffrey H. Hartman, *Wordsworth's Poetry, 1787–1814* (New Haven and London: Yale University Press, 1964), p. 158.

5. F. W. Bateson, *English Poetry: A Critical Introduction*, 2d ed. (London: Longmans Green, 1966), pp. 29, 59.

6. F. R. Leavis, " 'Thought' and Emotional Quality," 13:53–55, 54; Rosenthal and Smith, *Exploring Poetry*, p. 90.

7. Florence Marsh, *Wordsworth's Imagery* (New Haven and London: Yale University Press, 1952), pp. 55–56. See also Elizabeth Drew, *Poetry: A Modern Guide to Its Understanding and Enjoyment* (New York: Norton, 1959), p. 133.

8. Hugh Kenner, *The Art of Poetry* (New York: Rinehart, 1959), p. 132. Leavis, " 'Thought,' " pp. 54–55.

9. Brooks, "Irony and 'Ironic' Poetry," pp. 735–37.

10. Bateson, *English Poetry*, p. 29.

11. Drew, *Poetry*, p. 133.

12. Robin Skelton, *The Poetic Pattern* (London: Routledge and Kegan Paul, 1956), pp. 184–85.

13. Anna Freud, *The Ego and the Mechanisms of Defence* (London: Hogarth Press, 1948), pp. 16–17.

14. The most extensive presentation of this point of view remains my own earlier work, *The Dynamics of Literary Response* (New York: Oxford University Press, 1968).

15. Roy Schafer, *A New Language for Psychoanalysis* (New Haven and London: Yale University Press, 1976), pp. 241–43.

16. See, for example, Ulric Neisser, *Cognitive Psychology* (New York: Appleton-Century-Crofts, 1967); Jerry A. Fodor, Thomas G. Bever, and Merrill F. Garrett, *The Psychology of Language: An Introduction to Psycholinguistics and Generative Grammar* (New York: McGraw-Hill, 1974); Donald A. Norman, David E. Rummelhart, and the LNR Research Group, *Explorations in Cognition* (San Francisco: W. H. Freeman, 1975). See also my forthcoming "What Can a Concept of Identity Add to Psycholinguistics?," *Psychiatry and the Humanities*, vol. 3 (1978).

❧ 12 ❧

Toward a Reorientation of Psychoanalytic Literary Criticism

ALAN ROLAND

I

"IT'S A DEVASTATION!" Lionel Trilling, one of the first of the critics to use psychoanalysis, averred in his last years about psychoanalytic criticism.[1] Another, Leon Edel, so despaired over the misuse of psychoanalysis in literary criticism because of conflicting approaches to symbolic expression, that he strongly urged psychoanalysis to be confined to biography only.[2] More recently, Frederick Crews ran up the red flag over intrinsic, reductionistic tendencies in psychoanalytic criticism, warning that only the utmost caution can prevent the ubiquitous misuse of psychoanalysis.[3] And yet we are paradoxically faced with a swelling movement by literary critics as well as psychoanalysts to use psychoanalysis in criticism.

Is psychoanalytic literary criticism, then, simply a currently popular cul-de-sac? Or is psychoanalysis, rather a viewpoint pertinent to literary understanding, but one fraught with danger from hidden problems just beneath the surface of easy synthesis? If we are to speak of psychoanalytic literary criticism, rather than simply applied psychoanalysis—where one may romp freely without regard for the ecology of another discipline— then we must talk in the dialogue of a serious interdisciplinary effort. And such interdisciplinary explorations invariably lead into uncharted areas.

In particular, the psychoanalytic critic has a most difficult time in negotiating the straits between psychological reductionism and ignorance of the complexities of either psychoanalysis or aesthetics. The monster of psychological reductionism usually fells the critic through his reliance on an essentializing strategy[4] of reducing all motivation and content to the psychological or to infantile conflicts[5] or by his unquestioning acceptance of the basic assumptions of traditional applied psychoanalysis, assumptions that I hope to show reduce the literary work to a psychological framework, rather than expand the dimensions of the aesthetic experience. If this many-headed monster has not laid the critic low, then more often than not another sweeps into its vortex of ignorance the psychoanalyst unfamiliar with the basics of aesthetics, as well as the literary critic friendly to psychoanalysis but unaware of its theoretical and historical complexities. Even when the analyst-reader has some substantial grounding in criticism and the critic has taken psychoanalytic courses, there still remains the problem of not having acquired the sophistication and discrimination that comes from working in a field over many years. Such deficiencies, of course, are common to any interdisciplinary undertaking.

How then can some of the riches already attained in psychoanalytic literary criticism, and even applied psychoanalysis, be accounted for if the picture I have painted is so truly bleak? Ironically, the literary critic and psychoanalyst are remarkably similar in that their individual sensitivities, insights, and imagination often transcend their theoretical orientation in determining the validity of their work. Talent and flair often tend to prevail over methodology in these two fields. It is from just these individual gifts of perceptiveness and imagination that I suspect that much of the promise of psychoanalytic literary criticism has been realized. Are we then to chuck overboard all theoretical considerations, relying simply on raw intuition? Obviously not. No one would gainsay the need for a sound theoretical framework.

It is just to this need for a guide for better integration, rather than a new aesthetic, that I would like to address this paper. As a psychoanalyst with some grounding in literary criticism, I am under no illusion of the potentially perilous territory I shall be exploring, and rather expect that I too on occasion shall run up on the shoals. My confidence of some success, however, is predicated on my own work differentiating art from the dream,[6] experience in interdisciplinary collaboration on drama criticism, and familiarity with other very recent explorations into the creative process and primary-process thinking that are fraught with important implications for integrating psychoanalysis with literary criticism.

Before embarking in a new direction, discretion indicates a rather

careful examination of old pitfalls that have led so many astray. *In particular, I shall demonstrate, at times ad nauseum, how so much of psychoanalytic literary criticism and applied psychoanalysis is based on a certain
analogy of the work of art with the dream and daydream—an analogy that
must be seriously challenged because it interferes with valid criticism by
invariably pointing the critic toward reducing art to a psychological
framework.* I see this as the fundamental cause of reductionism, one that
leads the psychoanalytic critic down the garden path of invariably searching for infantile conflicts and latent content. In broad outline, I shall chart
how this basic analogy has influenced almost the entire field of psychoanalytic literary criticism, and how in recent decades this analogy has been
greatly reinforced by very facilely attractive formulations on the creative
process that have lured the critic astray and wrecked his efforts. These
formulations too are now open to serious question.

In the second part of this paper, I shall consider how literary critics
have been influenced by psychoanalysis, and especially by the basic assumptions and analogy just cited as they influence the development of a
new aesthetic by such critics as Simon O. Lesser, Frederick Hoffman, and
Norman Holland.[7] Finally, I shall cite new investigations that seriously
challenge the old world view, and offer sounder guideposts for a reorien-
tation in psychoanalytic literary criticism.

Let us take note of the historical particulars. With relatively rare exceptions, such as Rank's radical departure from Freud on the nature of art
and the artist,[8] psychoanalysts have generally followed Freud's initial orientation as developed in two seminal papers—the first on Jensen's *Gradiva*[9] and the other on "The Relationship of the Poet to Daydreaming."

In these writings, Freud uses the daydream and dream as a paradigm
for the literary work: forbidden wishes from unconscious, infantile fantasies of the oral, anal, phallic, and genital stages of development are
given disguised expression. Whereas the dream affords this disguised
expression through the dream work, or mechanisms of the primary process,[10] so that the forbidden wish is rarely recognizable in the manifest
content, the work of art accomplishes the same end through using elements of aesthetic form to distract the audience. In both cases, the con-
sciences or superegos of dreamer and audience are partially circum-
vented. The greatness of art then is the communication of powerful forces
and fantasies within the artist's unconscious to the audience without their
fully realizing it. Given this analogy of the dream to art, the psychoana-

lytic critic endeavors to ignore, or at best search through elements of form in a work to the "deeper," and of course to him more pertinent psychological content and meanings.

With this basic orientation serving as his polar star, the psychoanalyst has explored literature in three basic directions. As psychoanalysis has attained new complexities over the years, it has enabled the psychoanalytic critic to extend his forays in each of these directions. The more familiar undertaking has been to elucidate the universality in works of art of unconscious fantasies derived from the psychosexual stages of development. A classic example would be Ernest Jones's analysis of *Hamlet* in the light of the Oedipus complex.[11] An early variation of this was the analyses of myths in literature as shared unconscious fantasies of particular sociocultural groups. Such mythic critics with this psychoanalytic orientation, the most prominent pioneers among whom were Otto Rank and Geza Roheim,[12] are to be distinguished from the vaster body of critics who use a mythic analysis as derived from anthropology, religion, ethnology, and linguistics. Still another dimension to the psychoanalytic search for universal unconscious fantasy in art via the route of mythic exploration was added by Jung and his followers. The Jungian interest in archetypal figures and themes from the racial unconscious has been a major influence on literary criticism over the last half century, particularly in the work of such critics as Maud Bodkin, Leslie Fiedler, and Northrop Frye.[13]

A more recent preoccupation with universal unconscious fantasies in art, with important implications for criticism, is found in English schools of Freudian psychoanalysis, particularly in Melanie Klein and her followers. Here, unconscious fantasy is viewed as stemming from the interaction of a person's libidinal and aggressive drives with early familial interpersonal experiences or object-relations.[14] These early experiences are internalized in the psyche as internal objects (imagoes in traditional Freudian theory), and become the basis of unconscious fantasies supplementary to those derived from the psychosexual stages of development. While there has been considerable controversy over the particulars of Klein's contribution to psychoanalytic theory, her picture of the world of early object-relations or psychosocial stages of development has struck a most responsive cord in modern psychoanalysis. Other major theorists such as Harry Stack Sullivan, Erik Erikson, D. W. Winnicott, Ronald Fairbairn, René Spitz, Margaret Mahler, and Edith Jacobson, among others have dramatically enlarged the knowledge of early object-relations, so that this area is now an important part of contemporary Freudian as well as neo-Freudian psychoanalysis.[15]

The implications of this broadening approach to early object-relations and internalizations are several. For one, it makes available to the critic a far greater range of unconscious fantasy and emotional stages and experiences from childhood than the psychosexual only—which has figured so ubiquitously in psychoanalytic literary criticism. For another, it opens up a far broader study of the ego or self, with issues of self-image, identity, identification patterns, and narcissism—which has become the basis of the latest work of the psychoanalytic critic, Norman Holland. As I shall allude to below, these concepts are far more relevant for the psychoanalytic critic in considering much of avant-garde drama for instance than the traditional psychosexual fantasies. In still another vein, explorations into the ego or self have profound implications for a new theory of the primary process, and thus creativity as well—with considerable ramifications for psychoanalytic literary criticism, which I shall discuss in the third section.

A brief example of a Kleinian contribution to applied psychoanalysis—that of Joan Riviere's commentary on Ibsen's the *Master Builder*—is very much in order to illustrate its contrast with the more traditional use of psychosexual fantasies.[16] In Riviere's analysis, a character such as Solness's wife is seen as both a character in herself and as a representation of an internalized part of Solness's own psyche: the internalized mother who is destroyed by infantile greed. Hilda, too, is viewed as partly a manifestation of Solness: she is his "manic defense," denying all reality, particularly the destruction of his internalized object world. As important and novel as Riviere's analysis is, however, I must qualify that her contribution is still beset by the many-headed monster of psychological reductionism, i.e., there is no scanning of the rich imagery in the play for other levels of meaning with which the psychological viewpoint could be integrated, not to mention other aspects of form and structure.[17]

The second major direction in psychoanalytic literary criticism has been to investigate the unconscious motivation or psychopathology of a character in order to penetrate to the underlying meanings of a literary work. While earlier interpretations concentrated completely on character formation and motivation derived from the psychosexual stages of development, and most usually the Oedipal, later analyses have, with the newer contributions to psychoanalysis, become far more sophisticated. Thus, Phillip Weissman in a chapter of his book, *Creativity in the Thea-*

tre, analyzes Tennessee Williams's prostitute heroines in terms of problems of early object-relations as well as Oedipal difficulties.[18] Kurt Eissler in his work, *On Hamlet and "Hamlet,"* also adds considerable refinement to our view of the dynamics of Hamlet's superego and ego ideal and the effect of these on dramatic action.[19] Not only does Eissler try to use his understanding of Hamlet as a key to the exigencies of plot; he also sees the character as the embodiment of little-understood universal laws of the psyche. This approach contrasts considerably with the older one of seeing a character in literature or drama as a completely real, living person—the bane of earlier critics from both psychoanalytic and literary backgrounds.

The third and final direction that psychoanalytic criticism took, starting with Freud's work on Leonardo da Vinci, has been to relate the hidden psychological meanings in the work of art (either the unconscious fantasies or the analysis of character) to the author's life. An example of this is Kligerman's work relating *Six Characters in Search of an Author* to Pirandello's life and personality.[20] At its worst, treating the work of art as a chapter in the creator's psychobiography led to the reductionistic position that art, itself, is a manifestation of psychopathology, and can be understood simply by understanding the vicissitudes of an author's childhood. At its best, a sophisticated psychobiographical approach can help shed additional light on an author's work, and has been used to good effect by such a distinguished critic as Leon Edel on Henry James.[21]

Thus briefly reviewing the directions in which the psychoanalytic critic has set sail, it is time to assess some of the efforts of his forays. There is little doubt that a more sophisticated and penetrating psychoanalytic understanding of unconscious fantasy, of issues of the self and identity, of the wellsprings of character, and of the author's biography can all be of considerable value to criticism. But as Crews rightly noted, an increase of psychoanalytic knowledge and a sharpening of the analyst's tools may only help dig deeper the ditch of reductionism.[22] The issue still remains as to the uses of psychoanalysis in the critical endeavor. Even with significant advances in psychoanalytic knowledge, all too often the psychoanalyst has still equated the work of art with the dream and daydream, and continued his search for latent psychological meaning as the be-all and end-all of his efforts. In this, he has often been supported by major psychoanalytic views on form and creativity that more often than not have subtly carried over Freud's basic assumptions.

I would now like to turn to important psychoanalytic contributions to the theories of aesthetic form and creativity to assess the degree to which these approaches reinforce or contradict Freud's basic assumptions on aesthetics, and thus to the basic orientation of psychoanalytic literary criticism.[23] Early psychoanalysts such as Sachs basically followed Freud's view of form as disguise, but developed it in a more sophisticated way.[24] While Sachs viewed form in art as more elaborate than in the dream, he also saw it as a gateway to unconscious content—art thus restoring to the ego dissociated parts of the personality. His approach naturally led in the same direction as Freud's in searching for unconscious content. Of the early analysts, and perhaps the later ones too, Rank departed most radically from Freud's basic assumptions on form.[25] He saw form in a dual way: as the search for ego mastery over death in the artist's quest for immortality, and as the synthesis of the dualism between the individual and his society—form bearing the stamp of the collectivity. This latter concept of form presaged the important work of later analysts such as Kris and Alexander.[26]

Kris, coming to psychoanalysis from the field of art history, enlarged Freud's earlier conception of form as disguise and distraction by seeing it as partly determined by the conventions of culture and as a means of socially adaptive expression by the artist. Alexander also predicated changes in artistic style and form upon the fluctuating social climate; e.g., the movement into nonobjective art and literature as closely tied to a general disillusionment in the Western world in the twentieth century, resulting in a regressive turning within. Implicit in the work of Rank, Kris, and Alexander is the artist's conscious or unconscious identifications with certain groups of the collectivity in a particular historical period, which is then manifested in his work through its form and style.[27] Rycroft extends this notion to the artist's identification with and use of the symbols of the collectivity and other artists, rather than his own purely private ones—as in dreams.[28]

The main impetus in more modern psychoanalytic approaches to aesthetic form, comes, however, from the contributions of psychoanalytic ego psychology, particularly Ernst Kris's theory of creativity.[29] Kris's views on art and creativity are generally looked upon as the most definitive ones in psychoanalytic circles today, and have had considerable influence on art critics such as Gombrich and Ehrensweig, and literary critics as Hoffman, Lesser, and Holland.[30] Kris reinforced the bond between art work and dream work by equating artistic ambiguity, an important concept of the "new critic," William Empson,[31] with the overdetermination[32] of the primary process. Thus, the many-leveled meanings of a work of art are considered as basically similar to the overdetermined meanings of the primary process—as manifested in symptoms or a dream. In like manner, Kris also equated poetic metaphor, an integration of different levels of experience, with the metaphorical expression of dream imagery, where one presentation analogously stands for some more unconscious meaning of the latent content. He envisages the artist as regressing "in the service of his ego" to the imagery of the primary process with its variety of meanings, and then as progressing to the rational ego where secondary-process thinking cast derivatives from this primary-process exploration into aesthetic form.

Marshall Bush, in an essay, "The Problem of Form in the Psychoanalytic Theory of Art," summarizes the perspectives of Kris and other ego psychologists.[33] Bush derives from these contributions the conclusions that aesthetic form is a very high order of achievement of various ego functions and can be appreciated in its own right; and form is involved in an organic integration of diverse elements of content, analogous to the ego's attempt to integrate aspects of the id, superego, and outer reality into a workable synthesis. The implications for literary criticism, according to Bush, are on one hand psychological support for an appreciation of the formalist approach to aesthetics; and on the other, supplementary to the traditional psychoanalytic search for underlying psychological meanings and content, a further appreciation of the transformation, organization, and resolution of unconscious content through the manifestations of high-order ego functioning in aesthetic form.

The psychoanalytic view of form clearly pulls in two directions. To the extent that aesthetic form is related to the conventions, symbols, and historical changes in the collectivity, psychoanalytic understanding can enlarge upon the more universal meanings that are the essence of literary endeavor. However, when form is viewed as primarily the ego's conflict-involved way of handling and transforming unconscious material, in however elegant or refined a manner, the psychoanalyst tends once again to sift through the ego mechanisms (form) to the more unconscious or underlying psychological meanings as his final goal. And when this is reinforced by such a universally accepted theory of creativity as Kris's, that centrally locates creativity in the primary process—thus binding art work and dream work more closely together—then reductionism in psychoana-

lytic criticism becomes even more rampant. The possibility that the artist's ego could function in a relatively conflict-free way to produce new
meanings seems to be almost completely ignored by these psychoanalytic
critics.

The Kleinians, as is their wont, have a significantly different approach to creativity and thus to the function of form—one that is in some
ways closer to certain literary theories.[34] They view the central motivation
for creativity as stemming from the child's need to make reparation to the
maternal object during the depressive stage.[35] If the creative act is thus to
encompass destructive impulses, form is broadly considered as introducing order into chaos; in tragedy, order is based on the paradigm of the
reparation and restitution experience of early infancy resolving destructive
impulses toward the mother. The Kleinians use of this paradigm of early
childhood seems oriented toward the broader view of Kenneth Burke in
his chapter, "Beauty and the Sublime," that literature encompasses
threat, the poet being likened to a medicine man who deals with poisons,
but gives them in salutary doses.[36] Undoubtedly some of the more cur-
rent-day ego-psychological views described just above can also lend psychological credence to Burke's perspective on literary transformation.

II

How has the literary critic used psychoanalysis, and to what extent
have these major mappings of psychoanalysis influenced him? From the
second decade of the twentieth century psychoanalysis has indeed had
considerable influence on important literary critics such as Kenneth
Burke, Lionel Trilling, Stanley Edgar Hyman, William Empson, Robert
Gorham Davis, and Maud Bodkin.[37] For this generation of critics, psychoanalysis has been useful in a few main ways. One is to call attention to
primary-process mechanisms of displacement (splitting of characters, reversals, *double entendres*, and such), condensation, and symbolism, and
as these mechanisms are involved in poetic diction, atmosphere, and setting. Burke in particular sees the structure of a literary work determined
in part by unconscious factors.[38] He analyzes these by careful scrutiny of
the clustering and equations of images taken within the context of a given
work, or throughout the works of a writer.[39] Thus, important incongruities may arise between an author's overt intention and imagery that
unwittingly conveys other meanings. I should note parenthetically that

this close textual analysis of images, as well as of various other linguistic structures, is the hallmark of the French psychoanalytic approach to criticism. But, however much Burke stresses unconscious factors, he became rather critical of psychoanalytic literary criticism in its almost ubiquitous neglect of factors of form and communication, and of a variety of other meanings than the psychological—a criticism to which this paper is fully sympathetic.

Still other uses of psychoanalysis have been to delve into a character's motivation, or of defended against psychosexual fantasies, such as in Empson's analysis of the symbolism in *Alice in Wonderland;* or of the important use of archetypal themes by Maud Bodkin.[40] Then there is the important issue of the psychology of form as communication. In a critic strongly oriented toward psychoanalysis, such as Simon O. Lesser,[41] form is viewed as giving pleasure and/or regulating anxiety. This is in contrast to Burke's broader appraisal of the psychological function of form as the arousal and satisfaction of the audience's appetites, but in a refined and eloquent transcendence of emotions.[42]

In the last two decades, three literary critics have pushed the boundaries of psychoanalytic literary criticism further in comprehensive attempts to integrate literary criticism with psychoanalysis, and in evolving theories of criticism strongly derived from psychoanalysis. Frederick Hoffman does this in "Psychology and Literature," an appendix to his important book, *Freudianism and the Literary Mind;* Simon O. Lesser in *Fiction and the Unconscious;* and Norman Holland in his *Psychoanalysis and Shakespeare,* and more recently and thoroughly in his *Dynamics of Literary Response, Poems in Persons: An Introduction to the Psychoanalysis of Literature,* and *5 Readers Reading.* All three are considerably knowledgeable in traditional Freudian psychoanalysis, and all have been strongly influenced by the work of Ernst Kris. Since Holland's work is the most comprehensive of the three, and the most influential on the American critical scene today, I shall evaluate his attempt to elaborate a new aesthetic based on psychoanalysis—as developed in his *Dynamics of Literary Response.*

For Holland, artistic form is a valid, but nonetheless defensive transformation of unconscious impulses and fantasies from the various psychosexual stages of development into intellectual, moral, social, and religious meanings. His model comes from Kris's theory of creativity, of primary process being integrated with aesthetic considerations, socially or cul-

turally determined. It is also based on the psychoanalytic structural model
of the mind, particularly of compromises between the ego defenses and
the id fantasies wrought by the anxiety-provoking power of the cultural restrictions internalized in the superego. Considerations of early object-relations and various aspects of the self were originally conspicuous by their
absence, but in his most recent work, 5 *Readers Reading*—influenced
by Lichtenstein's work on identity[43]—they are much more fully present.
In any case, Holland's theory is basically a conflict-oriented one and tends
to view the literary work as a special type of compromise formation, not
totally unlike the formation of a symptom.

The explicitness with which Holland tries to relate aesthetic dimensions to his basic model of psychoanalysis, something the psychoanalytic
critic has usually neglected to do, is the most salient feature of his contribution. Thus, he views form as a structure tending to inhibit underlying
fantasies, in contrast to the dimension of language, which distracts the
superego to enable the underlying fantasies to gain expression. Meaning,
on the other hand, is seen more as facilitating sublimation of fantasies than
as an inhibitor of them. The reader's or spectator's identification with a
fictional character is in order to serve either a defense or a wish, depending on the particular traits of the character. Affects that are aroused by a
work of literature cluster around four categories of drive satisfactions,
derived from the four stages of psychosexual development—oral, anal,
phallic, and genital—combined with the presence or absence in the
reader of anxiety and arousal, and on whether his defenses are strong or
weak. This is a much more detailed working out of Lesser's concept of
form as primarily giving pleasure and/or regulating anxiety.

Holland's basic approach, then, is to penetrate through form, meanings, and imagery to the underlying psychosexual fantasies that "fuel" the
literary work; and then to appreciate how the formal aesthetic elements
either allow them expression or inhibit them, inciting the reader to experience his own fantasies and defenses. Thus, Holland emphasizes the communicative nature of art, and the psychological nature of the aesthetic experience—usually neglected by the psychoanalytic critic, and about which
Freud wrote only one paper, published posthumously in 1942.[44] However
important Holland's contributions are in his emphasis on the aesthetic experience and communication, his starting-point nevertheless is still the
Freudian notion of the dream and daydream dressed in aesthetics. The
more sophisticated note that Holland strikes that aesthetic form is defen-

sive transformation rather than disguise, simply results in a newer, much more subtle, and more thorough reductionism. Then there is Crew's incisive critique that Holland and other similar psychoanalytic critics have lost sight of art as being primarily meaning-creating.[45]

III

As persistent and pervasive as is the correlation of the literary work with the daydream and dream in applied psychoanalysis and psychoanalytic literary criticism, it can nevertheless be seriously challenged by Albert Rothenberg's groundbreaking work on the processes of creativity in highly recognized writers, and by my own work on dreams and art.[46] The central issue is that the literary work has much higher levels of integration than dream imagery, and aims at more universal meanings rather than particularized biographical ones. The literary work thus attains and expresses artistic meanings noticeably absent in the dream. More specifically, as I have carefully demonstrated, poetic metaphor—so crucial to the broader meanings in a literary work—is present in the dream in only incipient forms. It thus becomes apparent that Kris[47] wandered astray in equating poetic metaphor and metaphorical expression in dreams—the latter standing analogously for unconscious meanings in the latent content, with the former expressing a high-level integration of the concrete and abstract.[48] Similarly, upon careful scrutiny, it is possible to discern the elements for the making of paradoxes in the latent content of a dream, but never the real integration expressing the paradox.[49] Whatever true integration of antithetical elements from the latent content does take place is from the conscious creative work of analyst and analysand within the context of current psychical problems in the patient's life and/or therapy.[50] In considering literature and the dream, Coleridge's "extremes meet" is pertinent. But if literature is to be differentiated from the dream, then this declaration must be amended to "extremes meet meaningfully."

Rothenberg's work makes unmistakably clear that the integration of diverse meanings in a literary work through its various symbols and metaphors is of a qualitatively different nature from condensation in dream imagery—where there is little if any true integration of the component parts, and where meanings are derived from the dreamer's associations rather than from those of the listener. Thus, Kris's facile equation of ambiguity in literature with the overdetermination of the primary process is but a chimera that has tended to lure critic as well as analyst astray. Rothenberg, in ongoing studies of highly creative writers, has been able to identify a thought process that he terms "Janusian thinking"—crucial to literary creativity in enabling the writer to make high-level integrations of two or more antithetical elements.[51] An example he cites is O'Neil's use of multiple antithetical elements around the themes of salvation, death, and sexuality in *The Iceman Cometh*.[52] Since this cognitive ability clearly transcends primary-process thinking, he relates it to an imaginative or refined part of the secondary process—or what he sometimes terms as translogical cognitive processes. This must be emphasized as a radical change from Kris and other psychoanalytic theorists who place so much of the creative process in primary-process thinking.[53]

Rothenberg's findings clearly imply a rerouting of the basic assumptions underlying psychoanalytic literary criticism. They lend a psychological underpinning to the validity of the multiple meanings in a literary work in their fullest complexity, that should obviate the usual psychological gymnastics of trying to find the hidden primary-process conflicts or varied sublimating mechanisms. Thus, the abstract meanings of a literary work can be accorded a psychological legitimacy rarely acknowledged by the psychoanalytic critic.

Have I now reached the point of asserting that applied psychoanalysis and psychoanalytic literary criticism have gone so completely astray that there is little hope of any significant psychoanalytic contribution to literary explorations? Hardly so. There are obviously a variety of ways that psychoanalytic understanding have been and can be judiciously used in criticism. What perhaps needs further clarifying is on one hand the use of form and structure by the psychoanalytic critic; and on the other, the integration of insights derived from a depth analysis of character and relationship with other meanings of a work. I see no real need to amend a more literary view, such as Burke's that form in its broadest sense communicates the richness of intellectual synthesis and emotional integration in their fullest complexity—rather than as merely facilitating the expression or inhibition of infantile fantasies.[54] In fact, Rothenberg in a study of O'Neill's *Long Day's Journey into Night* and Miller's *View from the Bridge* revises Holland's "form is defense" to "defense is part of form:" the playwright's handling of the defenses of his characters becomes an important regulator of dramatic tension.[55]

The psychoanalytic critic can often use a variety of formal and structural elements in a work, when merited, for psychological meanings. These meanings, of course, do not in any way degrade other viewpoints derived from the formal elements, but are rather supplementary; and in fact, should be integrated with them—a task more often than not ignored by the psychoanalytic critic. The paper on Pirandello's *Six Characters in Search of an Author* and *Henry IV* by Roland and Rizzo in this volume is one example of this approach.

In *Six Characters* we took into account innovative, antinaturalistic elements such as the impotent and repudiating position of the playwright; the lack of any three-dimensional characterization; the unique and incongruous juxtaposition of two-dimensional, imaginary characters existing in fantasylike time and space with a supposedly real, but one-dimensional stage company: and a dramatic technique of alienation—the actors constantly stepping out of their roles. We also assessed the central metaphor of the quest of the imaginary characters for an existence, and the major paradox that although the six characters are more real than the stage company, they depend on the latter for their embodiment and realization. (For a detailed discussion of some of the meanings of these formal and structural elements, see our paper in this volume.)

The absence of three-dimensional characters in *Six Characters in Search of an Author* is thus perfectly consonant with the vision of an unrealized self. In a similar vein, Martin Esslin noted that part of Beckett's significant contribution was to find a new dramatic form and structure to incorporate the existential visions of Sartre and Camus around the vanishing self—which they themselves could not render dramatically effective because of their dependence on more traditional, naturalistic portrayals.[56]

Still another example of an innovative change in form involving characterization that cries for psychological elucidation is Pinter's *The Homecoming*. I have previously indicated that the key to following the play's seemingly absurd dramatic action is recognition of the character, Ruth, as both a character and noncharacter simultaneously.[57] She is both a real character, in herself, and acts as a puppet pulled by the strings of the unconscious, living imagoes in the five men of the dead wife and mother, Jesse. Thus, the seemingly absurd interactions of the men with her, and they with each other, are none other than the old patterned interactions of each of them with their old imago of Jesse, and in the light of this imago, to each other. Thus, the psychoanalytic concept of identification as the internalization within the psyche of early patterned interactions within the family is invaluable for understanding important aspects of the dramatic action in *The Homecoming*, which otherwise has baffled critic and audience alike. From a literary standpoint, this understanding can be used to elucidate Pinter's exploration of the roots of violence within the family as the basis of social violence—conveyed by the metaphor of the visitor.

Lest it be imagined that the approach envisioned here is only applicable to more avant-garde drama where the important meanings of the formal elements are often broadly psychological in nature, I would like to illustrate how Riviere's psychoanalytic analysis of Ibsen's *The Master Builder*,[58] if integrated with other meaning of the work, helps amplify it. In any truly adequate criticism of *The Master Builder*, dimensions must be elucidated of the place of the drama in Ibsen's work, and its relationship to his life; its relationship to Ibsen's sociohistorical values, such as the emphasis on self-realization and humanism versus outworn religious and other traditional doctrines; literary and mythic themes of the older man's search for youth and revitalization, and the sacrificial figure of Solness at the end with a wreath over his head; the plight of the creative artist in society; and the various aesthetic and dramatic devices used. However, I shall focus mainly on the central paradox of the builder of homes being a destroyer of homes.

On one hand, we have presented to us a great builder of churches and then homes—specially designed for their occupants. Whatever luck came Solness's way, he was undoubtedly a man of considerable talent, an artist. Moreover, the desolation of his own family can be easily taken on one level as the personal sacrifices of the creative artist, and his challenge to God as a movement toward more modern values of humanism and self-realization. Why then is there such a need for youth and rejuvenation, and such feelings of persecution when he is at the top and so greatly sought after? Here the psychological analysis of Riviere is very pertinent: he is a man possessed by the ambition of infantile greed, which has caused inner desolation and persecutory anxieties. His downfall is brought about not by his building or creating, but rather by his power urges to climb to the top. His images of his building are not involved in his destruction, only those of his climbing to the top.[59] Thus, art and power become too intertwined. Throughout the play it is reported how he has struggled to the very top from a poor background. And it is finally Hilda, who comes to him in hiking clothes with fantasies of his ascending ever higher, and who urges him to climb the tower in spite of his terror of heights—which brings about his destruction. Thus, the creative builder becomes the destroyer when too infused by power drives stemming from infantile greed. This may then be viewed as a metaphor for industrial man, who abdicates his human needs for the lure of power drives.

In a very limited way I have tried to show how the psychoanalytic critic can use important aspects of form for psychological meanings, when psychological meanings seem appropriate, and to integrate these meanings into a fuller analysis of a work. In like manner, the psychoanalytic critic may help clarify emotional communication as well. An example of this is Pirandello's use of alienation, wherein an actor involves the audience in his role, and then suddenly steps out of it. This original dramatic device induces in the audience the very feeling of being split that is also being communicated abstractly. Humor in Pirandello also serves in a related vein in emotionally involving the audience while simultaneously subtly drawing their attention to the incongruities and splits that are taking place. I may add, parenthetically, that the whole issue of humor in the Theater of the Absurd and its evocative communicative effects on the audience needs further study and elucidation.

However, the communication of emotion and fantasy in literature is a more profound issue for the psychoanalytic critic than the above discussion alludes to, and merits careful exploration. Holland's proposition that fantasies underlie literary works and emotionally fuel them is a most valuable one.[60] But it needs radical amending both as to the nature of fantasies or emotional states that are involved, and to a methodology to integrate them with the other meanings of a work. To carry out this criticism, I must first explicate some of the recent work on primary process by Pincus Noy and myself,[61] and then delineate a more adequate picture of the relationship of primary to secondary-process thinking in the creative process than Kris developed.

If we are to essay the varied riches and varieties of psychic experience, we must first distinguish the mechanisms of primary-process thinking from its function. The mechanisms of the primary process—those of displacement, condensation, and symbolization—were recognized early by literary critics such as Kenneth Burke and psychoanalysts such as Ella Sharpe[62] as being highly pertinent to poetry. But until the recent work of Pincus Noy and myself, the function of primary-process thinking was con-

sidered to be entirely that of allowing the forbidden wishes of the psychosexual fantasies to evade the superego or conscience for limited, disguised
expression—e.g., the Oedipal fantasy in *Hamlet* or *Oedipus Rex*. Thus,
the emphasis on primary process as *function* has always been on disguise
and distortion; in literary criticism, as the search for the disguised or
transformed expression of underlying fantasies. Used analytically for a limited dimension in a work—such as in Doubrovsky's analysis of the card
game in Sartre's *La Nausée* [63]—it renders clearer some of the affectual nature of a work. But as a be-all and end-all in itself, it results in what Crews
terms the debunking propensity. [64]

In the recent findings cited above by Noy and Roland, the function of
the primary process is *also* seen as giving analogous or metaphorical expression (as distinguished from poetic metaphor) to various aspects of internalization, relating to the ego or self and the superego. [65] This new view
of additional functions of the primary process is in keeping with the development of psychoanalysis from an early id psychology—primarily dealing
with fantasies of the psychosexual stages—to the structural hypothesis (the
interrelationships between id, ego, and superego), and now to the very
new developments in ego psychology, object-relations, self and identity,
and internalization theory.

From this expanded version of the primary process, it is easy to see
that fantasies fueling a literary work can be expanded far beyond those
dealing with psychosexuality alone. But elucidating these fantasies or
emotional states is not the end-point of the psychoanalytic critic's search
and research. Rather, it is to integrate them with the broader and more
universal meanings of the work, and to show how they are interrelated.

But to be able to use this valuable asset judiciously requires theoriz-
ing on the nature of the creative process—particularly the integration of
primary and secondary-process thinking. To rely on Kris's older formulation, [66] or even the later more sophisticated ones of Ehrenzweig and
Noy [67]—where the expressiveness of the primary process is integrated hierarchically with formal considerations governed by the secondary—is to
again be rerouted over the old terrain of looking to the daydream and
dream as the main stuff of art. If we take seriously Rothenberg's research,
then the major thrust of the creative process cognitively is rather in an
imaginative, refined part of the secondary process. And yet, at least in art,
if perhaps not in science, a rich use of the primary process is much in evidence.

I should like to present another perspective that the artist's expression of his inner world through primary-process thinking is yoked to the artistic visions and unusual integrations fashioned by "Janusian thinking." That is, that his innermost experiences, whether of psychosexual fantasy or some aspect of the self, are used in relationship to his more abstract and universal meanings.[68] The artist's method of tapping his or her more unconscious or preconscious sources, is, I suspect, through the very images that are laden with more universal meanings and artistic purpose; i.e., poetic metaphors may contain the personal metaphorical as well.[69] While artists undoubtedly work in very different ways, I still imagine that most create in a rather concentrated state of mind over a prolonged period in which abstract meanings, personal emotional states, and considerations of form are more or less integrated within the same state of mind. Of course, there are usually later revisions of the work that involve a sharpening of the formal elements; but even these revisions may encompass new meanings and emotional elements. The point of view I am elaborating is a very different formulation than that of Kris's "regression in the service of the ego."[70]

My perspective differs from Holland in that I see emotional states in literature as enabling the audience to experience emotionally on an individual level the artistic vision being communicated on a more abstract level, through various structures and formal elements. Thus, the task of the psychoanalytic critic is to use his or her depth understanding of these underlying emotional states in their organic relationship to the artistic purposes and vision of a work, rather than as end-points in themselves.[71] Or it may even be the lot of the psychoanalytic critic to point out that the underlying emotional fantasies may contradict the more abstract meanings—if such be the case.

An interesting example of this area of emotional communication is present in Pirandello's *Six Characters in Search of an Author*. A psychoanalyst, Charles Kligerman, astutely pointed out the primary-process nature of the inner plot of the six characters, with its intense, underlying childhood fantasies and meanings. However, being oriented toward the dream and daydream as constituting the meaning of literature, Kligerman completely denigrated the importance of the rest of the drama.[72] In Roland's and Rizzo's critical rendering of this drama, we have endeavored to demonstrate how the intense emotional states indirectly expressed through the inner plot are totally consonant with the more abstract meanings derived from the structure, formal devices, metaphors, and para-doxes of the total play.[73] To quote from our paper, "In this regard, we have already discussed the repudiation of the inner self by modern society as well as the artist's rejection of overly rigid theatrical conventions. . . . On all three levels, however, the individual experiences the loss of a firm social context through which he can establish his slowly unfolding iden-tity. We contend that the theme of repudiation, narcissistic injury, and deprivation pervading the inner drama charges the play's other levels with intense emotion. This emotion evokes a deeper, more personal response on the part of the audience than any of the work's other dramatic ele-ments and devices. . . ." The inner plot thus evokes in the audience in-tense emotions quite related to the overall artistic vision of the work, thus enhancing the artistic unity of the play.

In summary, psychoanalytic literary criticism has most often been shipwrecked by the dual dangers of psychological reductionism and of ig-norance—of psychoanalysis or aesthetics. The latter danger is one of the built-in risks of any interdisciplinary effort, and probably can only be over-come by increased knowledge of the other's field, and close collaboration. The former danger essentially derives from following the very prevalent but fallacious assumption relating the literary work to the daydream and dream. I have tried to cite newer formulations around the dream and art, and on the creative process, that help highlight the significant distinctions between the literary work and the dream. It is my hope that the new perspective will enable the psychoanalytic critic to use his psychoanalytic knowledge to enhance rather than reduce the integrity and vision of a work of art.

NOTES

1. Personal communication in 1974 upon being invited to participate in a program, "Psychoanalytic Literary Criticism: Promise and Problems," sponsored by the National Psy-chological Association for Psychoanalysis.

2. Leon Edel, "Hawthorne's Symbolism," in Leonard and Eleanor Manheim, eds., Hid-den Patterns, Studies in Psychoanalytic Literary Criticism (New York: MacMillan, 1969).

3. Frederick Crews, Out of My System (New York: Oxford University Press, 1976).

4. Kenneth Burke (1941), The Philosophy of Literary Form (New York: Random House, 1957).

5. Crews, Out of My System.

6. Alan Roland, "Imagery and Symbolic Expression in Dreams and Art," International Journal of Psycho-Analysis (1972), 53:531–39.

7. Simon O. Lesser, Fiction and the Unconscious (Boston: Beacon Press, 1957); Freder-ick Hoffman, Freudianism and the Literary Mind (Baton Rouge: Louisiana State University

Press, 1957); Norman Holland, *Psychoanalysis and Shakespeare* (New York: McGraw-Hill, 1964); Holland, *The Dynamics of Literary Response* (New York: Oxford University Press, 1968); Holland, *Poems in Persons: An Introduction to the Psychoanalysis of Literature* (New York: Oxford University Press, 1973); Holland, *5 Readers Reading* (New Haven, Conn.: Yale University Press, 1975).

8. Otto Rank, *Art and the Artist* (New York: Knopf, 1932).

9. Sigmund Freud (1907), "Delusion and Dreams in Jensen's *Gradiva*," *Standard Edition* (London: Hogarth Press, 1954), vol. 9.

10. Primary process thinking involves mechanisms of displacement—such as affect manifesting itself in areas other than where it belongs, reversal, and the like; condensation—of incorporating into one image a variety of diverse, unintegrated meanings, derived from the dreamer's associations; and symbolism—conveying basic aspects of the id.

11. Ernest Jones, "The Death of Hamlet's Father," *International Journal of Psycho-Analysis* (1948), 29:174–76.

12. Rank, *Art and the Artist*; Geza Roheim, "Myth and Folk Tale," in William Phillips, ed., *Art and Psychoanalysis* (Cleveland: World Publishing, 1963).

13. Stanley E. Hyman, "Maud Bodkin and Psychological Criticism," in *The Armed Vision* (New York: Knopf, 1948); Leslie A. Fiedler, "Archetype and Signature," in William Phillips, ed., *Art and Psychoanalysis* (Cleveland: World Publishing, 1963); Northrop Frye, *Anatomy of Criticism* (Princeton, N.J.: Princeton University Press, 1957).

14. In Freudian theory, interpersonal relations are conceptualized as "object-relations." This derives from the Cartesian philosophical distinction between *self* and *other* (object). This dualism has recently come under criticism by psychoanalysts such as Erikson, Lichtenstein, the Menakers, and Searles; and is beginning to give way to field concepts derived from ethology, such as the *Umwelt*.

15. Harry Stack Sullivan, *The Interpersonal Theory of Psychiatry* (New York: Norton, 1953); Erik Erikson, *Childhood and Society* (New York: Norton, 1950); Donald W. Winnicott, *The Maturational Processes and the Facilitating Environment* (New York: International Universities Press, 1965); Ronald Fairbairn, *Psychoanalytic Studies of the Personality* (London: Tavistock, 1952); René Spitz, *The First Year of Life* (New York: International Universities Press, 1964); Margaret Mahler, *On Human Symbiosis and the Vicissitudes of Individuation* (New York: International Universities Press, 1968); Edith Jacobson, *The Self and Object World* (New York: International Universities Press, 1964).

16. Joan Riviere, "The Inner World in Ibsen's The Master-Builder," in Melanie Klein, Paula Heimann, and Ronald E. Mony-Kyrle, eds., *New Directions in Psychoanalysis* (New York: Basic Books, 1957).

17. Riviere, besides ignoring other major dimensions of the play such as the plight of the artist in society, self-realization and humanism versus outworn religious and traditional doctrines, mythical themes of the older man's search for youth and revitalization, and the sacrificial figure of Solness, also neglected the main paradox of the play—the builder of homes being a destroyer of homes, as well as the varied imagery around climbing. Riviere's contribution would have undoubtedly been much more significant for serious criticism if she had attempted to integrate her work with any of these other dimensions of the play.

18. Phillip Weissman, *Creativity in the Theatre* (New York: Dell, 1965).

19. Kurt Eissler, *Discourse on Hamlet and "Hamlet"* (New York: International Universities Press, 1971).

20. Charles Kligerman, "A Psychoanalytic Study of Pirandello's *Six Characters in Search of an Author*," *Journal American Psychoanalytic Association* (1962), 10:731–44.

21. Leon Edel, *Henry James* (New York: Lippincott, 1953).

22. Crews, *Out of My System.*

23. Marshall Bush, "The Problem of Form in the Psychoanalytic Theory of Art," *The Psychoanalytic Review* (1967), 54:5–35.

24. Hans Sachs, *The Creative Unconscious* (Cambridge: Sci-Art Publishing, 1942).

25. Rank, *Art and the Artist.*

26. Ernest Kris, *Psychoanalytic Explorations in Art* (New York: International Universities Press, 1952); Franz Alexander, "The Psychoanalyst Looks at Contemporary Art," in William Phillips, ed., *Art and Psychoanalysis* (Cleveland: World Publishing, 1963).

27. Kenneth Burke introduces the same formulation by citing Pope's highly refined verse as related to the etiquette of a newly propertied class to which he belonged (*Philosophy of Literary Form*).

28. Charles Rycroft, "Freud and the Imagination," *New York Review* (1975), vol. 22.

29. Kris, *Psychoanalytic Explorations in Art.*

30. Edward H. Gombrich, "Psychoanalysis and the History of Art," in Benjamin Nelson, ed., *Freud and the Twentieth Century* (New York: Meridian Books, 1957); Anton Ehrenzweig, *The Psychoanalysis of Artistic Vision and Hearing* (New York: George Braziller, 1953); Ehrenzweig, *The Hidden Order of Art* (Berkeley and Los Angeles: University of California Press, 1969); Hoffman, *Freudianism and the Literary Mind;* Lesser, *Fiction and the Unconscious;* and Holland, *Psychoanalysis and Shakespeare, Dynamics of Literary Response, Poems in Persons,* and *5 Readers Reading.*

31. William Empson (1930), *Seven Types of Ambiguity* (New York: New Directions, 1947).

32. Overdetermination refers to the economic way in which the unconscious attaches a variety of meanings and motives to a particular image or symptom. The symptom is regarded as an unconscious compromise-formation of conflicting motives, whereas images in dreams are often a condensation of a variety of often unrelated thoughts and meanings, adduced by the dreamer's associations to the image. Such unconscious, non-logical, imagistic thinking is known as the primary process.

33. Kris, *Explorations in Art;* Heinz Hartmann (1939), *Ego Psychology and the Problem of Adaptation* (New York: International Universities Press, 1958); Ives Hendrick, "Instinct and the Ego During Infancy," *Psychoanalytic Quarterly* (1942), 11:33–58; David Rappaport, *Organization and Pathology of Thought* (New York: Columbia University Press, 1951); Robert White, *Ego and Reality in Psychoanalytic Theory: Psychological Issues* (1964), vol. 3.

34. Hanna Segal, "A Psychoanalytic Approach to Aesthetics," in Melanie Klein, Paula Heimann, and Ronald E. Mony-Kyrle, eds., *New Directions in Psychoanalysis* (New York: Basic Books, 1957).

35. In Kleinian theory, once the infant has internalized sufficient experiences of the good mother to be able to see her as a whole, and his aggression as stemming from himself, he experiences guilt over his aggression and then needs to make reparations to the mother.

36. Burke, *Philosophy of Literary Form.*

37. *Ibid.* Kenneth Burke, "Psychology and Form," in *Counterstatement* (Berkeley and Los Angeles: University of California Press, 1953); Lionel Trilling, "Art and Neurosis," in William Phillips, ed., *Art and Psychoanalysis,* (Cleveland: World Publishing, 1963); Stanley E. Hyman, *The Armed Vision* (New York: Knopf, 1948); William Empson, "*Alice in Wonderland:* The Child as Swain," in *Art and Psychoanalysis;* Robert G. Davis, "Art and Anxiety," in *Art and Psychoanalysis;* and Bodkin (Hyman, "Maud Bodkin and Psychological Criticism").

38. Burke, "Psychology and Form."

39. This methodology contrasts with the psychoanalytic analysis of dreams whereby the

patient must associate to each image, and these associations then gain meaning within the context of the patient's life and/or therapy situation.

40. Hyman, "Maud Bodkin and Psychological Criticism."

41. Lesser, *Fiction and the Unconscious.*

42. Burke, "Psychology and Form."

43. Heinz Lichtenstein, "Identity and Sexuality," *Journal of the American Psychoanalytic Association* (1961), 9:179–260.

44. Sigmund Freud (1915), "Some Psychopathological Characters on the Stage," *Psychoanalytic Quarterly* (1942), vol. 11.

45. Crews, *Out of My System.*

46. Albert Rothenberg, "The Iceman Changeth: Toward an Empirical Approach to Creativity," *Journal of the American Psychoanalytic Association* (1969), 17:549–607; Rothenberg, "Process of Janusian Thinking in Creativity," *Archives of General Psychiatry* (1971), 24:195–205; Roland, "Imagery and Symbolic Expression in Dreams and Art."

47. Kris, *Explorations in Art.*

48. I am indebted to Gino Rizzo for this distinction between poetic metaphor and the metaphorical, a distinction remarkably absent from the psychoanalytic literature.

49. Since almost everything upon this earth has an exception to the rule, the dream is no exception. There are indeed the very rare, creative dreams that do express a poetic metaphor or paradox, or an unusual scientific discovery. But these are explained by even Freud as being carried over lock, stock, and barrel from the preconscious creative processes of daytime, rather than as being intrinsic to dream work.

50. Alan Roland, "The Context and Unique Function of Dreams in Psychoanalytic Therapy," *International Journal of Psycho-Analysis* (1971), 52:431–9.

51. Rothenberg has more recently been able to confirm this same cognitive process in highly creative scientists as well.

52. Rothenberg, "The Iceman Changeth."

53. Kris, *Explorations in Art;* Ehrenzweig, *Psychoanalysis of Artistic Vision* and *The Hidden Order of Art;* and Pincus Noy, "A Theory of Art and Aesthetic Experience," *The Psychoanalytic Review* (1969), 55:623–45.

54. Burke, *Philosophy of Literary Form.*

55. Albert Rothenberg, "The Defense of Psychoanalysis in Literature," *Comparative Drama* (1973), 7:51–67.

56. Martin Esslin, *The Theatre of the Absurd* (Garden City, N.Y.: Doubleday, 1961).

57. Alan Roland, "Pinter's *Homecoming:* Imagoes in Dramatic Action," *The Psychoanalytic Review* (1974), 60:415–27.

58. Riviere, "Inner World in Ibsen's *The Master-Builder.*"

59. I am indebted to Professor Gary Keller for pointing out this distinction in an interdisciplinary drama seminar at the National Psychological Association for Psychoanalysis.

60. Holland, *Dynamics of Literary Response.*

61. Pincus Noy, "A Revision of the Theory of the Primary Process," *International Journal of Psycho-Analysis* (1969), 50:155–78; and Roland, "Context and Unique Function of Dreams." I am indebted to Susan Deri for her unpublished formulations on the primary process, which have so influenced my own point of view.

62. Burke, *Philosophy of Literary Form;* and Ella Sharpe, *Dream Analysis* (London: Hogarth Press, 1961).

63. Serge Doubrovsky, " 'The Nine of Hearts': Fragment of a Psycho-Reading of La Nausée" (this volume).

64. Crews, *Out of My System.*

65. For an example of this, see Roland's paper, "Context and Unique Function of Dreams."

66. Kris, *Explorations in Art.*

67. Ehrenzweig, *Psychoanalysis of Artistic Vision* and *Hidden Order of Art;* and Noy, "Theory of Art and Aesthetic Experience."

68. From personal experiences in etching and playwriting, it has become apparent that deeply buried emotional states can be used for artistic purposes—states that have not become conscious until much later through psychoanalysis.

69. I will elaborate on this important point in another paper, "Imagery and the Self."

70. Kris, *Explorations in Art.*

71. Burke has a somewhat similar formulation in discussing Coleridge's poem, "Dejection." "The poet would convey a sense of political foreboding. To do so effectively, he draws upon his own deepest experiences of foreboding" ("Psychology and Form," p. 83).

72. Kligerman, "Psychoanalytic Study of Pirandello's *Six Characters.*"

73. Alan Roland and Gino Rizzo, "Psychoanalysis in Search of Pirandello" (this volume).

❧ 13 ❧

The Double
and the Absent

—◆◆—

ANDRÉ GREEN

IF IT IS TRUE that the existence of motion is proved by the act of walking, a similar logic may relieve us of the need to justify applying psychoanalysis to the study of literary texts. There are, in any case, a considerable number of works which argue in favor of just such an approach.[1] The
act of walking, however, does not exempt us from posing questions about
our course. All the more since, despite authoritative contributions to the
field, the efforts of psychoanalytical criticism are greeted with such reticence. Freud himself experienced this. Today, psychoanalytical criticism
is even more thoroughly challenged—to begin with, by literary theorists
who criticize it for all sorts of reasons. They claim, for example, that it ties
the work too closely to an analysis of the author, even though many works
of psychoanalytical criticism deal exclusively with the text and leave aside
the always conjectural biographical approach. In cases where criticism
confines itself to the text, the psychoanalytical critic is blamed for at-
taching too much importance to one meaning of a work while neglecting
the others (social meanings, for example), even though the analyst has
always pointed out that his approach in no way claims to be exhaustive.
Finally, criticisms will be leveled at the fact that his perspective focuses
on the non-literary, and neglects the "literal" aspect of the work—as

Originally published as "Le double et l'absent," in *Critique* (May 1973), 312. Translated
from the French by Jacques F. Houis. Copyright © 1973 André Green. All rights reserved.
Reprinted by permission.

though the literal were not a means of gaining access to the non-literal which always underlies and shapes it.

If these complaints issued only from literary sources, we could ascribe them to a very natural reaction against an unpleasant intrusion. Inured as he is to this type of reaction, the psychoanalyst could simply ignore it and count on posterity to vindicate him. Unfortunately, he finds himself at odds with his own peers, his colleagues, who do not tend to approve of such excursions outside of the clinical realm. Thus, there seems to be a consensus that the analyst should stay put in his office, with his patients, and not overstep the bounds of his practice. We are told that there is no analysis but that of the transference, and that the transference is only found in analysis. Outside of these limits, it is said, there is only adventurism and even abuse of power on the part of the analyst. We should not, therefore, be surprised if psychoanalytical criticism, along with every other branch of applied psychoanalysis, is in a state of recession, considering the heights it initially reached during its first analytical generation with Freud, Jones, Rank, Abraham, Ferenczi, and others. But Freud's example alone is not justification enough. His work, from this point of view, is not exempt from criticism. Recently, one of our most brilliant Hellenists, J. P. Vernant, contested the psychoanalytical interpretation of *Oedipus Rex* and offered instead a sociopolitical one.[2]

This chorus of criticisms does not discourage us. Nothing so stimulates perseverence in an undertaking as to feel oneself the object of such reprobation. But what about concrete experience? Imagine an analyst: he has spent his day listening to a succession of patients, each with his particular neuroses, conflicts, defenses and often burdensome transference. When, finally, his workday is over and he returns to his family, he allows himself some distraction—sometimes by going to the theater or the cinema, or simply by reading a good book which is supposed to allow him to forget his work and his worries. But there is a catch. It is sometimes difficult to stop the psychoanalyzing machine, probably because psychoanalysis isn't just another job. To be a psychoanalyst is to have a psychoanalytical view of any experience. Some deplore this situation because, faced with this professional addiction, there isn't much room left for other things. I am not saying that it *must* be this way; I am saying that it often is.

To set our minds at ease we should note that it isn't *always* so, but only when the analyst is captivated, when the work, whatever it may be, has touched, moved, or even disturbed him. At this point the analyst often feels a need to analyse, to understand why he has reacted in such a way, and this is where his work of criticism, of "deconstruction" begins. This already limits the scope of his work. It is out of the question that he analyze a text to order; the request can only come from within—that is, if something *has already happened* between the text and the analyst. *The analysis of the text is an analysis after the fact.* However, since the text is not the author, how do we analyse it? Before answering this question we should, perhaps, show how an analyst analyses not a text, but a patient. The differences and the similarities will then emerge. The first difference between the analysand and the text is that the analysand is subject to a continuous and progressive analysis which precludes any possibility of turning back. During each session he communicates to the analyst what he is living, how he lives it in relation to the analyst, how he lives that part of himself which is shaped by his drives and his defenses; all this in the face of his ego, which is more or less organized and more or less related to external reality. Whatever the analyst comes to understand from this communication, he will choose to either keep to himself, or communicate to his patient in order to produce a "becoming conscious" which involves the analyst himself (interpretation of the transference). This interpretation will supposedly be related to the analysand's past but, even more, it will be based on everything the analyst has learned from the evolution of the patient's analysis. Every analyst knows from experience that what there is to comprehend in the patient's communication amounts to far more than he will be able to grasp. This is not only because, skilled as he may be, his capacity to understand is finite, but also because it is never possible to backtrack. Even if the analyst asks the analysand to repeat such and such a fragment of his communication, this second utterance will always be different from the first. It will always be *another story* and never a repetition. The psychoanalytical process, even if it is based on the patient's regression, always moves forward, even if the repetition compulsion seems to indicate stagnation. Progression is inevitable as long as the patient continues to live and speak. Time flows inexorably and the analyst, as Heraclitus puts it, never bathes twice in the same stream.

I have just mentioned regression, a major phenomenon that all the conditions of psychoanalysis seek to promote. Because of this regression, the patient's discourse, given its disconnected and rambling style, is sometimes unintelligible to the layman. Besides, the analyst does not listen solely with his ears, but with his entire body. He is sensitive to the words, to the tone of voice, to interruptions in the narrative, to pauses and to the entire emotional make-up of the patient's expression. Without the dimension of affect, analysis is a vain and sterile enterprise. Without a *sharing* of the patient's emotions, the analyst is no more than a robot-interpreter who would be better off changing jobs before it is too late. Today we know that the analyst must be able to bear the chaos of some patients, in order to enable them to emerge and build a certain ordered inner space, without which no kind of social existence is possible.

A recent work tells us that interpretation is not only the revelation of a hidden meaning but, in a certain sense, the creation of an absent meaning, the veritable invention of a meaning previously left, as it were, in abeyance.[3] A psychoanalytical interpretation relies to a great degree on the hypothetical, because it deals with the patient's internal psychic reality which is shaped by his fantasies. It is not, therefore, an historical interpretation as an historian would define the term, but a conjectural interpretation. Contrary to what Freud thought, the analysand does not contain an image of his past resembling that of a city buried in the sands, like some Pompei which one could recover almost intact but, rather, a reality warped by his own interpretations, both of reality itself and of the past, whose image does not remain pure but changes according to his own evolution. This does not mean, however, that the interpretations furnished by the analyst are unrelated to what this buried past actually was. Fantasy is also constructed around a core of reality, much in the same way that certain myths and legends, although transforming them considerably, tell of actual historical events. It would, in any case, seem that what is important in analysis is not that the analyst succeed, at any price, in reconstructing a puzzle, but that his interpretations help the patient free himself from the alienating burden he bears and, if possible, help him to utilize his energies in more productive ways. Thus analysis should lead to the *sharing of a truth supposed possible* between the analyst and the analysand, acknowledgement of which aids in their mutual emancipation. A clinical example should allow us to better understand what I have just said.

A patient arrived at her session one morning. She lay down and at first expressed a certain satisfaction, tinged with gratitude, with the preceding session. That session had concerned her dilemma, which was experiencing something with me and having to, at the same time, understand what was going on. She could not accept this dichotomy. Every time she found herself in one of these situations, she felt that she was failing to live up to the other. Thus, if after receiving something from me, she made an effort to understand, she felt as though she were withdrawing from me; if, on the other hand, she simply enjoyed herself, she would feel guilty for not having made the effort to understand. One could relate this to the difficulties she had in satisfying the two parts of herself: the one requiring an intense relationship with her mother, and the other wanting to obey the wishes of her father, a professor of mathematics. She herself had aspired to become a mathematician.

I had reminded her of her first dream in analysis, where a woman showed her a painting and analyzed it. In her dream, she had protested, saying, "Why bother? You need only to look at it and take it all in!" During the more recent session she told me (probably because the preceding session had been a good one in which she had accomplished analytical work satisfying to both of us, prompting me to furnish more interpretation than is my habit), that she had felt nourished, and that it was as if she still had reserves from the day before and that she needed time to digest them. After this expression of satiety and contentment, she stopped. As for myself, I was lighting my pipe, which she heard me do.

At that point, she began to speak again in an ironic tone, saying, "It's good, isn't it, that first pipe of the morning!" I should note that this patient was not my first patient of the morning. She knew that there had been someone before her and, therefore, that it was not necessarily my first pipe of the morning. It was apparent, from what she said, that she longed for my pipe, for this pleasure that excluded her, and may even have included someone else. The word "pipe" suggested two possible meanings: the first involved the fantasy of fellatio which the previous material had brought to mind; the second pointed to nutritional pleasure. I tended toward the second meaning because it seemed closer to the context of associations—related to the feeling of being nourished by the analyst. I therefore decided on the second meaning, because it seemed more highly cathected by the patient in the transference.

The day before, she had mentioned two occurrences. The first was a comment made by one of her friends, to the effect that her (the friend's) analyst, Dr. X, (to whom my patient had almost gone for analysis before deciding on me instead), really gave the impression of being interested in his patient; whereas my patient complained of my reserve and of the fact that, according to her, I had imposed a distance between us by not responding to her wishes. The second occurrence was that, upon hearing that my vacation would interrupt our analysis, she had reacted to my upcoming absence by deciding to join her sister on a trip to America, although her sister had planned to travel alone. In this I detected a displacement upon the sister, of a wish to be with the mother, by denying the disagreeable effect of separation.

I then understood the meaning of "the first pipe of the morning." It must have been related to the envy inspired by the first meal that her mother gave to her younger sister—her first feeding—after a night spent with the father. She had to accept losing the satisfaction of the breast and settle for the memory of satisfactions prior to the arrival of her sister (the reserves). Whereupon I told her that it seemed that she felt satisfied and full with the reserves from yesterday's nourishment, but the mere fact of hearing me light my pipe, which proved, to her, that I wasn't really interested in her, had been enough to make her hungry again and resentful. She accepted this interpretation and went on, speaking about her avidity. Among other things she alluded to her difficulties with her husband, to the fact that she reproached him for his lack of affection toward her, even though she was quite intolerant of his virility, demanding sexual relations when he did not desire any and refusing those that he proposed when he did desire them. The allusion to the trip to America—in other words, to the sister—allowed me to follow the momentum of the initial interpretation. I spoke to her about her hunger and the envy she felt toward her sister, as well as toward her friend who, with Dr. X, seemed to be better fed and more loved than she. I added that it seemed to me that, although she might have been perfectly sated, the mere fact of witnessing her sister's nourishment had been enough to annul her satisfaction. Rather than feel that she had something extra (the previous day's nourishment), she especially felt what was lacking (the first pipe). By wanting, at any price, to restore the balance, she only succeeded in creating a new imbalance which she then had to correct.

The patient felt very happy: "That's exactly it. That's extraordinary. I always wanted to equalize things between my sister and myself (to annul the difference, the fact that she was the oldest and her sister the youngest), so that we would be similar. When I gained weight, I wanted my sister to eat and to gain weight too, so that she would be exactly the same as me." We can see that through this behavior she defended herself against their respective ranking, and that she wanted them to be like twins in order to deny her sister satisfactions that she herself had to forego, when she couldn't enjoy them through identification. "If you are like me = not different from me, any pleasure you have, I also have."

This summary overview of analytical work should allow us to gain some insight into what the analyst does when he analyzes a text. For many reasons, through a curious reversal, it cannot really be said that the analyst analyzes a text. The literary text is the opposite of analytical discourse. It is a highly crafted product, even when it seeks to give an impression of free association. The text is reworked, erased, censored, the product not only of writing (*écriture*) but of one or several re-writes (one never knows how many times a text has been written), overloaded with interpretations, while whatever fails to suit the author has been excised or mutilated. Was this material taboo, or simply bad? Nothing here reminds us of the conditions of analytical work.

Why then even attempt it? All the more since the text, despite the efforts of modern typography, remains wedded to linearity. The text is a succession of phrases which differs from the living discourse of speech. Everything happens as if certain of the conditions of carnal speech, certain transformations (which will always be so many decantations, even if they masquerade as incantations) had produced this succession of grammatical sequences which we find in written language.

These inconveniences would discourage any attempt, if it were not for two circumstances which come to the analyst's rescue. The first of these is that the text is set and one can return to it repeatedly. This is just the opposite of what occurs in analysis where the repetition of a story will always yield another story. To be sure, a re-reading will never repeat a previous reading, but this only applies to the analyst who interprets. The text itself is sealed—and permanent; only within ourselves does it overflow.

The second circumstance is that any text, as crafted as it may be, always bears traces. Thanks to these traces, which always awaken something in the analyst-reader, an interpretation becomes possible, but never urgent as in analysis, never hurried as in the transference with its countertransferential inductions. With the text, there is always time for further reflection. The "publication" of one's thought does not embarrass the patient.

Moreover, since psychoanalytical interpretation involves a process of deformation of the subject's conscious intentions (it is what I have called a *delirious deconstruction* of the text,[4] causing it to irrevocably say what it has never said), we must recognize the fact that if someone is to be helped here, it is certainly not the author, who could not care less, but the analyst-interpreter, who helps himself through seeking to comprehend the emotions the text awakens within him. Thus the patient, the potential analysand, is not the author as everyone believes and fears, but the analyst himself.

This extreme subjectivity of psychoanalytical criticism nevertheless aims at a certain objectivity. To be sure, interpretation does not lay claim to absolute truth, but rather to an approximation of truth—but we have seen that the same could be said of analysis itself. The value of this approximation, once more, does not lie in analyzing the author, but rather in seeking to discover what underlies the text's effect on the potential reader. Thus the analyst-interpreter becomes that critic who is the privileged interlocutor, the mediator between reader and author, between the text as writing and its realization as reading. The text is therefore re-written by this reading. There have been many complaints concerning the abusive pretentions of the critic who substitutes himself for the author, but who can believe in the existence of an innocent reading?

Of course, most of the time the analyst has, at his disposal, only the definitive printed version, the one approved by the author, who has consented to furnish this veiled portion of his truth. It happens, however, that circumstances sometimes confirm an interpretation. What follows is a personal experience: While reading Henry James's *The Ambassadors,* the more I read, the more I felt that the key to the story could be found in the vicinity of the character who is not named: the dead father, who is never alluded to. I thought to myself that it was an indication of James's great talent, that he constructed this work around this absent reference which dictates the stylistic efficacy of the literary endeavor. Later on, while reading the *Notebooks,* I learned how James worked. He started with what he called "the germ" (I think we should read this word in its sexual rather than botanical sense)—an anecdote told in his presence, a news item, a conversation overheard at a dinner party, a trifle around which he spun his tale, like a patient spider.

Now, *The Ambassadors* is a privileged case, in that we possess three versions of this story. The first, a "germ"; the second, a project of unusual length (forty-five printed pages) sent to his publisher; and finally, the third version, the novel in its completed form. One can envision a very interesting study here, which would involve following the various transformations of the text, in this and other of James's projects, much as has been done in the case of *Jean Santeuil* as it relates to Proust's *Remembrances of Things Past.*

To return to the text, it was with great surprise that I noted the following. In the definitive version, Strether is the ambassador of Chad Newsome's mother, and he has a great stake in his mission. Its success will determine the feasibility of his own plans: to marry the rich widow, mother of the young man, Chad. He will eventually become Chad's ally, losing everything to insure the other's happiness, sacrificing even the love of another woman.

In the second version, the treatment, the character who directs the liberating remarks to the young man tells him, "*You,* you are young. Live! And free yourself from the burdensome duties that your family has heaped upon you." At first, he is anonymous: "A distinguished, older American." James will later call him Lambert Strether, and give him a double, Waymarsh, who will remain a faithful ally of the mother. The initial title was to have been *Les Vieux.*

What James tells us here about the character reveals the essential fact, about which he will have little to say in the final version: a failed father-son relationship between Strether and his child, left forever unresolved by the boy's death from an accident at the age of sixteen. In the final version, we find only a very discreet allusion to the "ambassador's" son. It is barely noticeable, whereas, in the *Notebooks*, James treats it as pivotal.

Now, if we go back to the "germ," "barely ten words" quoted in the *Notebooks* on October 31, 1895,[5] no more than a short story is being considered, inspired by an anecdote told by a friend, Jonathan Sturge, concerning a common acquaintance (Howell). The anecdote concerns a man who comes to Paris to spend a few days—a brief stay which is interrupted by the announcement of the illness or the death of his own father. The man has come to Paris from his own country to visit his son, a student at the Beaux-Arts. Here, the storyteller tells us how the man in question spoke the very words which are to serve as the keystone of the planned story: "Oh, you are young, you are young—be glad of it and live." This, he repeated insistently.

It is obvious that these words, reported to an acquaintance, are those which the father says, or wishes he had said, to his son. The series of transformations which follows becomes clear: the father-son relationship is eliminated; the rather banal initial opposition between a life of duty and conscience on the one hand and, on the other, the regrets inspired by the rediscovery abroad, especially in Paris, of his lost youth, gives way to the relationship between a writer and a wealthy widow whose son (his future stepson) is to be recalled to family duties and financial responsibilities. But the "germ" already signals the imaginary relationship between father and son. Indeed, James writes: "He has sacrificed someone, some friend, some son, some younger brother, to his failure to feel . . . the young man is dead. It's all over." The other young man, who is to be brought back to the fold, will precipitate the *volte-face* (James's term) leading the "father" to side with the son. We are thus finally confronted with the problem of loss.

The notation from the "germ" had to be stored in order that, one day (three or four years later), according to James, "the subject sprang at me, one day, out of my notebook." From then on the subject becomes autonomous, independent of his "germ," his narrator, and himself. "He has become impersonal." Such was the conception, the gestation, and the birth of what was, according to James, "the best of all my productions."

How will the text's effectiveness function? We have compared it to the analysand's discourse, with its diversity and, above all, its different registers, from the most carnal to the most spiritual, the most concrete to the most abstract, the most emotional to the most intellectual. We shall retain these distinctions, despite today's tendency to get rid of them, because they function on the level of experience. We noted that the analysand's discourse calls upon a variety of materials in order to express itself: word, thing and affect presentation, states of the body, acting out. This has enabled us to speak of a *polygraphy of the unconscious* as if it were using several writing systems to express itself.[6] However, just as, in the end, there exists a vectorization which, through a series of transformations, leads to verbalization, the text of life changes into the written text through the final transformation that is written language. Everything is resolved into sentences. In *The Pleasure of the Text*, R. Barthes recounts an interesting experience:

One evening, half asleep on a banquette in a bar, just for fun I tried to enumerate all the languages within earshot: music, conversations, the sounds of chairs, glasses, a whole stereophony of which a square in Tangiers (as described by Severo Sarduy) is the exemplary site. That too spoke within me, and this so-called "interior" speech was very like the noise of the square, like that amassing of minor voices coming to me from the outside: I myself was a public square, a *sook;* through me passed words, tiny syntagms, bits of formulae, and *no sentence formed*, as though that were the law of such a language. This speech, at once very cultural and very savage, was above all lexical, sporadic; it set up in me, through its apparent flow, a definitive discontinuity: this *non-sentence* was in no way something that could not have acceded to the sentence, that might have been *before* the sentence; it was: what is eternally, splendidly, *outside the sentence*. Then, potentially, all linguistics fell, linguistics which believes only in the sentence and has always attributed an exorbitant dignity to predicative syntax (as the form of a logic, of a rationality); I recalled this scientific scandal: there exists no locutive grammar (a grammar of what is spoken and not of what is written; and to begin with: a grammar of spoken French). We are delivered to the sentence, to the *phrase*, as we call it in French (and hence: to phraseology).[7]

The function of the text, reduced to the linearity of written language, is to resuscitate all that has been killed by the process of writing. In a letter to Strakhov, dated June 26, 1876, Tolstoy writes: "In everything, in almost everything that I have written, I have been led by the need to gather my ideas, each connected to the next, in order to express myself; but each idea expressed in words loses its meaning . . . the connections themselves are made, it seems, not by thought, but by another process; to directly reveal the principle of these connections is impossible . . . we can only indirectly . . . through words, describe types of activity, situations. . . ." Types of activity, situations, transformed by the process of writing where the unconscious plays a part, become words, connected and locked into sentences. "Locked in" and "connected" well express what is involved: a process of imprisonment, of containment—lodging a content in a container, W. Bion would say—and a concatenation involving only the resources of language.

It is here that we see the effective power of writing to promote affects of writing which undermine and compete with the affects of life. So great becomes our fascination with the affects of writing, that we sometimes prefer them to those of life. Writing and reading are passions. Structuralist criticism, inspired by linguistics, in an unprecedented experiment in formalization, attempted to bypass these effects of textual affect. The text shriveled up under this analysis which yielded nothing but a lifeless skeleton. Its flesh melted away. After taking a long detour, Barthes, who has had a great impact on contemporary French criticism, realized that these efforts were leading to a dead end. This is why textual analysis returns, like the repressed, to an analysis of the pleasure of the text. The psychoanalyst finds himself more comfortable with this manner of interpreting, where the pleasure of interpretation merges with the pleasure of reading and writing.

The most important question has yet to be answered. Why does one write? Why does one read? From where does this pleasure, which we call intellectual, come?

Writing (as Derrida, in his own way, has eloquently demonstrated) is, according to Freud, communication with the absent, the reverse of speech, which is rooted in presence. In psychoanalysis, the contrived conditions of the analytical situation seek to create a kind of present absence or absent presence. The analysand does not see the analyst; at times he may feel a loneliness bordering on despair because of the analyst's nonvisibility. The analyst, in turn, is made to feel like a parent who abandons his child. But he also knows that there is someone else, someone who is at the same time himself and yet not entirely himself, ready to assume any role the analysand attributes to him: father, mother, brother, sister or any other important figure of the past or present.

In writing, no one is present. To be more precise, the potential and anonymous reader is absent by definition. He might even be dead. This situation of absence is a prerequisite for all written communication. But here, absence is compounded by the fact that writing is *not* the transcribed speech of simple communication. Writing fashions this dimension of absence while it re-presents, while (in a certain sense) it renders present. In another sense, writing deepens this dimension of absence which endows it with its specificity.

Conversely, for the reader, the author is always absent. The text alone creates this quasi-presence or quasi-absence, much as the analyst does for the analysand. Even when we read a text whose author is known to us, he remains absent. Because as well as we may know him, the author never resembles the living being whom we meet and with whom we exchange, from close range or from a distance, banal or profound words. The author is a secret character. But is he, strictly speaking, a character?

He is unknown to all, to such an extent that one sometimes wonders how this person with whom we are dining, or playing cards or chess, could possibly be the same one who wrote such and such a book. This makes me skeptical of psychobiographical studies when they are considered more than a simple element of information meant to compliment our actual contact with the text. Even if he writes for me—if the work is dedicated to me—I will learn nothing about the work by quizzing its author. This is why the author, who values his double identity, is so often irritated by our analyses and, when he is interviewed, always leaves us perplexed. The demon of writing does not show himself to those for whom the writing is intended.

By the same token, the reader is never the same individual with whom I dine or play cards. He is, even when I witness his reading, absent, in a private space, out of reach. The work, as I have said elsewhere,[8] is in this no-man's-land, this potential, transitional space (Winnicott), this site of a transnarcissistic communication where the author's and reader's doubles—ghosts which never reveal themselves—communicate through the writing.

Ghost means death. And absence means potential death. What then does this pleasure have to do with death?

The act of writing is a strange act, as unnecessary as it is unpredictable, but for the writer it is also as tyrannical as it is inevitable. It may be that attempts at psychoanalytical interpretations have remained for too long on the level of preconscious meanings, by emphasizing the role of creation and even self-creation fantasies. Freud blazed a trail but did not follow it to the end. Melanie Klein, after him, saw in the act of writing a desire for repairs in the wake of the destructive instincts—if only because of the negation of the real world, which coexists with the desire to write. Winnicott, finally, placed the work in that potential space where it has the status of a transitional object, that arena of play and illusion between ego and object.

To this, we would like to add the notion that the work of writing presupposes a wound and a loss, a work of mourning, of which the text is the transformation into a fictitious positivity. No creation can occur without exertion, without a painful effort over which it is the pseudo-victory. Pseudo, because this victory can only last for a limited time, because it is always contested by the author himself, who constantly wishes to start over, and thus to deny what he has already done, to deny in any case that the result, as satisfying as it might seem, should be taken as the final product.

As Blanchot has shown us in *L'espace Litteraire*, the farther along in the process of creation, the closer the work draws to that point of inescapable silence, the "vanishing point" where the temptation to become silent lies. The work is bound by two silences: the one from which it emerges, and the one toward which it tends. Writing is suspended in the provisional space, which is the space of reading writing. This is why we feel not only that the text always says something since it breaks that silence, but also that what it chooses not to say is even more essential. We become conscious of it only when the last word has been read and we have closed the book. And we will then have to begin anew with another work by the same author or by another. Reading and writing constitute an uninterrupted work of mourning. If there is a pleasure of the text, we should bear in mind that it is a substitute for a lost satisfaction that we are seeking to regain in indirect ways.

It is said that there are writers who write joyously; we know that some works are read jubilantly. Does this invalidate our theory? No, because what we witness is a victory over a loss, a victory which may manifest itself as sacred fury, as dionysiac dance, as mystical ecstasy. We need only scratch the surface to discover, beneath the denial of anxiety, anxiety; beneath the negation of loss, the work of mourning. This is not to say that the author's anxiety or loss are what is involved, at least not exclusively and, in any case, not directly. We are talking about the text's anxiety and loss, about something which inhabits the text's space and emerges from within it; like a stream, with a distant source, which travels underground over a long distance before reaching the surface. Between anxiety and loss on the one hand, and the text on the other, there is something else: the unconscious. The author's unconscious, of course, but especially the text's unconscious. But how to prove it?

Structuralist literary critics, even those who have the most reservations concerning psychoanalysis, admit that a text possesses formal unconscious structures. The analysis of Baudelaire's "les Chats," due to the combined efforts of R. Jakobson and C. Leví-Strauss, was greeted with admiration. But where the Freudian unconscious is involved, there is a manifest reticence. This unconscious can be detected—I dare not say that it can be proven—and this, without necessarily referring to the author. This textual unconscious is present in the text's thematic articulations, its

brutal silences, it shifts of tone, and especially in the blemishes, incongruities, and neglected details which only interest the psychoanalyst. Traditionalist critics dissect a text with incredible care; philology holds no
secrets for them; their erudition is overwhelming. There comes, nevertheless, a time, a moment of truth, when one has to ask, "But, what does
this mean to me? How, why does this do something for me?"

Here is where ideology enters the picture. No matter how prudent
the traditionalist critic, he will eventually reveal the implicit system of
thought to which he adheres. His ideology can remain camouflaged only if
he has recourse to the ruse of "paraphrase criticism," which involves relating the contents of a work using other terms. We should remember, however, that the work is not a tissue of intentions, that nothing can replace
the study of the writing itself. Still, we cannot proceed without questioning the work, the text of writing, in terms of the text of life—not only in
terms of an author's life, but also of life as a common space shared by
human beings, in which the work takes root or circulates, if only in order
to reach its audience. This whirlwind or commotion of life which Freud
ascribed entirely to Eros, also includes a core of silence, a neutral navel
which life makes us forget as it winds itself around it.

I will hazard an example. It concerns, once again, one of those details
which often go unnoticed: a note to Proust's *The Sweet Cheat Gone*. The
captive has just escaped. Marcel desires her intensely and wants desperately to recapture her. The intensity with which he pursues her leaves
him no alternative other than to transform this escapade into the death of
the desired object. Anything goes: Saint Loup's embassy offering a "re-
ward" in the search for Albertine, the stratagem of replacing her with
Andrée, or of waiting for her to show willingness to return and then feign-
ing indifference, etc. But, at the beginning there is, above all, the intense
fantasy of seducing and winning her back with sumptuous gifts:

In addition to the automobiles, I was going to buy the most beautiful
yacht in existence at the time. It was for sale, but so expensive that no one
could afford it. And supposing, once it was bought, that we took four-
month cruises, its maintenance costs would still run to more than two
hundred thousand francs a year. We had a little more than half a million
per year on which to live. Could I sustain this for more than seven or
eight years? But no matter. When my income fell to fifty thousand, I
planned to kill myself and leave the remainder to Albertine. This was my
decision. It made me think about *myself*. Since the self lives incessantly,

always thinking about all kinds of things; since it is no more than the things it thinks about—when, by chance, instead of having all these things before it, it thinks suddenly about itself, it finds only an empty structure; something that it doesn't know; to which, in order to give it some reality, it adds the recollection of a figure in the mirror. That funny smile, that uneven mustache . . . that's what will disappear from the surface of the earth. In killing myself, I would no longer be able to think those things which constantly parade in my mind. I would no longer be on the surface of this earth, and I would never return; my thought processes would stop forever. My self seemed even more negative, now that I viewed it as something that had already ceased to exist. How can it seem difficult to sacrifice one's self to the one toward whom our thought constantly tends (the one we love), to sacrifice to her this other being about whom we never think: ourself? Thus, the thought of my death seemed to me, like the notion of myself, peculiar. In no way was it disagreeable. But all of a sudden, I found it terribly sad. Realizing that if I lacked access to more funds, it was only because my parents were still alive, I suddenly thought about my mother. And I couldn't stand the thought of what she would suffer after my death.[9]

Albertine has therefore left. And not in just any fashion—she leaves *during Marcel's sleep*. Already, in *The Captive*,[10] it is clear that Marcel has made the connection with the good-night kiss in Combray. The presentiment of Albertine's departure comes to him one evening when she refuses to return his good-night kiss before they part. Marcel then suggests that she stay at his side. The two lovers talk throughout the night, Albertine having rebuffed Marcel's advances. One evening, Albertine breaks her promise to Marcel, who fears drafts, and opens a window. He interprets this as a fatal sign. "In a state of agitation such as I hadn't experienced since that night in Combray when Swann had dined at our house, I spent the night pacing the hall hoping that the noise would attract Albertine's attention, that she would have pity on me and call me back, but I did not hear any sound coming from her room. In Combray, I had asked my mother to come." Here, Marcel does nothing. Perhaps he is paralyzed by waiting for sounds to come from a forbidden room. The rest of the passage shows Marcel identifying with his bedridden and dying grandmother.

Finally, Albertine's disappearance is noticed by Françoise, who informs Marcel of it when he awakens. His response is extraordinary: "Ah! Very well, Françoise, thank you; you did very well, of course, not waking me. Leave me for a while; I will ring you later."[11]

The author does not react much to it. But how can the serious reader not grant to this disappearance all the attention it deserves? In Combray, little Marcel feared, more than anything else, the separation from his mother at bedtime. A mother who, in the scene of the good-night kiss, seems to have no desire to join the father in the conjugal bed. Henceforth, sleep is the essential question for Marcel. *Remembrance* begins with: "For a long time, I used to go to bed early." Here night takes on two meanings. It is a space/time of loss, the possible disappearance of the love object. Albertine's example confirms this. It is also a space/time of pleasure shared with another, from which Marcel, little or big, is always excluded.

During that memorable night in Combray when the object is won, that is to say when its disappearance is warded off, the mother is united with the child *in reading*. (Proust always knew that his mother desired not Professor Adrien Proust, in whose presence she never failed to express the feelings of a perfect wife, but literature—to such an exent that she delayed the progress of her son's work, which only started, we should note, after her death. But I err, since I seem to confuse Marcel Proust and the Marcel who has no surname, a significant fact.) In light of this, what does *The Sweet Cheat Gone* reveal? It is that Albertine will be mourned via the second meaning of sleep, to the detriment of the first: namely, the curiosity concerning the pleasure the object takes in the hidden space/time of night. The dream, grounded in the void of sleep, repairs the wound, as Marcel confesses,[12] because it allows him to be the beneficiary of pleasures bestowed on another. Hence, the dream is the genuine past recaptured, since Marcel is sensitive to the power of condensation, to the speed with which he attains wish fulfillment. In the work, this becomes the mad search for proof of Albertine's infidelity, of her supposed homosexuality. No, Albertine is not Albert; she is a double of the mother, of a homosexual mother. This indicates, whereas it has always been underestimated, Marcel's (not Proust's) love for his father.

But only one side of the truth speaks here. The other remains silent. It involves the "empty structure" in which we see the expression of *negative narcissism:* the invisible shadow of the subject's image. Proust is concerned with the image in the mirror. What concerns us, now, is the exact counterpart of this situation. On one side is the subject and his image in the mirror—in other words, his double; on the other, a mirror without reflection, where the self-contemplative subject sees no image. This is the absent. The suffering of mourning is preferable to forgetting the loss. The whole of *Remembrance of Things Past* is centered around not memory, but the invincible power of oblivion. The writer is caught between the double and the absent: the double that he is, as a writer who produces another image of himself, exists in another world; and he is absent, he who emerges from silence and returns to silence. His absence is as essential to the constitution of the work as is his duality.

James, in a little-known story called *The Private Life*, expresses this opposition in terms of two artists. One is an author who has a private life but no public life (because, in society, he is a failure), while the other, a painter, shines in public but has no private life (because his paintings are drab and uninteresting). James concretizes these metaphors. The writer is actually two characters; one has a social life and the other writes. As for the painter, when he is alone, without an audience, he literally disappears.

The story is about creating, about the division of the subject which occurs therein, and about the need to erase images of the world creating out of a void. It also involves manifesting this void in the created product. In fact, the text's very positivity carves out this void. These two characters, Clarence Wauwdrey (the writer), and Lord Mellifont (the painter), must be joined if we wish to shed some light on the problem of creation. Writing, and reading—for what is reading-writing if not "the capacity to be alone in someone's presence" (Winnicott)?—show us their two sides: that of the image which fascinates us, and of that of the invisible which serves as the image's backdrop; that of the voice which captivates us, and that of the silence without which we could not hear it. The analyst searches for both.

A third example confirms this opposition. It is borrowed from Russian literature—a literature which, incidentally, is not particularly well endowed from this point of view. (We could probably find even better examples among German authors: Hoffman, for instance, to whom Freud referred in his work on the Uncanny.) I mention what follows in passing, keeping in mind that it deserves to be developed further, a possibility we will discuss later. Two works complement each other: Gogol's *The Nose* and Dostoyevsky's *The Double*.[13] In the first, the *negative hallucination* (of the partial object) is explicit. The hero looks at himself in the mirror and discovers that he has lost his nose; he searches for it until he finds it in the form of a whole object (a civil servant). In the other, Dostoyevsky describes not a mourning over the lost object, but persecution by the double who, through his intrusive positivity, replaces, *doubles,* the subject everywhere, always arriving at the subject's destinations before him, preceding him at all times.

These three examples are illustrations; we are not seeking to limit our argument to its explicit expressions. Rather, we should conceive of this as an ever-present structure, which certain writers of genius have made visible. But this structure is also at work *in* literary production, caught between persecution and mourning, between the double and the absent.

Psychoanalytical interpretation of reading-writing leaves many problems unsolved. Once its legitimacy has been established, one is still left wondering what gives a text its literary merit—because here the method is found lacking in discriminatory power. Must we conclude that this problem arises from an exclusively "literal" approach—not to say literary? Poetry offers us extreme examples of this situation. But in poetry, far more than in prose, condensation and displacement are explicitly at work. Everything happens as if the work tended toward a constantly shifting relationship between *veiling* and *unveiling.* Enough has to be said to preserve a *cell of intelligibility,* yet not so much for the language to become utilitarian and banal. *The text must follow the path of a difference constantly seeking its measure by imposing a detour on its message.*

We should specify that the text sustains two forces. For simplicity's sake, we will call "vertical" the one which springs from the body, from its depths, urging, "driving" the text; the other, which we will call "horizontal," is *the pressure that comes from language*—words, sentences and style receiving, through the very irradiation they provoke, recoil effects, caused by the very production of the text. But this pressure of language is neither abstract nor deserted. Not only do language and writing populate this space, but also all the writings which haunt the author: those of his masters, his rivals, his peers, and his potential successors. There remains, like a residue that cannot be eliminated, the radically retrenched space of writing; a space which functions as a limit, as a border which Lacan would term "littoral." Without this double perspective, something is always overlooked. If language alone is considered, affect becomes negativity and we cease to understand why Flaubert vomited while writing *Madame Bovary;* why Proust became more asthmatic as his work progressed; or why Kafka's anxiety hastened his death. If affect alone counts, we are left to ask, why does it occur in written form? Why doesn't the symptom suffice? Why this morbid obsession with writing?

There has been much discussion of the split in the subject, and no doubt our theory of the subject contributes to this point of view. But we must also concern ourselves with other forms of this split: the split of body and thought; and that of affect and idea, of which fetishism is the illustration. Yet, whether it is one or the other, both have the same function: filling the empty structure. Reading-writing, once the structure is filled, inhabits the interstice of this split, this potential space.

It is a space in which the problem of the Real is abolished (no one questions the reality of literary beings), at the juncture of outer and inner (it is a transitional space). It is a solitary space—furnished, however, with the presence-absence of the object: a space of the maybe (*neither yes or no, but that* may *be.*) For those who enter it, it is a space endowed with a power of fascination which can lead to a veritable descent into hell or ascent to heaven. The space of reading-writing is a purgatory.

The "genetic" relationship we have just established between the absent and the double (the 0 and the 2) contests any unitary theory of the subject. It reiterates the heuristic value of the split, but it grounds it in negativity. This succession, however, does not imply a chronological process. A retroactive reversal functions here, because while the double seems to succeed the absent, it is also possible to say that the double is erased by the absent. Sometimes this "erasure" will only affect one of the double's parts. (In mythology, when one twin is immortal, the other often is not.) Sometimes the suppression is radical, sparing neither partner. This reversal, which challenges the succession, can be regarded in terms of simultaneity, as if the double and the absent were produced in one stroke. The "Uncanny," Hoffman's *Unheimlichkeit,* but also Poe's, Nerval's, and many others', bears witness to this. Today, no doubt, science-fiction continues to develop this theme. Beyond these particulars, however, all writing is at stake: splits between author (person) and author (producer of text); between the author and the narrator; the author and his text; a given text and others (of the same or different authors). . . .

These remarks apply to non-contemporary texts. Contemporary texts (influenced, to some extent, by psychoanalysis), have, in so little time, so transformed the written language, that they require new techniques on the part of psychoanalytical criticism. This will be the work of the future.

But we can already see, in some contemporary literature, that anxiety and loss are compounded on the level of the writing. This loss mourned now seems to be that of the act. One writes to question the death of writing. One enters into the impossible situation of writing about the death of writing not to postpone it, but to hasten it. It is as if one believed this death inevitable, and that the only way of surmounting it were to submit to it and to contribute to it (much in the same way that one can control a scientific law by obeying it). To cite one more ruse employed by the double and the absent, I take as an example Rene Laporte's *Fuque*.[14] This book is no more than an essay on "Why write? Why write this rather than that? Why use these signs rather than others?" This remarkable essay is subtitled "A Biography," which we could tendentiously translate as: the writing of life or the life of writing.

Dismantling something can never account for its existence as a whole. What I gain from a certain perspective necessarily causes me to lose sight of what another perspective might reveal. We must accept the fact that the literary problematic denies us any total access to the literary object. The analyst will never deny that there is a space peculiar to literature, created by writing. The literary critic is, no doubt, chiefly interested in the question of writing creating itself. But the analyst will always question the constitution of this literary space, because it isn't writing, so much as what makes it possible, that interests him.

Concerning tragedy, Freud once commented that it is one of the pleasure principle's most remarkable triumphs to be able to extract pleasure from a show of pain. By virtue of this, we could say that any writing is tragedy, since from its pains, it manages to create pleasure, for the author himself—if not, where would he find the energy to write?—and for the reader, who prefers the company of books to any other and who finds great joy in reading sad stories. But why, then, do so many masterpieces lack joy?

We have seen that the work, as elaboration of anxiety and loss, is, in its very relation to death, the opposite of death. It opts for life's illusory clamor, as against the certainty of death; it prefers masochistic pleasure to brutal joy. In these times of a Dionysian revival, we are told to burn all books and all of culture, too, in order to rediscover some vital new human contact which would restore our lost eroticism. I would not be surprised if, in the middle of some dazzling Dionysia, a participant stands on the fringes of the crowd, keeping to himself, forgetting the others and forgotten by them, inscribing a sign on a surface, for an absent person.

And everything will start over again.

NOTES

1. Anne Clancier, *Psychoanalyse et Critique Littéraire* (Paris: Privat, 1973).

2. Jean-Paul Vernant, "Oedipe Sans Complexe," in *Mythe et Tragedie en Grèce Ancienne* (Paris: Maspero, 1972).

3. Serge Viderman, *La Construction de l'Espace Analytique* (Paris: Denoel, 1971).

4. André Green: "La Déliaison," in *Littérature* (1971), no. 3.

5. Henry James, *Notebooks*, p. 225.

6. André Green: "l'Affect," *Revue Française de Psychoanalyse*, 1970.

7. Roland Barthes, *The Pleasure of the Text* (New York: Hill & Wang, 1975), p. 49.

8. André Green, "Idealization and Catharsis," in *Times Literary Supplement*, September 29, 1972.

9. It is worth noting that Proust originally chose to paste this addition to the manuscript on page 469 instead of 465, where the editor had placed it, and which is indeed more logical. If this is a slip, how remarkable that it happens right where Marcel announces to Albertine his desire to replace her with Andrée. Thus the object (Albertine) is caught between the empty structure of the subject on the one hand, and, on the other, the object which succeeds it by replacing it. She is caught between two deaths, the not-yet and the no-longer.

10. Pléiade, 3:399.

11. Pléiade, 3:425.

12. Pléiade, 3:915. If one wishes to defend the notion of *Transversality* (Gilles Deleuze, *Proust et les Signes* [Paris: P.U.F., 1964]), one must also recognize the *verticality* which materializes the fall during sleep and in the dream. But then there is waking.

13. This parallel impressed the specialists. See G. Aucouturier's introduction to La Pléiade's *Dostoïevsky*.

14. Roger Laporte, "Le Chemin," *Fugue* (Paris: Gallimard, 1970).

❧ 14 ❧

Narcissism: The Freudian Myth Demythified by Proust

RENÉ GIRARD

IN HIS *On Narcissism: An Introduction,* Freud defines this notion as the attitude of a person who treats himself as an object of sexual love. He can also detect, he believes, an "object narcissism" in which the subject turns his libido not directly toward himself but toward love objects that "resemble" this subject too much to qualify as "real" objects. These objects must be viewed as mere appendages of the subject. Narcissism, in other words, is the condition of a subject who prefers never to get out of himself, even when he appears to do so.[1]

Freud likes to think in terms of a fixed quantity of libidinal energy that can be directed either toward the self, or a substitute of the self, on the one hand, or toward a "real" object, different enough from the subject, on the other. In the first case—narcissism—the libidinal energy goes in a circle, so to speak; it stays with the subject or returns to it. As a result this subject may be said to be self-contained or self-sufficient, whereas in the second case—"true object love"—the libidinal energy is discharged outside. The self is "diminished," "impoverished."

Still according to *Narcissism,* it is normal for children to be highly narcissistic; even adults should retain a certain degree of narcissism but not too much. An excessively narcissistic adult can be said to be "immature." Freud considers women and artists as especially prone to excessive narcissism. The notion of narcissism plays a major role in Freud's theory of art and the artist.

In the nineteenth century and in the first half of the twentieth, there is a large amount of philosophical and literary theory that corresponds rather closely to the views of Freud on the affinity between artists and the self-sufficiency labeled by him narcissism. A major difference, however, is that in many pronouncements by artists and writers, the condition described by psychoanalysis as excessively and pathologically narcissistic is presented as a positive asset, even as an ideal toward which the artist must strive if he has not yet truly achieved it. Between philosophers such as Fichte or Stirner, some major romantic and symbolist poets, and a prose writer like André Gide in twentieth-century France, we had many differences, of course, but we find also a common element; it could be summed up as a deliberate embrace and celebration of some or all features of "excessive narcissism." We often hear from these writers that loved objects are desirable and poetic only insofar as they become reflections of the poet's self. As soon as it is no longer suffused with subjective passion and imagination, reality becomes banal, vulgar, disappointing.

When Marcel Proust expresses himself directly in regard to desire, as if he were a psychologist, rather than through his fiction, he shares the narcissistic or individualistic ideology that was still widespread among intellectuals and artists during his lifetime. People, he writes, love primarily themselves, and they seek themselves in the objects of their desire. They endow the desired object with a mystery and beauty that really flows from themselves. The superior self radiates enough energy to transfigure commonplace reality into its own image, turning it into poetry. Only when the genuine *otherness* of outside reality breaks through to us does disenchantment occur. Reality does not come up to the high expectations of the self; it is less beautiful, less rich, less authentic, less substantial than the self's own private projections.

In his first novel, *Jean Santeuil*, which he never published, Proust portrays a young man who is intensely preoccupied with himself; the effect he produces on other people is almost invariably good. Jean Santeuil experiences desire—it is not an experience a brilliant young man would like to do without—but his desire never takes him beyond the boundaries of his own beautiful world. He is in love with a girl who has the same refined taste and leads the same beautiful life as himself; she frequents the same people, her aspirations run parallel to his.[2]

If we read the theoretical pronouncements on the nature of the self and of desire in *Remembrance of Things Past*, the great masterpiece

Proust wrote and published in the last ten years of his life, we find that they often remain very much as before. As long, therefore, as we base our judgment on Proust's theoretical pronouncements, wherever they may come from, or on his actual practice as a novelist in *Jean Santeuil*, we will find only material that appears to confirm Freud's conception of narcissism and its privileged application to both the artist and the work of art.

The only place where things are different is also the one that counts most from a literary standpoint, Proust's practice as a novelist in the great masterpiece. There, the fictional substance is quite new as far as desire is concerned; it no longer corresponds to the narcissistic model. It is the desire of a self that feels extremely "impoverished," even destitute. The word "impoverishment" is actually used by Proust, just as it is used by Freud in *Narcissism*, in connection with "anaclytic" or "object love." We may suppose, therefore, that between the two novels, Proust has shifted from "narcissism" to "object love." The fact, after all, should not surprise us since the Proust of the later novel is older than the Proust of the earlier one. "Object love" is constantly described by Freud as "more mature" than "narcissistic love."

This idea seems strengthened at first by the type of object that fascinates the narrator as well as the other characters in *Remembrance of Things Past*. Love-objects always give an impression of "blissful autonomy" or "self-sufficiency." They correspond to Freud's idea of "intact narcissism." It is no longer the subject of desire that is narcissistic as in the earlier novel, but its object. This sounds like a paradox but, if we turn back to *Narcissism*, we will see that the same paradox is present in Freud, too, and that it is a paradox of "anaclytic" or object desire.

It seems very evident that one person's narcissism has a great attraction for those others who have renounced part of their own narcissism and are seeking after object-love; the charm of a child lies to a great extent in his narcissism, his self-sufficiency and inaccessibility, just as does the charm of certain animals which seem not to concern themselves about us, such as cats and the large beasts of prey. In literature, indeed, even the great criminal and the humorist compel our interest by the narcissistic self-importance with which they manage to keep at arm's length everything which would diminish the importance of their ego. It is as if we envied them their power of retaining a blissful state of mind—an unassailable libido-position which we ourselves have since abandoned. The great charm of the narcissistic woman has, however, its reverse side; a large part of the dissatisfaction of the lover, of his doubts of the women's love, of his complaints of her enigmatic nature, have their root in this incongruity between the types of object-choice.[3]

If we go to the great descriptions of desire, in *Remembrance of Things Past*, Proust is going to look even more "mature" and Freud even more astute than the one and the other did up to this point. Down to almost every detail, it seems, everything corresponds to that "great attraction" that "one's person narcissism" exerts upon those "who have renounced part of their own narcissism and are seeking after object love."

Let us turn to a famous passage in *Within a Budding Grove:* the first encounter by Marcel, the narrator, with a group of girls he calls *la petite bande.* The scene is in the resort town of Balbec—Cabourg—in Normandy. Marcel's attention becomes immediately attracted by the adolescents because of the tightly knit appearance they give, and their contemptuous indifference toward anyone but each other.

> Though they were now separately identifiable, still the mutual response which they gave one another with eyes animated by self-sufficiency and the spirit of comradeship, in which were kindled at every moment now the interest now the insolent indifference with which each of them sparkled according as her glance fell on one of her friends or on passing strangers, that consciousness, moreover, of knowing one another intimately enough always to go about together, by making them a "band apart" established between their independent and separate bodies, as slowly they advanced, a single atmosphere making of them a whole as homogenous in its parts as it was different from the crowd through which their procession gradually wound.
>
> For an instant, as I passed the dark one with the fat cheeks who was wheeling a bicycle, I caught her smiling, sidelong glance, aimed from the centre of that inhuman world which enclosed the life of his little tribe, an inaccessible, unknown world to which the idea of what I was could certainly never attain nor find a place in it.[4]

Words like "autonomy" and "self-sufficiency" recur several times in the course of the description which extends in the novel over ten pages. There is not one feature in one writer which does not have its counterpart in the other. The girls, of course, are neither "great criminals" nor "humorists" but their behavior verges, at times, on juvenile delinquency, and Marcel immediately assumes that they are not "virtuous." They must have many love affairs, he speculates, in which they always play the commanding role; they are never the ones who get hurt. He also supposes they must be of a sharply satirical mind, and he is afraid they would make fun of him if they noticed his existence, something he both terribly fears and desires.

At one point, one of the girls climbs on the bandstand in the shade of which an old banker is sitting and she jumps over him, frightening her senile victim who is made more impotent still by the brief absence of his wife: she has left him to make him believe he can still manage by himself. Marcel too, has been temporarily freed from the surveillance and protection of his grandmother, and he visibly identifies with the old man. Fear is an indispensable ingredient in his desire, which is greatly inflamed by such a mixture of youthful arrogance and innocent cruelty. He imagines the adolescents as the very antithesis of what he, himself, is, invulnerable to the vicissitudes of existence, just as invincible in everything they undertake as he feels vulnerable and ungainly, unsuccessful and sickly.

Throughout the description the accent lies on the youthful inhumanity of the tightly knit little group. Just as in the case of Freud, the beloved narcissist is compared to animals that are not only graceful and cruel but above all completely indifferent to human beings. In Freud the animals are "cats and large birds of prey." In Proust they are sea gulls, as befits an episode that takes place on a beach. The metaphor is more elaborate but the significance remains exactly the same:

I saw coming towards me five or six young girls, as different in appearance and manner from all the people whom one was accustomed to see at Balbec as could have been, landed there none knew whence, a flight of gulls which performed with measured steps upon the sands—the dawdlers using their wings to overtake the rest—a movement the purpose of which seems as obscure to the human bathers, whom they do not appear to see, as it is clearly determined to their own birdish minds.[5]

The similarities between Proust and Freud are striking. And yet, a careful observer will note a difference which a little reflection will reveal to be crucial. Freud clearly implies that the people who have renounced part of their narcissism did so as a matter of choice, not because it is pleasurable to be sure but out of a sense of obligation. They have decided to become "mature" and "virile." They are the good people, in other words, they choose the path of duty.

With Proust, there is no such thing as a voluntary renunciation. "Blissful autonomy" and "self-sufficiency" are things the narrator never freely renounced because they were not his to renounce in the first place. As far as he can remember, his lot has always been an "impoverishment" so extreme as to amount to complete destitution, too painful certainly to be freely assumed.

Of what possession does the narrator feel deprived? Of the "blissful autonomy," of course, that the desired *other* seems to possess. It is quite clear in the case of *la petite bande*. The narrator does not desire any of the girls in particular but all simultaneously, at least most of the time. The very coherence of the group, its "tightly knit" character, gives it the appearance of self-sufficiency that the narrator would like to appropriate, that awakens his desire, in other words.

What Freud calls "intact narcissism" is the main, even the sole object of desire in the novel of Proust. Since "intact narcissism" is defined as perfect self-sufficiency and since self-sufficiency is what the subject of desire does not have and would like to have, there is nothing "incongruous" in the choice of "intact narcissism" as an object of desire.

With Proust, in other words, desire can be both self-oriented and other-oriented at the same time, because the main "business" of the impoverished or even nonexistent self is to acquire the richer self that it lacks, or, if you prefer, to become "self-sufficient" at the expense or after the pattern of the self it desires, a self that already is, or appears "self-sufficient."

Nothing is more logical, therefore, than the superficially paradoxical conjunction of self-centeredness and other-centeredness. Freud does not perceive that logic, or he refuses it because he insists on viewing what he calls "object-desire" as a selfless gesture, a deliberate and virtuous sacrifice of "self-sufficiency," rather than a fascination for an alien "self-sufficiency," forced upon us by a state of severe and involuntary deprivation in which human beings might generally find themselves in regard to that commodity. And yet, the possibility of that solution cannot be far from his mind since he observes "the great attraction" that "one person's narcissism has . . . for those other who have renounced, . . ." etc. The Proustian solution is almost visible, and yet Freud must not really see it because, if he saw it, he could not view the "great attraction" as an incongruity.

Could it be that Proustian desire is really "narcissistic" in Freudian terms, in other words that it focuses on objects "too similar" to the subject, too much like mirror images to deserve the badge of "true object-love." The following lines certainly do not support this narcissistic hypothesis:

The fact that we had, these girls and I, not one habit—as we had not one idea—in common, was to make it more difficult for me to make friends with them and to please them. But perhaps, also, it was thanks to those differences, to my consciousness that there did not enter into the composition of the nature and actions of these girls a single element that I knew or possessed, that there came in place of my satiety a thirst—like that with which a dry land burns—for a life which my soul, because it had never until now received one drop of it, would absorb all the more greedily in long draughts with a more perfect imbibition.[6]

This desire has nothing to do with the so-called narcissistic desire of Freud since it is not resemblance but an absolute difference that it seeks. And this absolute difference is the same thing, in the last analysis, as the self-sufficiency the other always seems to possess and the Ego never possesses. This grim vision of desire is as far from narcissism à la Freud as from the reassuring clichés of literary and philosophical individualism in the nineteenth and twentieth century, and yet, I repeat, Proust tends to revert to these clichés and to something very much like "narcissism," as a result, when he speaks about desire in the abstract.

There is another difference between Proust and Freud that we have not yet observed. In Proust, the "blissful autonomy" and the "self-sufficiency" of the desired object are not real. They are never experienced by anybody. They are a mirage of desire which confers them wrongly upon the desired object.

Not long after his first encounter with *la petite bande*, Marcel becomes acquainted with the girls, and their superhuman prestige evaporates. They look no longer like the superbly indifferent semigods he first imagined. Not even Albertine. If his infatuation with this one girl becomes lasting and obsessive, the reason lies in her presumptive unfaithfulness. A treacherous Albertine is crowned once more with the halo of inaccessible independence that, at the outset, radiated from the entire group. Marcel's thirst for the mirage of *being* reawakens. He becomes indifferent again if he can persuade himself that Albertine is loyal. Unfortunately, there are always new or old reasons to suspect foul play and, whenever one of these turns up, painful desire resurrects, even though there is no more faith in the "blissful autonomy" and "self-sufficiency" of Albertine. In other words, there is no such thing as a "real," objective narcissism for Proust. Narcissism, especially intact narcissism, is a projection of desire. No one can really be a self-conscious narcissist, a narcissist for himself.

To say that no one is a narcissist for oneself and that everyone wants to be one is to say that the self does not exist in the substantial sense that Freud gives to that term in *Narcissism*. But everybody is trying to acquire such a substantial self; everybody believes, more or less as Freud does, in the existence of the substantial self.

If the substantial self does not really exist, how can everybody believe in its existence? We already know the Proustian answer to that question. Everybody believes that someone else possesses the self he wants to acquire. That is why everybody experiences desire.

Snobbery in Proust operates exactly like erotic desire; as a matter of fact it can hardly be distinguished from it. A salon can become desirable only if it appears blissfully self-sufficient. And it will so appear only if it is sufficiently *exclusive,* if it excludes enough potential candidates whose very eagerness is interpreted as unworthiness. A salon is like a collective self at least for the outsiders, who desire to appropriate that self. It would be wrong, however, to conclude that the self is a purely subjective illusion. It is an illusion in which everybody, ultimately, collaborates and shares. Since every desire seeks self-sufficiency, no one really possesses it and an open display of desire amounts to a confession of nonbeing. Such an admission of failure places the imprudent and candid person who makes it in a position of inferiority. He finds himself unable to attract other people's desires, exposed to their contemptuous indifference, and, as a result, vulnerable to their own power of attraction.

Desire in the Proustian world is a one-way street that runs not from an objectively poorer to an objectively richer self but from whichever self, having first betrayed its own fundamental nothingness, enables the other self to maintain his show of indifference a little longer, and the show, as a result, will become a reality in regard to that first self.

Almost any encounter, therefore, presents itself as a kind of antagonistic parade. When people like Charlus meet other people like themselves they look a little like two male birds displaying their feathers, trying to look as impressively attractive as possible; each wants to awaken in the other the painful desire which, as a result, he himself will be spared.

It would be wrong to believe that the deceivers at this game are sharply separated from the deceived, that the world is neatly divided between the cold calculators and the innocent dupes. Everybody is a little of both; you must be a dupe of your own comedy to play it with conviction. The romantic and satanic vision of the cold calculator, of the totally lucid manipulator of other people's desires, is a more sophisticated version of the narcissistic illusion.

The preceding remarks place us in a position to give a Proustian reading of the road traveled by Proust from *Jean Santeuil* to *Remembrance of Things Past*. In the first novel, we recall, the hero seems to possess the "blissful autonomy" that would make him a narcissist in the eyes of Freud. This hero manages to see himself much of the time, as if he had already reached the goal of his desire, as if the beautiful self-sufficiency toward which he aspires were already achieved.

This hero is also a successful rendition of the various models that were popular at the time. *Jean Santeuil* is much more of a period piece than *Remembrance of Things Past*. The historical interest it arouses as well as its apparently healthy and well-adjusted hero made it quite popular when it was first published in the fifties. Some critics have suggested that it might be the better of the two novels written by Proust. This view, however, did not prevail. The earlier novel fails miserably, much of the time, in the area where the second most strikingly succeeds—the description of desire. *Jean Santeuil* simply does not convey the subjective experience of desire.

The reason for this failure obviously lies with the self-sufficiency of the hero. Wherever there is self-sufficiency there is no desire; the notion of a narcissistic or self-sufficient desire is a contradiction in terms. The weakness of *Jean Santeuil* in regard to the evocation of desire suggests that the only conception of desire that really works, aesthetically, is the opposite one, the one that underlies *Remembrance of Things Past*.

Does it mean that the author of *Jean Santeuil* was unacquainted with the type of desire that the later Proust so successfully portrays?

If we adopt the conception of the later Proust, we will realize that the reverse must be true; it means that the author was still too much under the grip of his desire, even when he wrote his novel, to abandon the half-strategic, half-sincere pose of self-sufficiency demanded by that desire. He had to represent himself "on top" of every situation, already enjoying the commanding position that we always feel about to acquire through the success of our desires, but that in reality belongs only to the desired object.

Thus, narcissism appears like a valid concept, in the case of *Jean Santeuil*, only because the novel is false, because it is a strategic extension of desire, a mere reflection rather than a revelation of that desire.

In both novels there is a great theater scene in which the main focus of interest is not the stage but the box in which the aristocrats and other prestigious people are seated. The two scenes are similar enough to be recognized as one and the same, and yet they are strikingly different. The difference will make my point clear.

In *Jean Santeuil*, the hero, Jean, is with the "beautiful people" inside the box; he is the center of flattering attention; an ex- but still very famous king helps him straighten his necktie; all the ladies crowd admiringly around him, just as in a television advertisement for an after-shave lotion. In *Remembrance of Things Past*, the narrator is outside the box, looking at the Duchess of Guermantes with desperate desire, feeling a thousand light years away from the divinity. The enclosure of the box symbolizes an autonomy and self-sufficiency that now belong exclusively to the object of desire, insofar as that object remains inaccessible. The difference between the novel that does and the novel that does not represent desire convincingly becomes manifest in these two perspectives. To regard it as a difference in narrative technique only as most critics would now do is to miss the point entirely. In the great novel, the novelist places his narrator, i.e., himself in the position of the rejected outsider, he assumes humiliation and exclusion; this is what the author of *Jean Santeuil* is unable to do; the truth hurts too much to be faced.

What we have in *Jean Santeuil* is only one of the countless manners, of course, in which the mediocre writer can escape the knowledge of his own desire, the practical knowledge that Proust achieves only later and that nourishes the greatness not only of *Remembrance of Things Past* but of the few literary works that can be called its equals in regard to the description of desire.

Thus, the inferiority of *Jean Santeuil*, relative to *Remembrance of Things Past*, is revealed as an inability of its author to realize that the "blissful autonomy" exists nowhere, not even in the desired object. What prevents the first Proust from reaching its own genius is very close if not identical to the belief of Freud in something he calls "intact narcissism."

This suggests that the critique of *Jean Santeuil*, from the perspective of the last Proust, should extend to *Narcissism*. If we go back to the passage quoted above, we will see that it calls for some kind of analysis. There is something defensive and self-righteous about it. Freud obviously counts himself among the high-minded people who have "renounced part of their narcissism" in order to "seek after object-love." This renunciation was necessary, we are given to understand, to make the invention of psychoanalysis possible. It had to be performed for the benefit of all mankind, but there was nothing pleasurable about it.

Freud must be one of these people, therefore, who feel an attraction for the "intact narcissism" of the coquette. He speaks of this attraction as an "incongruity," something a little odd, no doubt, which he is too observant to pass up but which is not important enough to deserve a full investigation. He does not say why this attraction should occur, except, perhaps, for the striking sentence: "It is as if we envied. . . ."

This envy is presented as something that cannot be real because the renunciation of Freud to the narcissistic position is deliberate. The question is: how does one go about freely renouncing the unassailable libido position of narcissism? Freud does not say. If the renunciation were not deliberate, if the lack of "blissful autonomy" were the major predicament of the psyche, the same terrible ordeal that it is in Proust, we would understand that desire must be a perpetual effort on our part to escape from that predicament, and we would not find "incongruous" at all the choice of objects that seem to enjoy that blissful state of being. We would understand with Proust that it is the universal law of desire.

The dutiful man who freely renounces narcissism is a mask. The blissfully decorous playboy of *Jean Santeuil* is also a mask. The two masks are different. The man who passionately embraces narcissism is not the man who virtuously rejects it, but the difference is not so important as it always seems since the narcissism embraced in one case and renounced in the other does not really exist. The Freud who invents narcissism as something of which he himself is deprived reaches deeper into the essential *abjection* of desire than the Proust who was still a *mondain*, but not as deep, I am afraid, as the Proust who had renounced his *mondanité;* and is not the same thing at all as renouncing a narcissism that never was ours in the first place for us to renounce. Freud, it seems, never gave up his belief in the narcissism of others, in an objective narcissism that the naughty and seductive people who do not heed the voice of duty must tremendously enjoy.

Behind the seething puritanism of our passage, a desire analogous to the desire generated in the narrator by the first encounter of *la petite bande* cannot fail to be at work. And the concept of *narcissism* is a projection of that desire. The "blissful self-sufficiency" of *intact narcissism* is perceived by Freud not as his own experience, no doubt, but as the real experience of other people, flighty women, bohemian artists, and so on. Whereas the narrator understands after a while that the self-sufficiency of *la petite bande* is the same old mirage of desire that a prolonged acquaintance will dispel, Freud is really taken in, and the mythical nature of the object to which he feels so greatly attracted remains hidden from him. The result of that continued delusion is *narcissism*, a theoretical construct for which psychoanalysis claims scientific status but which is really mythical. I personally believe that the descriptions of desire in *Remembrance of Things Past* and a few other literary works amount to a critique of narcissism which is really decisive and much more "scientific" than anything psychoanalysis has to offer on the same and related topics. It is unfortunate, to be sure, that this critique remains implicit and that the writers who achieve it regress to conceptions more literary but really equivalent to the theory of narcissism when they try to become their own theoreticians. That is the reason why we must not remain content with their theoretical pronouncements on the matter, and we must go to the real substance of their work.

You will perhaps object that the juxtaposition of self- and other-centeredness that we find in Proust is not only possible with Freud but that it is also the rule, since no one can be 100 percent narcissistic and addicted to self-love or altruistic and addicted to object love. Even the "normal" personality must retain a certain amount of narcissism. Thus, there will be a certain amount of infantile narcissism even in the man who succesfully graduates to object love and vice versa.

This is true, indeed, but Freud nevertheless ends up with something quite different from Proust because his models remain mechanistic. The libidinal energy can be allocated in different proprotions between the self and the other, but it remains a fixed quantity; as a result, you cannot increase the share of the one without diminishing the share of the other and vice versa. This conception leaves no room for the fundamental paradox of human desire, which is, I repeat, that the more morbidly self-centered an individual becomes the more morbidly other-centered he also becomes.

The substantial self and the quantitative conception of the libido are great obstacles to the understanding of desire. They turn it into meaningless pardoxes and therefore compel us to disregard aspects which the Proustian conception makes perfectly intelligible. The deficiencies of Freud's models are widely suspected; what is not realized, however, is that the choice of such models must be forced upon Proust by his continued belief in the reality of *self*-sufficiency, which is the same, really, as his belief in a substantial self. These various beliefs function, on the whole, like the primitive conception of *mana*, or sacred energy. The substantial self is crystallized *mana*. That is why any discharge of libidinal energy that is really "spent" outside and does not return to the self, as in the circular pattern of narcissism, constitutes, for that self, a material "impoverishment."

We have the same thing exactly in many Polynesian religions. If you spend too much of your *mana* you may exhaust your supply. In such a system, the person with an "intact narcissism" is the one who, for some reason or other, manages to hoard the stuff of which the gods are made in greater quantities than anyone else. No wonder he appears more desirable than anyone else. He is more like a god than anyone else. That is why the man with an "impoverished narcissism," as Freud says, would like very much to be among them, to be one of them, but he feels they are too divine not to be inaccessible. The divinity of the primitive god is the same thing as the "blissful self-sufficiency" of Freudian narcissism or the *schöne Totalität* of German idealism:

. . . the supposition that I might some day be the friend of one or other of these girls, that their eyes, whose incomprehensible gaze struck me now and again, playing upon me unawares, like the play of sunlight upon a wall, might ever, by a miraculous alchemy, allow to interpenetrate among their ineffable particles the idea of my existence, some affection for my person, that I myself might some day take my place among them in the evolution of their course by the sea's edge—that supposition appeared to me to contain within it a contradiction as insoluble as if, standing before some classical frieze or a fresco representing a procession, I had believed it possible for me, the spectator, to take place, beloved of them, among the godlike hierophants.[7]

Behind its scientific appearances, the energetic model of Freud really means exactly the same thing as the literary metaphors. The only difference is that the novelist does not believe in his metaphors; they reveal a process of transfiguration akin to the primitive sacred and understood as such by the novelist, whereas it remains hidden in *Narcissism* behind the myth of a really self-sufficient narcissism.

Freud is obviously a greater poet and Proust a greater analyst of desire than the "specialists" in the respective fields of poetry and analysis have ever realized. The most characteristic aspect of a "poetic" talent is that it reaches farther and deeper with such devices as metaphors and other figures of speech than with conceptual thought. Proust is certainly closer than Freud, here, to the conceptual truth of his own metaphors. The metaphors are really the same in both writers, and they often murmur, in the text of Freud, the truth that Proust certainly makes explicit, at least up to a point, the truth or rather the untruth of narcissism, the impossibility of a self-conscious narcissism that would remain "blissfully autonomous."

All the living creatures Freud associates with "intact narcissism," small infants and animals, are deprived of a full human consciousness. These metaphors really suggest between narcissism and human consciousness an incompatibility amounting to an impossibility.

If narcissism reflects a desire still too intense to acknowledge its own projections, the popularity of this theoretical concept in modern psychology, sociology, and literary criticism should not surprise us. Freud himself says that only mystified concepts that buttress the illusions of our desires are readily acceptable to vast throngs of people.

It is not the ineffable nature of the work of art that makes narcissism useless as a critical tool; it is its mythical nature. How could the concept of narcissism help us understand *Remembrance of Things Past* since the level of understanding that generates the concept is lower than the best passages in the novel?

The modern mind is easily seduced by the prestige of terms that sound technical. Even with those readers who know both Proust and Freud and whose mind is not prejudiced against literature, the scales will remain weighted in favor of Freud. He, alone, provides us with the labels around which our incipient and still formless intuitions can crystallize. As soon as the word "narcissism" comes to our mind, we perceive that it corresponds to certain elements that are really present in the text of the novel and we almost inevitably feel that the right solution has been reached. How could Freud be wrong about narcissism since we, ourselves, can diagnose narcissistic aspects in the text of Proust?

In reality the concept of narcissism acts as an obstacle; it arrests our thinking at the point where Freud arrested his; it confirms our natural tendency, the tendency of all desire to consider "self-centeredness"—and "other-centeredness"—as separate poles that can become dominant in separate individuals. Our intuition will remain not only incomplete and partial but grossly misleading. The superiority of the great novelist, which lies in the perfect identity of self-centeredness and other-centeredness, will remain invisible or it will be perceived only as the "paradoxical" but ultimately unimportant and "rhetorical" nature of literary talent.

Freud claims somewhere, and he is right, that he was the first to attempt a systematic investigation of relationships that, before him, were the monopoly of creative writers. Thus, we cannot exclude *a priori* the possibility that some writers at least did as well or even better than Freud. To consider this a possibility has nothing to do with the mystical cult of literature per se or with a blind rejection of psychoanalysis. It does not mean that Freud was not a great man. As we said earlier, Proust tends to regress to a lower level of intuition, much lower than Freud, as soon as he tries to become his own theoretician.

Strangely enough the literary critics do not seem very interested in the possibility I am trying to explore. A little reflection will show that this lack of interest is almost inevitable. The literary critics, since Freud, have either been Freudian or against Freud. If they are Freudian, they will never place the literary text on the same level with that of Freud. Even the most sophisticated among them, the ones who now carefully refrain from practicing a *psychanalyse sauvage* of literary texts, have not yet reached the point where they could regard those texts as a possible source of theoretical insights.

If the critics are against Freud, they perceive the failure of psychoanalysis in its literary applications but they usually ascribe it to some divine or inane *littérarité* that would lie beyond the more or less "sordid truths" exhibited by their Freudian colleagues. It really means, in practical terms, that they have tacitly surrendered the theme of desire, in literary texts, to their adversaries. For years they have tried to convince themselves that the area of common interest between Proust and Freud is of little or no relevance to their pure essence of literature, and they have now succeeded. Most critics of Proust will embrace any topic and work it literally to death rather than even allude to the one subject that occupies Proust most of the time: desire. The dresses of Madame de Guermantes, the texture of Albertine's skin, the Platonic essence of the hawthorne bud, pure consciousness, the "undecidable" nature of the sign, the frequency of the imperfect subjunctive, the divorce between words and things, anything will do as long as they can get away from that implacable and rigorous mechanic of desire that remains at all times the principal affair of the novelist.

All the other topics are interesting, of course, but their real significance is subordinated to desire and can be understood only in its context.
It is not the "ineffable" or at the opposite end, the purely "rhetorical" nature of the work of art that makes narcissism useless as a critical tool; it is
the faulty and misleading nature of the concept. The bluntness of this one-
sided instrument ratifies our natural propensity to cancel out the genius
we do not possess, the paradoxical understanding that shocks our own
desire.

An unwritten law divides all texts in two categories, the ones that do
the interpreting, and the ones that are there mostly to be interpreted, like
Remembrance of Things Past. Our great critical revolutions have not yet
succeeded in overturning that law, or even in questioning it seriously,
probably because our identity as literary critics depends on its perpetua-
tion.

Far from questioning that ultimate taboo that justifies our professional existence, our most recent critical fads and fashions have emphasized the alleged specificity of literary language, its difference with the
language of "real" knowledge.

I personally feel that the language of both literature and the social
sciences tends to become more specific as it becomes mediocre. Weak
creative writers no less than weak researchers must resort to visible signs
of "specificity" as they become less and less sure of their own competence
within their own chosen field of endeavor. The less we have to say, in
other words, the more jargon we tend to use.

This is not the case with such people as Proust and Freud. The text
of *Narcissism* shows that Freud is no less literary than Proust and Proust is
certainly no less psychoanalytical than Freud. There is a difference, however: Proust did not coin the specialized vocabulary that would have been
out of place in a "novel" and Freud did not resort, most of the time, to the
sort of transposition that frees the novelist from the constraints of straight
autobiography.

Between the intuitions and limitations of psychoanalytical theory on
the one hand, and of great literature on the other, there is a gap that we
must bridge. Literature and psychoanalysis in the best sense need *each
other*. My intention is not to build up Proust against Freud, or even less
"literature" against "psychoanalysis," but to facilitate a dialogue between
the two, a dialogue of equals that has never occurred so far, and through
the fault of literary critics, really, as much as of psychoanalysts. Most

critics do not have enough confidence even in the greatest literary texts to hear the theoretical voice behind them and to make it explicit.

The relationship between texts, the role of active interpreters or passive "interpretees" which they must play in regard to each other should be decided on the basis not of some *a priori* decision that labels the one "theoretical" and the other "literary" but of that dialogue of equals I have just mentioned; only a fair encounter will reveal the relative power of each text in regard to the other.

It seems to me that a fair enough encounter between *Narcissism* and *Remembrance of Things Past* must reveal that the whole theory of narcissism is one of the most questionable points in psychoanalysis. We were irresistibly drawn, I believe, to adopt the vision of the last Proust, if not his theoretical views. This vision alone makes the itinerary of the writer intelligible, from the relative mediocrity of the first novel to the genius of the second. A writer's career can be an intellectual experience of major dimension, a genuine conquest of the mind to which even the most sympathetic Freudian readings remain invariably blind.

We found that this Proustian vision gives to one text of Freud at least, the same privileged access that psychoanalysis promises in the case of the literary work but fails to deliver. Thus, after countless Freudian readings of Proust, we can propose, for a change, a Proustian reading of Freud. The idea at first sounds whimsical, but it can be shown, I believe, that *Remembrance of Things Past* is not the only literary work that provides the base for a critique of narcissism. Comparable results could be obtained with the work of Cervantès, of Shakespeare, of Dostoevsky, and also of Virginia Woolf, to name one other novelist among the contemporaries of both Freud and Proust.

We have no time for these works, but Proust is more than enough, I trust, to show the ease with which a great writer can see through defense mechanisms still visibly at work behind the slightly sanctimonious tone of the man who, curiously enough, discovered defense mechanisms in the first place.

Quite reminiscent of our *Narcissism* passage is the attitude of Swann towards the "cocotte" Odette de Crécy, his constant rationalization of jealousy as "mature commitment to object love." Swann is one of those people who can be surprised to see the nicest human beings fall in love with the most disreputable characters. Like Freud, he finds his own irresistible attraction to Odette an inexplicable "incongruity." And he does not investigate the matter too searchingly. He is too well-bred for such a course, too genteel, and secretly afraid, perhaps, of what he might discover.

The irony of Proust is evident in all this, as well as in the exclamation that concludes the volume on *Swann in Love,* the magnificent *cri du coeur* of the man who remains deluded to the end and still defines the love-object in terms of a narcissism quite alien, he feels, to his temperament and even his erotic inclinations: "To think that I have wasted years of my life, that I have longed for death, that the greatest love I have ever known has been for a woman I did not really like, who was not in my style!" *(une femme qui ne me plaisait pas, qui n'était pas mon genre!)*[8]

As a fictional personality, Swann is quite remote from Freud, of course, and from the flavor that gives our text on *Narcissism* its charm as literature, a rather Herr-Professorish charm in a slightly *Blue Angel* sort of way. We are not dealing, therefore, with mere character similarities. What Proust derides, with gentle humor, is an extremely widespread delusion, the same, evidently to which the mythical psychic entity known as *narcissism* owes both its existence and persistent popularity.

NOTES

1. Sigmund Freud, "On Narcissism: An Introduction," in *General Psychological Theory* (New York: Collier Books, 1963), pp. 56–82.

2. Marcel Proust, *Jean Santeuil* (Paris: Gallimard, 1952), 3 vols.

3. Freud, "On Narcissism," p. 70.

4. Marcel Proust, *Within a Budding Grove,* trans. C. K. Scott-Moncrieff (New York: Vintage Books, 1970), p. 271.

5. *Ibid.,* p. 267.

6. *Ibid.,* p. 272.

7. *Ibid.,* p. 272.

8. Marcel Proust, *Swann's Way* (New York: Vintage Books, 1970), p. 292. The theoretician of narcissism is still, like Swann but unlike Proust, in the position of the desiring subject, *because he does not know it.* In order to confirm this point, I will quote, in *Narcissism,* the lines that come immediately before and after the passage discussed above. They speak for themselves:

A different course is followed in the type most frequently met with in women, which is probably the purest and truest feminine type. With the development of puberty the maturing of the female sexual organs, which up till then have been in a condition of latency, seems to bring about an intensification of the original narcissism, and this is unfavourable to the development of a true object-love with its accompanying sexual over-estimation; there arises in the woman a certain self-sufficiency (especially when there is a ripening into beauty) which compensates her for the social restrictions upon her object-choice. Strictly speaking, such women love only themselves with an intensity comparable to that of the man's love for them. Nor does their need lie in the direction of loving, but of being loved; and that man finds favour with them who fulfils this condition. The importance of this type of woman for the erotic life of mankind must be recognized as very great. Such women have the greatest fascination for men, not only for aesthetic reasons, since as a rule they are the most beautiful, but also because of certain interesting psychological constellations. . . .

Perhaps it is not superfluous to give an assurance that, in this description of the feminine form of erotic life, no tendency to depreciate woman has any part. Apart from the fact that tendentiousness is alien to me, I also know that these different lines of development correspond to the differentiation of functions in a highly complicated biological connection; further, I am ready to admit that there are countless women who love according to the masculine type and who develop the over-estimation of the sexual object so characteristic of that type. (pp. 69‘–71)

It is on such texts, rather than on the more exotic and harmless myth of *Penisneid*, that the critique of Freud from a woman's standpoint should focus. The position of Freud toward women is basically the same as the sadomasochistic position of the homosexual object in Proust. The only difference, once more, is that Proust knows it and Freud does not.

❧ 15 ❧

"The Nine of Hearts": Fragment of a Psychoreading of La Nausée

SERGE DOUBROVSKY

I HAVE SELECTED for our attention a rather insignificant detail in a rather famous scene: the scene at the café, the "Rendez-vous des Cheminots," where Roquentin finally experiences Nausea with a capital "N": "Things are bad! Things are very bad: I have it, the filth, the Nausea."[1] Along with the print, Nausea here assumes capital importance: it attains a status which is *clinical,* as the symptom of a malady, *ontological,* as the revelation, through this malady, of the subject's mode of being-in-the-world, and *aesthetic,* as the call to salvation through art, which is offered here by the "rag-time with a vocal refrain" and which will be taken up again by the "book," the "novel" planned by Roquentin in the conclusion. Sartre produces a discourse which "totalizes," or rather, which progresses by a process of totalization until the moment when Roquentin can say "I understood that I had found the key to Existence, the key to my Nauseas, to my own life." Fictional language is equipped, is coupled with a metalanguage which is imperious, even imperialistic, and which seems, from the beginning, to exclude commentary, or, what amounts to the same thing, to include it. For years, the critical result has been paraphrase. After the wealth of explanations offered by the narrator himself

Translated by Carol A. Bové.

(an ironic, post-Proustian tribute?) what more or better, or simply, what else, can be said of Nausea than what is said in the text? What remains for the critical eye to see? Nothing, certainly, except this unimportant detail: the Nausea scene closes upon a card game which is fairly intricate, and the game itself, just at the moment when Roquentin gets up, closes upon an exclamation by the "dog-faced young man": "Ah! The nine of hearts." This paper is therefore entitled: " 'The Nine of Hearts': Fragment of a Psychoreading of *La Nausée*."

At the level of stylistic analysis, you might call it a purely realistic effect; verisimilitude in the narrative code demands that a card game be played, preferably *manille* or *belote*, in a French café in the provinces. From this point of view, the ace of clubs or the nine of hearts would do the trick equally well. For me, psychocriticism begins right where other forms of criticism stop: at the production, in the text, of an insignificant detail which cannot be accounted for by either the Sartrian metatext or by another metadiscourse. Sartre might certainly just as well have written: "Ah! The ace of clubs" or the "nine of hearts" with the same narrative-stylistic effect. It remains that he has written "nine of hearts," and it is precisely this *remains* which remains for the critical eye to see, all the more since, strangely enough, this card, displayed right in the middle of the table, *is not seen* by the players: "One of the players pushes a disordered pack of cards towards another man who picks them up. One card has stayed behind. Don't they see it? It's the nine of hearts." What is insignificant now begins to signify, since the invisible card which is right in front of their eyes is perceived only by Roquentin. This perception must in turn be perceived, and, one hopes, penetrated, by the psychocritic.

Don't worry, I'm not going to do or redo "The Purloined Letter" act, nor will I play or replay some "instance of the card." Abandoning for now this signifier at the end of its chain (which is, in this discussion, our own since it closes precisely the narrative sequence of the café), and hoping to find it later in its place, let's leave Lacan for Freud and direct our attention straightaway to sex. Like Roquentin, as a matter of fact: "I was coming to screw but no sooner had I opened the door than Madeleine, the waitress, called to me: 'The patronne isn't here, she's in town shopping.' I felt a sharp disappointment in the sexual parts, a long, disagreeable tickling." Before it makes your head "whirl," it "tickles," then, uncomfortably, in a definite erogenous zone. Like honor, Roquentin's penis is "ticklish" and of course, only what is by nature delicate, vulnerable to attack, can be ticklish in this way. Now, it strikes us immediately that there is a lack of proportion between the process which sets off Nausea (what in Sartrian terms might be called the "teleological circuit" of fornication: "I was coming *to screw*") and Antoine's usually very lukewarm ardor for the owner: "I dined at the *Rendez-vous des Cheminots*. The patronne was there and I had to screw her, but it was mainly out of politeness. She disgusts me a little, she is too white and besides, she smells like a newborn child. . . . I played distractedly with her genitals under the cover" (p. 59). Without having read Freud, we rightfully wonder why, when the *owner is not there*, he experiences such "sharp disappointment" in a zone which, when she *is there*, is, we must admit, hardly erogenous. Why this "long uncomfortable tickling" in a penis which is definitely more ticklish than it is capable of being tickled? Having read Freud, of course, we may wonder whether there is not an unconscious denominator common to the two complementary and antithetic sequences (*I was coming to screw*/*I had to screw her*), an operating chart common to the pleasure which is disappointed or received, or again, having read Mauron, we wonder whether the two texts are not superimposable.

Once the act is more or less completed, sequence 2 (*I had to screw her*) produces something which makes the analyst happy: a "dream": "I let my arm run along the woman's thigh and suddenly saw a small garden with low, wide trees on which immense hairy leaves were hanging. Ants were running everywhere, centipedes and ringworm. . . . Behind the cactus and the Barbary fig trees, the Valleda of the public park pointed a finger at her genitals. 'This park smells of vomit,' I shouted" (p. 59). Since we cannot go into the problematic of the written pseudo dream, which is not a dream, but can be analyzed as if it were (see Freud, *Gradiva*), and since we don't have the time to undertake a detailed analysis, we will confine ourselves to two remarks: (1) The "dream" subsequent to the consummation of the sex act shows the vagina to be an extremely anxiogenic source, precisely the *nauseating* site of a nightmare ("this park smells of vomit"); (2) if we grant the traditional Freudian decoding, vermin-children, in dream language, we understand the nature of Roquentin's "disgust" for the owner who "smells like a newborn child." The parturient organ of the woman anticipates the final horror of a kind of swooning fecundity (the chestnut-root scene): "My very flesh throbbed and opened, abandoned itself to the universal burgeoning. It was repugnant" (p. 133). *Throbbing, opening, abandoning itself:* Roquentin experiences his final

Nausea as if his entire body had become *the female organ,* which is, moreover, "burgeoning," in gestation. It's an absolute nightmare. For whom? "I was coming *to screw* her." For a man. Recalling sequence 1, we observe that the disappointment of a kind of ticklish masculinity is accompanied by another symptom: "at the same time I felt my shirt rubbing against the tips of my breasts and I was surrounded, seized by a slow, coloured mist . . ." (p. 18). Usage demands that the word "breast" (and the Robert dictionary, I venture to add, confirms it), especially in the plural and in the expression: "the tips of my breasts," refers to a fundamental signifier of femininity, one of its essential appendages and endowments. A man usually speaks of his chest. Everything occurs, then, exactly as if this radical disgust for the female sex, projected as dream at the end of the completed sexual act, is introjected as *fantasy* in the aborted act, the failure to screw being in no way a failure to *enjoy* but a failure to *prove:* from the minute I become unable to prove that I am a man, *I am immediately transformed into a woman.* Such is the logic of Sartrian fantasy which thoroughly regulates the unfolding of Nausea. We could demonstrate in detail, in its four successive stages (stone, café, little Lucienne, and chestnut-root scenes), the inevitable progression of the fantasy, experienced in the merry-go-round of ambivalence, "whirling" from disgust to desire. That is, the fantasy is experienced as a number of stations of the cross at which the man-woman stops, obsessed by the sudden, forced substitution of a female sex for a precarious, masculine one: "How strange it is, how moving, that his hardness should be so fragile" (p. 22). This constitutes, at one and the same time, a malady and a remedy, since, in short, by assuming a femininity which makes you nauseous ("the viscous puddle at the bottom of *our* time"), it is a question of bartering actual masculinity for a kind of inexpugnable, imaginary one, inscribed in the symbolic domain: the "steel band" of music or the "beautiful," "hard as steel" story into which Roquentin dreams of transposing himself.

Those who are suspicious of this analysis can at least give credence to "Sartre through Flaubert," or, if they prefer, to "Sartre: A Self-Portrait." Thus, by reading Sartre reading Gustave, we reread precisely *La Nausée:* "Flesh is complete inaction . . . now, according to Gustave, pleasure arises from a kind of swooning abandonment, from a passivity which is ready and willing; the woman feels pleasure because she is taken. She feels desire, too, of course, but in her own way . . . female desire is passive waiting. The text speaks for itself: if Gustave wants to be a woman, it is because his partially female sexuality demands a sex change which will allow the full development of his resources" (*L'Idiot de la famille*, I, 684).[2] In this respect, Antoine is Gustave's guilty conscience. "The text speaks for itself," said Sartre: yes, especially when it believes it is talking about the Other. Let's take a look at Sartre as he imagines Flaubert looking at himself in a mirror: "At the start, out of his natural passivity, he creates the *analagon* of a femininity which is concealed . . . it is possible for him, at the cost of creating a double illusion, to imagine that he is someone else, who is caressing an actual woman—himself—behind the mirror. . . . There are two *analoga* here: his hands, his reflection. In the latter, he apprehends only his caressed flesh, overlooking insignificant details like his penis or his youthful male chest" (*L'Idiot de la famille*, I: 693). In this "Sartre through Flaubert," then, we surprise Jean-Paul as he rewrites precisely the progression of Nausea, that is, the progressive feminization of his flesh, which goes from his *hands* (stone scene), to his *face* in the mirror ("An entire half of my face yields . . . the eye opens on a white globe, on pink, bleeding flesh" [p. 17]), preceding the entrance into the café where the narrator suddenly "loses" the insignificant detail which is his *penis* and where his *youthful, male chest* becomes "the tips of his breasts." The discourse of fiction and the discourse of criticism display a strange kind of intertextuality/intersexuality. In fact, if Madame Bovary is a man disguised as a woman (*Critique de la Raison dialectique*, p. 90), there is no reason why Antoine Roquentin cannot be a woman disguised as a man. But if we prefer to believe "Sartre: A Self-Portrait," let's listen to him directly as he answers the formidable questions of the formidable Simone: "Now then, Sartre, I would like to question you on the subject of women . . . you've never talked about women . . . how do you explain that?" "I think it stems from my childhood . . . girls and women formed, in a way, my natural milieu, and *I have always thought that there was a kind of woman in me*" (italics mine).

But, not as "natural" as all that, as *La Nausée* demonstrates, and this reticence on the subject of women is in no way innocent, analytically speaking (I'll leave ideology to Simone). At the level of unconscious discourse, *La Nausée* fills precisely the strange gap in the writer's conscious discourse, and the trio "Antoine—Jean-Paul—Gustave" reveals more about it than Sartre would like to say or to admit to himself. We know that the notion of "bisexuality," introduced both as a major and as a poorly defined element in Freudian thought, receives a good deal of attention from psychoanalysts, at least from those of the Psychoanalytic Society of Paris, which devoted its April 1975 meeting to it. According to a recent report by Dr. Christian David, every successful cure implies the integration of the subject's psychic bisexuality; inversely, he tells us: "every serious threat concerning sexual identity or integrity is likely to lead to a variety of disturbances to psychic organization, to the point of psychosis" (*Report*, p. 52). And the French psychiatrist Kreisler formulates the same idea in a vocabulary which is of particular interest for us: "Belonging to a sex constitutes one of the firmest kernels enabling the personality to cohere, and sexuality may be the most primitive and most powerful form rooting us in existence" (*Report*, p. 52). That Roquentin's final Nausea takes place in front of an eminently phallomorphous root ("the bark, black and swollen, looked like boiled leather . . . this hard and compact skin of a sea lion" [pp. 127–28, 129]) clearly indicates that the form taken by the subject's existential crisis consists in a kind of rooting in masculinity. "I am not at all inclined to call myself insane," writes Roquentin. He shouldn't feel this way, especially at a time when neurosis is terribly devalued and when only psychosis gives status to the writer.

The critic, however, is not a psychiatrist, and the diagnosis (if you wish, the "construction" element) is of interest only if it produces something equivalent to the stream of new, repressed material which Freud sees (*Construction in Analysis*, 1937) as the touchstone of a correct interpretation. Here, this equivalent would be the increasingly thorough integration of metonymically discrete elements of the text into a coherent, metaphoric sequence. At bottom, a psychoreading simply establishes what may be called a rigorous logic of details, to the extent that the logic which underlies the possibilities of the narrative is reinserted into the operation of the fantasy. If we fold erotic sequence 1 (I was coming to screw) down upon erotic sequence 2 (I had to screw her), we might say that the masculine obligation which has been fulfilled avoids the crisis of sexual identity, if it is true, according to R. R. Greenson's remark, that "the adult neurotic behaves as if the sex of his sexual object determined his own sex." But traces of the signifiers' first logic subsist in the second: no sooner does the Valleda in the public or public garden point to her genitals as the "sinful parts," in this way reassuring the male sleeper, than upon waking, the latter hears the owner say to him: "I didn't want to wake you up . . . but the sheet got folded under my backside . . ." (p. 59). The syntagmatic order is revealing: this vestige of "daytime" sets off *immediately afterward*

another "dream" in the fictional text, a dream in which the "backside" signifier proliferates, having been repressed as a simple detail pertaining to
the "real" in the vigil scene (the fold in the sheet). The obsession is fully
manifested: "I gave Maurice Barrès a spanking. We were three soldiers
and one of us had a hole in the middle of his face. Maurice Barrès came
up to us and said, 'That's fine!' and he gave each of us a small bouquet of
violets. 'I don't know where to put them,' said the soldier with the hole in
his head. Then Maurice Barrès said, 'Put them in the hole you have in
your head.' The soldier answered, 'I'm going to stick them up your ass' "
(p. 59). Once again, a detailed analysis is impossible here. Let us mention
only the triple associative constellation: head with hole—put up your
ass—bouquet of violets, and, with a movement reversing the first, let's
fold it back upon erotic sequence 1.

In the café where we left him, we find Roquentin in the throes of
Nausea, flopping on the bench: "The bottom of my seat is broken. . . . I
have a broken spring. . . . My head is all pliable and elastic, as though it
had been simply set on my neck; if I turn it, it will fall off" (p. 19). Having
become the "little, detachable object," the "broken spring," the head of
which turns to the point where it risks falling off, reveals severe castration
anguish at the source of Nausea: in vertigo, Roquentin actually *experiences* his head *as a penis,* facing the castration threat which takes aim at
his narcissistic identification. "I dropped to a seat, I no longer knew
where I was": the text, however, *knows* exactly where he is; when he (his
head) drops, Antoine is in the spot where the "seat is broken." Now, in
the crude slang which is dear to Sartre, "se faire défoncer" (to get
buggered) designates the greatly feared act which transforms the masculine subject into a "queer." The anguish of castration, which feminizes,
causes a return to a vulnerability which is fundamental to him: the anus is
the male's vagina. Disgust (desire) for the female sex becomes interiorized
in the phantasmatic register as the obsession to possess a potential feminine sex, which is actualized in Nausea. The fear of castration is accompanied by a severe complementary fear of sodomization. Let's not forget
the answer to Maurice Barrès who tells the soldier to put the bouquet "in
the hole you have in your head" (the soldier's head with a hole in it,
Roquentin's head which has been cut off): "I'm going to stick them up
your ass." Now what is stuck up this ass, if I may inquire? A bouquet of
violets. The obsession with sodomization, experienced as feminization
(fantasy being, along with common sense, the most widely shared thing in

the world, Roquentin finds himself here in the excellent company of Freud's President Schreber who is "God's wife") is, moreover, designated, in the Sartrian text, by a special signifier, *violet*, since, let's not forget, Roquentin's Nausea is also a *colored* vertigo: "I saw the colors spin slowly around me. . . ." A thematic analysis of the signified would easily show that, in the Sartrian text, this color is the emblem for a sexuality which is feminine and lethal (a case in point, the cashier with whom Roquentin spontaneously identifies: "she's red haired, as I am; she suffers from a stomach disorder. She is rotting quietly under her skirts with a melancholy smile, like the odour of violets given off by a decomposing body" [p. 55]). We are, then, less surprised than Anny at this aesthetic repugnance on Antoine's part: "You swore indignantly for a year that you wouldn't see *Violettes Impériales*" (p. 140). But, still more important, violet is the Sartrian color for a formidable female sexuality even at the level of meaning: as *viol* (rape), as *violated*. This is affirmed in the next stage of Nausea when the narrator identifies with "little Lucienne" after he has done so with the putrescent cashier: "Little Lucienne was raped [*violée*]. Strangled. Her body still exists. . . . *She* no longer exists. Her hands . . . I . . . there, I. . . . Raped [*Violée*]. A soft, bloody desire for rape takes me from behind . . ." (p. 101). The very ambiguity of the expression: "bloody desire for rape" (to rape, to be raped?), which is none other than the ambivalence of active/passive desire, is momentarily resolved for the benefit of a transsexualization which is phantasmatically assumed by way of the *place* where desire takes hold of the subject: *from behind*. There is in this an exact symbolic equivalence between the way that he experiences his flesh as feminine ("My body of living flesh which murmurs and turns gently, liquors which turn to cream . . . the sweet sugary water of my flesh" [pp. 101–2]) and his universal Schreberian sodomization: "existence takes my thoughts from behind and gently expands them *from behind*; someone takes me from behind, they force me to think from behind . . . he runs, he runs like a ferret, 'from behind' from behind *from behind*, little Lucienne assaulted from behind, violated by existence from behind . . ." (p. 102). Little Lucienne, having reappeared just in time as the last link in the chain of verbal delirium, is necessarily "assaulted from behind," if Roquentin is to be able to "become" her. Here, according to the law which Freud assigned to the development of the dream sequences of a single night, which progress from what is most hidden to what is most manifest, all elements of the Sartroquentinian phantasma appear unrepressed in the delirious writing (desyntaxization, de-grammaticalization, decodification in the narrative indicating that "textual work" is fulfilling sexual impulse). We have not yet arrived at that point, and in the café scene, the elements mentioned only show through some-thing else, are a little obscured, hesitant: like cousin Adolph's *suspenders* (the traditional emblem, if ever there was one, of proletarian machismo, the Gabin-suspenders of the Prévert-Carné films), which "hesitate" be-tween blue and mauve ("You feel like saying, 'All right, *become* violet and let's hear no more about it' " [p. 19]). But, at this stage, and it is for this reason that they are discussed, that is, written about, the suspenders can-not, *do not want to* become violet; and where Robbe-Grillet formerly saw naive anthropomorphism in Sartrian description, we see the very clear, precise inscription of fantasy, which already articulates "the time of violet suspenders and broken chair seats" (p. 21) in a strangely condense form. The drive which is yearning and delirious is controlled by the call already mentioned to a kind of imaginary masculinity, to this "band of steel, the narrow duration of the music which traverses our time through and through" (p. 21), whose effect is indicated as specifically as is its cause: "When the voice was heard in the silence, I felt my body *harden* and the Nausea *vanish*" (p. 22) [italics mine]. A contained drive, we might say, but also one in which a dangerous and latent feminization is retrieved not only in the *female* vocalist's song, but in the very reaction of the vet-erinarian's little girl listening to the music: "Barely seated, the girl has been seized by it: she holds herself stiffly, her eyes wide open . . ." (p. 22). A phallic, female child, we might say, in whom what holds itself stiffly is a woman's penis. We are hardly surprised that the book's final solution constitutes a kind of fetishism of art.

Yet the café scene doesn't end with the disappearance of Nausea under the spell of the music; it closes upon that innocuous card game which demanded our attention in the beginning, less innocuous, perhaps, for being *manille*, if we consider that Nausea originally attacks the *main* (hand), which is punished later on ("I . . . stab the knife into the palm" [p. 100]). Having averted obsession with sodomization, Roquentin has yet to confront the threat of castration, in order that the well-known "mascu-line protest" be complete. It is this second phase of the phantasmatic operation that is carried out vicariously in the card players scene. When the "great, red-faced man" throws down his diamond *manille,* the "dog-faced young man" immediately trumps him (this head, like that of a domesticated, male animal, is an improvement over Roquentin's "pliable," "elastic" one): "Hell. He's trumped" (p. 23). You *coupe* (trump) in cards; you also *coupe* (castrate) on the analyst's couch; and there, when it comes to the father, there's no cutting out. It's precisely he who appears, only to disappear in his most classic form: The outline of the *king of hearts* appears between his curled fingers, then it is turned on its face and the game goes on. Mighty king, come from so far, prepared by so many combinations, by so many vanished gestures. He disappears in turn so that other combinations *can be born*, other gestures . . ." (p. 23). The unexpected lyricism in this passage has no meaning in terms of the "realistic" code of a narrative in which Roquentin is not known to be a great "cardomaniac" or "manillephile." On an Other Stage and in another code, the reading is perfectly logical: the "son" castrates *(coupe)* the "father," liquidates the Oedipal complex by reversing the threat; in order that the son *be born*, the "king of hearts" disappears, as Mr. de Rollebon does later on (another imaginary murder of the father). Dubbed male, consecrated truly virile, he is struck by an otherwise unexplainable "emotion" which we can well understand: "I am touched, I feel my body at rest like a precision machine" (p. 23), a rest which is well deserved after such transexual terrors. We understand equally well the stream of memories which suddenly overwhelms Roquentin precisely at this point in the phantasmatic chain: "I have . . . plunged into forests, always making my way towards other cities. I have had women, I have fought with men . . ." (p. 23). In keeping with a masculinity which is from now on homologized, reassured concerning his two essential attributes, the screwer-fighter is at peace with his "human machine": it is normal that he *should see* what others *do not see*, since this is the site of his fantasy: the *"neuf de coeur."*[3] "New of heart," he can set out once again ("That's it, I'm going to leave") and best foot forward, except, alas, for putting his foot in it. It's the card which "has stayed behind": "someone takes it at last, gives it to the dog-faced young man. . . . Ah! The nine of hearts" (p. 23). There is certainly reason for this surprise. As far as the fantasy's resolution is concerned, you are not "given" masculinity, you have to "take" it yourself, that is, undertake it, unless you have "stayed behind," or as we say, "are left back." Not knowing what to do with it and not having yet decided to transmute or to "transmalize" it into writing, "the young man turns and turns the nine of hearts between his fingers" (p. 34). But, along with this failure, there may already be the promise of a (re)solution to come, since, next to the young

man, "the violet-faced man bends over a sheet of paper and sucks his pencil."

NOTES

1. Quotations are from Lloyd Alexander's translation of *La Nausée* (New York: New Directions Paperback, 1964). I have altered a few passages, especially some of Mr. Alexander's
sexual terminology, which often lacks the "thrust" of the original.

2. My translation.

3. *Neuf*, of course, means both "nine" and "new" here.

❧ 16 ❧

Psychoanalysis in Search of Pirandello: Six Characters and Henry IV

ALAN ROLAND
and
GINO RIZZO

I

FEW DRAMATIC WORKS have so challenged the modern imagination as Pirandello's *Six Characters in Search of an Author* and *Henry IV*. Over the years, critics and audiences have endeavored to understand these enigmatic and profoundly psychological works only to discover still deeper and more complex layers of meaning. It is hardly surprising, then, that the better-known of the two works, *Six Characters*, has attracted a recent flurry of critical attention based on psychoanalysis,[1] a dimension of psychology not so readily available to an earlier generation of Pirandello critics.

To assess the contributions of the psychoanalytic critic is to confront the promise and the problems of traditional applied psychoanalysis; even more pertinent is the need for a more valid critical endeavor that can still encompass psychoanalysis. The most fruitful of the insights generated by a psychoanalytic approach has been Kligerman's study of the inner plot of the six characters,[2] a strategy generated by Ernest Jones's analysis of the play-within-the-play in *Hamlet*.[3] This analysis in turn reflects the importance ascribed by Freud to the dream-within-the-dream, a structure which classical psychoanalysis interprets as yielding the fullest and deepest expression of infantile fantasies, wishes, and conflicts.[4] Kligerman insightfully assessed the inner plot and the six characters as expressing qualities of the primary process,[5] in contrast to the full development of character and the rationality of dramatic action characteristic of the secondary process. He was then able to delineate a variety of infantile psychological themes.

The promise of this psychoanalytic approach became transformed into a problem in criticism the moment Kligerman dismissed the rest of the play as being of little consequence—mere "comic badinage between actors and characters, and a great deal of philosophical discussion of reality and art. . . ."[6] Wangh[7] and Jacobs[8] followed suit, but differed in their interpretations of the inner plot; the former stressed pathological Oedipal jealousy, while the latter focused on pre-Oedipal deprivation. The extreme emphasis laid by these critics upon the inner plot can now be dismissed as mere exaggeration reflecting their concern with plumbing the depths of the psyche rather than subjecting the *artistic* work to critical analysis. This emphasis stems from an explicit psychoanalytic assumption that the greatness of a literary work lies not in its artistic vision and the aesthetic experience it affords, but rather in the author's ability to communicate on a subliminal level to his audience intense and universal unconscious infantile conflicts.

Another major cul-de-sac into which the Pirandellian psychoanalyst-critic has unwittingly wandered is the formulation that form and structure basically function as defensive transformations of infantile fantasies.[9] Thus Wangh viewed the particular amalgamation of structures in *Six Characters* as a layering of resistances to disguise and defend against the expression of intense infantile conflicts and passions. This type of analysis adds little to our overall understanding of the play as an artistic and dramatic work; at best, it serves to illumine the inner struggles of the playwright.

As the psychoanalyst-critic is beleagured by problems in aesthetics, the drama critic interested in psychoanalysis is beset by the complexity of new contributions in the field. Eric Bentley first initiated a more valid critical approach by incorporating the insights of Kligerman with attempts to encompass the philosophical discussions and the total dramatic action of *Six Characters*. But in turning to the "avant-garde" position of R. D.

Laing,[10] Bentley analyzes *Six Characters* as being concerned with schizophrenia. "I am arguing that it is not a philosophical play at all because the philosophy is harnessed to a non-philosophical chariot. *The content is psychopathological from beginning to end.*"[11] (Italics ours.) Bentley concludes by drawing attention to the dialectical relationship existing between the indeterminate nature of the six characters with their loose temporal and spatial contexts, and the utter one-dimensional concreteness of actors and director moving within a clear specificity of time and place. But he is content to observe that as indeterminate as the six characters are, they are ironically far less one-dimensional than the supposed "real" personages drawn from life; and that this reversal functions as one of the play's major comic devices.

Are we then justified in averring that *Six Characters in Search of an Author* is a play about schizophrenia? Or even that it is about pathological jealousy or emotional deprivation? We think not. In our judgment, *Six Characters* explores modern man's fate in a way far more extensive and profound than a work primarily engaged in studying individual forms of psychopathology. A more valid use of psychoanalysis in Pirandello criticism would maintain the critic's sensitivity to the subtleties of form and structure, while incorporating the contemporary psychoanalyst's knowledge in the areas of identity and the self. A thoughtful examination of the structure of *Six Characters* is very much to the point in beginning our analysis, to be followed by important, recent considerations on the nature of splitting.

Six Characters unfolds within the shell of naturalistic form. Six characters appear at the premises of an acting company who are rehearsing the Pirandello play, *Rules of the Game.* The characters become involved in a dramatic encounter depicting their desperate attempts to become realized on stage after their author has repudiated them. Naturalistic structure and dramatic tension are initially sustained by the characters' efforts to persuade the company's manager to stage them. Their endeavor meets with success, and they then proceed to enact the drama of their own story. But naturalism, as it is generally understood, ceases at this point to provide the dominant dramatic structure.

The play's antinaturalist stance is exemplified by the position of the author in relation to the play. The Pirandellian author fails to assume his classical role as teacher, prophet, or as central intelligence; rather the playwright is now disclosed as being impotent and repudiating. Rejection of the naturalistic mode is further evidenced by the fact that the six characters are in themselves only two-dimensional figures unlike the characters found in naturalistic drama; indeed, the actors, manager, and stagehands are one step further removed from the dominant mode in that they are but one dimensional stereotypes. The play is thus totally unsuited to method techniques of any kind and hardly lends itself to complex forms of characterization.

The movement in dramatic form from naturalistic to antinaturalistic structure is significant in that it allows the characters to project themselves as *psychological processes,* rather than as characterization suitable for individual, depth-psychological analysis. As Bentley noted, the six characters exist within a paradoxical situation. While they are far more real and passionate than the members of the acting company, they nevertheless exist within a fantasy, primary-process realm in contrast to the "real" secondary-process universe of the acting company. In this fashion, the play's two levels of reality are linked to each other within a structure of juxtaposition and overriding incongruity. Moreover, there is the further paradox that while the six characters are more real than the stage company, they nevertheless utterly depend on the latter for their realization.

As the naturalistic action progresses, we gradually find ourselves standing in a hallway of mirrors where multilevel vantage points reflect reality's many facets. Thus, a considerable part of the incongruous interaction between actors, manager, and characters could have occurred just as easily in Act II as in Act III, and vice versa. As Kligerman astutely observed, only the inner plot involving the six characters demonstrates a highly structured development.

Other modifications of naturalistic structure may be found in any number of experimental devices introduced by Pirandello into the dramatic structure. First, we note that all the actors in the cast and particularly the six characters experience a marked sense of alienation from their roles. From roles played to thoroughly engrossed audiences, the actors suddenly step forth as persons, thereby destroying the traditional illusion of character. Second, we observe that the play is presented as process—it is presented in the making, unfolding contemporaneously with the desperate search of the six characters for existence and embodiment. Then, the work has been termed a comedy although its incongruities are not only humorous but painful and tragic as well. In this way, the old form of comedy is transformed into what may properly be called a "grotesque." [12]

Overt themes in *Six Characters* deal with the nature of theater and the creative process. More specifically, the play expresses the conflicts between the author and his work, and between the work and its meaningful embodiment on stage. However, we see this exploration into the life of the theater not as an end in itself, but rather as paradoxically related to life itself, which is theater. Pirandello's choice of only one- and two-dimensional characters at once suggests an exploration of the psychological processes and existential dilemmas which beset twentieth-century man.

The psychoanalyst might well object that such an approach ignores profound psychological considerations. *The aim of our methodology, however, will be to use psychoanalysis to elucidate the psychological aspects of the play's central metaphors, paradoxes, and structures—those symbolic forms that make the work universal—rather than to isolate psychological content as an end unto itself.*[13] Thus we seek to integrate the "depth" approach of psychoanalysis with more properly literary ends to achieve what we consider a valid form of psychoanalytic literary criticism.

With this orientation in mind, it becomes evident that the inner drama of the six characters in quest of author and existence must be viewed not only in terms of its psychological import, but as a crucial metaphor as well as structural element of intrinsic value in and of itself. As projections of the creative imagination and symbolic expressions of the inner self juxtaposed with social role, the six characters assume an importance that transcends the limits of their own drama. By contrast, Shakespeare's "play-within-the-play" in *Hamlet*—integral as it is to the work—is of far less consequence as an overall structural element than the inner plot of *Six Characters*.

Prior to interpreting *Six Characters*, we must clarify "splitting," a key psychoanalytic concept of considerable complexity. Splitting involves many of the most salient contributions of contemporary psychoanalysis, ones highly relevant to an understanding of Pirandello—with distinctions to be made that have yet to be discussed in psychoanalytic literary criticism.

One well-known definition of the term refers to the splitting of a single character into two or more others. The operation involves the primary-process mechanism of displacement and may be utilized to sharpen characterization. The notion of splitting has been understood and applied over the years by a number of psychoanalytically oriented critics—first and foremost Kenneth Burke in "Freud and the Analysis of Poetry."[14] A refinement in our understanding of splitting by displacement is to be found in a paper published by Sheppard and Saul in 1958.[15] Their findings have suggested to us that the splitting of characters by displacement occurs at times not merely for fuller dramatic effect, but as encompassing important defensive mechanisms. Thus, where a particular character may display the socially approved facets of a given personality structure, any number of other characters may express its reprehensible and blameworthy aspects. Splitting by displacement then is an indispensable methodological tool to understand both the significance of the inner drama of the six characters and the play as a whole.

A more recent interpretation of splitting—one that differs radically from the primary-process mechanism of displacement—is associated with concepts of identity and the self. In the popular as well as literary imagination, splitting is frequently equated with schizophrenia. But while the notion of schizophrenia as a metaphor for the madness of modern life may be highly evocative, it may also distract from clarifying the real nature of social madness.

Splitting as related to identity and the self is indeed a complex issue, but we may delineate directions most relevant to *Six Characters* and *Henry IV* by drawing upon the significant work of a variety of analysts who have explored this area, such as Erikson, the Menakers, R. D. Laing, H. Lichtenstein, Helen Lynd, Schachtel, Searles, and Winnicott; and more recently Kernberg and Kohut.[16]

Splitting has a variety of faces, but they all eventually involve crucial defects in that essential psychological achievement, a meaningful and fulfilling adult identity: i.e., the integration of vital aspects of the inner self with the multiple options of social role. Thus, the individual strives to integrate the inner self of childhood and adolescence with commitment and involvement with major adult social roles (in love, friendship, and work), value systems, and the dominant skills of a given era.[17] Such identity syntheses by no means imply adjustment only to a given society, but often striving to change prevailing patterns of life. Except for the rare individual who can stand alone, however, identity is sustained and developed through repeated reciprocal relationships, where supportive reactions of others mirror back to the person whom he or she is trying to be. Thus, identity, while being profoundly individual, paradoxically matures only within the society of others.

Serious splits in the self may develop from two broad directions; each can seriously impair a fulfilling identity. One involves historical eras such as the present, of rapid, pervasive changes throughout society. For the psychoanalyst and critic to comment on such changes in depth without the collaboration of the historian and social scientist would obviously be presumptuous. However, certain broad outlines seem already clear. When major patterns of social life change extremely rapidly, and certain supportive systems disintegrate while others become highly impersonal; and when value systems, too, become fragmented, outmoded, or denigrated, then involvement with and commitment to social role and value system become much more difficult. Further, little supportive mirroring from others may cause great strife in the individual in his effort to maintain a meaningful identity synthesis. Thus, painful splitting may be then experienced between social role and the inner self.

Even when new societal interrelations become more flexible, and new opportunities are forthcoming, splitting may result. In these cases, the new roles may be at considerable variance with expectations and values internalized during childhood from the social reality of another generation. A case in point are the rapidly changing opportunities for women to combine serious career commitments with marriage and motherhood—a new dual-role identity often at considerable odds with the older-style housewife model.

Splitting also occurs where society insists on the maintenance of rigid social codes inappropriate to changing times and needs, and enforces its demands with techniques of shaming or disapproval.[18] A further distinction must be made between Western countries—where rapid social change has been generated within their own traditions—and countries such as India and Japan, where ancient indigenous cultures have been confronted, occupied, and either stimulated or forced to change by societies operating from a totally different cultural frame of reference. Enormous splitting is present in urban-dwellers in these two countries, who may identify with highly conflicting value systems and roles. Such splits, however, may also become a spur to new levels of integration in the unusual individual.

If one major dimension of splitting is generated by rapid social change, the other is related to the childhood splits in the self. This also presents several different aspects. Where parents are unable to relate to their child as an individual—often due to rigid social expectations of their own strong narcissistic needs—a split develops between the true self of the child and the necessity for presenting a false self.[19] This false self may then substitute for the realization of the truer needs and feelings of the individual, resulting in pervasive social facades, and foreclosing any genuine self-fulfillment. When the usual conscious splitting between social facades appropriate to a variety of roles and the inner self dissipates into unconsciously compulsive and pervasive role playing, then a gaping cleavage is present in the self—a major Pirandellian concern.

Related to the true self/false self dichotomy is deeply wounded narcissism with its desperate compensatory mechanisms. The mother who lacks empathy, who is so self-preoccupied as to be unable to retain any strong inner image of the child, or who develops rejecting, sadistic attitudes toward the child, fosters intense feelings of worthlessness and greatly depreciated self-images.[20] The child desperately compensates for the lack of self-worth with a number of narcissistic maneuvers in order to restore a modicum of self-esteem—maneuvers which often prove to be ultimately self-destructive. Narcissistic compensations are highly relevant to *Six Characters* and *Henry IV*, and will be delineated below in a variety of specific instances. Particularly relevant is the creation of an idealized self,[21] which is gradually implemented by roles around which an adult identity crystallizes.[22] Such idealized role identities, while allowing a modicum of self-worth, ultimately destroy the possibility of genuine fulfillment of adult needs in a variety of relationships.

Attendant upon many if not most instances of intense narcissistic hurt are masochism and depression.[23] Masochism in this form is the idealized hope of gaining love from a rejecting and/or sadistic parent by becoming one day lovable. The quest is futile and the masochist unwittingly seeks out love partners all too similar to the only ones he had known. When deprivation is even greater, illusory hope yields to the despair of depression.

Still another major process of splitting relates to childhood needs to preserve good aspects of the self and of parental imagoes, and to get rid of all the bad images. This often results in adult role relationships in which others are often sharply split into idealized or denigrated figures—either all good or all bad.[24] When this type of splitting becomes involved in group phenomena, a destructive process involving the "ins" and "outs" occurs, with considerable projection of all that is bad onto the "outs."

Although this summary of splitting as related to identity and the self is of necessity a sparse one, it nevertheless focuses on the inner life of the individual. Otherwise, we are left with the alternative of sociologies in which masks and roles are seen as completely constituting the self, and the individual's unique humanity disappears.

We may now be in a position to apply some of our considerations to an analysis of the play. The central metaphor of the work is the search by the six characters for an author, or more properly, their quest for existence. The central paradox is a simple yet profound one: while these creatures of the imagination are more "real" than so-called real people, they remain nonetheless thoroughly dependent on the latter for their embodiment. Without the author, or in his stead, the manager and his actors, there can be no existence. Moreover, the author and subsequently the theater manager are the ones who by the end of the play actually reject them, a rejection that is carried one step further in their repudiation by the actors themselves. For when the actors finally do determine to bring the six characters to actualization, the situation turns into so obvious a farce that the characters in turn repudiate the actors.

What then is the meaning underlying the metaphor, and how is the central paradox to be resolved? In our view, the metaphor is primarily a symbol for modern society in which the sociocultural contexts—as products of rapid social change, disjointedness, and the disintegration characteristic of many industrial, technological, and urban societies—interfere in any number of ways with the ability of the inner self to realize itself through an identity integrated with meaningful social roles and value systems.

To exist, to have an identity is to participate in meaningful relationships. In fact, the dominant metaphor of the play, as we have seen, rests upon repudiation—which we interpret as symbolizing repudiation in the modern world of meaningful self-realization. The author, for example, impotent and unable to embody his characters, concludes by disowning them; this is reflected in the Manager's and Father's impotence in their own roles. The author thus becomes a metaphor for the inability of the creative self to achieve self-realization.

A speech by the son in the third act suggests, however, that the author's disowning of his characters is due to more than mere impotence. With its rigid and outworn conventions, the theater—understood as a metaphor for society—is unable to tolerate and accept deeper manifestations of the inner self; thus, the author is impelled to withhold his creations just as the son is impelled throughout the play to withhold himself from involvement with others. The conception of the author then as simply impotent or withholding is far too limited an interpretation of his true role. With his power to create the author holds the tools which allow him to portray not only the human condition but the human impasse as well. He thus becomes an alienist or therapist, in the sense Ben Nelson uses the terms in discussing the absurdist playwrights.[25]

On a manifest level, the attempt by the actors to enact the roles of the six characters describes the impossibility of entering into genuine communication with the inner self of another. On another level, the play's comic incongruity reveals the enormous split between modern man's role-playing facade—represented appropriately enough by the actors as players—and his inner, truer self—symbolized by the six characters. The divorce between social facade and inner self is further evinced by the Son's distaste when the actors too closely approach to observe him during Act III; he accuses them of "freezing" his image. Here, social role is portrayed as a Procrustean Bed for whatever of the self's inner urges lie concealed within. That not a single three-dimensional character appears in the play is perfectly consonant with its vision of modern man as a fundamentally unrealized being. In this regard, *Six Characters* anticipates the later work of Beckett and other absurdists, obsessed by what they perceive as modern man's nearly total loss of self.

Splitting is further conveyed to the audience by Pirandello's use of humor, briefly alluded to above, and his highly original manipulation of audience response. Alienation and identification, as audience response, occur as the actors—and particularly the six characters—successively demonstrate both intense involvement and subsequent dissociation from their roles; where involvement creates a dramatic situation, dissociation allows its analysis and examination. Concomitantly, the audience's initial identification with the actors is suddenly interrupted and its involvement suspended. The use of this device produces a feeling of being split, thus inducing in the audience a psychic response consonant with the play's meaning and content.

The play's humor depends principally on the juxtaposition of incongruous elements. As such, it represents the fundamental mode by which the split between social role and inner self is dramatically conveyed. Indeed, one could go so far as to assert that an important reason for the play's artistic success is its use of humor to convey what is expressed philosophically and psychologically as an essentially tragic situation. The theme of splitting of the self is clearly developed in the dialogue, and especially in those speeches where the Father dramatically confronts the Manager with the illusoriness of his existence, or where he discusses the mutability of time or where he ultimately challenges the Manager to tell him whether he really knows who he is.

Before we examine the inner drama of the six characters both in terms of more profound psychological levels of meaning and as it relates to the central metaphors and paradoxes of the play, it would be well to reiterate our previously stated position which insists that the psychoanalytic approach *must* operate within the larger context of a work's *artistic* framework and not vice versa. In a somewhat analogous fashion, dreams are analyzed as they relate to the specific contexts of the therapeutic experience and overall life situation rather than as isolated phenomena.[26] The task of the investigator is to see to what extent meanings underlying the inner drama of the six characters correlate or clash with the central dramatic metaphors and paradoxes, neither severing the inner drama from the total play nor extrapolating meaning exclusively from the inner drama as attempted by the psychoanalyst-critics.[27]

In analyzing primary-process material, such as the inner plot, each of the characters as well as their interrelationships must be viewed as fragments of a single psyche, or more correctly, of a state of mind subjected to splitting as a displacement process, in keeping with our first definition. Further, the sequence of the inner drama must be examined in terms of its underlying meaning. We would note, in particular, that only two phases of the overall drama are actually presented, and that it is around these two incidents that the ensuing dramatic action centers. The first of these episodes is the scene at Madame Pace's where the Father goes to have sex with a "poor girl of refined family,"[28] and is only prevented from doing so when the Mother surprises him with the Stepdaughter and intervenes. The second episode is the fountain scene at the Father's house, where the Son rejects the Mother, the Child drowns, and the Boy shoots himself. The rest of the drama is narrated, but in such a way that the psychological relativism of individual viewpoints is made self-evident.

An examination of the inner drama reveals the presence of traditional Freudian themes. By way of example, we need only cite the Father's incestuous feelings toward the Stepdaughter, the murderous impulses experienced by the play's younger siblings toward one another, and the attendant feelings of guilt, anguish, and remorse—all discussed by Kligerman.

Nevertheless, we would suggest that a close examination of the inner drama's key episodes discloses underlying themes of repudiation and deprivation.[29] The audience first becomes aware of their presence in the Father's repudiation of the Mother, sending her off with his former employee. Her departure, however, is perceived by the Son as abandonment—reflecting an earlier abandonment when he had been banished by the Father to the countryside as an infant. From the start, the relationship between Father and Stepdaughter is strongly marked by deprivation. Loneliness and emptiness impel him to follow her near her school. His later visit to Madame Pace's—the scene of incestuous sexuality—is clearly brought forth by his sense of being unloved and unlovable to women.

FATHER: . . . Ah! what misery, what wretchedness is that of the man who is alone and disdains *debasing liaisons!* Not old enough to do without women, and not young enough to go and look for one without shame. Misery? It's worse than misery; it's a horror; for no woman can any longer give him love; and when a man feels this. . . .[30]

Deprivation here is expressed antithetically in terms of the conflict experienced by the Father: against his acute feelings of loneliness is posed his need for human contact, and his attempt to resolve the conflict unwittingly ensnares him into a fundamentally incestuous relationship. Moreover, when confronted and crossexamined by the Manager, the Stepdaughter readily admits that her complaint against the Father is not his desire to have sex with her but his implicit abandonment of the family long before.

STEPDAUGHTER: For one who has gone wrong, sir, he who was responsible for the first fault is responsible for all that follows. *He is responsible for my faults, was, even before I was born. Look at him, and see if it isn't true!*[31] [Italics ours.]

In view of this new interpretative framework, Bentley's contention that the Father's philosophizing merely functions as a schizophrenic defense against being overwhelmed and deluged by the world becomes untenable. Concomitantly, we reject as our only alternative the argument that speech must be interpreted on a purely philosophical level. Rather, we prefer to view the content of the Father's musings on the split nature of the human psyche as being consonant and integral to the structure of the dramatic action. His persistent self-justification and his suffering, in this view, would be interpreted as compensations for damaged narcissism or low self-esteem resulting from rejection and deprivation. From this perspective, the Father may be readily seen to depict in his own person only certain aspects of an entire psychic spectrum which is represented by the six characters and their story *in toto*, rather than by the in-depth characterization of any single *dramatis persona*. Applying the concept of the defensive splitting of characters, the Father, as a more central dramatic character, evinces the more acceptable emotions of anguish, guilt, self-justification, and remorse; while the Son, a more subsidiary character, displays a punitive detachment from the Mother and others, and the Boy, who plays no part at all till the end, implicitly manifests murderous rage with its attendant guilt.

Deeply wounded narcissism is reflected in other patterns of response in both Father and Son. The Father's behavior, for instance, in sending off his wife after noting some unspoken attachment on her part, is paradigmatic of one kind of narcissistic compensation resulting from a state of deprivation: "If I can't have everything, I shall take nothing," he seems to say. Similarly, the Son's persistent aloofness is an attempt to punish his Mother, and, as such, is another typical narcissistic compensation against fears of renewed rejection. "Since you rejected me once, I shall continue to punish you for the rest of my life regardless of what you now have to offer me."

The progression of thematic material from the scene with the Stepdaughter to the last episode by the fountain, which as Kligerman points out marks a regression from Oedipal incest material to pre-Oedipal themes of sibling murder and guilt, suggests even more directly the theme of deprivation and accompanying murderous feelings. The normal wish to do away with younger siblings in order to enjoy the exclusive love and attention of the parents is greatly intensified when the parents themselves are emotionally depriving. It is interesting here to note that as deeper and more unacceptable feelings are allowed to emerge, the protagonist is no longer the Father, but either the Son or the Boy. The Father experiences anguish, suffering, and loneliness, but not rage. The Son, on the other hand, through his unusual detachment and withdrawal, implicitly reveals his avoidance of precisely those deep-seated feelings of rage. However, the dramatic material also portrays the Son's disdainful and angry rejection of his younger half-sisters and brother as well as his rejection and punishment of the Mother for her abandonment of him and for bringing sibling rivals into the world. Here, then, splitting by displacement would appear to assume a defensive function. A similar kind of displacement mechanism is clearly operative in the Child's implicit murder by the Boy who stands by and in no way attempts to save the younger sister from drowning. The Boy's subsequent suicide then may be viewed as giving utterance to the guilt he harbors over his murderous impulses. The inner drama closes as the Son, Father, and Mother draw together anew, now that the two youngest children have been permanently disposed of and the Stepdaughter has run off. Thus, rather than simply depicting, as Wangh has speculated, aspects of a long-buried Oedipal relationship,[32] the play's inner drama expresses a basic wish to eliminate the three younger siblings.

Rather than now relating the meanings underlying the play's inner drama to events and relationships in Pirandello's life—as Kligerman did in a paradigmatic application of psychoanalysis[33]—our objective is to examine the manner in which such meanings can be effectively integrated into an analysis of the total play. We turn to Norman Holland's valuable notion that every valid literary work is constructed upon an underlying emotional fantasy which evokes a deep personal response in the audience.[34] But while Holland confines these fantasies to those characteristic of the various psychosexual stages of early childhood, we would expand the scope of his theory to include those emotional states deriving from the internalization of early childhood experiences, and in particular, from close family relationships.

For us, the inner drama of the six characters is ultimately concerned with the most primal form of repudiation a human being can experience, the repudiation of a child by his mother and all the pain attendant upon such a rejection. The young child's identity, self-worth, and very existence depend almost totally upon his or her enjoyment of a reciprocal relationship with the mother. As Winnicott cogently puts it, it is impossible to speak of the infant alone, but only of the infant *and* mothering figure.[35] This theme is echoed throughout Pirandello's hall of mirrors and is rejoined by echoes of similar themes of a more properly philosophical and artistic nature. In this regard, we have already discussed the repudiation of the inner self by modern society as well as the artist's rejection of overly rigid theatrical conventions that would become a Procrustean Bed for his creative impulses.[36] On all three levels, however, the individual experiences the loss of a firm social context through which he can establish his slowly unfolding identity. We contend that the theme of repudiation, narcissistic injury, and deprivation pervading the inner drama charges the play's other levels with intense emotion. This emotion evokes a deeper, more personal response on the part of the audience than any of the work's other dramatic elements and devices, of which it is the underlying focus. The successive stages of emotional arousal and frustration experienced by the audience, as remarked by Wangh,[37] and deriving from the play's ambiguous structure and ending, may be viewed as still another form of deprivation consistent with the play's overall technique. To our way of thinking, Pirandello's use of the inner drama reflects his ability to mold past experience and inner conflict into metaphoric expression designed to further his own artistic vision rather than to produce the necessary catharsis predicated by applied psychoanalysis.[38] Thus, the fully integrated valences of Pirandello's hall of mirrors—its reflection of the plights of the child, modern man, and the artist himself—is a many-figured tableau where psychological content and dramatic form and structure continue to reinforce and illumine one another.

II

Written directly after publication of *Six Characters* and generally regarded as Pirandello's second great work, *Henry IV* directly confronts the theme of madness. Are Eric Bentley[39] and Martin Wangh[40] correct in assuming that madness, masochism, and jealous rage are indeed the boundaries of Pirandello's vision in a limited tragicomedy? Or again, does this awesome drama deal with yet another facet of modern man's desperate but frustrated yearning for self-fulfillment? Given the complexity of the plot, a brief synopsis may be the necessary premise to any analysis of the work.

Where in *Six Characters* we found a constant juxtaposition within the *present* of the six characters and members of the acting company, *Henry IV*, on the other hand, constantly juxtaposes *past and present time*. The play moves backwards in time from the present into the medieval past of the German court of the Emperor Henry IV while the characters alternately enact the roles of present and past existences. This juxtaposition has come about accidentally some twenty years prior to the drama's present context when an unnamed individual, participating in a masquerade as the Emperor Henry IV of Germany, took an unwitting tumble from his horse, bumped his head on a rock, and became consequently mad. He had assumed this disguise, we are told, because the woman who was the current object of his affections, the Marchioness Matilda of Spina, and who at the time had rejected his love, had assumed the masquerade role of the Marchioness Matilda of Tuscany. The particular form of madness assumed by the protagonist consists in his deeply rooted belief that he is indeed the Emperor Henry IV, that he is frozen into Henry's twenty-sixth year of life despite the passing of time.

To comfort and succor her mad brother, a wealthy sister of the protagonist decides to redo her solitary Italian villa as a medieval German court. She hires people to serve as courtiers, including four men who will play the important roles of Henry's counselors, and she has them all richly and appropriately costumed for the occasion. The one incongruous element of the latter-day court, but central to the play as dramatic device and metaphor, consists of two large contemporary portraits of the unnamed man and the Marchioness Matilda, outfitted as Henry IV and the Marchioness of Tuscany, which had been painted twenty years before at the time of the masquerade.

Henry is now fifty years old. The dramatic action is precipitated by the sister's death a month previously, and her dying words to her son, Charles Di Nolli, begging him to leave no stone unturned in his efforts to bring his uncle back to sanity. She herself thinks she has discerned signs of recovery. Di Nolli, faithful to his mother's last wishes, calls in a Dr. Genoni to perform the cure. The doctor, an alienist or psychiatrist, devises a remarkable type of shock therapy. He invites to the scene the heroine of the past masquerade, the Marchioness Matilda, together with her daughter, Frida, who is identical to the portrait of her mother done so many years before, and Di Nolli. The daughter and Di Nolli are to enact the past and present images of the Marchioness Matilda of Tuscany and Henry IV, coming alive from within the frames of their portraits, and thereby shocking Henry into an awareness and perception of reality. Also present is the Baron Tito Belcredi, the Marchioness' present lover and most probably a rival to Henry at the time of the masquerade.

The action of the play itself is relatively straightforward. The state of affairs is amusingly conveyed by three present-day Italians, dressed as Henry's counselors, to an utterly confounded neophyte. The "therapeutic troupe" then arrives. The Marchioness, glimpsing her portrait, is arrested and deeply moved by its frozen image of her youthful self and its uncanny resemblance to her daughter, Frida. For their meeting with Henry, the guests array themselves in medieval dress in different roles of the period. Henry then enters dressed in sackcloth, the sign of his penitence and self-abasement at Canossa. He alternately attacks Belcredi as his enemy, Peter Damian, and expresses tender feelings toward the Marchioness, begging her to free his miserable self transfixed as the twenty-six-year-old Henry. Act I closes as Henry exits leaving the Marchioness deeply moved and overcome with feeling.

Act II opens with a recall of the encounter with Henry, a discussion highlighted by the Marchioness' startling disclosure that she intuitively senses that Henry has indeed recognized her and that the hostility he has demonstrated toward Belcredi springs from discovering the latter to be her lover. In a new exchange between the Marchioness and Henry, the former takes pains to illustrate that, in her historical role no more than in the masquerade of twenty years ago, was the Marchioness as hostile to Henry as he imagines. As soon as they depart, Henry rages to his counselors, irate that the Marchioness should presume to appear there with her lover, *clearly revealing his awareness that both counselors and visitors are role-playing in his presence.* Nevertheless, despite apparent insight, when the counselors invite him to live in the present, Henry refuses. His unwillingness to do so denotes his reluctance to surrender the role of Emperor and master puppeteer in whose hands lies the power to manipulate the roles of others.

The doctor's strategem is implemented in the third act. From the frame of the portrait, Frida calls to Henry. Henry initially responds with fears of renewed madness, but these quickly change into violent and passionate calls for revenge at seeing himself the butt of the commpany's unmerciful ruse. Belcredi, apprised by the counselors of Henry's "sanity" and acting against Genoni's promptings, begins to prod Henry for trifling them and making sport of their quite serious efforts to help him. Henry counters by declaring that for twelve years he had indeed been mad, but that upon recovering, he had perceived that life had passed him by: ". . . not only had my hair gone grey, but that I was all grey, inside. . . . I was going to arrive, hungry as a wolf, at a banquet which had already been cleared away. . . ."[41] His beloved had been taken from him; to return to a world maliciously taunting him as "Henry IV" would have been too painful. The realization of the chasm lying between his unlived life and theirs is profoundly agitating and awakens in him the yearning to possess the Marchioness as she had been, in the image of her daughter, Frida. The climax of the play follows swiftly as Henry embraces Frida, ordering the counselors to seize the others—an order which the counselors much to their amazement proceed to carry out. Belcredi then breaks loose begging Henry to "leave her alone," exclaiming that he, Henry, is "no madman." "I'm not mad, eh!"[42] retorts Henry, drawing his sword and plunging it into Belcredi. Continuing to taunt Henry, Belcredi, fatally wounded, is borne offstage by the others. Henry then summons his counselors and standing like a wise man in their midst, utters the play's closing lines, transfixed forever in the role of the Emperor Henry IV.

It is our contention that *Henry IV*, like *Six Characters*, responds to an artistic vision considerably broader than either Bentley or Wangh envisaged with their emphasis on psychopathology. The play's structural aspects disclose more profound, extensive levels of meaning which must be integrated with precisely the themes of madness, masochism, deprivation, and jealousy analyzed in their respective essays.

Henry IV, like *Six Characters*, is shaped in a naturalistic mold. Similar to the earlier play as well is the juxtaposition of two sets of characters. In *Six Characters*, however, spatial dimensions and characterization are juxtaposed within a contemporary time scheme. In very different fashion, the characters in the later play are juxtaposed in their changing roles across a diachronic time scheme, rapidly moving from the present to a remote historical past, thence to twenty and finally to eight years prior to the dramatic action. That the themes of *Henry IV* can be expressed as jealousy, insanity, masochism, and deprivation should not alter the fundamental consideration that these themes are depicted within thoroughly unique temporal and role structures. The unusual nature of the play's temporal structure is emphasized by the characters' changing names and roles. The young man who at twenty-six assumed the name and role of Henry IV is known by no other name in the drama, despite the fact that during its second half he exists consciously within the present. His name is *only of the role*. On the other hand, there are four characters—Frida, Di Nolli, Dr. Genoni, and Belcredi—whose names are *only of the present* although each plays a role in the past. In the case of the Marchioness, her first name, Matilda, is the link between the contemporary figure and the historic Matilda of Tuscany. Finally, there are the four counselors each with a double set of names corresponding to the character's historical and present-day identity: Harold/Frank, Landolph/Lolo, Ordulph/Momo, Berthold/Fino. It is inconceivable that Pirandello would have assigned such past, present, or double names to characters completely at whim. It becomes necessary, therefore, to assess the significance of this unusual relationship between time and role, an analysis that can only proceed in conjunction with a basic study of the play's central metaphors and paradoxes. A few comments about how these differ from those of *Six Characters* are also pertinent.

The paradox that "life-in-theater" is "theater-in-life" is transformed in *Henry IV* into "life-of-madness" is "madness-of-life."When the two (Pirandello) plays are compared, the later one appears rather close to the Laingian view of sanity-in-madness and madness-in-sanity.[43] The play's central metaphor is the portrait, the image that captures, freezes, and evokes in us the feelings of a past self. The metaphor anticipates the structural development of the drama: an unknown individual is frozen, first by tragic accident and then by psychological necessity, into an old self, or more precisely, into an idealized, grandiose image of that past self; at the same time he is unable to fulfill the yearnings and needs of his real self, and half-mad, half-sane, he lives on until one last tragedy freezes him forever into the portrait of his past.

The Doctor explains the significance of a portrait as the reflection of a past self:

DOCTOR: Quite right! Because a portrait is always there fixed in
                    the twinkling of an eye: for the young lady something
                    far away and without memories, while for the Mar-
                    chioness, it can bring back everything: movements,
                    gestures, looks, smiles, a whole heap of things.
DONNA MATILDA. Exactly![44]

A few pages on, Belcredi muses on the relationship between the portrait and Henry, frozen forever into the role of Holy Roman Emperor.

BELCREDI: . . . look at him—(points to the portrait)—ha! A smack on
           the head, and he never moves again: Henry IV for ever![45]

An important metaphor in *Six Characters*, that of role-playing as theater, becomes transformed in *Henry IV* into the *masquerade* or the wearing of masks in life. Pirandello uses this metaphor to portray his perception of the cleavages or splits in the self.

HENRY: . . . We're all fixed in good faith in a certain concept of ourselves. However, Monsignor, while you keep yourself in order,
holding on with both your hands to your holy habit, there slips
down from your sleeves, there peels off from you like . . . like a
serpent . . . something you don't notice: life Monsignor!
(Turns to the Marchioness) Has it never happened to you, my
Lady, to find a different self in yourself? Have you always been
the same? . . .[46]
. . . you, you, my Lady, certainly don't dye your hair to deceive
the others, not even yourself; but only to cheat your own image a
little before the looking-glass. I do it for a joke! You do it
seriously! But I assure you that you too, Madame, are in masquerade, though it be in all seriousness. . . .[47]

The compulsion to don masks is a clear sign of madness, just as the
unconscious choice of masquerading through life rather than living it is a
clear sign of Laing's madness-in-life. The play's true dramatic conflict,
therefore, begins not when Henry tumbles from his horse and awakens
unwittingly convinced that he is Henry IV, but rather twelve years later
when he realizes that he is *not* the Emperor at all, when his profound
needs force him to remain frozen behind a mask of which he is fully conscious. Parenthetically, Henry seems himself aware of some of his life-
thwarting needs. When invited by Ordulph to switch on the electric light,
he passionately demands his old lamp, clinging to it as to a fate that has already been ordained in history, eschewing the anxiety and chaos of an existence to be lived in the present.

ORDULPH: Well, then shall I turn it on now (the electric light)?
HENRY IV: No, it would blind me! I want my lamp![48] . . . the men of the
twentieth century are torturing themselves in ceaseless anxiety
to know how their fates and fortunes will work out! Whereas
you are already in history with me. . . . And sad is my lot,
hideous as some of the events are, bitter the struggles and
troubled the time—still all history! All history that cannot
change, understand? All fixed forever![49]

We are now in a position to relate the play's unusual temporal and role
structures to its metaphors and central paradox. The meaning of these
structures is clarified if we consider, as we did in our analysis of *Six Characters*, man's profound need to forge an identity through meaningful
relationships with others. In dramatic terms, then, the juxtaposition of
roles and time sequences conveys Pirandello's belief in the cleavages of
the self, *particularly as they reflect the conflict between the individual's*

yearnings for self-fulfillment and his life-thwarting need to masquerade in various roles. Henry IV, known in the play only as Henry IV, illustrates madness as a life frozen into his mask. He stands in contrast to the others, particularly the "therapeutic troupe," who masquerade wildly through life dissipating all chance of self-fulfillment. When Henry regains awareness twelve years after his initial fall, his need to persevere in masquerade allows us to perceive that his only context for identity is to abide as Henry IV.

The Marchioness Matilda, as her single name implies, is remarkably similar in all three of her past, present, and historical roles, demonstrating throughout her ambivalent rejection and sympathy for Henry. The last group of characters—Dr. Genoni, Frida, Charles Di Nolli, and Tito Belcredi—play their historical roles clumsily; they are clearly rooted in the present. In fact, the function of this last group is rather similar to that of the professional actors in Pirandello's earlier play whose inept attempts to fill the roles of the six characters underscore even more markedly the split between self and role. Finally, we must consider Henry's philosophy, which in our view is fully consonant with the dramatic depiction of splits in the self, and the conflict between self-actualization and the need for masks. The latter emerges in a number of speeches, particularly the one where he mentions the Irish priest brimming with life as he dreams but who upon awakening reverts to the mask of the zealous and stodgy clergyman.

HENRY IV: . . . Look here, doctor! I remember a priest, certainly Irish, a nice-looking priest, who was sleeping in the sun one November day, with his arm on the corner of the bench of a public garden. He was lost in the golden delight of the mild sunny air which must have seemed for him almost summery. One may be sure that in that moment he did not know any more that he was a priest, or even where he was. He was dreaming. . . . A little boy passed with a flower in his hand. He touched the priest with it here on the neck. I saw him open his laughing eyes, while all his mouth smiled with the beauty of his dream. He was forgetful of everything. . . . But all at once, he pulled himself together, and stretched out his priest's cassock and there came back to his eyes the same seriousness which you have seen in mine: because the Irish priests defend the seriousness of their Catholic faith with the same zeal with which I defend the sacred rights of hereditary monarchy![50]

In this connection, we would also remark about the allusion to prostitutes who sleep with Henry under the guise of being his wife and who burst into strident laughter when he calls them Bertha of Susa: in bed, naked, we can throw off our masks.[51] Thus, a remarkable similarity of theme can be discerned in both *Henry IV* and *Six Characters*. *However, where underlying meaning in the latter was focused on the impossibility of the inner self to find realization within a social context, Henry IV hinges upon the tragic assumption of masks in social roles, masks which ultimately destroy any chance for inner realization.* As in *Six Characters*, the reader stands in the same hall of mirrors where diverse aspects of the self and its splits are reflected endlessly back and forth. Or perhaps the image is rather that of a many-faceted gem that we turn over and over in the palm of our hand to examine. Pirandello's exploration of the human psyche in *Henry IV* leads him to the threshold of modern man's profoundly existential dilemma: his need for masks even at the price of his own self-fulfillment.

In assessing Pirandello's exploration of the modern dilemma of the self, we must indicate another formal aspect of *Henry IV*, one which differs sharply from the earlier play: the presence of three-dimensional characters rather than the exclusively one and two-dimensional figures of *Six Characters*. With this important difference in mind, we can now examine character interaction and characterization, particularly as they relate to Henry. *Rather than elucidate Henry's psychopathology alone, our task will essentially be to investigate the relationship between character and the existential conflict over man's self-fulfillment.*

The true drama of Henry's madness is the paradox of his *need to masquerade,* however conscious he may be of its fictive character and however destructive and unfulfilling his role. Wounded narcissism, masochism, and deprivation—those haunting specters of childhood pain—together with man's profoundly universal need for an identity, drive Henry on to his final destruction. Even the Oedipal rivalry and jealousy experienced by Henry toward Belcredi are colored by rejection (by the Marchioness), deprivation, and repudiation (the same constellation of themes present in *Six Characters*, where they appear reinforced by the Father's search for the Stepdaughter). Thus Henry's reaction to regaining awareness of his old self is filled with imagery of deprivation.

HENRY IV: Not only had my hair gone grey, but that I was all grey inside. . . . I was going to arrive, hungry as a wolf, at a banquet which had already been cleared away.[52]

We may even speculate that Henry's rejection at the hands of the Marchioness twenty years before is by implication merely a repetition of a still earlier maternal rejection. For Henry is portrayed as a man of deep inner coldness, or in more properly psychoanalytic language, as a man without a warm maternal internalization or presence.

BELCREDI: . . . Evidently, because that immediate lucidity that comes from acting, assuming a part, at once put him out of key with his own feelings, which seemed to him not exactly feelings, but like something he was obliged to give the value there and then of—what shall I say—of an act of intelligence, to make up for that sincere cordial warmth he felt lacking. So he improvised, exaggerated, let himself go, so as to distract and forget himself. He appeared inconstant, fatuous, and—yes—even ridiculous sometimes.[53]

That Henry was attracted to a woman seemingly incapable of loving him indicates the extent to which masochism forms an integral part of his personality. But it is masochism motivated by what contemporary psychoanalytic thinking posits as the child's urgent need to sustain at all costs, with a rejecting, neglectful, or sadistic mother, a love relationship that at best is extremely tenuous.[54] Unless he or she can achieve this, the child faces a life of utter deprivation and futility, a life of despair and depression. Later, as an adult, he is unconsciously drawn to similar masochistic love relationships because he inwardly experiences such relationships as being the *only* ones he is capable of having. His self-abasement obscures the true nature of the rejecting love object and affords some small hope that if he can but himself change, the other will then love him.

In view of Henry's masochistic relationship with the Marchioness, it is hardly accidental that Pirandello should freeze his protagonist into the role of Henry IV during the latter's twenty-sixth year. This is the time, we will recall, when in order to rescind his excommunication and to prevent his being deposed by the Imperial electors, he had been forced to abase himself before both Marchioness and Pope. For had Henry not humiliated himself before the temporal and spiritual powers of the eleventh century at this time, existence would have stretched before him, a terrible void of nothingness. Masochism of this kind also tinges the relationship between Belcredi and the Marchioness, although it functions there as a lesser motif reflecting what is in Henry a dominant theme.

However important the function of rejection, deprivation, and masochism as psychic determinants of Henry's personality, his actions as a dramatic character yet proceed from quite another though related source. To us it seems quite evident that they are motivated by Henry's profoundly wounded narcissism—another familiar theme from *Six Characters*. As noted earlier, against this wounded narcissism or painfully low self-esteem, the individual contrives a system of compensatory defenses intended to make his life at least minimally endurable. Henry's major defense is clearly the implementation of a grandiose, idealized self-image into an adult role-identity, thus foreclosing fulfillment of any genuine needs for human closeness.

While most of the play's dramatic action is contingent upon the fanciful scheme devised by Dr. Genoni, there are in fact three events which occur without apparent premeditation. The first such incident occurs in Act II as Henry, in high fury, reveals his awareness of the doctor's ruse by disclosing the real identities of the Marchioness and her lover. The other two incidents occur during Act III; the first, when Belcredi mocks Henry for trifling with the company despite their having taken their parts quite seriously; and the second at the end of the play when Henry, after seizing Frida, and instigated by Belcredi's taunting accusations that he is not mad at all, becomes a murderer. In all these instances, the fundamental motivation must be understood as originating in the need to recompense profoundly wounded narcissism.

Let us examine the first of these three incidents. A closer look reveals that paradoxically Henry confesses his awareness of his surroundings *not* at the time of any new rejection by the Marchioness, but just at the point when Matilda demonstrates affectionate and sympathetic feelings toward him.

DONNA MATILDA: . . . (looks at him; then very softly as if in confidence) You love her still [Matilda of Tuscany, but referring to herself]?

HENRY IV: (puzzled) Still? Still, you say? You know, then. But nobody knows! Nobody must know!

DONNA MATILDA: But perhaps she knows, if she has begged so hard for you.[55]

The reason for Henry's apparently bizarre reaction lies in his adoption of one of the most self-destructive forms of defense against wounded narcissism—a mechanism one desperately clings to in order to prevent any further painful disappointment after severe rejection and deprivation have already occurred. "If I can't have everything, I'll take nothing," is the paradigm on which this kind of defense is modeled. Already present in the Father in *Six Characters*, it sounds a more dominant chord in *Henry IV*. Needless to say, so desperate a measure to preserve one's self-esteem ultimately leaves the individual completely empty-handed.

Turning to the last scene, Henry's actions are clearly motivated by a last attempt *to preserve the final vestiges of a narcissistic compensation for feelings of utter worthlessness.*

HENRY IV: (remains apart, peering at one and now at the other under the accusation and the mockery of what all believe to be a cruel joke of his, which is now revealed. He has shown by the flashing of his eyes that he is meditating a revenge . . .).[56]
BELCREDI: We've had enough of this joke now.
HENRY IV: Who said joke?
DOCTOR: (loudly to Belcredi) Don't excite him, for the love of God!
BELCREDI: (without lending an ear to him, but speaking louder) But they have said so (pointing to the four young men), they, they!
HENRY IV: (turning around and looking at them) You? Did you say it was all a joke?[57]

HENRY IV: All by itself, who know how, one day the trouble here (touches his forehead) mended. . . . Ah!—then as *he* says (alludes to Belcredi) away, away with this masquerade, this incubus! Let's open the windows, life once again! Away! Away! Let's run out! (Suddenly pulling himself up) But where? And to do what? To show myself to all, secretly as Henry IV, not like this, but arm in arm with you among my dear friends.[58]

Already Henry has confessed that even eight years ago he was afraid to venture into the world for fear of the ridicule that would greet him. With these words, he reveals the extreme and continuing fragility of the compensatory mechanism.

One final issue of central importance is now to integrate our analysis of Henry's narcissism with the play's overall artistic vision. Expressed otherwise, how are we to reconcile wounded narcissism with the need to masquerade in roles that sever and truncate our lives and keep us from achieving self-fulfillment? In *Henry IV*, the need to don masks and to structure one's entire existence around an assumed role is perceived by the author as a response to narcissistic wounds sustained again and again. *In lives where relationships affording meaningful existence and identity to the individual are lacking; where love relationships with mother and family and later lovers and friends are extremely tenuous; where relationships in work and community are impersonal and removed; where the individual experiences life as inner emptiness and himself as worthless, a semblance of self and self-worth are achieved by masquerading in various roles.* But at what cost to his fragile humanity does man sustain this vicarious mode of living.

Thus we find that *Henry IV*'s unusual temporal and role structures, its metaphors and central paradox, can be fully integrated with the work's three-dimensional characterization and philosophy. What emerges is a unified artistic vision, a message at once powerful and tragic for modern man. Its intuitive grasp of his need to yield to self-destruction through masquerade and self-deception surely anticipates by decades similar conclusions of an empirical, scientific nature. *Henry IV* performs the magical feat so often noted by Freud:[59] it reveals the vision that mysteriously crystallizes in the mind of the poet.

NOTES

1. Eric Bentley, "Father's Day," *Tulane Drama Review* (1968), 13:57–72. Theodore Jacobs, Discussion of Martin Wangh's paper on Pirandello, presented at the New York Psychoanalytic Institute, January, 1974; Charles Kligerman, "A Psychoanalytic Study of Pirandello's *Six Characters in Search of an Author*," *Journal of the American Psychoanalytic Association* (1962), 10:731–44; Martin Wangh, "Underlying Motivations in Pirandello's *Six Characters in Search of an Author*: A Psychoanalytic View," *Journal of the American Psychoanalytical Association* (1976), 24.

2. Kligerman, "Psychoanalytic Study of *Six Characters*."

3. Ernest Jones, "The Death of Hamlet's Father," *International Journal of Psychoanalysis* (1948), 29:174–76.

4. Sigmund Freud (1900), *The Interpretation of Dreams* (New York, Basic Books, 1955).

5. The primary process, as more fully manifested in such psychical products as dreams, is traditionally characterized by displacement of affects, condensation of disparate trends of thought into a single image, and expression of instinctual impulses through symbols; and as a result of these mechanisms, there is often overwhelming illogic in temporal, spatial, and causal dimensions. This is in contrast to the secondary process where logical cause-and-effect relationships in realistic time and space prevail.

6. Kligerman, "Psychoanalytic Study of *Six Characters*," p. 732.

7. Wangh, "Underlying Motivations in *Six Characters*."

8. Jacobs, Discussion of Wangh's paper. The second discussant at the New York Psychoanalytic Institute Meeting was Martin Bergmann, but he spoke from notes, and his remarks have not been made available.

9. See Norman Holland's *The Dynamics of Literary Response* (New York: Oxford University Press, 1968) for a more comprehensive exposition of this point of view.

10. Ronald Laing, *The Divided Self* (Baltimore: Penguin Books, 1965).

11. Bentley, "Father's Day," p. 71.

12. As it pertains to drama, an acceptable formulation of the term "grotesque" is the one suggested by the Polish critic, Jan Kott, *Shakespeare Our Contemporary* (New York: Doubleday, 1964), p. 141: "This dispute about the tragic and grotesque interpretations of human fate reflects the everlasting conflict of two philosophies and two ways of thinking; of two opposing attitudes defined by the Polish philosopher, Leszek Koakowski, as the irreconcilable antagonism between the priest and the clown. Between tragedy and grotesque there is the same conflict for or against such notions as eschatology, belief in the absolute, hope for the ultimate solution of the contradiction between the moral order and every-day practice. Tragedy is the theatre of priests, grotesque is the theatre of clowns."

13. Leon Edel, "Hawthorne's Symbolism and Psychoanalysis," in Leonard and Eleanor Manheim, eds., *Hidden Patterns; Studies in Psychoanalytic Literary Criticism* (New York: Macmillan, 1966).

14. Kenneth Burke, "Freud—and the Analysis of Poetry," in *The Philosophy of Literary Form* (Baton Rouge: Louisiana State University Press, 1941).

15. Edith Sheppard and Leon Saul, "An Approach to a Systematic Study of Ego Function," *Psychoanalytic Quarterly* (1958), 27:237–45.

16. Erik Erikson, *Identity, Youth, and Crisis* (New York: Norton, 1968); Esther and William Menaker, *Ego in Evolution* (New York: Grove Press, 1965); Laing, *Divided Self*; Heinz Lichtenstein, "Identity and Sexuality," *Journal of the American Psychoanalytic Association* (1961), 9:179–260; Helen Lynd, *On Shame and the Search for Identity* (New York: Science Editions, 1958); Ernest Schachtel, "On Alienated Concepts of Identity," *American Journal of Psychoanalysis* (1961), 21:120–31; Ronald Searles, "Concerning the Development of an Identity," *The Psychoanalytic Review* (1966), 53:507–30; D. W. Winnicott, *The Maturational Processes and the Facilitating Environment* (New York: International Universities Press, 1965); Otto Kernberg, *Borderline Conditions and Pathological Narcissism* (New York: Jason Aronson, 1975); Heinz Kohut, *The Analysis of the Self* (New York: International Universities Press, 1971).

17. Erikson, *Identity, Youth, and Crisis*.

18. Laing, *Divided Self*, and Lynd, *On Shame and the Search for Identity*.

19. Winnicott, *Maturational Processes*.

20. Kohut, *Analysis of the Self*, and Edmund Weil, "The Origins and Vicissitudes of the Self-Image," *Psychoanalysis and the Psychoanalytic Review*. (1958), 45.

21. Kohut, *Analysis of the Self*.

22. Schachtel, "Alienated Concepts of Identity."

23. Annette Overby and H. Freudenberger, "Patients from an Emotionally Deprived Environment," *Psychoanalytic Review* (1969), 56:299–312.

24. Kernberg, *Borderline Conditions*.

25. Ben Nelson, "Avant-Garde Dramatists from Ibsen to Ionesco," *Psychoanalytic Review* (1968), 55:505–12.

2(Alan Roland, "Imagery and Symbolic Expression in Dreams and Art," *International Journal of Psychoanalysis* (1972), 53:531–39.

27. Jacobs, Discussion of Wangh's paper; Kligerman, "Psychoanalytic Study of *Six Characters*", and Wangh, "*Underlying Motivations in Six Characters.*"

28. Luigi Pirandello, *Six Characters in Search of an Author* and *Henry IV* in Eric Bentley, ed., *Naked Masks: Five Plays by Luigi Pirandello* (New York: Dutton, 1952).

29. Important aspects of our analysis reflect more closely Jacob's rather than Kligerman's or Wangh's views. Our thesis assumes an expanded conceptualization of primary-

process functioning derived from Roland's work on dreams ("Imagery and Symbolic Expression in Dreams"), as well as Noy's important reconceptualization of the primary process. Pincus Noy, "A Revision of the Psychoanalytic Theory of the Primary Process," *International Journal of Psychoanalysis* (1969), 50:155–78. Such a conception not only incorporates the classical view that primary-process displacement, condensation, and symbolism give disguised expression to hidden impulses and wishes; but also, that they give metaphorical expression to aspects of the self and old internalizations of childhood familial relationships.

30. Pirandello, *Six Characters*, p. 229.

31. *Ibid.*, p. 259.

32. Wangh, "Underlying Motivations in *Six Characters.*"

33. Kligerman, "Psychoanalytic Study of *Six Characters.*" Kligerman correlated dramatic actions with biographical events such as the incestuous theme between Father and Stepdaughter in *Six Characters* with Pirandello's over-attachment to his own daughter and the discovery scene at Madame Pace's with the confrontation of Pirandello's father in an affair.

34. Holland, *Dynamics of Literary Response.*

35. Winnicott, *Maturational Processes.*

36. By having the *Rules of the Game*—a naturalistic type drama in rehearsal at the beginning of *Six Characters*—replaced by this new open-structured play of the six characters, Pirandello suggests that he would defy and prevail over long-established theatrical conventions.

37. Wangh, "Underlying Motivations in *Six Characters.*"

38. The assumption that the artist creates to have a necessary catharsis is common in applied psychoanalysis, and is incorporated into Kligerman's essay, "Psychoanalytic Study of Six Characters."

39. Bentley, "Il Tragico Imperatore," *Tulane Drama Review* (1966), 10:60–75.

40. In his paper, "Underlying Motivations in Six Characters," Wangh relates similar themes in *Henry IV* to *Six Characters.*

41. *Pirandello, Henry IV*, p. 203.

42. *Ibid.*, p. 207.

43. Laing, *Divided Self.*

44. Pirandello, *Henry IV*, p. 152.

45. *Ibid.*, p. 159.

46. *Ibid.*, p. 169.

47. *Ibid.*, pp. 169–70.

48. *Ibid.*, p. 193.

49. *Ibid.*, p. 195.

50. *Ibid.*, p. 205.

51. This allusion to Henry's use of prostitutes reiterates one of the earlier play's central motifs; the meeting of the Father and Stepdaughter at the small-town bordello where he is a well-known client. The theme of prostitution in both works is used in part to highlight the male protagonists' incapacity to sustain a true love relationship with one woman; it is also used to provide a dramatic context in which the individual's masks may be torn away: thus, in *Six Characters* the Father's secret jaunts to the bordello are exposed, while in *Henry IV*, the prostitutes jeer at the entire masquerade.

52. Pirandello, *Henry IV*, p. 203.

53. *Ibid.*, pp. 157–58.

54. Esther Menaker, "Masochism as a Defense Reaction of the Ego," *Psychoanalytic Quarterly* (1953), 22:205–20.

55. Pirandello, *Henry IV*, p. 187.

56. *Ibid.*, p. 199.
57. *Ibid.*, p. 200.
58. *Ibid.*, pp. 202–3.
59. Freud, "Relationship of the Poet to Daydreaming."

NAMES INDEX

Abraham, K., 272
Adler, S., 208
Alain-Miller, J., 57
Alexander, F., 254
Althusser, L., 56
Anzieu, D., 45
Aristotle, 130, 142

Backes-Clément, C., 56
Barthes, R., 12, 280-82
Beckett, S., 332
Bentham, J., 119-20
Bentley, E., 324-25
Blake, W., 183
Bion, W., 281
Blanchot, M., 284
Bruno, P., 56
Buber, M., 132
Burke, K., 256-57, 263

Carnovsky, M., 209
Castoriadis-Aulagnier, P., 46
Chambers, W., 179, 181, 187
Clurman, H., 200, 204-5, 207-8, 215, 225
Coleridge, S., 259
Comte, A., 131
Crane, H., 126
Crews, F., 248, 253, 264

Dali, S., 58
David, C., 317
De Gaulle, C., 49

Deleuze, G., 12, 292
Derrida, J., 12, 282
Dolto, F., 44
Donne, J., 237
Duncan, R., 245

Edel, L., 185, 248, 253
Einstein, A., 158
Eissler, K. R., 38, 253
Eliot, T. S., 237
Emerson, R. W., 119
Erikson, E. H., 2, 166; disciplined subjectivity, 178; dream-analysis, 191, 201; identity and identity elements, 190-91, 230, 243; interpersonal model, 242, 251; intimacy, 219; Luther, 186; play, 183; psychohistory, 180, 184

Favez-Boutonnier, J., 44
Ferenczi, S., 272
Fichte, J., 294
Flaubert, G., 289, 315-16
Fliess, R., 87
Foucault, J., 12
Freud, A., 30, 239-40
Freud, S., 2; America, 22; art, 185, 254; behaviorism, 131; death drive, 16-17; dream-within-the-dream, 324; French psychoanalysis, 13-14, 19-20; individual consciousness, 236; International Psychoanalytic Association, 26; interpsychic model, 242; Jung, 131; lay analysis,

LITERARY WORKS INDEX

SUBJECT INDEX

Abbreviation, 132

Absent, 292; in literature, 290-91; psychoanalysis, 282; writing, 282-83, 288-89

Abstinence, 88

Action: consciousness, 130; definition of, 117; dreams, 130; language, 120, 243; poetry, 140; principle of duplication, 130, 138, 142; relationship to motion, 119, 122-23, 125, 133, 139-40; self, 118, 121; symbolic, 117-18

Actual neuroses, 88, 91

Adaptation, 32-33; Erikson, 242; French criticism of, 63-64

Aesthetics, 312; experience, 167, 324; inevitability, 225; psychoanalytic literary criticism, 248-49, 266; reaction, 154

Alienation, 104; aesthetic, 197; as dramatic device, 261, 263, 332; identifications, 32; in contemporary theater, 229; in Pirandello, 326; self, 112; subject, 57

Alienist, 332

Ambiguity, 254, 259

American: businessman, 212; Dream, 203, 206; frontier, 206

American Psychoanalysis, attitudes toward French psychoanalysis, 1; comparison with French psychoanalysis, 11-12; image of French psychoanalysis, 3; new clinical observations, 2

American Psychoanalytic Association, 4-5, 23-24; Chicago Psychoanalytic Institute, 28; ethics, 29; institutional structure, 27-28, 30;

International Psychoanalytic Association, 26-27; medicalized psychoanalysis, 37; nonmedical members and women, 28; political positions, 29; standards for training, 27-28

Anomolous phenomena, 163

Anima, 217

Anthropology, 36; cultural, 244

Antithesis, 6, 150-51, 158, 259-60

Anxiety: death instinct, 93; in contemporary literature, 291; writing, 284, 291

Applied psychoanalysis, 248-50, 259-60, 272, 323, 336-37, 350

Archetypes, 132; imagery, 137; in psychoanalytic literary criticism, 257; polaristic thought, 135; psychoid nature of, 137; *unus mundus*, 137

Art: dreams and daydreams, 7, 249-51, 253-55, 259, 264, 266; freedom, 224; individualization, 166; integrity, 221; *La Nausée*, 312, 320; *Master Builder*, 262; narcissism, 293, 295; playwright, 182; psychoanalytic literary criticism, 250-51, 253, 255, 324; Saroyan's viewpoint, 186; self, 111, 113

Artist: as priest, 215; biography, 185; Cleo in *Rocket to the Moon*, 203, 211, 214, 216-17, 222-23; collectivity, 155; conflicts of, 219-20; creative processes, 146, 149, 163, 179, 185, 188, 200, 227, 255; duality between individuality and collectivity, 165-66; duality between life and creation, 167; identifi-

DATE DUE

MAR 9 '89			
SEP 27 '91			
MAN 31 '92			
GAYLORD			PRINTED IN U.S.A